(continued from front flap)

and old-style military officers, businessmen and technocrats, as well as the democratic reform movements. But for all the talk of a "revolutionary" situation in Latin America, the author writes, the goals of the majority of the Latin Americans are really very moderate. They want a society similar—in principle—to that of the United States.

This is the reality that lies behind the virulent anti-Americanism so widespread in Latin America today. There are many valid reasons for this anti-Americanism, as the author shows in his analysis of U.S. policy—both official and unofficial—toward Latin America. But anti-Americanism is also used by the ruling minorities to obscure the fact that the majority of the people are outside the mainstream of Latin American life. And it is to this majority, the author argues, that the United States should direct its attention and its aid.

Mr. Alba's analysis of relations between the United States and Latin America—past and present—is admirably balanced. But he is equally pointed and provocative on such subjects as Latin American psychology, students and intellectuals, Castro and Castroism, the Latin American "new left," Latin American business practices, and the politics of military coups. To all these topics, and many more, he brings the sort of understanding that Americans must acquire if they are not going to be increasingly baffled and frustrated by their "good neighbors" to the south.

# THE LATIN AMERICANS

THE

LATIN AMERICANS

Víctor Alba

FREDERICK A. PRAEGER, *Publishers*
New York • Washington • London

FREDERICK A. PRAEGER, PUBLISHERS
111 Fourth Avenue, New York, N.Y. 10003, U.S.A.
5, Cromwell Place, London S.W.7, England

Published in the United States of America in 1969
by Frederick A. Praeger, Inc., Publishers

© 1969 by Frederick A. Praeger, Inc.

All rights reserved

Library of Congress Catalog Card Number: 69-10513
Printed in the United States of America

Author's Note

Many books on Latin America give the impression of dealing with imaginary men and not with men of flesh and blood. The present book is an attempt to explain Latin America through its inhabitants. It is not a detailed study of every aspect of each Latin American country but a composite view of the present-day situation in Latin America, of how it arose, and of the possibilities for future change. In a work of this sort, generalizations are inevitable and even desirable, for they help put into proper perspective details that may seem important at first glance but that in the long run are of merely anecdotal interest.

Notes have been kept to a minimum, but I have provided in their stead a fairly extensive reading list. As for the statistics, they are so diverse and contradictory, and they date so quickly, that it seemed best to refer to them as little as possible.

The treatment is fundamentally historical, since in few parts of the world is there such a clear and immediate relation between the present and the past—one might almost say, between the future and the past. In each period, I have tried to pay more attention to questions of social structure, living standards, and governmental relationships than to picturesque detail and sterile data. I am not concerned that the reader who has finished the book shall know a great many facts about Latin America, but that he shall be in a position to understand the facts he encounters in his subsequent readings.

Finally, I have wanted to give an objective presentation and a sincere one, because although I am a Latin American, I am so neither by birth nor by upbringing, and this has enabled me to experience the problems of Latin America from within and to analyze them from without.

All of which may be summarized: this book has been written not simply to inform but to make the appeal of Latin America infectious. For Latin America, as perhaps no other part of the world, can only be understood if one feels a certain passion for it; the passion need not be excessive.

As usual—but more than usual, in this instance—I want to thank my editor, Marcia Case, whose help in organizing the book has prevented it from being as chaotic as Latin America itself often appears to be (but is not).

V.A.

May, 1969

Contents

AUTHOR'S NOTE	v
I. IS THERE A LATIN AMERICA?	3

Latin American Unity • Latin American Diversity • The Hard Life • The Riches of Latin America

II. IS THERE A LATIN AMERICAN?   17

The Aborigines • The Indians • The Conquistadors • The Negroes • The Immigrants • Relations Between the Races • Population Growth • Urbanization • The Psychology of the Latin American

III. HOW DID LATIN AMERICA EMERGE?   48

The Pre-Columbian Peoples • Explorers and Conquistadors • The Founders • The Colonial Structure • Indians, Friars, and Bishops • The Rebellions of the Encomenderos • The Indian Rebellions • The Negro Rebellions • The Creole Rebellions • The British, French, and Dutch in America • Independence

IV. WHY HAS LATIN AMERICA NOT CHANGED?   104

Organization of the States • The Church and the Land • Latifundism • The Abolition of Slavery • Industrialism and the Middle Class • Foreign Investment • The Caudillos

Contents

V. WHAT DO LATIN AMERICANS WANT? 138
The Composition of Society • The Labor Movement • Radicals and Populists • Militarism • The Mexican Revolution

VI. WHERE IS LATIN AMERICA GOING? 172
Standard of Living • Economic Thought • Economic Policy • The Business World • The Mixed Economy • Finance • The Treasury • Inflation • Financing • Production of Goods • Foreign Capital • Foreign Trade • Foreign Aid • Economic Integration

VII. IS LATIN AMERICA IN THE WORLD? 233
The Aspiration to Isolation • European Interventions • Relations with the United States • United States Interventions • Latin American Interventions • Latin American Diplomacy • Latin America in International Organizations • From Pan-Americanism to Inter-Americanism

VIII. WHO WANTS SOCIAL CHANGE? 277
The Isolated Revolutions • Bureaucratization of the Revolution • The Alliance for Progress • The Case of Cuba • The Normalization of Disorder • Nationalism and Stability • For or Against Social Change? • How Can Development Be Accelerated?

IX. WHAT DO LATIN AMERICANS THINK? 333
Way of Life • Poverty as Educator • The Formalization of Life • Students and Intellectuals • Cultural Expression

READING LIST 368

INDEX 379

THE LATIN AMERICANS

CHAPTER I

Is There a Latin America?

One of the commonplaces most frequently encountered about Latin America is the statement that it does not exist—that differences in climate, culture, and degree of development between Uruguay and Nicaragua are as great as those between Korea and Switzerland.

The denial of Latin America's existence is almost symbolic of what we might call Latin America's drowning in clichés. There is probably no continent whose image has been distorted as Latin America's has by tourist folklore, old saws, and prejudice. Hardly has the name "Latin America" been pronounced than there leap into mind various images that have nothing to do with reality but that together embody the ideas we are used to entertaining about Latin America: laziness in work, passion in love, fanaticism in religion, rhetoric in culture, personality cult in politics, backwardness in the economy, poverty in the streets, chivalry in behavior, deceit in business, chaos in government, women shut up at home, vivacious songs and dances, sleepy and mysterious Indians, the all-devouring jungle. . .

This is not Latin America. There is a bit of all this in it, but it is much more; in the long run, it is very different from what these conventional images suggest.

The reality of Latin America is varied and, above all, different from the reality the North American is accustomed to seeing around him. Different in physical aspects, in ways of working and living, in ways of thinking and of expression. Hence, it is a reality that cannot be understood merely on the basis of statistics and description. Latin America must be interpreted if it is to be understood. Otherwise, the reader will find it impossible to comprehend what is happening in its twenty-two nations or to anticipate future developments in them. Measured with a North American yardstick, Latin America appears to be an eccentric continent, full of surprises and inconsistencies. Measured with a Latin American yardstick, it is consistent, predictable, and orderly. This book will try to persuade the reader that Latin America should not be measured with a North American yardstick.

Latin American Unity

Latin America does exist as a unity. Indeed, no other continent presents so high a degree of unity. In Asia, we find civilizations, languages, degrees of development, and lines of historical evolution that are completely different from one another. There is nothing in common, nothing that could be called characteristically Asian, between Arabia and Korea, or between China and India. Similarly, in Africa, there is little in common between a Bantu and a Berber, between Madagascar and Algeria, or between Egypt and Angola. In Europe, despite a common historical development, there are today greater differences between Portugal and Switzerland, or between Ireland and Greece, than between any two Latin American countries.

Language is an important factor contributing to Latin American unity. Spanish is spoken in eighteen of the twenty-two Latin American republics. Portuguese is spoken in Brazil, French in Haiti, and English in Guyana and Trinidad and Tobago. But the Spanish- and Portuguese-speaking peoples have no difficulty in understanding one another because of the similarity of the two languages.

This alone establishes a very important common denominator. But other factors just as important as language contribute to Latin American unity. All derive from the fact that society in the Latin American countries was molded by several common influences. The differences between the various countries, and even between the various regions within a country, derive from certain differences in the material on which these influences were brought to bear. In some places the Spaniards found relatively advanced social structures, and in others primitive tribes; Spanish influence had different effects, naturally, where the conquistadors conquered empires and where they conquered scattered tribes. But in any case, the Spanish influence—and also the Portuguese—was sufficiently strong and lasting to produce, over and above the diversified elements, some common factors that have endured and have become increasingly marked. So that in spite of the division of Latin America into countries, there is today more uniformity, there are more shared Latin American traits, than there were in the colonial period.

As we shall see, the most characteristic, the most Latin American feature of Latin America—more than the language, more than its folklore, more than its ways of life or its religion—is the social structure. And it is this social structure that will explain for us not only the fundamental unity of Latin America, but also its cultural and even its economic unity.

It is not possible, however, to have an entity of hundreds of millions of people, inhabiting several million square miles, without a certain diversity. In Latin America, the diversifying factors are plentiful.

Latin American Diversity

Latin American unity is first of all the result of human action, it is a social product. Latin American diversity is a product of nature, of geographic and climatic factors that man often cannot influence even with the most modern techniques.

From north to south, from the Rio Grande to Cape Horn, Latin America measures 7,000 miles. There is great variation in the width of the region, from 50 miles at the Central American isthmus to 3,200 miles at the widest part of South America, across Brazil and Peru. At its widest point, it extends over 47 degrees of longitude, as against 58 for the United States. All in all, Latin America's surface is nearly two and one-half times greater than that of the conterminous United States.

Latin America lies not south but southeast of the United States. Indeed, most of South America is further east than Florida. Lima, Peru, for example, is in the same time zone as New York City; Mexico City is only two hours behind New York; Caracas and Buenos Aires are in the same time zone as San Juan, P.R.

The 8 million square miles of Latin America occupy an intermediate position in the Atlantic. Recife, at the eastern tip of Brazil, is 1,700 miles from Dakar in Africa, but 3,700 miles from New York and 3,100 from London. (The coastal configuration of South America has given rise to the theory that it was once joined to Africa, whose northwestern bulge would have fitted into the Caribbean.)

Geologically, the hemisphere is young. The Andes mountain range belongs to the Cenozoic Age, although in central Brazil there are some mountains of the Mesozoic and Paleozoic ages. For the entire length of the South American continent, the Andes form a vast highland, or altiplano. The highest point in the Andes, Mt. Aconcagua, on the border between Argentina and Chile, rises to 22,835 feet, the highest point in the Western Hemisphere. The Andes highlands are bordered by a coastal fringe on the Pacific side and by plains, or llanos, and forests on the Atlantic.

In Latin America, the centers of population—cities and regions of high demographic density—are near the coast, in the highlands, and in some cases on the banks of the great rivers. Latin America's history and economic life have been played out on longitudinal margins, never exceeding 400 miles in width, that lie along the coast. Even the cities of the altiplano are no more than 400 miles from the sea. Cities and provinces in the interior are thinly settled. The spread of population has not been toward the interior but along coastlines and rivers. The plains have not brought unity, as in the United States, but separation.

The physical features determine the type of crops grown in each region and also the manner of farming. Plantations are abundant on the Pacific coastal fringe, whereas on the

Andean heights extensive latifundios, or great landed estates, are the rule. The plantations and the latifundios did not appear where they did by chance; the differences in physical conditions made mechanized farming profitable on the coastal plains but difficult and expensive in the isolated Andean zones.

Geography has also caused differences in the people. In the nineteenth century, great masses of Europeans migrated to the thinly settled plains of the southern part of the continent. In the mountainous countries, which had a stable and organized Indian population, land was not plentiful; and in the tropics, the climate made life difficult for the European—who, on the other hand, found in the region around the Río de la Plata and in Chile, for example, temperatures and seasons like those of his native country. Geography determined the migration of many Chinese and Japanese to the Pacific coast, and the climate favored the importation of Negro slaves to the tropical coastal regions on the Atlantic. All this accounts for significant differences in the ethnic composition of the various Latin American regions.

There are also profound psychological differences among the inhabitants. The people of the highlands tend to be reserved and introverted, suspicious and active; they give a general impression of sadness. The people along the coast are outgoing, extroverted, imaginative, and give a general impression of happiness. A resident of Mexico City, 7,000 feet above sea level, is more like a resident of Bogotá, 9,000 feet high, although they are thousands of miles apart, than he is like a person from Veracruz, 280 miles from Mexico City but on the coast.

Perhaps the most basic diversifying feature of Latin America, which is often forgotten but which is inescapable in its history and its everyday life, is its enormous size. Brazil is not only larger than the continental United States, it is bigger than all of Europe west of the Soviet Union. Argentina is about one-third the size of the entire United States; Mexico is three times the size of Texas; Bolivia is ten times the size of Ohio. Mexico City is as far from Buenos Aires as London is from New Delhi, and the mouth of the Amazon is as close to San Juan as it is to Rio de Janeiro. The Amazon, which is 105 miles wide at the mouth, is navigable for a distance only a little shorter than that between New York and Los Angeles.

Moreover, communications in Latin America are poor. With a surface more than double that of the United States, Latin America has only a little more than 500,000 miles of railroads (compared to 3.5 million in the United States), and these are antiquated. Argentina, southern Brazil, and Mexico are the only areas with railway systems of genuine importance, and they are far below the needed level.

The mountains and the jungles make the building of railroads (and highways) expensive and technically difficult. To build railways across the Andes is a fantastic undertaking. The line from Santiago to Mendoza goes through mountain passes 10,000 feet high and in winter is often blocked by snow. The highest railroad in the world runs from Lima to the Cerro de Pasco mines; it has sixty-five tunnels, sixty-seven viaducts, and sixteen major zigzags in a stretch of 250 miles.

Roads are also scarce and in poor condition. In 1966, there were only 650,000 miles of roads in all Latin America, many of them unpaved. The Pan-American Highway, which is eventually to reach from one end of the continent to the other and to pass through every country, is almost completed (lacking only a stretch between Panama and Colombia), but it is far from being entirely paved.

River travel, except on the Paraná, the Amazon, and the Orinoco, is inadequate and disorganized. Air transport is increasingly plentiful, but it is also expensive, since each country wants to have its own national airline, which is considered a status symbol.

The result of all this is isolation and provincialism. For the majority of Latin Americans, the world is reduced to the small territory through which they are able to travel without having to pass great natural barriers. The jetliner and the small plane have overcome this isolation in only a few cases; poverty keeps most of the people in the same state, as regards communication, that prevailed when the Spaniards came.

The Hard Life

Nearly 80 per cent of Latin America lies in the tropics. Only the height of the mountains makes it possible to endure the tropical climate; most of the cities founded by Spaniards in the tropics are several thousand feet above sea level: Mexico City, Bogotá, La Paz. Tropical ports were not really important until a few decades ago, when public-health techniques made it possible to do away with the plague, malaria, and other tropical diseases. Only in the south, where the climate was more favorable and where there were adequate bays, were such important coastal cities as Buenos Aires, Rio de Janeiro, Valparaiso, and Callao founded.

Farming in the tropics is exhausting, not only because of the heat but because the crops must be protected against encroaching vegetation. Extraction of materials from the jungle —rubber and chicle, for example—still presents almost incredible aspects of brutality and suffering.

If life in the tropics is uncomfortable and dangerous, the heights are scarcely more hospitable. At 9,000 feet in the Andes, one suffers from the *sorocho,* a feeling of weakness accompanied by dizziness and palpitations. Physical effort is difficult; in La Paz, no one ever hurries through the streets. To make matters worse, because of the topography, many cities of the altiplano have steeply sloping streets; even automobiles need engine adjustment to prevent a loss of power. Many of Latin America's mines are at high altitudes, and this makes working them particularly difficult. The high altitude has less effect on the Indians born on the altiplano— the only people able to work there—but even so, the Indians who work in the mines of Bolivia and Peru grow old in a few years and at forty are so worn out that they must seek a different occupation.

In the tropics, air conditioning—where economic and power resources make it possible—can alter the working environment and put an end to the "softening" caused by the heat, whose consequences are as devastating to productivity as the *sorocho* is in the mountains. But no means has been found for conquering the latter.

Water is the cause of other perils that could in great part be conquered if economic means were available.

Latin America's rivers are among the largest in the world. The Amazon, 3,000 miles long, carries more water to the sea than the Mississippi, the Nile, and the Yangtze combined and is navigable for 1,000 miles by transatlantic vessels. The Paraná, which drains the southern watershed, connects Bolivia and Paraguay (through its tributaries) with the sea; it joins with the Uruguay River to form the Río de la Plata when it empties into the Atlantic between Buenos Aires and Montevideo. The Magdalena River gives the region around Bogotá access to the coast and is navigable for its entire length of 1,000 miles. In Venezuela, the Orinoco River turns the llanos into fertile pastures; the world's largest deposits of iron ore have been discovered along its banks.

There are also large lakes, although they are smaller than those in the United States or Europe. Lake Maracaibo, in Venezuela, which has an outlet to the sea and is thickly dotted with oil wells, is the largest on the continent; it is almost as big as the state of New Jersey. Lake Titicaca, between Peru and Bolivia, 12,500 feet above sea level, is larger than the state of Delaware. In Argentine Patagonia, a salt lake, Salinas Grandes, 131 feet below sea level, marks the low point of Latin America.

But all this is merely a matter of statistics. In fact, these great rivers and lakes, the many rapid streams that fall from the Andes to the Pacific, and the mountain lakes in their age-old craters are little used for navigation because of the scarcity of canals, or for irrigation or power production because of the lack of dams and irrigation systems.

Only 2.5 per cent of the world's electric power is to be found in Latin America, which covers 15 per cent of the land surface of the globe. And although they are agricultural, the Latin American countries have only very recently begun to utilize their water resources, for reasons we shall examine later. The result is that there are vast sterile belts of land almost as desolate as deserts. The plains of the Gran Chaco are no more productive than the Patagonian mesa, which has only ten inches of annual rainfall, or rocky Tierra del Fuego in the extreme south. The Atacama Desert in Chile, possibly the driest spot in the world, and the Altar Desert in northern Mexico are totally barren, although the latter is beginning to yield cotton, thanks to the persistence of the peasants, who have irrigated it at considerable cost to themselves.

Two great ocean currents wash the shores of Latin America. The Atlantic Gulf Stream has little effect. But the cold waters of the Humboldt Current, in the Pacific, dry out part of the coastal lands of Peru and Chile and envelop the coastal cities in a stubborn fog (the *garúa*).

Traditionally, Latin America has relied on rain. Except in the south, where we find the four seasons of the temperate zones (although snow is rare, except in the southernmost tip), there are only two seasons in Latin America: the dry and the rainy. Each lasts half a year—the rainy season from October to March in the south, and from March to October in the north. But the six months' rainy season is irregular, the dry zones are increasing (chiefly as a result of deforestation), and formerly fertile lands are poor today: for example, La Laguna in Mexico, or the northern pampas in Argentina. In other places, the excessive rainfall—80 inches annually in the Amazon country—produces such fertility that cultivation of the land requires a constant struggle against the jungle. In many places, the rains wash the minerals out of the soil. Floods are frequent and devastating, while the rapidly growing cities suffer from a shortage of water.

There is an abundance of freaks of nature in Latin America, and these are reflected in folklore. There are trees whose "shade"—actually, the poisonous powder given off by the leaves—puts a man to sleep and kills him, and there are fish, like the piranha of the rivers flowing from the Andes to the Atlantic, whose sharp teeth can turn a body into a skeleton in a few minutes. The jungle, although it does not have the "big cats" we consider typical, like the lion and tiger, has plenty of jaguars, which the Indians held in fear and wonder, and pumas, which Latin American *pueblo* dwellers called lions. The Indians also attached great religious importance to snakes, which figure frequently in Aztec mythology (the god Quetzalcoatl was represented as a plumed serpent, a concept that gave D. H. Lawrence the title for a novel about Mexico); the snakes were dreaded by the conquistadors, who were accustomed to the far less dangerous reptiles of Europe. The black widow spider and the scorpion are also much more poisonous than the European varieties, and are still nightmares to the peasants. The peasants are ignorant of the deathdealing bacteria and insects, but they suffer greatly from them: gastrointestinal ailments caused by bacteria in the water, amebic dysentery, serious infections produced by tiny insects that get into the soles of the feet and work themselves into the bloodstream, and sight-destroying enconiosis, spread by an insect that lives on the coffee plant. On the other hand, malaria is on the way to being eradicated, and yellow fever has been almost conquered.

Technical and medical progress has thus made it possible to eliminate many of these natural hazards, although little advantage is taken of these advances because of the high cost. But there are other obstacles against which science has been powerless. In the central cordillera of the continent—the Sierra Madre in Mexico and the Andes in South America—a hundred major volcanoes and thousands of minor ones constitute an ever-present menace, for many are active and erupt from time to time. For almost two years, in 1963–64, Mt. Iguazu, in Costa Rica, covered a part of the country with ashes, destroying crops, paralyzing industry, and causing a genuine economic crisis. One could not walk through the streets of San José, the capital, day or night, without being covered with ashes; the plumbing and drainage systems were stopped up by ashes. And where there are volcanoes there are also earthquakes: they are frequent in Chile, Peru, and Ecuador. The ancient capital of Guatemala, Antigua, lies in ruins from an earthquake in the eighteenth century, and Concepción, in Chile, was almost destroyed in 1965. The Pacific coast is especially prone to earthquakes and, at times, tidal waves. The Caribbean islands are never safe from late-summer hurricanes.

Nature, obviously, would seem to be savagely hostile to man in Latin America. The very grandeur of the landscape, with its lofty mountains and distant horizons, depresses and dwarfs man, leaving him with a sense of futility, and the unending recurrence of natural catastrophes tends to breed fatalism.

The Riches of Latin America

Yet Latin America has great riches. The Indians of the pre-Conquest period were kept from realizing this by their lack of technical knowledge. The Spaniards, within the limits of the technology of their time, exploited some of Latin America's wealth. In the nineteenth century, when industrialization enabled men to seek out and profit from the continent's hidden riches, the prevailing social system hindered such development, since the ruling classes were interested only in exploiting the land. It was foreign capital that, in small measure, began to utilize the true riches of the continent.

The flora and fauna of Latin America are abundant: the task of classifying them has only just begun. This abundance is reflected in the national coats of arms, many of which display an animal or plant characteristic of the country: Guatemala shows the brilliant quetzal bird (which also gives its name to the unit of currency); Peru, the llama; Uruguay, the sheep.

Indian corn (maize), the potato, the tomato, tobacco, and many tropical fruits are native to America. The Mayas smoked tobacco through their noses. For the Aymará Indians in what is now Bolivia, potatoes were like bread; they dried and preserved them for winter—as they still do. Corn is still the basic food of many Latin Americans.

Columbus took to Cuba the seeds of the sugar cane, which the Arabs had introduced into Spain. The Spaniards also brought with them from the Old World rice, wheat, and oranges, among many other plants. They also introduced into the New World the banana from Africa and the mango from the Philippines.

The Indians were familiar with rubber, which they used to make balls with which they played a kind of basketball. Until 1870, rubber was produced only in Brazil, Peru, and Colombia, but in that year an Englishman, Sir Henry Wickham, took with him several thousand seeds which, planted in London, produced nurseries for the plantations soon to be established in Ceylon, Indonesia, and throughout Southeast Asia. The quinine of Peru, Ecuador, and Colombia was also taken out by the Dutch, French, and English, who cultivated it in their colonies. In 1727, a Portuguese ambassador stole coffee beans from the Dutch in Surinam, who were cultivating it secretly; carried to Brazil, coffee became that country's principal product.

Today, there are great harvests of bananas and other tropical fruits, coffee, sugar, and cotton. Brazil produces nearly half the world's supply of coffee, and the Caribbean islands account for almost one-third of its sugar.* Chile has excellent wines; Ecuador's cocoa is famous. Corn, the staple food of the people, is grown everywhere, and so to a lesser degree is wheat. But only very recently has there been an attempt to introduce new crops or improve existing ones, or to satisfy the needs of the domestic market.

Scarcely one-third of the surface of Latin America is arable; scarcely half of that is cultivated; a quarter of that half is used for grazing. The richest farmland is concentrated in a few regions, like the Bajío in Mexico; the 300-mile semicircle of pampas around Buenos Aires (where the black soil reaches a depth of 12 feet); the Colombian and Venezuelan llanos (the latter used almost wholly for cattle-raising); and the lowlands of southern Brazil. Near the Pacific coast, plantations make good use of the land, but in general the agricultural yield is low, the land is wasted, and only the indispensable minimum is cultivated—again as a result of social causes. Still, in some parts of Latin America it is not unusual to harvest two and even three crops a year.

The animals that are the basis of modern agricultural wealth in Latin America were brought in by the conquistadors: the horse, cattle, and sheep. The Spaniards also brought with them chickens, asses, pigs, dogs, and cats. (The only animal that did not acclimate was the camel, either in colonial times or in the nineteenth century, when it was tried as a means of transporting immigrants across the Isthmus of Panama.) The horse had existed in a wild state in Latin America, but had disappeared by the time the Spaniards arrived. Today, it is essential for farming and above all in cattle-raising, which is a major industry in Argentina, Uruguay, Venezuela, and Colombia. The *llaneros* (in Colombia and Venezuela), the gauchos (in Argentina, Brazil, and Uruguay), and the *huasos* (in Chile) are—like the cowboys of the American West—excellent horsemen. (For a gaucho, the worst conceivable fate is the loss of his horse. In the Argentine army, during the last century, gauchos who received the death penalty were sentenced instead to serve in the infantry.)

* Latin America produces the following percentages of the world supply of these crops:

coffee	70%	meat	40%
bananas	60	cocoa	35
linseed	50	sugar	30
rare woods	45	cotton	12

The lumber industry, although little developed, has caused significant deforestation in the regions around Latin America's cities. Moreover, the scarcity of coal has made it necessary to use wood for cooking, which has increased the deforestation. But there are still more than 2 million square miles of rare woods and more than 1,500 varieties of hardwood growing in Latin America. The quebracho of Chile and Argentina is much in demand for making railroad ties, and Peruvian balsa is used in ship-building. Cinchona bark yields quinine. Tropical woods are still much used by cabinetmakers. But, at the time when the lumber industry might have thrived, lack of transportation facilities hampered it, and today, with the appearance of plastics, wood is losing its usefulness.

The subsoil of Latin America is much richer than the topsoil, but it has been little and poorly exploited. The Spaniards concentrated on gold and silver, which served to finance their wars in Europe (and, indirectly, to ruin their country). Available techniques did not make possible the discovery of Latin America's huge deposits of other minerals; even if these had been discovered, they could not have been used, since Europe had plenty of minerals and its industry at that time was well supplied with raw materials. The growing industries of the eighteenth century opened up new markets for minerals, but Latin American society was exclusively oriented to exploitation of the land, and its leaders were not interested in extending the sources of wealth. Exploitation of the existing mines, however, was continued. The needs of the industrial countries induced foreign entrepreneurs to explore Latin America further and to exploit new sources of wealth. Being foreigners, they were interested in making the greatest possible profit without concerning themselves with the future or the interests of the Latin American countries—an attitude that, in certain cases, has had serious economic consequences and, as we shall see, ended by producing extreme nationalistic reactions among Latin Americans.

More than 10 per cent of the world's tin now comes from Bolivia. Venezuela provides the greater part of the United States' imports of iron, Chile of copper. Caribbean bauxite represents more than half of the world's supply. Mexico, Bolivia, and Peru supply the greater portion of the world's silver. (Two mines in Mexico alone—in Guanajuato and

Pachuca—yield one-third of the silver used in the world today.) In the last fifty years, Mexico and Venezuela have developed a mighty oil industry; oil has also been found in Colombia, Peru, Brazil, Argentina, Chile, Ecuador, and Bolivia, although still not in quantities sufficient to meet the needs of these countries.* There is also little coal in Latin America; it is found only in Mexico, Colombia, Brazil, and Chile.

Latin America's potential wealth is far greater than its actual riches. Venezuela is the world's second largest producer of oil, but experts say that there is more oil under Bolivia than in all the rest of South America. Chile's copper reserves account for about one-third of the world's supply. There are known to be iron reserves of about 5 billion tons, in addition to 80 billion tons of available potential reserves, nearly all of high quality; these represent one-third of the world's reserves. The most important deposits are those of Minas Gerais and Matto Grosso in Brazil, which represent more than 80 per cent of the Latin American reserve. The salt deposits of Zipaquira, in Colombia, extend over several thousand square miles and are several hundred feet deep.

Alexander von Humboldt, the German scholar and writer who traveled throughout Latin America in the early nineteenth century and wrote about its geography, flora, and fauna, said that Latin America was like "a beggar sitting on a bench of gold."

* Latin America produces the following percentages of the world supply of these minerals:

nitrates	65%	copper	25%
vanadium	50	oil	18
silver	45	tin	12
antimony	45	gold	7

CHAPTER II

Is There a Latin American?

When you ask a Latin American where he comes from, he answers with the name of his country. He never says that he is a Latin American. Consciousness of being Latin American is restricted to small groups of urban intellectuals, businessmen, and students.

In physical appearance, a Bolivian Indian and a half-Italian, half-Galician stevedore on the waterfront of Buenos Aires look as unlike as a Scandinavian and a Greek. But in their reactions, their customs, their scale of values, and their aspirations there is a common denominator. Above all, there is identity in the social systems and social structures of nearly all the Latin American countries. The resident of Buenos Aires who considers himself more European than Latin American, and the Ecuadorian peasant who does not consider himself an Ecuadorian at all but simply a Quechua, are products of a similar type of society that has conditioned their culture and determined their differences and similarities. In this sense, it may be said that while the Latin American does not exist subjectively—very few see themselves as Latin Americans—there does exist a Latin American type of society that unites its component members and gives them a fundamental uniformity.

The Latin American people and their society are the products of four widely differing ingredients: the indigenous peoples, the Spanish and Portuguese conquistadors and colonizers, the Negroes, and the later European and Asian immigrants. These peoples, mingled, have shaped Latin American society. And a Latin American, obvious as this may seem, is a person who lives in this society.

The Aborigines

Many theories have been advanced concerning the original Americans. Some say that the first inhabitants of the continent came by land from Europe in an epoch in which the two continental masses were joined. Others think that they came from Europe, but by sea. Another theory assigns an Asian origin to the Americans, and this also has supporters in two camps: those who believe the first inhabitants came from Asia over a land bridge (possibly today's Bering Strait), and those who think they came by sea. There are still more theories. Some speak of Atlantis, a lost continent that might have existed in the present Atlantic Ocean. Lord Kingsborough, who financed expeditions to the Mayan ruins, maintained that the Indians were descended from one of the lost tribes of Israel. Finally, there are those who maintain that man originated in South America, from which he gradually spread north and east to Africa and Europe and west to Asia. The Argentine archeologist Florentino Ameghino (1854–1911) was one of those who thought that the American continent was the cradle of mankind.

None of these theories is simple fantasy. Every one is based on Indian legends, archaeological discoveries, ancient navigators' maps, or on the narratives of classical literatures. Sometimes a theory rests on coincidence, like the fact that Mayan pyramids, although quadrangular rather than triangular, otherwise resemble those of Egypt. Other theories are based on phonetic similarities between the ancient languages and those of Europe (for instance, the Aztecs, in their language, Nahuatl, called their god *teo,* which resembles the

Greek word *theos*), or on the fact that the symbol of the sun, which appeared on the imperial flags of China and Japan, is also found on those of Costa Rica, Cuba, Ecuador, Honduras, Nicaragua, Panama, and El Salvador.

The theories about the South Americans' Asian origin, while less daring, are scientifically sounder than the rest. Archaeological remains recently discovered in Ecuador bear a surprising resemblance to objects used in China centuries ago, and this has given rise to a theory that the original population—or possibly a later colonization—was Chinese.*

But in any event, one thing is certain: there were human inhabitants in the Western Hemisphere 10,000 years ago. Proofs include a skull discovered in Mexico whose age could be estimated by means of carbon-14. What we know about these peoples comes to us through the Spaniards, who collected legends, literature, and history about the epochs that preceded their arrival.

The Indians

At the time of the Spanish Conquest, highly organized Indian societies existed in two extensive regions in Latin America: Mexico and Central America, and the Andean regions of South America. In the rest of the hemisphere, the Indians lived in tribes of differing degrees of social organization and technical development: some were scattered, some nomadic, some were the remains of conquered or subjected groups, and some were savage tribes in the first stages of permanent settlement. Some were agricultural societies, others were made up of hunters and fishermen. Between 150 and 200 different dialects were spoken.

But the indigenous inhabitants had certain traits in common: none knew about the wheel or the use of beasts of burden (if we except the llama, the alpaca, and the vicuña in the Andes, all little used and only for the lightest loads), and they had few metal utensils or tools. This lack of technological progress put them at a considerable disadvantage

---

* Many Latin Americans seem to be upset by the assertion that they have Asian origins. Paul Rivet, a French ethnologist who propounded this theory, made many enemies on account of it. The reason, though not one to be openly admitted, was obvious: the Latin Americans considered Asians inferior and did not want to be descended from them.

against the Spaniards. Moreover, the two major peoples the Spaniards encountered—the Incas and the Aztecs—were in a period of social disintegration: their rigid social systems constituted a barrier to progress, and protests and rebellions occurred. The Aztecs were also what we of today would call imperialists; this weakened their capacity to resist, since they could not rely on their subject peoples to oppose the Spaniards, who appeared to them as liberators.

It has been said that there was no mass slaughter of the Indians in Latin America because the Catholic conquistadors had a zeal for converting them that the Protestant colonizers in the North lacked. It is not certain that this can be historically supported. We should seek the explanation rather in a series of diverse but related factors. For one thing, the Spaniards wanted Indians to work the land and the mines, since they had come to America not to be farmers, miners, or servants but to be gentlemen; the Puritans who landed in New England, on the other hand, wanted to till their own lands and so had no need of the Indians. Moreover, the Englishman had never been one to mix racially, and he also came to America with his family; the Spaniard came without a wife and with his country's long tradition of racial intermixture behind him, and from the beginning intermarried with Indian women. Finally, in North America the Indians were scattered and nomadic and more difficult to manage than those in Mexico and Peru. We must not forget that in those parts of South America where the Indian tribes were savage and the Spaniards and Portuguese had no contact with them except by force of arms, there *was* slaughter.

To understand the Indian influence in Latin America today, we must take into account the fact that after the Spanish Conquest the indigenous upper classes largely disappeared, and only the mass of lower-caste people remained. Those who survived, therefore, were the least cultivated part of society. Moreover, because they had lived in submission to Inca and Aztec types of theocratic feudalism, they lacked initiative and personal ambition. The Indians had a collectivist outlook: for them, one's individual existence was bound up in the collective being. Imagine, then, the psychological shock caused by their compulsory adaptation not only to a new religion and a new language, but especially to new methods of work and a new social organization, all of which led to the emergence of individual life.

In some places, there was violent resistance to the changes produced by the Conquest. The Araucanians in Chile, groups of Aztecs in southern Mexico, and savage tribes in various places struggled for years and sometimes for centuries against the Spaniards. When Mexico won its independence, the Yaquis of the Pacific coast had not yet submitted. And as we shall see, there was no lack of Indian rebellions in the colonial era, some of which had as their avowed purpose the restoring of native government. But the most widespread type of resistance took psychological forms. It consisted in the Indian's adapting himself to the new society and the new religion while secretly retaining his old personality and even his old beliefs.

The direct influence of the Indian societies on colonial society and culture, and on modern Latin American life as well, consists basically in little more than certain cultural vestiges, especially in verbal expressions, religion, and the plastic arts. Certain forms of communal ownership of land (the *ayllu* in Peru, the *ejido* in Mexico) have also survived to our times. And some local political forms (the cacique) still exist, albeit in distorted form.*

But the Indian influence in modern Latin America is so apparent and important not because the indigenes and mestizos (mixed Indian and Spanish) have preserved Inca or Aztec traces, but because adaptation to Spanish colonial society distorted the Indian's outlook and obliged him to adopt certain attitudes that have persisted and have affected the mestizos too. When we come to speak of the psychology of the Latin American, we shall see that it has its roots in this adaptation of the Indian to a new and hostile society—the seemingly invincible and overwhelming society of the Iberian colonizers.

Naturally, these Indian characteristics are influential in proportion to the size of the Indian population (actually, to the number of people who live like Indians, since many mestizos are Indian in customs, culture, and speech). "Pure"

---

* The cacique was originally an Indian ruler, or chief. The Spaniards made use of him in their colonial administration, and in time the word came to mean a local strong man, or political "boss."

Indians account for 8.5 per cent of Latin America's total population, but in some countries this percentage is much higher: in Bolivia, 70 per cent; in Peru, 47 per cent; in Guatemala, 41 per cent; in Ecuador, 38 per cent; in Mexico, 9 per cent. But if we take into account the way of life rather than physical appearance, the percentage of "Indians" is much higher. A small part of the Indian population (about 870,000 persons) is savage; in Brazil, nearly all the Indians live in scattered tribes outside of civilization. Nearly half of Latin America's Indians do not speak Spanish or Portuguese, which further isolates them from the mainstream of Latin American society.

The Conquistadors

What was the incentive that sent the Spaniards and Portuguese to the New World?

They were seeking adventure and wealth, of course. The conquistadors were, to some degree, men of the Renaissance, which began in Spain before the rest of Europe, for the Spaniards received Hellenic ideas through the Moors and Jews at a time when Italy knew nothing of them. The taste for danger, the desire for adventure, the sense of power were all strong motives for these men.

But above all they were seeking—many perhaps unconsciously—a place where they would not be forced into a subordinate station in life. We must realize that for the Spaniard of that period, the end of the reconquest from the Moors also meant an end to the possibility of receiving lands and titles as a reward for services rendered in war: in other words, an end to what had for centuries been the chief impetus to social mobility. A Spaniard who in Spain was not a member of the elite, not a member of the governing class, accepted and shared the values of his society according to which nobility was based on excellence, was won by and expressed in action. An aristocratic title was not a guarantee of nobility but merely signified an external, formal obligation to behave as befitted a nobleman. But nobility was expected of every Spaniard. "The poor man has nothing but his honor," says the proverb. One went to America, then, in quest of a chance to rise, to prosper, without staining one's honor. America offered every man the means of showing his worth. In America, it was possible to realize the Spanish ideal that everyone's nobility should be self-made.

This may seem very "literary," but all the historical evidence indicates that these moral values—of which the Spaniard of that time did not consciously think—furnished the primary incentive for the exploration, conquest, and, later, colonization of Spanish America. Of course, this does not mean that the conquistadors were above greed, ambition, cruelty, or brutality.

The conquistadors were often the younger, untitled sons of noble families, who captained groups of peasants hastily turned soldiers, inured to work and fatigue, and able to learn quickly and to adapt themselves to unfamiliar climate and labor. They were obstinate about taking with them into the tropics the ways of life and attitudes that had been theirs in Spain. The Spaniard does not change; he produces change. He adapts himself to things in order to go on being himself. Thus it was that in the Indies he founded cities that were like Spanish towns, he created institutions similar to those established by the medieval *cartas pueblos*,* and he showed the same willingness to mingle his blood with that of the Indians as his forebears had shown during the successive invasions of the Peninsula.

The conquistador brought with him from the Peninsula a special social and political attitude: individualism combined with a certain characteristic sense of community. In Spain, every man who was not a serf thought of himself as an *hidalgo*, a member of the nobility. He was independent, his rights were well defined by law and tradition, and he considered himself the equal of any authority. "We who are of as great worth as You and who, joined together, are of greater worth than You," was the formula the Aragonese used in swearing allegiance to their king. Every Spaniard, and every Portuguese, felt that he was the equal of the viceroy or the leader of his expedition. This led to dissension, division, rebellion. But at the same time, the Spaniard and the Portuguese were part of a very solid living community with a long tradition—the municipality, which also had rights well defined by law. The Spaniard was accustomed to expressing his

---

* The *cartas pueblos* were granted by the Castilian king to settlers on lands reconquered from the Moors and conferred on them the right to govern their own communities.

opinion in community affairs and to taking part in the *cabildo abierto,* or town meeting. In the towns he founded in America, these assemblies were held for the discussion of important affairs. Most of the colonies' decisions to declare independence early in the nineteenth century were adopted in the *cabildo abierto.* And, as white women were few in America and ran as great risks as the men, the women also had a voice in the assemblies and, hence, a more important role in society than was granted them in Iberia, although they led the same kind of life, restricted to their homes.

The Spaniards had lived for centuries with Arabs and Jews. In Spain, many Arabs continued to live, accepted and respected, in the lands reconquered from them, just as many Christians had remained when the lands were first occupied by the Arabs. Moreover, the Spaniards themselves were the product of a mixture of many peoples: Iberians, Celts, Phoenicians, Greeks, Carthaginians, Romans, Visigoths. The idea of racial purity was foreign to them (although they substituted for it the idea of religious purity; their equivalent of "pure white" being "old Christian," that is, Christian for many generations and not a convert from Judaism or Islam). In southern Portugal, which had been depopulated by the struggle with the Arabs, many Negroes were imported from Africa and formed a good part of the population of the region of Algarves; in Lisbon, at the time of the conquest, half the population was Negro.

Thus it was natural that the conquistadors should mingle with the Indians, especially in the early epochs, when Spanish and Portuguese women were scarce, if they were present at all. The social standing of the children of these mixed unions depended on whether or not there had been a marriage, but the custom of recognizing bastards was general in Castile and Portugal and took root in America, too. Hence, whereas in North America there was hardly any mingling of Indian and white, in those parts of South America and Mesoamerica where Indians lived in organized societies, mestizos were numerous and ended by forming the majority of the population. There were also unions between whites and Negroes, especially in Brazil and Cuba.

The Spaniards and Portuguese also transferred to the New World their economic and administrative systems (as we shall see in Chapter III). In this sense, Spain and Portugal were

—like the Rome of centuries earlier—countries that were not satisfied with colonizing but that turned their colonies into parts of their own civilizations. When Rome fell into decay, Gaul, Spain, Dacia, Illyria, and Italy were Romanized, yet when British and French imperialism ended, India was not wholly Anglicized and Algeria was not Gallicized. But when the Spanish and Portuguese colonies in America declared their independence they were, on the whole, on the same cultural, economic, and social level as the mother countries.

A consequence of this was that the colonizer was not the classical colonial archetype but a Creole, a Spaniard born in America of Spanish parents, or the son of such a Creole. He felt himself to be a Spaniard—although he had often not even been to Spain—yet when the time came for independence, he also considered himself an American and could take part in the separation from Spain without grief or any sense of loss, since Spain and America were the same to him. Spain, for him, was *in* America.

The Portuguese who came to America was in some respects different from the Spaniard. He was not seeking new lands to settle in but new commercial routes. He came not to populate but to govern. So, in Brazil, the importation of slaves began early and grew to considerable proportions, and society was more feudal than in Spanish America. The Portuguese gentlemen went to America to rule—and then returned to Portugal. And unlike the Spanish peasant, who went to America to make himself a gentleman, an *hidalgo,* the Portuguese peasant left his country to escape servile status; in Brazil he preferred to change occupations, settle in a coastal city, and become an artisan, a status that made him free.

The Negroes

The Negroes were not native to America, as were the Indians, and they did not go there voluntarily, as did the Spaniards and Portuguese: they were brought to America as slaves.

The first Spaniard to set foot on Peruvian soil, Alonso de Molina, brought with him a Negro servant, and the astonished Indians made friendly attempts to clean the man's skin. In 1503, before the depopulation of Hispaniola (the site of present-day Haiti and the Dominican Republic), the Crown granted permission for the importing of Negroes, and in 1517 Charles V granted a concession to import 4,000 slaves to one of his Flemish favorites. A large part of the early contingents escaped when they reached South America and joined the Indians. From that time on, the mingling of Indians and Negroes was steady; the children of the two races were called zambos. By 1550, half the population of Cuba consisted of Negroes from the Congo and Mozambique.

Thanks to their inherited immunity to yellow fever, the Negroes were useful in the tropical lowlands. It was their labor that made possible the sugar and tobacco plantations of Cuba, the banana plantations of Central America, and the plantations of the Brazilian Northeast. Where there was no shortage of Indians, the colonists were less interested in having Negroes. When the Council of the Indies issued orders to employ Negroes in the Mexican mines, the viceroy replied that the Spaniards did not want them because the cost of transporting and guarding them was too high. But it became fashionable everywhere to employ Negroes as house servants.

The Portuguese, who had set up slave camps in Lagos even before the discovery of America, were the chief importers of African labor. The disproportion between the size of Brazil and of Portugal stimulated the desire to import Negroes, all the more since many of the Brazilian Indians were savages who fled to the interior at the white man's approach. But the slave trade was not exclusive with the Portuguese: the English, French, and Dutch did a thriving business populating the Antilles with Negroes. Curiously, the period of greatest importation of slaves occurred not in the early colonial period but in the late one: in the decade 1790–1800, about 75,000 Negroes were brought each year into Latin America.

The slaves came from various parts of Africa, but since a single shipload was intended for one city or region, the Negroes were able to retain their tribal customs and beliefs, which were then adapted to the new surroundings. Haitian voodoo has a different origin and very different characteristics from the voodoo of Bahia (where it is called *candomblé*), or from that of Cuba (where it is known as *santería*). The Brazilian samba is descended from a Bantu dance, but the Cuban rumba is of Congolese ancestry; and experts say the Argentine tango is as African as the rumba or bossa nova. In Brazil, there are small groups of Negroes who speak Arabic and whose religion is a blend of Catholicism and Islam;

these are the Males, descendants of Mandingos from the western Sudan, converted to Islam before their capture.

The Negro's situation in colonial Latin America was the typical one of slavery; as we shall see, he frequently rebelled against it. But the newly independent countries soon abolished slavery; Brazil was the last Latin American country to do so, in 1888.

Today, the Negro population is as large as that of the Indians: about 8.5 per cent of the total. But the Negroes constitute a color pattern of greater density and more definite limits than that of the Indians. It is restricted to Brazil; coastal Peru, Ecuador, Colombia, and Venezuela; the Atlantic coast of the Isthmus of Panama; Cuba; Haiti; the Dominican Republic; Guyana; British Honduras; and the Antilles. Brazil has the largest number of Negroes, although the percentage of the population that is Negro is higher in the islands of the Caribbean. Haiti and the Dominican Republic, especially, are largely made up of Negroes. The Negro presence probably explains some characteristic Caribbean traits: a sophisticated sense of rhythm, a manner of speaking in shouts and bursts, a certain joyfulness of expression that contrasts with the sadness of inhabitants of countries with a heavily Indian population.

The Immigrants

During the colonial period, there was steady immigration of Spanish and Portuguese to Latin America. Many of the colonists intended to remain only for a short time, but most of them, except for the bureaucrats and military men, stayed.

Spain and Portugal tried to prevent all immigration to Latin America except their own. Exceptions were made for Catholics who had suffered Protestant persecution; the liberator of Chile, Bernardo O'Higgins, was the son of an Irishman who had emigrated for religious reasons. Exceptions were also made in the case of artisans, which in practice changed into special privileges for certain Italian and German merchants. Columbus had two Italian pilots, and several Italians were accepted as physicians in the new cities. Sebastian Caboto (1476?–1557) and Amerigo Vespucci (1451–1512), who gave his name to the new hemisphere, were respectively Venetian and Florentine, and both were pilots major. The flow of Italian immigration to Latin America may be said never to have ceased, for it still goes on today. On the other hand, there were very few French, because of fear of the expansionist ambitions of their king, although a French sailor and adventurer, Santiago Liniers (1754–1810), became governor of Buenos Aires. Catalans, who were forbidden to come to the colonies until the eighteenth century, generally tried to find a place in America as soldiers or servants of the Crown (for example, Amat, a viceroy of Peru), or as members of religious orders (like the great figure of early Californian history, Fray Junípero Serra). Jews were forbidden entry into the colonies but some managed to mock the prohibition by disguising their origin; others won permission from Philip II to settle in Mexico, where they founded the city of Monterrey under the leadership of Luis de Carvajal. These Sephardic Jews lived apart, concealing their origin, but even so they were not always safe from the Inquisition. (Centuries later, Jewish immigrants to Mexico came upon small communities of Indians of Jewish faith, perhaps converted by Carvajal.)

In the first years after independence, many Latin American politicians favored immigration. "To govern is to populate," said the Argentine statesman Juan Bautista Alberdi (1810–84). But this was true chiefly in the south—in Argentina, Brazil, Chile, Uruguay—and much less so in countries with a large Indian population, like Peru and Mexico, where an attempt was made to preserve the restrictions of the colonial era.

Most immigration after independence was for economic reasons; people came to a new land to better their lot. But there were also waves of political immigrants fleeing persecution in Europe.

In the nineteenth century, when there were no passports or visas, it often happened that those who wanted to go to America—young men from the cities, families from the country, artisans thrown out of work by industrialization—made their way to a European seaport, asked the price of passage, and boarded a ship whose passage they could afford. When the ship reached South America, the immigrant was in a position very different from that of an immigrant to the United States. The standard of living in the United States was not lower (at times it was higher) than the one the immigrant had left behind; but in Latin America, the immigrant found workers who lived on a lower level than his had been in the Old World, and peasants who were virtual serfs. Thus he could not continue to be a laborer or farmhand but had to find an occupation that would at least permit him to live at the level he was accustomed to. So the immigrants generally turned to commerce, to skilled labor, or to farming on their own—in other words, they changed occupation. A few Latin American governments gave land to immigrants; in other cases, the immigrants bought land at low prices. But except in some parts of Chile, Brazil, and Argentina, the number of immigrants who devoted themselves to agriculture was low; the majority of immigrants settled in the cities.

This was not the case with Asian immigrants, many of whom gave up a standard of living no higher than that of the Latin American masses. Chinese and Japanese immigration has been significant on the Pacific Coast and in Brazil. Early in the twentieth century, the Mexican government encouraged the immigration of several thousand Korean peasants to work on the sisal plantations in Yucatán; those Koreans who survived their slavery mingled completely with the Mayas and have left virtually no traces.

Other immigrants have included Syrians and Lebanese, usually known as "Turks" because they came when their countries still formed part of the Ottoman Empire. The "Turks" were primarily merchants (who introduced door-to-door instalment-plan selling to Latin America). Although in the big cities they tended to stay together, in the villages they integrated with the population. President Plutarco Elías Calles (1877–1945) of Mexico and the Bolivian vice president and miners' leader Juan Lechín were descended from families of "Turks."

Anglo-Saxon immigration has been minor. A few hundred persons from the British Isles (mostly from Ireland) settled in Argentina and Chile, and a few people from the United States have retired to Mexico. But most English-speaking immigrants in Latin America are temporary residents, who do not become a part of the country's life but live in comfortable and luxurious colonies in the cities in which they chance to settle.

Political refugees have come to Latin America in waves. One wave was of those who fled Europe after the swift collapse of the 1848 revolutions; another consisted of people persecuted during the Paris Commune of 1871. Later, many Spanish anarchists and republicans who did not want to fight in the Moroccan wars found asylum in Latin America. These immigrants exerted considerable influence on the labor movement in Latin America. At the end of the nineteenth century, and during the first half of the twentieth, many Jews from central Europe came to Latin America, fleeing first tsarist pogroms and later Nazi anti-Semitism. Today, the largest Jewish community is in Argentina, where there are about 450,000 Jews. Argentina is also the Latin American country in which anti-Semitism is most thoroughly organized.

After the Spanish Civil War, many exiled Spanish republicans took refuge in Latin America, particularly in Argentina, Cuba, and Mexico. Their influence was strong, especially in cultural life, for many were professional men and intellectuals who found employment in the universities and in journalism. Several of the most important publishing firms in Latin America were founded by Spanish republican refugees.

At the end of World War II, there was another, much smaller wave of political immigration composed of Nazis and Fascists fleeing the European trials against war criminals. Many found asylum in Paraguay and in Argentina, where they had a certain amount of influence in the Perón regime.

About 100,000 displaced persons, that is, persons who had to leave their country during or after World War II and were helped to resettle by the United Nations, were accepted in Latin America, one-third of them in Argentina.

Immigration for religious reasons has been much less frequent. Mennonites from Canada and Russia founded colonies in Paraguay and in northern Mexico, where there are also some Mormon settlements. These groups keep to themselves and probably do not number more than 30,000 persons all told.

A few figures will give an idea of the importance of immigration in Latin American history.* Between 1850 and 1950,

---

* All statistics for years before 1950 are only approximate: they are incomplete, and, moreover, until World War I, no visa or special permit was required for entry into any Latin American country.

17 million persons entered Spanish America, of whom 7 million went to Argentina. Convenience was a determining factor here, since more than half the ships that crossed the south Atlantic sailed for Buenos Aires. Two million immigrants went to Chile, 1.5 million to Cuba, 1 million to Uruguay, and 500,000 to Mexico. These immigrants came from Italy (6 million), Spain (4 million), Portugal (1 million), Russia (500,000), the Far East (1 million), the Near East (500,000), and various other areas and countries, and included 500,000 Jews of different nationalities. The Germans are statistically important only in southern Chile.

Between 1850 and 1950, Brazil received 4.7 million immigrants, of whom 1.5 million were Italian, 1.4 million Portuguese, 600,000 Spanish, 230,000 German, and the rest mostly Asian; in addition to a heavy Japanese immigration in the twentieth century (187,000 persons), there was a considerable importation of Chinese coolies in the years following the abolition of slavery, in 1888.

In the years immediately after World War II, European immigration to Latin America rose, despite numerous restrictions applied by the Latin American governments. After 1955, the flow of immigration dropped, except from Spain and Portugal, countries whose underdeveloped economies and outdated social systems encouraged the desire to emigrate. Many immigrants still come from Italy, mostly relatives of those already settled in the New World. Of the 26,-000 persons admitted to Latin American countries in 1949, for example, 18,000 were Portuguese, Spanish, or Italian; in 1953, of 42,000 admitted, 30,000 came from those three countries.*

Relations Between the Races

Latin America's demographic statistics are not much to be proud of. In some countries—Uruguay, for example—censuses were not taken for years, and in others, dictators who believed it would increase their prestige often gave orders to add on a few hundred thousand people to the final figures. But such extravagance is becoming a thing of the past, and today

---

* The figures are derived from studies collected in Margaret Bates (ed.), *The Migration of Peoples to Latin America* (Washington, D.C., 1957).

it is possible to establish accurate figures about the size and ethnic composition of the Latin American population.

In the middle of the seventeenth century, roughly 80 per cent of the population of Spanish America was Indian, 7 per cent Negro, 6 per cent white, 4 per cent mestizo, and 3 per cent mulatto. At the time of independence, 46 per cent of the population was Indian, 26 per cent mestizo, 19 per cent Creole, 8 per cent Negro, and 1 per cent Spanish.

Today, the Indian population is 8.5 per cent of the total population of Latin America. Of these, more than 90 per cent live in the Indo-Latin countries—Peru, Bolivia, Ecuador, Guatemala, and Mexico.

The Negro population is also 8.5 per cent of the total. The majority of Negroes are in Brazil, the Caribbean countries, and Panama.

The whites—to the extent to which it is possible to say who is white—compose 44.7 per cent of the population, but only at the southern tip of South America does the white predominate.

Mestizos, mulattoes, and zambos compose 38.3 per cent of the total population.

It is impossible to say, therefore, that the population of Latin America is white, Indian, or Negro. The only realistic statement would be that Latin America is inhabited by a population in the process of interbreeding. The mixture of races continues year after year, generation after generation (although there are some, like the Germans and the Anglo-Saxons, who steadfastly refuse to marry nonwhites). In reality, many who consider themselves white are really mestizos or mulattoes; many who consider themselves Indian live like mestizos, and vice versa. "Pure" whites probably make up only 10–15 per cent of the population, and even this "purity" is questionable—assuming it is worth the trouble to question it—since when Spaniards, Portuguese, or southern Italians come into the picture there is a great probability of earlier racial mixture.

However, it is possible to point out that the division of the population into ethnic groups is congruent to a division into social groups. Thus—in general—it may be said that the whites form the sectors of the population that are best off: the great landholders, bankers and industrialists, a high percentage of the professional people and intellectuals. Mestizos and mulattoes constitute the bulk of the middle class. Indians and Negroes form most of the working and peasant classes. Mestizos, of course, are to be found in all classes, and in some countries—like Mexico—Indians are, too. It is also clear that in countries with small Indian or Negro minorities, it is the whites who are found in all classes—as in Argentina, Uruguay, and parts of Chile and Costa Rica. But the *predominance* of one racial type or another in each group is unquestionable.

This fact has given Latin American racism a special aspect, which differentiates it from the racism found in other countries, notably the United States. In Latin America today, there is no legal racial segregation. One will not find anywhere that nonwhites are forbidden to use the same facilities as whites or to attend the same schools. Latin American segregation is de facto segregation, and it is difficult to distinguish racial motives from economic or social ones. Who can say why Indian children in Ecuador usually go to public schools while white children go to private, and better, ones? Is it because of the color of their skin or because of the difference in family income? There are restaurants to which no Indian or Negro ever goes, but is this a matter of color or because the prices are beyond the reach of Negroes and Indians?

White racism, then, is less overt in Latin America than in other regions because there is so little social mobility. Since the Indian, the Negro, and in some countries even the mestizo have so little chance of rising in society, the whites at the top do not bother to remain aloof from fellow citizens who have virtually no chance of overtaking them.

Latin American racism is subtle and concealed. And Latin Americans boast, of course, that they are not racists. The racism is not imposed or regimented but simply occurs and is accepted without being talked about; in this way any struggle against it is obviated, since it does not exist in the public consciousness. To understand this is to take a big step forward in understanding Latin American psychology. For the same phenomenon—acceptance of a de facto situation the existence of which does not excite anyone's attention and which is not sanctioned by law but is solely a product of custom—is found repeatedly in other aspects of life.*

The character of Latin American racism can best be shown by describing some of its phenomena, rather than by attempting to define it. This racism manifests itself in many different ways.

The language itself indicates the degree to which Latin Americans are conscious of skin color. There are dozens of names to distinguish different mixtures and degrees of darkness of skin. Mestizos are called *ladinos* in Guatemala; *cholos* in the Andes; *mamelucos, caboclos,* and *curibocas* in Brazil. Mulattoes are called tercerons, quadroons, octoroons, etc., depending on the proportion of Negro blood. One might also be, to cite only a few of the possibilities, *pardo* ("brown," a mixture of Negro, white, and Indian in Brazil); *castizo* ("pureblood," mixed mestizo and white); *chino* (literally, "Chinese," mixed *morisco* and white); *salto atrás* ("backward leap," mixed *chino* and Indian); or *lobo* ("wolf," mixed *salto atrás* and mulatto).

The Creole speech of Haiti includes 107 words for gradations of skin color and variety of feature; each group is disdainful of the components of the darker or less "pure" groups, except that during the periods when Negroes were in power, darkness was a sign of superiority. There are certain Latin American countries in which to say "Indian" is the same as to say "peasant"; there are others where *guajiro* or *jíbaro* (local words for "peasant") mean the same as "Negro" or "mulatto." In quite a few Latin American countries, kinky hair is called *pelo malo* (bad hair).

There is a saying among people of dark skin, "My grandfather was Spanish, too," to indicate their difference from "pure" Indians or Negroes. Satirizing this tendency, the Pe-

* On occasion, however, Latin American governments have adopted more or less openly racist measures. For example, until 1948, Negroes of the Atlantic coast of Costa Rica were forbidden to leave the Department of Limón to live in other parts of the country. In Cuba, the revolutionary government of 1934 forbade the entry of Haitian peasants (who worked for lower wages) and deported those already in the country, instead of insisting that they be paid decent wages. Several Latin American countries have passed laws limiting the immigration of Chinese and Japanese. There is a certain racism, too, in the laws depriving the illiterate of the vote, for it is known that the illiteracy rate is very low among whites and very high among Negroes and Indians.

ruvian Manuel González Prada (1848–1918) wrote the following epitaph:

> Here lies Manongo,
> Of pure Latin race:
> His mother came from China,
> His grandfather from the Congo.

In Brazil, in regions where the Indians were never serfs, local aristocrats tend to emphasize their Indian origins, since this gives them the prestige of being "old Brazilians." But in the Amazon region, where the Indians were once serfs, mestizos are looked down upon.

In Latin American help-wanted advertisements, photographs of applicants are often demanded.

In Cuba, where the mulatto petty bourgeoisie is considerable, the old and very conservative newspaper *Diario de la Marina* published a society column about this class under the headline "Café au Lait."

In the Dominican Republic, there is a saying, "Being white is a profession." In Dominican schoolbooks, the portrait of one of the founders of the country, Francisco del Rosario Sánchez (d. 1861), is shown in such a way as to make it impossible to tell the color of his skin. There one may also read that the dictator Ulises Heureaux (1876–1938) was "Negro in feeling and in color, white in manners and mind."

Simón Patiño (1862–1947), the owner of the richest tin mines in Brazil, which he discovered when he was a mule driver, was an Indian (although this did not induce him to provide decent working conditions for the miners); he was never able to gain admission to the clubs in La Paz. General Rafael Trujillo (1891–1961), for thirty years dictator of the Dominican Republic, was a mulatto; he was blackballed when he sought membership in a men's club in Santo Domingo. The Peruvian dictator General Manuel Odría (b. 1897) was not admitted to a men's club in Lima because he is a mestizo.

Guyana affords an example of racism converted into political ideology. Cheddi Jagan (b. 1918), who is of (Asian) Indian origin, won the Indian vote of the country—chiefly landholders and merchants—despite his pro-Communist ideology; Guyana's Negroes, mostly peasants and laborers, supported a leftist anti-Communist party; and the whites backed a party of the right.

There has been more discrimination against Negroes than against Indians. Indeed, racial prejudice is not limited to whites. Indians look down upon Negroes when the latter are in the minority. The mestizo policemen of Lima, for example, maltreat arrested Negroes, considering them virtually guilty because of their color. It might be said that this tendency began in the sixteenth century, when Bartolomé de las Casas defended the Indians and proposed that for their protection Negroes be imported to do heavy labor. Colonial laws established prohibitions pertaining to freed Negroes: they were, for instance, forbidden to wear jewels or hats, both signs of nobility. In 1796, the municipal government in Caracas asked that mulattoes be forbidden to use the title Don, because it "concealed the user's dishonorable slave origin and the stain of illegitimacy."

In Brazil, where there was a certain racial tolerance—it was said that "God made whites and Negroes, but the Portuguese made mulattoes"—the imperial family retained freed Negroes as part of the court and invited them to palace festivities. For a short time (1909–10), there was even a Negro president of the republic, Nilo Peçanha. But with this chance exception, Negroes have never occupied important posts in Brazil.

In 1953, it was necessary to pass a law outlawing racial segregation in Brazil, a sure sign of its existence. In deluxe restaurants and stores in Brazilian cities, one never sees a Negro waiter or clerk, nor is there ever a Negro nurse in the private clinics. Although he is today accepted in sports, there was a time when Negro soccer players in Brazil had to use light makeup. In that country, however, it has become more and more true that, as the proverb says, "The Negro with money is not black, and the white man without money is not white."

For many years, there was active controversy among intellectuals over the Negro contribution to Brazilian culture. The prevailing opinion was that of Artur Ramos (1903–49), who held that the cause of Brazil's backwardness was the high proportion of Negroes in the population. Even the mulatto novelist Machado de Assis (1839–1908) believed that the Negro influence had been a negative one. The sociologist Gilberto Freyre (b. 1900) modified this general opinion and underlined the importance of Negro and mulatto contributions to the development of Brazil. A similar controversy took place in Cuba, where Negroes were socially, though not politically, segregated until 1950. The studies of the ethnologist Fernando Ortiz (b. 1883) did much to point up the Negro contribution to "Afro-Cuban" culture.

Ethnic diversity has given many theorists a pretext for supporting the oligarchic structure of Latin American society, saying that given their past and their biological nature, the Indian and Negro cannot be expected to create stable democratic institutions. Even "liberals," like the Argentine sociologist José Ingenieros (1877–1925), argued that immigration establishing the numerical superiority of the white race was the only way to modernize Latin American society—this despite the fact that Argentina itself was living proof that a virtually all-white population does not automatically achieve either political stability or social justice. A Bolivian essayist, Gabriel René Moreno (1836–1908), wrote: "The Inca Indian is good for nothing. But he represents a mass of passive resistance. . . . If in any way the mass of Indians were to play a part . . . it would probably be by the passive route of more or less rapid disintegration." And José Hernández (1834–86), poet of the Argentina gaucho, wrote of the Indians on the pampas:

> The Indian clings to his barbarity;
> Don't hope to change him.
> To wish to make himself better
> Doesn't go with his rough ways.
> The barbarian only knows
> How to get drunk and fight.

Even among those who seek to rise above racist concepts, we find an occasional bad aftertaste. For example, the Mexican writer José Vasconcelos (1882–1959), who was very influential in the 1920's, wrote a book entitled *La raza cósmica (The Cosmic Race)* in which he said that there had occured a fusion of races in Latin America that would lead to a universal race.*

One exception must be noted, however: Mexico. Although there is a certain amount of racial discrimination in social

---

* These examples, and many others, will be found in *Hipocresía y discriminación racial,* in *Panoramas* (Mexico City), No. 16 (July-August, 1965).

life and in groups with an oligarchic tradition, Indians and mestizos are to be found in all sectors of Mexican life. The dictator Porfirio Díaz (1830–1915) was a dark-skinned mestizo, and President Benito Juárez (1806–72) was a full-blooded Indian. The Revolution of 1910 opened the doors to the last fields that had been closed to nonwhites: large-scale landowning and industry. Outside this last bastion, nonwhites had been, since independence, eligible for any office. No doubt this may be explained by the fact that Indians and mestizos were active in the struggle for independence and that since the mid-nineteenth century the largely mestizo middle class has been the most powerful political element in the country.

Population Growth

No exact idea can be formed of the number of inhabitants of pre-Columbian America, but it has been estimated that there must have been about 10 million persons in all of Latin America. In the seventeenth century, there were probably 7–12 million persons in Latin America; when the Spanish colonies became independent, about 20 million; at the end of the nineteenth century, about 70 million; in 1920, 90 million; and in 1940, 130 million. By 1960, the population had reached nearly 210 million, approximately equal to the number of inhabitants of the United States and Canada at that time; by 1965, the population was estimated at about 240 million.

With the exceptions of Haiti and El Salvador, whose population density is among the highest in the world, many areas of Europe, Asia, and the United States have a population density greater than that of Latin America. Within a single Latin American country, we may find regions with only one or two inhabitants per square kilometer, and others with 2,000. The average is 7.7 Latin Americans to the square kilometer. On the whole, Latin America today is one of the more sparsely populated areas in the world.

What *is* significant is that the population growth in Latin America is greater than that of any other part of the world. The rate of population increase in Latin America is 2.8 per cent per year. The rate is not uniform: Costa Rica has the highest, about 4 per cent per year; Guatemala, the Dominican Republic, Mexico, and Venezuela approach this figure.

From 1900 to 1930, population in the temperate zones grew more rapidly (thanks in part to considerable immigration), with Argentina, Uruguay, Cuba, and Brazil in the lead. From 1930 to 1940, the lead passed to the countries of the tropics and the Caribbean; after 1940, Brazil, Mexico, and Central America show the highest population growth rate. Since 1940, immigration has not been a significant demographic factor; the causes of population growth are entirely internal.

What are these causes? Of course, they may be expressed in statistical terms as the variation in the birth and death rates. At the beginning of the century, the birth rate varied, according to country, from 40 to 50 per 1,000, and the death rate from 25 to 30 per 1,000. Up to 1930, the mortality rates diminish gradually; after 1930, they diminish much more rapidly. In 1960, several countries had death rates not quite half those of 1900. At the same time, the birth rate has remained stationary, except in Argentina, Uruguay, Chile, and Cuba, where it has decreased. This means that the cause of the population explosion is not that proportionately more people are being born, but that fewer are dying.

The fall in the death rate has been greater for the lower age groups, infants and young people. This accounts for another characteristic of the Latin American population: its youth. Forty per cent of the Latin American population is under twenty years of age; only 7 per cent is over sixty. Although life expectancy has risen steadily over the last half century, it is still only forty-three years for men and forty-nine for women.

For purposes of comparison, we may note that the birth rate in the United States is 25 per 1,000 and the death rate is 10, so that this country shows a rate of natural population increase of 15. In Latin America, the rate of increase varies from 22 to 32 (although Argentina has a rate of 15). When we consider that with a rate of natural increase of 25 the population doubles every twenty-eight years, it is possible to see the magnitude of the problem.

How will this situation end? Specialists calculate that if the present rate continues, Latin America, inside of a century, will have 5 billion inhabitants. No less fantastic is the estimate of 38 billion inhabitants by the middle of the twenty-second century. Such figures are beyond the real possibilities; even supposing that, thanks to technological advances, there would be food enough for all these Latin Americans, they would have to eat it standing up for lack of room.

More realistic is the calculation for the year 2000. At that time—if the current population growth rate continues—Latin America will have more than 500 million inhabitants. At present, the population of Latin America constitutes 6.9 per cent of the world's population; in 1920, it was 4.7 per cent; and in the year 2000, unless the situation is altered, it will represent 10 per cent.

The Latin American population explosion is a peculiar phenomenon, the causes of which have not yet been satisfactorily explained. As is usual with most social phenomena, it has been both cause and effect of a situation that is also a peculiar one and that will be discussed in other chapters of this book. The population explosion has made the solution of Latin America's problems more difficult. Those that could have been solved half a century ago by energetic means will, in future, demand a much more complex and expensive activity, a situation aggravated by the fact that until now no one has proposed an efficacious solution to the problem of the population explosion itself.*

Urbanization

At present, the Latin American population is undergoing an important change: it is rapidly becoming urbanized.

There have always been large cities in Latin America. The cities found by the conquistadors—Tenochtitlán (where Mexico City is today) and Cuzco (Peru)—were as large and as densely populated as any European city of the sixteenth century. In colonial times, Mexico City, Lima, and Buenos Aires were comparable to European capitals. But the urban population was only a very small part of the whole. The rural

---

* For further documentation on the problem of population growth, see the books on which the figures cited here are based: Bates, *op. cit., passim;* and J. Mayone Stycos and Jorge Arias (eds.), *Population Dilemma in Latin America* (Washington, D.C., 1966), chap. i.

population, however, was not as scattered as it was in the United States, but was gathered around the haciendas and in small provincial towns.

The growth of these towns and cities was slow in the nineteenth century, when Latin America was essentially agricultural. But in the present century, especially in the last thirty years, the migration of people from countryside to city has speeded up, and today Latin America is going through a period of concentrated urbanization, with all its attendant problems.

Before 1940, the growth of cities was significant only in Argentina, Uruguay, Chile, and Cuba, and even in these countries it was confined mostly to the capitals. After 1940, and especially after 1955, the flow of inhabitants from the country to the cities grew increasingly heavy. In 1947 (with the four above-mentioned exceptions), the urban population did not exceed 20 per cent. In Venezuela, this index of urban population leapt from 18 to 47 per cent in twenty years. The larger the city, the faster its growth. There are capitals that have doubled their population in the last twenty years and that are absorbing a large percentage of the population of the country.* Few capitals today contain less than 10 per cent of the population of the country. In 1940, there were only four cities in Latin America with more than 1 million inhabitants; in 1960, there were ten.

Latin America is more urbanized than Asia or Africa; 32 per cent of its population lives in cities of more than 20,000 inhabitants, whereas the percentage for Africa is 13 and for Asia, 16. This percentage is still far from the 46 per cent of the United States and the 40 per cent of Europe (excluding the Soviet Union). Characteristically, urbanization in Latin America has taken place in a society whose social and economic structure bears little resemblance to that of the United States, Europe, or the Soviet Union. The causes of urbanization, as we shall see, have been not so much a matter of industrial development as of relative agricultural decline.

* In 1960, Mexico City, with its 4.5 million inhabitants, represented 13.4 per cent of the total population of the nation; Buenos Aires, with 6.7 million, represented 33.8 per cent; Santiago, with 1.9 million, 25 per cent; Havana, with 1.4 million, 21.8 per cent; Lima, with 1.4 million, 14.5 per cent; Caracas, with 1.3 million, 17.7 per cent; Montevideo, with 1.1 million, 45.9 per cent; San José, with 318,000 inhabitants, 24 per cent; Panama City, with 273,000, 25.4 per cent.

The Latin American countries are still predominantly rural, however. Excepting Argentina, whose urban population accounts for 63 per cent of the total, all have a rural majority. In Mexico, for example, 27 per cent of the population lives in the cities; in Colombia and Venezuela, 34 per cent; in Chile, 33 per cent; in Peru, 20 per cent; in Brazil, 19 per cent.

The differences between the urban and the rural areas are profound. In all of Latin America today, there are two entirely different ways of life, two mentalities, two cultures: the rural and the urban.

The Psychology of the Latin American

It might seem that all these differences—social, racial, of ways of life, of age—would make it impossible to speak of the Latin American as a single type. However, these differences notwithstanding, it is possible to identify the Latin American. In reality, it is easier to identify a person as a Latin American than as a national of a particular country.

Within each Latin American country, there are profound differences among the inhabitants in their skin color, cultural tradition, social position, standard of living, ideals. But these differences, in one form or another, are repeated in all the countries. Hence, though it is more difficult to point out the psychological characteristics of the "average" Latin American, it is quite possible to describe the characteristics of the worker in all Latin American countries, those of the middle sectors, and those of the ruling class. The differences are not so much vertical, between countries, as horizontal, between social strata. In the United States, the psychology of a laborer, a farmer, a businessman does not differ in any important respect. In Latin America, there are considerable differences, and these differences are found in every part of the continent, so that it is possible to speak of a Latin American peasant, latifundist, or intellectual, and to identify him without any great risk of error.

Yet it is also true that there is a typical Latin American, even though he is less schematized than the cliché of literature and the motion pictures, which portrays him as slender, dark, elegant, voluble, ceremonious, amorous, and passionate. What is this type like, in terms of a denominator common to all social groups in all the countries?

Perhaps the most common and profound characteristic derives from the fact that, as was pointed out earlier, the Latin American lives on two different planes at once, one of action and the other of word or thought. He acts in one way and thinks in another. This is not hypocrisy but an involuntary attitude, a product both of the need for self-defense that the Indian felt in the presence of the conquistador and of the psychological ambivalence to be found in all people of mixed blood. Even when the Latin American has a single racial origin—white, Indian, Negro—the fact that he lives in a society in which his single origin is an exception makes him adopt mental attitudes proper to those of mixed ancestry.

There is a widespread impression that people in Latin America are less honest than those in the United States. But we must not forget that what a Latin American says does not have to correspond exactly to what he does. The Latin American, for instance, holds women in high esteem, honors his mother, and treats the female sex with ceremony. At the same time, and without being conscious of any incongruity, the Latin American, as head of a family, as husband, as son, behaves in a way that seems to belie his attitude of esteem and that, to Americans or Europeans, appears irresponsible and even offensive. For the Latin American man, and his Latin American wife, the divergence of word and action is natural; the wife would feel cheated if she were not accorded the outward signs of respect and amazed if this respect were translated into action. The institution of the *casa chica*—the second, nonlegalized family kept by many Latin American husbands—is an example of this dual attitude.

In politics, this ambivalence is shown by the ease with which Latin Americans accept the idea that once a law has been promulgated to solve a problem, the problem ceases to exist—no matter how obvious the persistence of the problem, either because the law is not enforced or because the "solution" has not solved anything. Latin Americans constantly speak, in utter good faith, of constitutionality, in a continent where every year two or three constitutions are violated, altered, or simply annulled. And they boast, for example, that

Latin American social legislation is among the most advanced in the world, untroubled by the fact that poverty, exploitation, and even servitude continue because such legislation is poorly enforced, or not enforced at all. For the Latin American, accustomed to the Spanish legalistic spirit, the law itself, rather than its application, is the solution. Thus the recurrence of problems sincerely considered as solved, and the repeated passing of laws dealing with the same question.

As we shall see in subsequent chapters, the average Latin American has never had the power to decide his own destiny. Deprived of the opportunity to act, he has taken refuge in word and thought. If he cannot act, he can compensate for this by talking, and in Latin America this has given the word greater importance than it has elsewhere.

The same origin helps to account for other Latin American traits: the tendency to spend rather than to save for the future, and the fondness for gambling and betting. In Cuba, before Castro, there was a lottery every day; in Mexico, there is one three times a week. The Latin American tends to let chance decide his destiny, as if he were so convinced that outside forces determine his life that he wants to emphasize this by playing his own games of chance.

At the same time, the Latin American quickly resorts to violence in an attempt to solve his problems. Latin America has a long tradition of violence, going back to the colonial period. Today, the demonstrations that end in fights with the police, the bloody strikes, the elections accompanied by bullets are not rare. It is not that the Latin American is more bloodthirsty or cruel than other peoples, but that since the paths of action are closed to him—the means of resolving his problems, collective or personal, by law or the normal play of pressure and counterpressure—he is compelled to resort to drastic expedients, that is, to express in shouting and shooting what he is unable to express through legal means. The Latin American is no more violent than other men—in many places, especially in regions with a large Indian population, he is probably more resigned, passive, and pacific than the generality of men—but the society in which he lives often leaves him little else but violence with which to defend his interests and rights. (It is not insignificant that there has never been a pacifist movement in Latin America or the use of nonviolence for political ends. Gandhi was never a popular figure in Latin America.)*

These tendencies are reinforced by another Latin American trait that is found in the character of the pre-Columbian Indian and also in the Spaniard: a lack of fear of death, the making of death a constant companion, an accepted and familiar part of everyday life. The cult of death is common. In Mexico, where it assumes extreme forms, there are banquets and fiestas in the cemeteries on All Souls' Day, and death is an important element in folklore—as witness the sugar cookies in the form of a skull—and in everyday speech, in which dead children are referred to as "little angels." The lack of fear of death is also why we find in many parts of Latin America, in greater proportion than elsewhere, the crime without motive, without profit to the slayer.

Bearing all this in mind, it is not surprising that the Latin American is an insecure man who tends to express this insecurity in abrupt and harsh ways. In the United States, insecurity is accepted as normal, and one resorts to the psychoanalyst to cure it. In Latin America, insecurity would be unbearable if it were admitted, if one gave the impression of being insecure. Latin American insecurity, individual or collective, requires, first of all, that it be hidden, that one dissimulate, that he present himself as being very secure.

On the individual plane, this insecurity is shown, above all, in the concept of *machismo* (maleness), an attitude very common among Latin American men, which leads them to consider it a diminution of their virility to give in, compromise, make peace, or accept that they are in the wrong.

On the collective level, insecurity is displayed in a negative type of nationalism and in resentment of powerful countries (in the past, in the southern part of the continent, of Great Britain and now, everywhere, of the United States), or, on the

---

* Yet it should also be said that in any city in the United States there are more cases of violence than in a comparable city in Colombia, Mexico, or Venezuela, and that the history of the United States is as full of violence as that of any Latin American country. The United States had the violence of its revolution, that of the conquest of the West, the Civil War and Reconstruction, the great strikes at the end of the nineteenth century, later the Irish riots in the cities, and now those of the Negroes. The difference is one of style: in the United States, the cause of violence is what it is said to be, for social or political reasons. In Latin America, it appears cloaked in religious or idealistic motives.

other hand, in admiration of "virile" nations like Nazi Germany or Stalinist Russia.

It is possible that this insecurity is also the cause of the Latin American's living in the past with an intensity other peoples reserve for the present. For a cultured Latin American, the nineteenth-century struggles between liberals and conservatives, and even events that took place before the Conquest, are matters about which he can be as passionate as if they were contemporary. It is possible to divide Latin American intellectuals into two large groups: the pro-Spanish, who champion the colonial cultural heritage, and the anti-Spanish, who would restore the pre-colonial cultural tradition. When, in 1950, an archaeologist announced the discovery in Mexico of the tomb of the last Aztec chieftain, Cuauhtémoc, there was a fierce argument about the authenticity of the remains; archaeologists who questioned it were accused of being traitors to their country. The figure of the caudillo Juan Manuel de Rosas (1793–1877) still serves as a banner for the Peronists in Argentina, nearly a century after his downfall.

For the Latin American, in short, the past forms part of the present; he does not accept it as something that is over and done with, that can be viewed objectively. Perhaps this is logical, since, as the history of Latin America shows, the present is not fundamentally different from the past, nor are today's problems very different—except in the way they present themselves—from those the historic figures tried to solve.

In this society in which past and present are confused, to express a nonconformist, minority opinion has always been risky. Those who have wished to do so—and there have been many—have had to rely on circumlocution, parable, obscuration in order not to arouse an immediate reaction on the part of the Church, the authorities, the rightminded. If we add to this mental necessity the baroque tradition of Spanish literature, we will have an explanation for the manner of speech—especially the public manner—of the Latin American, which always appears prolix, endless, and obscure.

The Latin American's sense of time is different from the North American's. The Latin American considers it natural, even inevitable, to spend time and words on what to him is simple politeness but what to the American is a waste of time and sounds like flattery to boot. The Latin American does not see himself as ceremonious, gesticulatory, and voluble, but merely as polite, and he would consider it a discourtesy not to show a certain human warmth in the most casual relationship.

This warmth, the sense of humor of the Latin American —who is always ready to make fun of himself but rarely willing to be made fun of—his verbal imagination, which converts his language into a tapestry of images but makes it imprecise, and his obsession with sexual matters, which he disguises with romantic tinsel (a trait he no doubt shares with other peoples molded by a hermetically Catholic culture), these things give the Latin American a quality that cannot be expressed in English but which is best described by the Spanish word *simpático*. He is also often a charmer, despite his chronic mistrustfulness and his touchiness about things that are inoffensive to a North American.

It annoys him, for example, that the United States has monopolized the name America (which was not even used, originally, in reference to North America), and he feels cheated when he hears someone call himself an "American" not because he was born in the Western Hemisphere, but because he is a citizen of the United States. And it undoubtedly bothers him even more that he himself now says "American" when referring to a citizen of the United States.

Moreover, this creates the problem of finding a name to apply to himself. "Latin American"—a term coined in the United States, which has since become general—does not satisfy the educated Latin American because it excludes an entire part of his antecedents, the pre-Columbian, and because he considers it the product of an Anglo-Saxon wish to degrade the Spanish influence in America. The term "Hispano-American" does not include Brazil or Haiti. "Ibero-American" includes Brazil but leaves out Haiti. Both ignore the Indian contribution. "Indo-American" would perhaps be the best word, because it takes into account that which is Indian as well as that which is American, that is, deriving from the colonial period. But the use of "American" by the people of the United States distorts the meaning of the word. The Latin American feels as if the United States had stolen his family name.

This is only a detail. But the very fact that it has any importance may be symbolic of the Latin American personality.

CHAPTER III

How Did Latin America Emerge?

When, in the sixteenth century, the Spaniards began to explore and colonize the New World, the Indians of what are now Mexico, Guatemala, Colombia, Ecuador, Peru and Bolivia had a more advanced social organization and a higher standard of living than the Indians of what is now the United States.

When Spain lost its American territories at the beginning of the nineteenth century, the former British colonies, which had won their independence less than half a century earlier, had reached a stage of development that was not superior to that of the Spanish viceroyalties. The Spanish colonies had a better bureaucratic organization, greater resources under exploitation, a larger population, and universities and other cultural media that were lacking in the north. The cities of the south were larger, more luxurious, and more accessible than those of the north. The wealth of the ruling classes was greater. It may be said, without exaggeration, that the Spanish colonies began their career of independence under better conditions and with more initial advantages than the British colonies.

Today, however, a century and a half later, the comparison is by no means favorable to the Spanish- and Portuguese-speaking countries. In 1965, the gross national product of all the Latin American countries was $80 billion; that of the United States was $740 billion. The Latin American country with the highest per capita income was Argentina, with $830; in Bolivia, at the bottom of the list, the per capita income was $126. If we remember that in the United States anyone with an annual income of less than $1,540 was considered poor, we will have some idea of the discrepancy between the two continents.

What has happened to make Latin America fall so far behind the United States, or, rather, to keep it from progressing as far as the United States?

Many answers to this question have been suggested. Some say the cause is the lack of coal, since only 1 per cent of the world's output is mined in Latin America; on the other hand, oil and hydroelectric resources are plentiful. Others attribute the lag to the limited supply of raw materials, but Brazil has more raw materials than Japan, Italy, or France, and the same may be said of other Latin American countries, though not of all. Others maintain that the high altitudes or the tropical climates lower productivity and retard agriculture. But the Incas built a center of civilization at 9,000 feet, and their agricultural production was probably greater than that of the same region today; and the same may be said of the Mayas, who lived in the tropics. Some seek the answer in political factors, arguing that the balkanization of the continent, its division into numerous rival units, is the cause of the lag. But many Latin American countries are larger and have greater resources than most European nations, which are further divided by differences of language, culture, religion, and by historical rivalries more profound than those in Latin America. A geography that makes communication difficult is another explanation, although the geography of the United States a century and a half ago was no more favorable to progress, and that country had the added disadvantage of being largely unexplored, whereas nearly all Latin America had been traveled, described, and even mapped. The mixture of races is considered—and by not a few Latin Americans—another cause of the lag, but other countries have mixed races without any retardation of their rate of progress.

Undoubtedly, there is no single reply to the question. Many factors have contributed to the backwardness of Latin America. But the fact that such diverse factors have converged in Latin America in a single historical epoch suggests that we must seek the fundamental explanation in history.

To give a résumé of the history of Latin America is no easy task. For one thing, the enormous wealth of detail, of legend, of interesting events and characters often conceals the essentials. In the United States, it is possible to single out a few people and events that in themselves explain that country's evolution. In Latin America, there are more than twenty countries, and the history of each swarms with caudillos, battles, rebellions, civil wars, and boundary disputes. I shall try here to trace the main lines in Latin American history, leaving out many names and details, however picturesque they may be.

One more thing: the written history of Latin America has serious defects. The most serious is partiality. Spanish historians tend to try to justify Spanish colonial rule. Latin American historians, according to their ideological tendencies, flatter the liberals or the conservatives and attribute all blame to the Spaniards, the Indians, the Anglo-Saxons, or, today, to the "imperialists" or the Communists. Until World War I, North American historians, and most European ones, seem to have written about Latin America with the idea not so much of understanding it as of creating an unfavorable image of Spain (what Spanish historians call the Black Legend). Only in the last thirty or forty years do we find an attempt at impartiality and serious investigation.

The reader who wishes to increase his knowledge of Latin American history should begin with modern works of a general character. Not until he has found his touchstone in them should he turn to works about particular countries, or those written before World War I, because it is best that he see each country in the broadest Latin American context and be able to interpret the works of earlier historians in the light of today's research and synthesis.

The Pre-Columbian Peoples

Until a few decades ago, all that was known of the history of the pre-Hispanic American peoples was what the Spaniards were told by the Indians or deciphered from the Indians' hieroglyphics. More recently, archaeology has furnished information about these peoples' way of life, and the use of carbon-14 and other methods of dating antiquities has enabled us to establish a chronology that is a bit less uncertain; even so, little is known about the historical events preceding the Conquest. But we do know that the Aztecs and the Incas were only the last of a long succession of peoples and cultures. The high tableland of Mexico and Central America was the stage for the history of one series of these peoples; the Andes mountain range, from Ecuador to northern Argentina, was the other region in which there were Indian societies of complex organization.

From south of Veracruz to Guatemala and Honduras, the Mayas—a collection of tribes belonging to the language group known as Maya-Quiché—developed a very interesting civilization. It is believed that the Mayas were settled in these regions by about 1000 B.C. The Mayas appear to have been descended from an earlier people, the Olmecs, who settled in what is now Veracruz, in the forests near which have been found enormous stone carvings with almost Oriental features. Even earlier, another people, whose sculpture has Negroid features, lived in this region; for want of another name they are called Ventas, from the place in which their relics have been found.

There are many Mayan ruins belonging to different epochs: in Copán (Honduras), in Petén (Guatemala), and in Chichén Itzá and Uxmal (Yucatán). Temples and houses were covered with pictures, and it is thanks to these, to codices collected (and sometimes later destroyed) by the Spaniards, and to legends transcribed by Spanish chroniclers that we know something about this race of people, who may be considered the most advanced, the most subtle, the most "modern" of all the American peoples of pre-Hispanic times.

By about 750 A.D., the Mayas had built large, well-laid-out cities, had a numerical system (based on the figure 20, that is, using the zero), a very exact calendar, hieroglyphic writing (which was later partly converted into a phonetic system and which no one has yet been able to decipher, although from time to time a Russian or German scholar appears with the claim that he has), an architecture that is considered technically advanced for its time, and an active coastal trade using small sailing craft. They also had an obsession with cleanliness and bathed several times a day, a habit that greatly impressed the Spaniards.

The Mayan religion and Christianity had certain similarities: baptism, belief in a god who would come in human form to save his people, congregations of monks and nuns under special vows, and belief in a life beyond the earthly one. There was no human sacrifice in this religion until it was introduced, around the twelfth century, by the Toltecs.

The Maya priest-rulers were probably intellectuals rather than warriors; they undoubtedly founded a society based on slavery. It seems that, on one occasion, a popular rebellion drove the nobles out of the cities. The latter formed a confederation, in the Greek manner, and the priestly aristocracy finally recovered their dominion with the aid of mercenaries from the north, the Toltecs. Again, the people revolted, attacked the cities, and drove out the nobles. When the Spaniards arrived, the Mayan tribes were scattered and weak, although a number of them fled into the jungle and held out against the conquistadors for a long time. But the memory of their former grandeur remained alive with the Mayas; in the eighteenth century, an unknown author, possibly the Indian Juan José Hoil, wrote the *Book of Chilam Balam,* in which he recalled Mayan customs "before the invaders taught us to fear and before they took honey from the flowers of others to make their own bloom."

Around the years 1000 to 1200 A.D., the Toltecs ruled central Mexico, from their city of Tula. They worshiped a white god, Quetzalcoatl, a messiah who was to come from the east. Warriors and builders, they were long credited with the majestic ruins of Teotihuacán, near the present site of Mexico City; but today it is thought that this city, with its great pyramids, palaces, and boulevards, was the capital of another people, of whom we know almost nothing, who lived there around the third and fourth centuries of our era.

There were many more Indian peoples scattered throughout the territory that is now Mexico: the Zapotecs and Mixtecs in the south, who built the splendid cities of Monte Albán and Mitla; the Tarascans in the north; the Otomís and Tlaxcaltecs in the east, and the Huastecs in the northeast.

All these peoples were conquered by the warlike Aztecs from the north. The coming of the Aztecs is recent—around 1325. After a period of acclimatization, they allied themselves with other tribes speaking their language (Nahuatl), who had founded Texcoco, Tacuba, and Atzcapotzalco (today suburbs of Mexico City), and began to enlarge their territory. They overcame other peoples and imposed tribute—ornamental plumes, cotton cloth, and cacao seeds, which they used for money. They also took prisoners, who were slaughtered in the human sacrifices called for by their religion, according to which the sun demanded victims as a condition of his appearance.

Eventually, the Aztecs established an empire that extended from the Pacific coast to the Atlantic, and from northern Mexico to Central America. Its capital was Tenochtitlán, a kind of Venice built on the islands of a shallow lake in the Valley of Mexico; partially destroyed by Spaniards, it was rebuilt as Mexico City.*

Aztec society was theocratic, and its monarch was the chief priest. The ruler Itzcoatl (d. 1440) institutionalized Aztec religion around the figure of the warrior god Huitzilopochtli. The Aztecs also adopted the gods of the peoples they encountered. Among these were Quetzalcoatl, the patron of arts and agriculture, and Tezcatlipoca, patron of violence and evil; these two gods fought each other, and the former won only after covering himself with a leopard skin and disguising himself as a warrior.

Aztec society was based on a system of clans or *calpullis,* which were virtual agrarian communes, each of whose members received a parcel of land. The inheritance of property won as booty soon appeared among this warlike people, and with it came class divisions based on wealth and not on the social function of the individual. Their wars also demanded a certain specialization of labor and resulted in the appearance of trades—armorer, weaver, fashioner of plumed articles —and the establishment of what we may consider genuine guilds. In Tenochtitlán, every guild was assigned to a section

---

* According to legend, the Aztecs settled in Tenochtitlán because the eagle they were following perched on a nopal cactus, where it caught a serpent in its claws—signs they considered good omens. The Mexican seal shows the cactus, eagle, and serpent.

of the city. There was no money, except in the form of cacao seeds, since wages, properly speaking, did not exist. Artisans were freemen, and were subject only to military service. In the country, however, we find the *tlacotli*, the man expelled from his clan (as a judicial punishment or for violation of some tradition), whose parcel of land was taken away, thus obliging him to work another's land; he was not a slave, for he could change masters and his descendants retained membership in the clan, but he was neither serf nor freeman, since legally he formed no part of society, which ignored him; in today's terms we should call him a nonperson. There were also captive slaves, employed in the fields, in public works, and as porters in the transportation of goods on their backs; they were also destined to be sacrificial victims.

Culturally, the Aztecs adopted much of the knowledge and many of the beliefs of the Mayas and Toltecs. Much attention was paid to the arts and letters (and Aztec hieroglyphics, unlike those of the Mayas, have been deciphered). One of the kings of Texcoco, Netzahualcoyotl (1402–72), who combined the qualities of both David and Solomon, wrote ethical poetry and erotic songs; some of them have a singularly modern flavor. The sovereign Moctezuma I (d. 1469) sent expeditions to explore the snows of the two volcanoes near Mexico City (Ixtaccihuatl and Popocatepetl) and established a botanical garden.

The active and dynamic Aztecs were to some extent like the Romans; they had a pantheon to which they admitted the gods of peoples they conquered, they devoted themselves to commerce and systematized their customs. The Mayas resembled the Greeks, leaning to contemplation, poetry, and science. In this respect, the Toltecs enacted the role the Persians and Egyptians had played in ancient Mediterranean society.

At the time the Mayas were writing their poetry, two civilizations predominated in South America. In the highlands around Lake Titicaca lived a people of whom little is known but whose astonishing monuments—huge, stiff, cold, decorated with abstract motifs—have been preserved. We call these people by the name of one of their ruins: Tiahuanaco. Earlier, another culture had flourished in this area, that of the Chavín. Other cultures flourished on the coast: archaeologists call them Wari, Chimú, and Nazca. These peoples were farmers, worked in gold, built forts; they left only beautiful ceramic objects, decorated with scenes of hunting, fishing, dancing, and battle.

In the south, as in the north, the peoples in the highlands created artistic forms that were heavy and severe, which might lead us to believe that they cultivated ugliness in order to impose respect or terror; the people of the lowlands show a sense of humor, and their ceramics, their genuine caricatures, with a mixture of human and animal figures, are examples of an art that today we would call surrealistic.

About the ninth century, the Tiahuanacos came down to the coast, and their harsh artistic forms (and, no doubt, their ways of life) were blended with the more genial ones of the coastal peoples. But they promptly fell into a decline and made way for a renascence of the Chimús and Nazcas in the lowlands, and for the first appearance of the Quechuas in the highlands.

The Quechuas probably came down to the Cuzco valley in the eleventh century, when, according to legend, the emperor Manco Capac founded the city of Cuzco. By the fourteenth century, all the peoples of this region had been overcome by the Quechuas. The supreme head of the Quechuas bore the title Inca, which led the Spaniards to call the entire people by that name.

In the time of the Chavín and of the Waris, there was a common influence over all of what is today Peru and Bolivia. With the Incas, this extended as far north as Ecuador and as far south as the northern part of Argentina. The Incas also controlled the Aymarás, a numerous and active group south of Lake Titicaca. The Inca empire's final extent was 1,500 miles from north to south and almost 400 miles from east to west. When the Spaniards arrived, there must have been about 8–9 million subjects in the Inca state.

Inca influence, rather than political or military, was cultural and probably religious, with a cult of gods represented by cat figures. Doubtless this carry-over, or cultural interchange, as we should call it now, aided the extraordinary expansion of the Incas. And no doubt the Incas realized this, for their armies included propagandists or teachers—the *amautas*—who fanned out over lands that were marked for conquest, talked to the inhabitants, and often persuaded them to submit. Thanks to the *amautas,* a great part of the Inca expansion was accomplished without major battles.

The Quechua language was imposed on all the conquered peoples. This helps us to understand the ease with which a handful of Spaniards was able to seize such a great empire, for peoples who had been compelled to learn the language of the Incas had no cause to object to being forcibly taught another equally strange language, Spanish.

The Incas, unlike the Aztecs, were virtual monotheists who worshipped the sun as the supreme being (the Inca, who was chief high priest, was considered the incarnation of the sun), although their temples contained images of the moon and a certain divine character was ascribed to natural phenomena. The Incas did not practice human sacrifice or ritual cannibalism. They were familiar with confession, fasting, and prayer.

The social structure of the Incas has been described as socialistic. In reality, it was theocratic, with a controlled economy and state ownership. Inca society was much more firmly controlled than the Aztec or, probably, any other society of the time. It was divided into clans, whose supreme head—the Inca or Capac—was elected from the clan of "children of the sun," whose members formed a theocratic, military, and bureaucratic aristocracy. The priests formed a true separate class. The people consisted of the common subjects and the *mitimacuna,* members of conquered groups. The Inca was proprietor of all the land; he leased one-third of it to the peasants who, in payment, had to work the third lot belonging to the Inca (in other words, the state), and the third that belonged to the "sun" (the temples and the priests). Whatever was left over from the sun's harvest was used for public welfare (caring for the aged, children, and so forth), which was highly developed. Officials and soldiers were fed from the Inca's granaries. There were no great fortunes and no inheritances, for the personal property of every subject was buried with him.

If it were possible to make a comparison with European society of the period, we might say that the Inca's subjects were serfs, with the obligations of labor and military service.

Properly speaking, there were no artisans, since each family was expected to produce clothing and utensils for its own use as well as for the priests, soldiers, and officials. There were no guilds. Money was unknown, and barter was forbidden.

The life of these peoples was hard. Mountain agriculture is difficult, especially in regions with frequent dry spells. The peoples who preceded the Incas had developed techniques of irrigation and built canals and, perhaps even more important, had done their planting in terraces on the slopes. Although this entailed enormous labor, it also prevented erosion and facilitated irrigation and the profitable use of the land. There was no terrace farming among the Aztecs or in any other part of America. (Nor is there any today, for the custom disappeared and throughout Latin America farming is done on the slopes, with serious erosion and low productivity.)

The Incas had no writing, but communicated by means of *quipus,* cords with an arrangement of knots to indicate meaning. The capital was connected with the rest of the empire by an extensive network of messengers, called *chasquis.* By means of relays, the *chasquis* could deliver a message from Quito to Cuzco—a distance of 1,250 miles—in only five days. Roads and highways were numerous and excellent, despite the difficulties presented by the steep mountains of that region; there were frequent transfers of population in order to colonize conquered regions.

Inca architecture and applied arts—pottery and weaving—were as fully developed as the Aztecs', as witness the impressive ruins of Cuzco, Tiahuanaco, and Machu Picchu, among hundreds excavated. Architectural techniques were considerably advanced; walls and ramparts were built without cement but so carefully fitted that it is impossible even now to slip a knife blade between the stones. Literature was less abundant, confined as it was to oral transmission. The Spaniards were thus unable to collect as many elements of historical information as in Mexico, and no documents like the codices of the Mayas and Aztecs have been preserved.

In the rest of the continent lived other peoples who had reached a certain level of social organization, although not to the point of "modernity" represented by the Maya, Aztec, and Inca societies. What is today Colombia was the territory of the Chibchas. The Chibchas were good farmers and miners, mining salt, copper, and emeralds as well as gold; it is known that they had a fairly complete system of weights and measures. Cowardly or defeated warriors were compelled to wear women's clothing, and women had the right to give six lashes to delinquent husbands. Apparently their religion included human sacrifice.

The chiefs of the Chibcha tribes would meet on the shores of Lake Guatabita and, as a sign of respect for the god of water, cover their bodies with gold dust and submerge themselves in the lake, so that the water might have the gold. It was the abundance of gold among the Chibchas that gave rise to the legend of El Dorado, the fabled land where houses were fashioned of gold and paving stones of emeralds, in search of which a good many conquistadors undertook arduous marches that led, if not to El Dorado, at least to the discovery of new regions.

The Chibchas seem to have been a commercial people, and they occupied a pass along the route that must have joined the Incas to the peoples farther north. Indications of interchange and communications between the Incas, the Chibchas, and the Mayas have been found. So the Chibchas must have been, in a way, like the Hebrews of the ancient Orient, a trading folk who were at the same time prepared to fight to defend themselves against their neighbors.

Little is known of the Manabís of Ecuador, but it is known that the Arawaks, who lived in what is now western Venezuela, were among the earliest agricultural peoples on the continent. They have been compared to the Phoenicians, for Arawak relics have been found in Florida, the Amazon jungle, the Orinoco basin, and in various islands of the Caribbean. It is believed that other peoples, still in existence, are their descendants, for example, the Jívaros, Toscanás, and Uros.

Similarly, peoples living in the Amazon valley appear to be descended from the primitive and aggressive Caribs, who annihilated the Arawaks and Chibchas. The Caribs gave their name to the Caribbean Sea, as well as giving us the word cannibal. Their barbarian invasion of the most advanced peoples of the Andean regions must have been extensive, since it is believed that their descendants include the Sirionós of Bolivia, the Purúes and Yapuras of Peru, and the Chirianás of Orinoco.

There were other nomadic and warlike peoples who lived in the pitiless cold climates: the Magallanicos, who were fishermen of the southern Chilean islands; and the Onas, Tehuelches, Puelches, and Chechenetes of Tierra del Fuego, who continued to move up to the Argentine pampas where, centuries later, the Spaniards and the Argentines finished them off.

Other peoples were warlike but settled: the Guaranís of today's Paraguay, the Araucanians of Chile, and the Yaquis on the Pacific coast of Mexico. All these peoples resisted the conquistadors with greater tenacity than the more civilized groups but with no greater success, though some managed to remain isolated until the eighteenth century. But their impact on history was slight.

Over and above their cultural and social differences, all these peoples shared certain common traits that help us to understand the ease with which they were conquered: on the one hand, their technological lag, on the other, a common philosophico-religious outlook that reflected an attitude toward life that today we would call fatalistic. The Indians had no notion of progress. They did not believe that human existence could be altered or society modified; everything was static, unchanging, and wholly subject to the will of the gods, upon whom mankind had no influence.

The Aztecs believed that the universe had been destroyed four times: once by tigers, once by the winds, again by fire, and a fourth time by water. Each successive destruction had produced a new humanity, a race of men who inherited nothing from their ancestors. The tigers had destroyed a race of giants, the winds had changed men into apes, the fire did away with the men; and in order to recreate the sun, after the fourth destruction, the reunited gods established sacrifice of the new men to make sure that the new sun would rise every morning. This symbolic way of expressing philosophical concepts was taken literally by ordinary Indians (as by ordinary men in all religions). In their view, the conquistadors came, quite simply, to produce a new destruction. The alacrity with which the Indians submitted to the Spaniards may be partly explained by the fact that they were surprised at not being destroyed and found submission a small price for a survival that must have seemed miraculous.

Explorers and Conquistadors

The question "Who first discovered America, the Vikings or Columbus?" is a subject of unending discussion. For the understanding of Latin America, the important point is that the Spaniards and Portuguese implemented the discovery, conquering and later colonizing the new lands.

On October 12, 1492, Christopher Columbus (1436–1506), who had put to sea on August 3 from the little Spanish port of Palos de Moguer, arrived at what is today Watling Island in the Bahamas, which he named San Salvador and which the inhabitants called Guanahani. On the same voyage he discovered Cuba, which he called Isla Juana in honor of the daughter of his patrons, the king and queen of Spain, and Haiti, which he named Hispaniola. On his second voyage (1493–96), he discovered Puerto Rico and Jamaica. On his third voyage (1498–1500), which came after that made by the Italian Giovanni Caboto (John Cabot), Columbus reached the coast of Venezuela and for the first time set foot on the mainland. He thought he had found paradise, but he was arrested by an officer appointed to take his place, and returned to Spain in his own ship in chains. Vindicated, he made his final voyage in 1502–04, which took him to the Atlantic coast of Central America. Despite his title of Grand Admiral of the Indies—as the new lands were known—Columbus was not a conquistador. He took possession of new lands and carried strange articles and people back to Spain, but others were to assume the task of founding cities and establishing governments.

Columbus died believing that he had reached India, but the Spaniards soon became convinced that they had found a new continent. In 1513, Vasco Núñez de Balboa (1475–1517) crossed the Isthmus of Panama and discovered the Pacific Ocean, which he called Mar del Sur, or South Sea. Like many other conquistadors, he ended his life by being executed on the very lands he had discovered. The circumnavigation of the globe by the Portuguese Ferdinand Magellan (1470–1521), in the service of the king of Spain—a voyage that was completed by the Basque Juan Sebastian de Elcano (1476–1526), when the leader lost his life in the Philippines—proved the existence of the new continent and at the same time furnished empirical proof that the earth was round.

In 1500, another Portuguese, Pedro Alvares Cabral (1460–1526), en route to India by way of Africa, had reached the coast of Brazil and planted the flag of Portugal there. In 1516, Juan Díaz de Solís (d. 1516) reached the mouth of the Río de la Plata, which he mistook for a freshwater sea; he was slain and eaten by the Indians.

After this period, there were no more voyages of pure discovery. Once the Spaniards had founded their first cities—in reality, simple villages (*pueblos*) surrounded by palisades, which, in general, kept on good terms with the nearby Indians—the expeditions of conquest began: expeditions no longer undertaken simply to find new lands but to obtain gold, found cities, and establish colonies.

A series of expeditions sailed from Hispaniola and from Cuba to conquer the new lands. Later, Darien (Panama) and New Spain (Mexico) were added to these as expeditionary bases. The expeditions were usually financed by private individuals, who settled with the captains of the expeditions on a percentage of the booty and other wealth they obtained. The lands discovered went to the Crown, but the Crown granted the conquistadors a given share, to be distributed among the members of the expedition. So these explorations had a side that was strictly commercial, one of adventure, still another imperialistic, and one that in modern terms would be called patriotic. The expeditions were comparatively small; apparently, there were only three occasions on which more than 1,000 Spaniards were gathered together in one place. The death rate among the conquistadors was high; it is estimated that more than 80 per cent of the expeditionaries perished.

The expeditions were sent everywhere. In 1513, the governor of Puerto Rico, Juan Ponce de León (1460–1521), discovered Florida while in search of the legendary fountain of youth. Seven years later, another expedition to North America ended disastrously; its sole survivor, Alvar Núñez Cabeza de Vaca (c. 1490–c.1557), wandered for years over what is now Texas before reaching Mexico, where he wrote the chronicle of his incredible journey. Hernando de Soto (1495–1542) was lost in South Carolina and Arkansas for three years before he discovered the Mississippi River, on whose wooded banks he died. Francisco Vásquez de Coronado (1500–54), setting out from Mexico, searched for El Dorado in the north and apparently got as far as Nebraska before returning, disillusioned, to New Spain.

The legend of another El Dorado in South America caught the explorers' fancy. In search of it, Gonzalo Jiménez de Quesada (1496–1579) reached the Colombian antiplano, where he founded Santa Fe de Bogotá in 1539; at that time, he had only 160 of the 900 soldiers who had left the coast with him. Setting out from Peru, other captains went south into the interior. Pedro de Mendoza (1487–1537) brought fourteen vessels to the Río de la Plata, founded Buenos Aires, and sent his captains up the Paraná. He died on the return voyage to Spain. Buenos Aires, only a fort at the time, was abandoned by its starving garrison and it was not until 1580 that an expedition coming down from Asunción was able to restore the city.

But the most incredible expeditions of all were the conquests of Mexico and Peru.

The coasts of the Gulf of Mexico were visited in 1517 by Francisco Hernández de Córdoba (1475–1526) and a year later by Juan de Grijalva (d. 1527). When the news about Mexico and its civilized peoples reached Cuba, the governor, Diego de Velásquez, authorized Hernán Cortés (1485–1547) to organize an expedition. Velásquez later withdrew his permission, and Cortés had to leave the island secretly. When he reached Veracruz, he sank his ships in a way that would permit him to refloat them (and thus avoided having to leave a garrison) and, with an army of 555 men and 16 horses, advanced on the interior.

The history of the conquest of Mexico, as told by the soldier-chronicler Bernal Díaz del Castillo (1496–1584), is as exciting as any novel. It may be summarized thus: Cortés made friends of the Indian tribes and married an Indian princess—called La Malinche by the Indians and Doña Marina by the Spaniards—who served as his interpreter and adviser. He entered into an alliance with the Tlaxcaltecs, who were at war with the Aztecs; sighted the city of Tenochtitlán through a pass between two volcanoes; was received by the Aztec ruler Moctezuma II (d. 1520), and became his friend. Cortés later put Moctezuma into prison and seized his gold; he was obliged to flee from the city, laid siege to and occupied it, and then, in a series of brief campaigns, conquered the surrounding territory. From there he sent out his captains, some to the north and some south to Yucatán and Central America. Cortés founded cities, established headquarters in Cuernavaca, received titles from the king, divided lands among his men, and finally returned to Spain by order of the king, where he carried on a long quarrel with the imperial bureaucracy.

Cortés was tough, skillful and determined, as were all his men. He was a good governor and built up what was to be one of the two great Spanish colonies in America: it was then called New Spain.

The man who conquered the other great Spanish colony, Peru, was a very different sort. Francisco Pizarro (1475–1541) was, like Cortés, a native of Estremadura, but of more plebeian origins. Cortés had attended the University of Salamanca for two years, but Pizarro could barely read. Pizarro took part in Balboa's expedition and then formed a company with the priest Fernando de Luque and another expeditionary, Diego de Almagro, for the purpose of exploiting the southern lands. In 1532, he landed on the coast of what is now Peru and went up into the Andes, becoming the first man to reach the mountain range from the West. (Some years earlier, Alejo García, a Portuguese member of an expedition exploring the coasts of Brazil, had penetrated the jungle and reached the Bolivian Andes, where he was slain by Indians.)

If Pizarro was able to conquer the Inca empire in a short time and with only a few men, it was largely because of the dissension he found, for two brothers—the sons of the Inca Huayna Capac—were disputing the throne. The division weakened resistance to the Spaniards and provided them with allies. Pizarro captured and executed the Inca Atahualpa and then crushed a rebellion by the last Inca, Manco Capac II. He did not have long to enjoy his triumph, for a rivalry sprang up between him and Almagro, and Pizarro was slain by one of his associate's partisans. His brother Gonzalo (1502–48) succeeded to the command. In flight from this strife,

Pedro de Valdivia (1500–54), who had already conquered Venezuela, marched south, founded Santiago de Chile, and began a war against the Araucanians, in which he lost his life.

The Spanish expeditions competed in a desperate race to find new lands and riches. It seemed as though the enormous American territory was not big enough for them all. When one of Pizarro's captains, Sebastián de Benalcázar (1495–1550), marched north by way of the Andes, founded Quito, and entered Colombia, he met on the way Pedro de Alvarado (1485–1541), Cortés's lieutenant, who had conquered Guatemala and then proceeded south in search of El Dorado. When Gonzalo Jiménez de Quesada founded Sante Fe de Bogotá, he met nearby the forces of Benalcázar and those of a German, Nicolaus Federmann, which had come up from the Venezuelan llanos.

If we trace the expeditions of the conquistadors on a map, it seems incredible that they could have traveled so far (most of the way on foot, for they soon lost their horses in the jungles), through forests, across rivers and deserts, among hostile tribes. And it is even more incredible that they also built forts and founded cities in these isolated places; that from these centers new expeditions should fan out; and that, in time, organized colonies should spring up. And they did all this enveloped in heavy clothing and armor, plagued by hunger, eating unfamiliar fruits and meats, attacked by reptiles and insects. They were ambushed by Indians, oppressed by the sun by day and by icy winds at night, sometimes maddened by the effect of the heights. Yet they never failed to enter in their notebooks the route they were following, their expenses, their booty, the things they saw—finally to deliver their information to the king and to render their accounts to the men who financed the expeditions.

Some of these men knew how to write, and they left chronicles that are astonishing not only for what they relate—and which today are our chief source of information about the events of the time and about the Indian peoples—but for the direct and natural manner of the telling. They wrote as if discovering new peoples, entering gardens whose trees had "golden leaves" (as happened to some of Pizarro's soldiers in Tumbes), marrying princesses, learning new languages, and receiving titles were everyday affairs. Bernal Díaz's chronicles of the conquest of Mexico; the life of Christopher Columbus by his son Ferdinand (1488–1539); Gonzalo Fernández de Oviedo's (1478–1557) fourteen-volume *General and Natural History of the Indies;* the first history of the New World by the Italian Pedro Martín de Anglería (1455–1526), who was employed by the Council of the Indies in Seville and who took notes on everything told him by those returning from America—these are only a few of the works that describe with great vividness the extraordinary details of the Conquest.

By about 1550, hardly a quarter of a century after the first conquistadors landed on the mainland, and less than seventy years after the discovery of the New World, most of Latin America had been conquered, and cartographers could trace its general outlines on their maps.

The new lands, which extended more than eighty degrees on both sides of the equator, made Spain a world power and the world's first empire since the Roman. Spain oriented itself toward the West, across the Atlantic. Portugal, which had more promising lands in the Orient, oriented itself toward them. But both transferred to the New World the systems and customs that had prevailed in the Old.

The Founders

The first thing that the Spaniards did in the New World, once they had subdued the Indians, was to found a city. The survivors of the battle gathered and, according to legal procedure (the Spaniards were sticklers for juridical formula and ceremony), declared a city established, gave it a name, and elected officials. La Paz, in Bolivia, was founded in 1548 by seven Spaniards; one of them was elected mayor and two others were made judges. Lima—originally called the City of the Kings—one of the great urban centers of the colonies, was founded after a mass. As soon as they had given the customary cheers for the king, the founders rounded up the local Indians and ordered them to begin work on the city walls.

It often happened that the Indians destroyed the new city and slew the inhabitants. But more Spaniards always arrived to restore it. Along the coasts, the Spaniards did not build true cities but mere hamlets that could serve as ports. As soon as a port was established, they began to build vessels, for hurricanes wrecked many ships and the Spaniards did not like to feel cut off from their home country. But the coast was hot and unhealthful, and the Spaniards preferred to live in the highlands, where the climate was more like that of Spain. Thus in time the Andes became dotted with towns that closely resembled those in Andalusia, with houses built around patios and a central plaza on which stood the church and the town hall.

The founders of these cities were not noblemen or people of any great culture. (Nor were the priests who accompanied them, and who often acted as notaries to draw up the agreements that incorporated the expeditions, exactly the cream of the Church.) The conquistador was a man of the people; a younger son who would not inherit the family property in Spain, or perhaps an artisan weary of the monotony of city life, or a soldier who had retired when the wars against the Moors ended. These men were willing to perform any task, and able to perform many. The conquistador who fought one day might the next day take his tools and make furniture for his house, or teach the Indians to make bricks of clay and straw for the walls of the new city.

In Spain, he had either participated in the government of his municipality or had observed how others did it. He knew something about the privileges the king granted his own and, without actually thinking about it, expected equal privileges and similar methods of government in his new city. So the *cabildo,* or elected town council, and its complement, the *cabildo abierto,* or town meeting, to discuss important matters, developed immediately and spontaneously in America. The conquistadors established a dictatorship over the Indians, but among themselves, they lived democratically.

At first, the magistrates for the *cabildos* were elected by the people. Later, it became customary for the magistrates, when their term was up, to designate their successors. The law gave Indians the right to hold this office, but the naming of Indians was exceptional. The royal authorities were forbidden to intervene in the elections for the *cabildos,* but they often did so. In the same manner as royal authority dominated and lessened the power of direct municipal democracy in Spain, the *cabildos* in the Indies submitted to the viceroys. The early democratic character of the *cabildos* dwindled, not only in reflection of absolutist tendencies in Spain, but also because, although the conquistadors and colonists were men of the people, their descendants did not want to be. But, as we shall see, the *cabildos* played an important role in the struggle for independence.

The Spaniards also transferred to the New World their peculiar type of agrarian feudalism. The Iberian Peninsula had been conquered by the Arabs early in the eighth century. For seven centuries, the Christian kings of the north were kept busy winning back the territory in a series of wars, maneuvers, and agreements. As lands were recovered from the Moors, the king created nobles and bestowed titles and land upon the combatants. Although in the political realm, feudal relations between king and nobles, and nobles and their vassals, had never really flourished in Castile, feudal relations between the owner of land (the lord) and his peasants (or serfs) developed once the struggle against the Moors came to an end, and the agrarian situation in Spain became a wholly feudal one.

The same experience was repeated in the Spanish colonies in America. With the end of the Reconquest, the Spaniards gave their support to Columbus' expedition. And when the Spaniards reached the new lands, Columbus and his men, and those who followed in later expeditions, applied the same policy of giving titles and lands to the conquerors. Possession of the land was taken in the name of the king, and the lands were assigned to those who invaded them, also in the name of the king. Thus, Hernán Cortés was made Marquis of the Oaxaca Valley; he received 25,000 square miles of land in which there were twenty-two settlements and 115,000 Indians. Francisco Pizarro received the title Marquis of the Conquest, and lands on which there were 100,000 Indians. In 1580, the Río de la Plata region was divided among sixty-four Spanish captains. Bit by bit, these dominions broke up, and it became possible to buy American lands in Seville and Lisbon. This was the beginning of latifundism, which, as we shall see, has characterized Latin American society to the present day.

At first, when the commander distributed land to his soldiers, he also gave them Indians to work it. The Indians were not given as slaves but were "loaned," as unpaid labor, to the conquistador. The Crown, however, was interested in the Indians as tax-paying subjects; this, aggravated by religious and legal polemics over the condition of the Indians, was a constant cause of friction. The compromise solution found was the *encomienda*. Under this system, the colonizer was charged to protect the Indians he received and to educate them in the Catholic religion; in return, he could demand labor from them. This included not only labor on the land, but also in mines, and so on. The Council of the Indies had expected by this device to transform the Indians into faithful and loyal subjects, for the privilege of the *encomienda* was in theory not to be passed on to the grandson of the *encomendero*. But in fact new *encomiendas* were granted, and the system lasted until the eighteenth century. The *encomienda*, which was intended as a provisional instrument of protection, was changed into a permanent institution for exploitation. We shall see that similar things happened to other Latin American institutions.

Not all those who came to the New World received land and Indians, of course. Beginning with the first wave of colonists, there were artisans and skilled craftsmen. Although they organized guilds and guarded their privileges and trade secrets as jealously as they had in Europe, they did train many Indians and Negroes in their crafts and so created a local labor force that was technically no different from that of the motherland.

In Brazil, there had been, properly speaking, no conquest. The territory the Portuguese discovered in 1500 was thinly populated by scattered Indian tribes. The first Portuguese settlements were trading posts along the coasts, which exchanged various goods with the local Indians; chief among these was brazilwood (*pau-brazil*), which gave the country its name. Not until 1530 did the Portuguese Crown send an expedition, under Martim Afonso de Souza (d. 1564), who founded the first town and colony in Brazil.*

---

* The *bandeirante* (flag-bearer), who in the seventeenth and eighteenth centuries explored the Brazilian interior in search of gold and Indians, occupies a place in Brazilian history equal to that of the Spanish conquistador.

The king of Portugal then divided Brazil horizontally, or from east to west, into twelve zones, and granted the exploitation of each to a *donatario,* or grantee. Some of the land grants were larger than Portugal. Each grantee had the right to all the land in his zone, within which he was a feudal lord. The grantees were expected to finance the exploration, conquest, and administrative organization of the lands in their keeping; sometimes, the Portuguese Crown was unable to find persons disposed to accept grants of land.

In exploiting the new land, the Portuguese adopted the system used in the island of Madeira, where sugar was cultivated. The first sugar plantation was established in 1532, and a new form of exploitation, the sugar plantation worked by slaves, was born. Sugar became acceptable merchandise in Europe, and paid for the colonizing of Brazil.

The Brazilian cities were founded half a century later than those of Spanish America, and were not true cities, since their only inhabitants were soldiers, bureaucrats, and artisans. The owners of the plantations lived in their large houses on the fazendas, and began to move to the city only when the Portuguese Court was installed in Rio de Janeiro, in 1807, in flight from Napoleon.

The Colonial Structure

In 1519, the Emperor Charles V* declared the lands of the Indies united with the Crown of Castile. ("Spain" did not exist at that time. Although united under a single crown, Castile and Aragon-Catalonia continued to exist as two separate kingdoms. Castile alone had discovered America—although it was with the help of Aragon-Catalan financing—and she meant to colonize it.)

America was thus not regarded as a colony but as a property of the Crown. It was the king who established the liaison between the new lands and the old. This special relationship, proper to an epoch in which the concept of nationhood was lacking, was the framework of the administrative structure of America.

The seven centuries of war against the Arabs had given the

---

* Charles V (1500–58), Holy Roman Emperor; as King of Spain, he ruled as Charles I.

Castilian Crown much more power and authority than was customary in the rest of Europe. Over the years, a complex administrative apparatus, efficient and loyal to the king, had grown up. When the need arose to govern the new lands of the Indies, it was only necessary to enlarge this apparatus, forming new institutions and creating new offices. The entire administrative system for the Indies was created in the first fifty years after Discovery; while lands were still being conquered in the south, administrations were already in full operation.

The principal body governing the Indies was the Council of the Indies, which had its seat in Seville. The council, created in 1518 and given definitive form in 1534, was modeled upon a similar body that, together with the king, made the laws for Castile. The Council of the Indies made laws for the Indies; proposed candidates for administrative posts in America, both civil and ecclesiastical; organized fleets and armadas; sat in judgment on matters of *residencia* (that is, heard the complaints of subjects against the viceroy when his term had ended); directed military affairs; and was the final court of appeals. It was customary to appoint several members of the council from among former officials who had served in America, and inspectors were regularly sent out to study the situation in the Indies. The legislative activity of the Council was enormous; several compilations of its laws were made, the best known of which was published in 1681.

In America, the king was represented by the viceroy. The viceroy supervised the execution of laws drawn up by the Council of the Indies and appointed local civil and ecclesiastical officials. Although he was supposed to hold office for only three years, his term was often longer. At the end of it, he was answerable for his stewardship before the Council of the Indies.

New Spain (Mexico) and Peru were the first viceroyalties. Later, New Granada (Colombia) and the Río de la Plata became viceroyalties. Other regions—Guatemala, Venezuela, Cuba, Puerto Rico, Santo Domingo, Chile, Louisiana, and, for a time, Florida—were governed by captains generals or by governors. The frontier areas were under *adelantados*.

The judicial system in America was based on a court known as the *audiencia*. The first *audiencias* consisted of three or four judges, but over the years the number steadily grew. There was an *audiencia* in every viceroyalty, captaincy general, or governorship. In addition to their judicial functions, the *audiencias* were also responsible for military, religious, and financial inspections, and served as advisors to the viceroys. There were frequent jurisdictional disputes between the *audiencias* and the viceroys, however, especially since the *audiencia* communicated directly with the royal *audiencia* in Spain, which in turn communicated directly with the Crown.

There were also, in the New World, special tribunals of the army, the treasury, the Church, and the Inquisition (which was of much less importance in the New World than in the Old).

Most of the officials were sent from Spain. This in time gave rise to rivalry between the *gachupines* (Spaniards born in Spain)* and the Creoles (Spaniards born in America), because the latter resented having administrative careers closed to them. However, the fact that the officials did not settle permanently but had a limited stay in America, at the end of which they had to give an account of their stewardship, contributed a certain degree of independence to their authority.

Moreover, the Court understood that not all Spanish laws and customs could be applied to the New World. It therefore decreed that while the laws of Spain should serve as models for those made for the Indies, the laws and customs of the Indians should be respected, wherever they were not contrary to the Catholic religion. The Court also took into account the differences among the regions of the Indies, realizing that the same type of government was not suitable for savage peoples and those who were highly organized. Thus the authority of the viceroys was made flexible, and a court of appeals was established so that there should be mutual checks and controls. This system did not always work, for its corruption paralleled that of the Court itself.

There was also an autonomous local regime for the In-

* In the north, Spaniards who were not born in America were called *gachupines,* a word of unknown etymology still used in Mexico to designate Spanish immigrants who go into business; in the south, they were called *chapetones,* from *chapeta,* or "pink cheeks," which the Spaniards usually developed in high altitudes. In Spain, Spaniards who settled in America were called *"indianos";* this name is still given today to Spanish emigrants to the New World who make a fortune and then return to the Peninsula.

dians, who were governed by their cacique; it had fewer functions and less power than before the colonial period, but preserved its hereditary character. The town councils of these villages were, on paper, composed entirely of Indians; the reality was often quite different.

Over the years, the system changed little. But by the eighteenth century, there was so much discontent that the "enlightened ministers" of Charles III reorganized it. In 1786, the *intendencias* (supervisory boards) were created; they absorbed economic, fiscal, and even police and judicial functions.

To protect its economic interests in the New World, Castile established a monopoly on trade with its lands in America. All Indies trade was regulated by a Board of Trade (*Casa de Contratación*), founded in 1503. Trade could be carried on only through the ports of Seville and Cádiz in Spain, and through a few ports in America. Two expeditions a year went to America: one to New Spain (Mexico) and the other to Tierra Firme (South America). Both were protected against pirates by an armada. In the eighteenth century, Charles III extended the privileges of trading to eleven Spanish and twenty-four American ports, but did not lift the monopoly.

The Court also imposed many and varied taxes on the new lands. There were taxes on imports (the *almojarifazgo,* the ancient Arab name); on foodstuffs (the *sisa,* so unpopular that the word came to mean what servants kept for themselves when they did the marketing); on metals and precious stones (the *quinto real,* or royal fifth, 20 per cent on all products extracted from the ground); the tax on agricultural products (the *diezmo,* or tithe; in theory, nine-tenths of this went to the Crown and one-tenth to the Church, but in reality, much more often went to the Church); and on sales (the *alcabala*). Indians were exempted from paying the *diezmo,* but they did pay a tribute.

There were also state monopolies on such goods as playing cards, salt, spices, mercury, and tobacco.

The revenue from all these taxes was sent to the Board of Trade in Seville. Once a week, the Council of the Indies met to examine the accounts, make fiscal decisions, and assign the use of that part of the revenues that went back to America to pay administrative and military expenses. After 1526, every viceroyalty, governorship, and captaincy general had its own budget; any surplus was earmarked for the aid of colonies that showed a deficit. As we shall see, these taxes were the cause of a long series of rebellions by colonizers and Indians alike.

Obviously, this fiscal system had extensive control of the economy. This is significant, for it created in Latin America the tradition of relying on state intervention in business; the planned or directed economy is a Spanish heritage so deeply rooted as today to be considered natural and even essential. No small contribution to this was made by some colonial corporations, like the Guipuzcoana company, to which Charles III granted the economic control of Venezuela.

Yet it should also be said that the colonial administration tried harder to exploit riches that were already known than to discover new ones. There was considerable development in mining, especially in the silver mines, which were more "modern" than European mines of the time. Progress was also made in metallurgy. But in general, the natural wealth —as it was understood in that era—was so great, the fertility of the soil so astonishing to people accustomed to the tired soils of Europe, that there was little interest in seeking new sources of wealth or in modernizing the utilization of those that already existed.

In Brazil, too, the administrative system was based on the concept of the colony as a property of the Crown, which was represented by a viceroy resident in Bahia, the capital until 1763, and subsequently Rio de Janeiro. Brazil was divided into eight captaincies general and eight governorships. The Church was administered by an archbishop and five bishops. The municipal assemblies, similar to the *cabildos,* were democratic in origin, but they lost this character even more rapidly than the Spanish ones and became mere bureaucratic mechanisms. We must also remember that until the nineteenth century, Brazil consisted essentially of a fringe of settlements along the coast and that there were scarcely any Portuguese in the interior. The principal problem of the Portuguese authorities was to combat the incursions of the Dutch, French, and British into Brazil.

The tendency of both Spanish and Portuguese policy in the Indies was clearly assimilative. Colonization was not the spontaneous activity of small groups of dissenters, as it was in the United States, but was directed and controlled by the state. And since few details were known about the only comparable historical antecedent—the Roman—Spain and Portugal had to invent their policy. The simplest way was to transfer to the Indies the administrative systems of the mother country, just as the colonists transferred their way of life. This had conflicting consequences. On the one hand, it impeded the spontaneous development of Latin America in its own fashion; on the other, it established a real equality between the motherland and the Indies. A few decades after the Conquest, the Indies boasted a modern civilization that had not arisen there and had not evolved through any intermediate stages.

It is very difficult to judge the political and, especially, the social realities of Latin America in the colonial period. In 1735, two learned Spaniards, Jorge Juan (1713–73) and Antonio de Ulloa (1716–95), were sent to inspect the colonies. They wrote a "secret report," which was not made public until 1826, in which they said, among other things, that "the Indians have become slaves, and are in a state of slavery so oppressive that those Africans whom the force and right of the colonies have condemned to servile oppression may consider themselves comparatively fortunate." Years later, the German scholar Alexander von Humboldt (1769–1859), after traveling over the continent, wrote that "the Indian tiller of the soil is poor but free," and judged him better off than the European peasant.

The problem of the Indians, of course, had presented itself from the beginning. The Castilian Court had the same ambivalent attitude toward the Indians as the conquistadors: it wanted to save souls and at the same time to acquire wealth and territory. The Court viewed the Conquest both as an apostolate and as a business, and royal policy constantly shifted between the two alternatives: the economic and the spiritual. But if one of the Court's principal preoccupations in the New World was to protect the Indians from the conquistadors, the chief burden of defending the Indians was assumed by the Church.

Indians, Friars, and Bishops

We can imagine the astonishment of the Indians when they came upon a group of strange white men, clad in armor and carrying odd weapons, when they saw one of these men draw his sword, touch the ground, and then heard him read aloud a document of whose meaning, of course, they had no idea. This document, called the *Requerimiento* (Requirement) embodied the conditions the king or his deputies had stipulated for the expeditionaries and the formula by which the latter took possession of those lands in the name of the Crown and assured the Indians of royal protection. The *Requerimiento* was a very long affair; in addition to the legalities, there was, for the benefit of the Indians, an explanation of the creation of the world, a résumé of the Old and New Testaments, an explanation of Catholic dogma, and an exhortation to adopt that religion. If the Indians, bored or puzzled, went away, the Spaniards went right on with the reading. Only when it was completed could the spot be considered duly conquered.

This was not a mere exercise in judicial futility. It shows that the Spaniards, to their considerable credit, had their doubts as to the legality of the Conquest. They had come for booty—for gold, lands, and titles—but also to conquer souls, and they wanted to do this in a way that did no violence to their deeply rooted feeling for legality. Early in the colonial period, several viceroys ordered an investigation on the legal title of the Incas and the Aztecs to their lands.

On this point, there were two schools of thought: that of Juan Gínes de Sepúlveda (1490–1573) held that discovery and military occupation were a means of creating sovereignty over a territory that, once conquered, became *res nullius* and whose inhabitants were to be treated as beasts of burden without rights or protection under the law. The other school, that of Francisco de Vitoria (1486–1546), considered that America was the property of its inhabitants and that their paganism was no reason to make war on them. It might be said that Vitoria inspired the legislation of the Indies and Sepúlveda its application. (In effect, however, Pope Alexander VI had already recognized the right of Spain to the new lands in his bull of 1493, which divided the world between Spain and Portugal.)

On his return to Seville from his first voyage, Columbus took with him several Indians, whom he sold as slaves. But Queen Isabella forbade this traffic in people she considered her subjects. In 1503, Nicolás de Ovando (c. 1469–1518), governor of Hispaniola, wrote to the Queen that if the Indians were not compelled to work no gold would be mined—and it would also be impossible to christianize them. The Court then authorized the division of the Indians among the conquistadors, but at the same time ordered that they were to be clothed, fed, and instructed in the Catholic religion: this was the beginning of the system of the *encomienda.* Ovando then devoted himself to rounding up the Indians for division. The island was soon depopulated, chiefly as a result of the diseases, especially smallpox, that the Spaniards brought with them and to which the Indians were particularly susceptible.

In 1515, an uprising of Indians who had been angered by bad treatment persuaded the bishop of Hispaniola, the Dominican Bartolomé de las Casas (1474–1566), to speak to the king. Las Casas proposed that Spanish peasants be sent to till the soil side by side with the Indians, in colonies under the supervision of friars. He also proposed that Negro slaves be imported from Africa, since they were more accustomed to heavy labor and also since the fact that they cost money would induce their owners to give them better treatment (a proposal he later withdrew). Las Casas' colonization plans were tried out in Venezuela, but without success.

About 1542, Las Casas returned to Spain and presented to the king his *Very Brief Account of the Destruction of the Indies,* a denunciation of Spanish maltreatment of the Indians. At first, Las Casas scored a triumph. Charles V promulgated the New Laws of 1542, which offered protection to the Indian and revoked or limited the *encomienda:* no new *encomiendas* were to be granted, and when the present *encomenderos* died their Indians were to revert to the Crown. Yet despite his initial success, Las Casas' efforts ended in failure, for the New Laws were never enforced. After Las Casas, the defense of the Indians went on an ad hoc basis, and no longer on the question of principle—the right of the Indians to be free—as the Dominican bishop had wanted.

Augustinian, Dominican, and Franciscan friars had come to the New World almost from the beginning of the Conquest: they arrived in Mexico three years after the conquest of that country. Everywhere, they faced an enormous task: to convert millions of Indians who spoke a strange language, and to overcome the mistrust of the *encomenderos*.

Until the missionaries could learn the native languages, they tried to convert the Indians by signs and through interpreters. This had two results: it created a favored caste, the Indian interpreters, who enjoyed certain privileges not only because of their closeness to the priests but also because, in the eyes of their fellow countrymen, they possessed magical powers; and it brought about a perversion of doctrine. We know, for example, that when a priest explained to the Inca Atahualpa that God was both one and three, the interpreter translated this as if God were one plus three, that is, four gods.

The friars faced other problems in converting the Indians. The Indians did not believe in reward and punishment, in heaven and hell. The Indian thought in terms of his clan, the Spaniard in terms of his individual self. Whereas the dying Spaniard confessed his faults in order to win personal salvation, the Indian confessed his faults to neutralize the evil influence of his death upon his clan.

In converting the Indians, the friars made use of many native beliefs, simply giving them new names. In the course of time, there was produced a very special syncretistic religion: Catholic in rite (in places where the rites were observed) and even in liturgy, but still Aztec or Inca in the temper of worship and the figure of the god. In many places, for centuries, Indians would hold their own wedding ceremonies immediately after the Catholic one, and it was the same with baptisms and funerals. In recent years, when it has been necessary to move the Spanish wayside crucifixes to make way for modern highways, the engineers have often found clay images of the ancient idols buried in the bases of the pedastals.

The missionaries also imposed on the Indians standards of sexual behavior completely alien to their tradition, and this doubtless was one cause of the falling birth rate in the first generations after the Conquest. Indian women were required to dress in the Spanish style, and all Indians had to wear clothes to mass; often, they would take them off as soon as they left the church and returned home naked.

But the friars played a notable role as civilizers in the New World. Not only did they defend the Indians against the voracity of the colonists, but they also taught them Spanish, built schools, and founded hospitals.

Most of what is known of the pre-Columbian cultures comes to us through the works of the monks. It is true that the friars destroyed pyramids and artifacts of the native cultures—the first bishop of Mexico, Juan de Zumárraga (d. 1533), boasted in a letter that he had destroyed 500 temples and 20,000 idols and had burned the hieroglyphics of the royal library of Texcoco. But they were also interested in the Indian heritage. Thus, Fray Bernardino de Sahagún (c. 1500–90) wrote a history of New Spain, after fifty years of investigation and the study of several Indian languages; Fray Toribio de Benavente (d. 1568), whom the Indians called Motolinía ("poor man"), wrote a history of the first twelve mendicant friars in Mexico, as well as grammars of the native languages.

The friars also employed the Indians to build their churches and convents, and thus played a great part in teaching them modern skills and techniques. This accounts for that strange mingling of European technique, Catholic themes and images, and characteristically Indian or African taste that we see in colonial architecture and religious art and that gives them so much personality.

About 1572, the Jesuits began to arrive in the New World, fired with the zeal of a new order. It was the Jesuits who founded many of the schools, libraries, and universities in colonial America, who set up printing presses and encouraged the circulation of books and ideas.

Their most notable work was done in what are now the eastern provinces of Paraguay, where they organized *reducciones,* or city-states, in which they gathered the Guaranís, tilled the soil side by side with them, and with an almost military discipline taught them the catechism, technical skills, and semi-Western ways of life. (The *reducciones* were mistrusted by the people of Asunción, who felt that the existence of communes of virtually free Indians would encourage the subjected ones to ask for privileges.)

Around 1700, when the Brazilian *bandeirantes* attacked the *reducciones* and carried away thousands of Indians to work in the recently discovered gold mines, the Jesuits won the king's permission to arm the Guaranís and to organize them into a militia, which spread over the pampas of Paraguay, Uruguay, and northern Argentina. These militiamen were the distant ancestors of the gauchos, and this, as well as their having the use of arms, explains the fighting qualities of the Paraguayans in the long war with Brazil, Uruguay, and Argentina in the nineteenth century. When the Jesuits were expelled from Spanish America, in 1767, the Indian communes were dissolved and the jungle grew over the former villages. But the idea of isolationism and of paternalism in government lived on and inspired the policy of the first president of Paraguay.

By the seventeenth century, missionary zeal in the New World had almost entirely vanished. We begin to find in the Church the same conflict of interests as among the colonists. In addition to its spiritual and cultural labors, the Church pursued material ends. To the convent-forts built in the early decades of the Conquest—whose lands were cultivated jointly by friars and Indians—were added new lands worked by the Indians alone. Each convent, like each ecclesiastical unit, owned land and houses and had Indians to work them. By the eighteenth century, one-fifth of the Spanish colonial lands was in mortmain. In Lima, a city of 25,000 persons, one-third of the buildings belonged to the convents; there were six monasteries and six nunneries, with 200 Franciscans, 250 Dominicans, 200 Jesuits, and 150 Augustinians. In the Ecuadorian city of Cuenca, with 500 Creole inhabitants, there were four monasteries and one nunnery; the people called the city "Valley (*Cuenca*) of the Clergy". Quito, with 3,000 whites and mestizos, had eight convents of friars and three of nuns, in addition to seven churches, one of them, that of the Jesuits, fabulously wealthy. In Mexico City, there were no fewer than twenty monasteries and sixteen nunneries.

In the villages, the priests often imposed special taxes, and fixed the price of religious services as they saw fit. One of the most frequent demands in the rebellions of the Indians, and also of the Creoles, was the reduction of the cost of religious services. The peasants in many villages went into debt to maintain the tradition of the fiesta—a collective celebration paid for by families in turn—which the parish priest would encourage and exploit, since he was paid for all the religious functions around which the fiesta revolved. The peasants supported the local parishes. When Juan and Ulloa visited Peru in the mid-eighteenth century, they found a parish in a *pueblo* near Quito that received 200 sheep, 6,000 chickens, and 50,000 eggs every year. Such abuses were condemned by many laws, which forbade the friars to own businesses and lands in their own name, to operate mines, to beg, and to gamble. Priests were expressly forbidden to have concubines and children. But these prohibitions were of little use.

In the capitals of the viceroyalties, the Church was the ally of the royal authorities; in provincial towns and *pueblos,* it was the ally of the Creoles; in the hamlets, the parish priest was the real authority. In zones bordering on regions inhabited by savage Indians, or in unexplored areas, the monks were often the only authority, since after the original enthusiasm of the conquistadors had been lost, the bureaucrats objected to being sent to places distant from the cities. It was missionaries who made the "conquests" in the eighteenth century: men like the German Jesuit Eusebius Kind (d. 1710), who explored Lower California, and a Franciscan from Mallorca, Fray Junípero Serra (1713–84), who founded many missions in what is now California, as well as the city of San Francisco. These were centers of devotion and power.

The Church in the New World followed the same evolution as in the Old. In eighteenth-century Latin America, we find, as in Spain and the rest of Europe, a divided Church, with violently dogmatic bishops and Voltairean abbots, with parish priests who denounced the works of the French encyclopedists (which were imported secretly) and priests who expounded the doctrines of d'Alembert and Diderot and protected Creoles engaged in scientific research. Although the Church generally sided with the secular authorities in combating rebellions, and also in opposing independence, some members of the clergy were sympathetic to the independence cause, as were the Jesuits. The Jesuits were expelled from Spain and from Spanish America in 1767; many of them settled in Italy, where they became the first Latin American patriots. It was Jesuits exiled in Italy who were the first to use the name "Mexico" to designate what they had come to regard as their own country. One of these, Francisco Xavier Clavijero (1731–87), wrote in Italian an *Ancient History of Mexico,* which is probably the first cultivated expression of Latin American nationalism.

The Church was involved in everything that happened in the colonies. Its internal rivalries and disputes with the viceroys were the woof of colonial history into which were woven the other events in the life of the colony: pirate attacks, and rebellions of Creoles, Indians, and Negroes. For if the three centuries of colonial life passed without any sensational events, they were rich in adventures, struggles, and protests.

The Rebellions of the Encomenderos

From the very beginning of the Conquest, we find two opposing forces: the royal authorities, and the conquistadors or *encomenderos.* In Spain, men had won nobility and territory by fighting the Moors and taking their land. In America, the Spaniards expected the same rewards for the same sort of activity against the Indians. When the king attempted to pass laws governing the new lands, to send deputies, or to levy taxes, the conquistadors rebelled and, as a result, frequently returned to Spain in fetters or were hanged by order of the king in the very country they had conquered in his name.

The first rebellion took place as early as Columbus' fourth voyage. After landing in Jamaica, a group of sailors, headed by Francisco de Porras, deserted the admiral, founded their own city, and held out for a year before surrendering to the Crown. Cortés began the conquest of Mexico by disobeying the governor, Velásquez; he later defeated the soldiers Velásquez sent against him, and they joined his small army. After conquering Tenochtitlán, Cortés crushed a rebellion by Cristóbal de Olid (1488–1542) in Central America, and another by his countrymen in the capital, who hanged the governor Cortés left behind when he moved south. In Peru, Pizarro had his associate Almagro hanged; in return, the latter's friends assassinated Pizarro, in 1541.

In 1542, the New Laws were passed for the protection of the Indians. These laws, as we have seen, had as their purpose the abolishment of the *encomienda*. They also made it compulsory to obtain permission to buy lands from the Indians; a Spaniard found guilty of a crime was punished more severely if the victim were an Indian than if he were another Spaniard; the payment of wages in kind was forbidden. In order to get sufficient revenue from the new lands, the colonial authorities often tolerated stretching of the law. But this did not prevent rebellions.

One of the first to revolt was Gonzalo Pizarro, brother of the conquistador, who rose up against the viceroy who had brought with him the text of the New Laws and imprisoned him. To keep the rebellion from spreading, the Court suspended the New Laws until 1548, when Gonzalo Pizzaro was arrested and beheaded, even though he had resisted the advice of his supporters to marry an Inca princess and proclaim Peru's independence. Four years later, the New Laws were again put into force in Peru. Francisco Hernández Girón (d. 1550) immediately led a new rebellion; when he saw that he could not win, he began to free the Indians, hoping to form them into an army; but the *encomenderos* then joined with the viceroy and defeated the rebels who were jeopardizing their privileges. In Mexico, Martín Cortés, son of the conquistador, was jailed for conspiring to expel the viceroy charged with enforcing the New Laws. In Asunción, the settlement of conquistadors rose, jailed the *adelantado* sent by Spain to impose the New Laws, and shipped him off to the Peninsula. For twenty-six years, this colony existed outside the authority of the Crown. In other places, colonists refused to receive the Spanish envoys. Only Chile, which was caught up in the struggle against the Araucanians, was free from rebellions against the Crown.

The rank-and-file soldiers sometimes found dramatic ways of expressing their point of view. In Peru, according to the chronicler López de Gómara, a group of them confronted the viceroy who was to impose the New Laws. They surrounded him silently, merely displaying the marks of the Conquest: their toothless gums, their scar-covered bodies, their amputated limbs.

But the formula that satisfied both the legalistic spirit of the Spaniards and their reluctance to apply the New Laws was found by Sebastián de Benalcázar, the founder of Guayaquil. After reading the laws in open assembly, Benalcázar bowed before the royal seal as a sign of respect for the king, indicated that execution of the laws would be "inconvenient" for the colonists, and enunciated a phrase that in the course of years would be repeated whenever the colonists wanted to resist a law without breaking with the Crown: "It is respected but not complied with."

The most astonishing of the early rebellions was that of Lope de Aguirre (1518–61). Aguirre was a commoner who had taken part in the conquest of Peru and in the uprising of Hernández Girón (in which he became known as "the man with the lame right foot"). This did not prevent him from joining an expedition organized by the viceroy to rid the city of what today would be called agitators. But in Amazonas, the expeditionaries revolted, and their leader proclaimed himself king. Aguirre killed him and took his place. He then gathered his companions together and told them: "We must make war on the king's cities, where the real El Dorado is. There we'll find women, gold, and weapons." When his men began to thin out, killed by wild animals and disease, Aguirre recruited a force from among the fierce Marañon Indians, along the Orinoco. He then wrote to Philip II: "Now we have truly found out in these kingdoms how cruel you are and that you are a breaker of faith and word. And look you, King and Lord, as a just king you can have no rights in these lands, where you took no risks, until those who have toiled and sweated in these lands have first been rewarded." In another letter, he announced that he was establishing his own kingdom: "I have renounced obedience to you, cruel and ungrateful King, to make the most cruel war upon you. I solemnly swear, I and my two hundred Marañons, that we shall not leave you one minister alive." Aguirre eventually settled on Margarita Island, where he was finally captured and beheaded. But in a sense, he had made the first declaration of independence in America.

The Spanish rebels wanted two things: the right to govern the conquered lands, and the right to exploit the Indians. They failed to win the former, for the power of the royal authorities grew stronger with each rebellion. But if feudalism lost the political battle it won the economic one, for the New Laws were never enforced and the *encomienda* persisted until Charles III finally abolished it in the eighteenth century.

The Indian Rebellions

The Indians under the *encomienda* had to work wherever the *encomenderos* sent them, and without pay.

Those Indians who were not under the *encomienda* were subject to the *repartimiento,* or *mita,** a system of forced labor under which the Indians had to serve periodically in mines, fields, workshops, fisheries, on public works, or as domestic servants—all without pay, and often far from their *pueblos*. Indians who worked in the mines had a quota set for them, and those who did not meet it were punished; they had to buy their own food, the coca they chewed, and even the candles they used in their work from shops run by the mine owners. By the eighteenth century, one-seventh of the Indians of Peru were subject to the *mita,* one-fourth in New Spain, one-third in Chile, and one-twelfth in Paraguay and the Río de la Plata.

But the Indians who lived in *pueblos* under the authority of their traditional cacique were no more fortunate. In each *pueblo,* there was a friar who served as "Protector of the Indians." But as time went on, he neither protected nor taught but forced the Indians to till his land. A viceroy of Peru, López de Zúñiga y Velasco, advised the king in a letter: "It would be better if Your Majesty would order that there be less sending over of friars and that, if they are sent, they should not be young men, but old men of good life and example."

All Indians payed a tribute, collected by the *corregidores,* who were entitled to keep a percentage of what they collected. These officials usually kept two accounts: one, based on the Indians' ability to pay, was shown to the royal authorities; the other, more grasping, was actually imposed on the Indians. Failure to pay incurred whipping and other punishments. If the *corregidor* owned a latifundio, the defaulting Indian was sent to work on it.

The Court made some attempts at reform, beginning with the New Laws of 1542. In New Spain, the viceroys Marquis of Nancera and Fray Payo Enríquez de Rivera forbade cor-

---

* The system of forced labor was known as the *mita* in Peru, the *repartimiento* elsewhere.

poral punishment. In the sixteenth century, a viceroy of Peru, Andrés Hurtado de Mendoza, authorized the caciques to arrest whites who disturbed the peace in their villages and prohibited the transporting of Indians to climates different from their native one. The viceroy Lope García de Castro tried to prevent the systematic tipping of justice in favor of the whites. Viceroy Antonio de Mendoza of Mexico fixed the total daily hours of work in the mines, ordered the payment of wages to free Indians or those under *encomienda,* and established the *ejido* system to protect the Indians' comunal lands.

The Indians knew that if they were to get any help, it would have to come from the ministers of the Crown; their enemy was not the king or the viceroy, but the *encomendero,* the teacher, the *corregidor*—that is, the Creole. (Later, when the Creoles rose against the Crown to declare their independence, the Indians formed the bulk of the royalist forces.) When the *corregidor* established a monopoly on the sale of merchandise in his district; when a slow-working Indian was sent to labor in a workshop to pay his tax debt out of his wages; when, at the All Souls' Day fiesta, each inhabitant of the *pueblo* paid, one after the other, for the same uncorked bottle of wine that was offered to the dead, the Indian said to himself that if the king knew of these injustices, he would put a stop to them. Hence, the Indian rebellions generally began with a proclamation of loyalty to the king, and only when the authorities suppressed it—and where there was still a lingering memory of ancient Indian sovereignty—did there appear the desire to create an Indian state. Only Brazil was free of Indian revolts; its few Indians had been driven inland by the colonists; when the latter needed labor and no Negroes were available, they sent expeditions of *bandeirantes* to capture the Indians, who were then subjected to virtual slavery.

The first important Indian rebellion was that of the workers in the Tepic mines in New Spain, in 1598. In 1680, the Indians of Tehuantepec, New Spain, rebelled and for eight years were in command of the region. In Mexico City, in 1692, a famine led to a Creole rebellion during which an Indian lost his life. When the guilty Spaniard was not punished, the Indians in the city set fire to the town hall; this is probably the only example of a revolt by urban Indians. In 1761, the

Mayas of Yucatán, led by Jacinto Canek, rose against the excessive tribute and their owner's right to whip them; eight of the rebels were quartered.

There were also rebellions in the other viceroyalties. For ten years, from 1640 to 1650, the Calchaquíes of Tucumán carried on a real war against the governor who had offended their caciques. In 1723, in Chile, there was a widespread rebellion against official maltreatment. In 1752, the Guaranís rebelled against the treaty between Madrid and Lisbon that ceded to Portugal regions in which the Jesuits had founded *reducciones;* after a three-year struggle, the treaty was annulled. From 1761 to 1773, the Indians of the Hacha River in New Granada fought to bring about the discharge of certain oppressive officials, but the latter scattered them and brought in Indians from other places.

The most significant Indian rebellions occurred in regions in which the memory of the Inca government lingered, and in which there had been maintained, around the legends, some vague national feelings. In these places, the leader of a protest would claim to be a descendant of the Inca and would move to establish an Indian government or kingdom.

The first of these "nationalist" rebellions broke out in 1655 in Tucumán, where Pedro Bohórquez (who took the name of Inca Hualpa) fought for twelve years in the mountains until he was captured and beheaded. From 1736 to 1750, the mestizo Juan Santos (Inca Atahualpa) headed a miners' uprising in Oruro, which demanded lower tribute and the reduction of fees for religious services. The same demands caused the most spectacular of the Indian rebellions, that of Tupac Amaru.

The Indians in the Peruvian province of Tinta, exasperated by the exactions of the *corregidor,* killed him. The cacique of one *pueblo,* José Gabriel Condorcanqui, hurried to Lima to ask pardon from the viceroy. He failed to receive it. Upon returning to the *pueblo,* he arrested the new *corregidor,* brought him to trial before the Indians, and hanged him. He then took the rifles of the *corregidor*'s escort and formed a guerrilla band of Indians. The bishop of Cuzco hastily organized a battalion of priests and asked Lima for reinforcements. In several encounters between the two forces,

José Gabriel was victorious. He proclaimed himself Tupac Amaru II and organized a new government; his wife, Micaela Bastida, was the brains of it. At the head of 40,000 Indians he tried to take Cuzco, but failed. Meanwhile, another revolt broke out in Catavi (Bolivia). The rebellion spread until José Gabriel was taken prisoner. He was tried and executed with thirty-seven of his followers. Before his death, he said to the visitor sent by the viceroy: "The only conspirators are you and I; you by oppressing the people and I by having tried to liberate them from such tyranny." A brother of José Gabriel kept up the struggle, was offered a pardon, and surrendered. Some days later he was tried and executed, with the assistance of the same bishop of Cuzco who had accepted his surrender. The rebellion had been brief—from November, 1780, to March, 1782—but it left a deep impression, one that still remains.

The Negro Rebellions

The Negro rebellions are of a different character from those of the Indians. The Negroes were not seeking smaller taxes and better government. They were slaves, and the fundamental question was one of freedom or slavery. The Indian wanted to modify his servitude, the only condition with which he was familiar before or after the Spanish Conquest. The Negro, who had been free, wanted to do away with his slavery. Often, the Negroes fled their owners and organized their own rudimentary states.

The colonial slaveowner could sell his slave as chattel, could separate him from his family, could punish him by flogging, and could even order his execution. An extensive slave code existed, but these laws were seldom enforced. And although Pedro Claver (1582–1654), a Catalan friar, was proclaimed a saint in the nineteenth century for his unfailing help to the Negro slaves, it was very unusual to find priests as interested in the well-being of the Negroes as they were in that of the Indians. The chief thing that protected the Negro was the tendency of the colonists to have children by Negro women as well as by Indian ones.

For the Negro, therefore, the king and his officials could not be regarded as protectors. Hence, when he rebelled, the

Negro showed no respect for the Crown, and when the struggle for independence began, Negroes fought in the hastily recruited insurgent armies. (The Liberator José de San Martín was one of those who praised his Negro battalion.)

As early as the sixteenth century, Mexico had known an uprising of the Negroes of Orizaba, headed by a Negro called Yanga. To end their rebellion, they were allowed to form a *pueblo* of their own, San Lorenzo de los Negros, and the importation of slaves was suspended for several decades. In the same period, in Central America, Negroes fled to the forests and survived by attacking the trade caravans; when the expeditions sent against them failed, their leader, Bayano, was granted permission to found a kind of autonomous city, Santiago del Principe; in 1574, they were granted freedom in order to avoid another revolt. On the Mosquito Coast, many runaway Negro slaves, who had mingled with the Indians, created principalities and exacted tribute from the pirates who landed there. Sometimes, the Negroes helped the pirates, however; when Sir Francis Drake landed at the port of Callao, the Negroes of Lima went en masse to the coast to welcome him.

The tendency of the Negroes to found kingdoms of their own was soon evident. As early as 1555, Negroes working in the gold mines at Buria, Venezuela, revolted and set up a kingdom that lasted until their monarch's death in battle. In the seventeenth century, slaves in the same gold mine, led by a certain Miguel, founded another kingdom; it was crushed by armed force. And in 1795, the Negroes of Coro revolted, aroused by the propaganda of French Jacobins who had been deported to Guiana after the Thermidor. In the same year, slaves in Uruguay established a kingdom on the island of Yi in the Río de la Plata.

The most notable Negro rebellions occurred in Brazil: one of them lasted sixty-five years. In the northeastern region of Palmares, Negroes who had fled the fazendas joined together to establish settlements that were known as *quilombos;* these *quilombos,* with their chiefs and councils, gradually formed a kingdom. Two generations of Negroes lived there in liberty, from 1630 to 1695, although the second generation was subject to a virtual dictatorship of its own chiefs (called *zumbís*). The Negroes of the *quilombos* bartered with the whites in Palmares. In 1678, there was a revolution, when king Ganza Zumba concluded an agreement with the whites; his captains deposed him, redivided their lands, and continued the war. The Dutch, when they occupied Pernambuco, organized an unsuccessful expedition against them, and the Portuguese organized fourteen. The Negroes were finally conquered by an army of *bandeirantes* from São Paulo. But the legend arose among the Negroes that the last *zumbi* had not died and that he would return to free them.

It was Negroes who introduced republican ideas into Brazil. In 1789, the mulattoes of Minas Gerais, led by Joaquim José da Silva Xavier (1748–92), known as Tiradentes (tooth-puller, because he was a dentist), rose in protest against an increase in taxes and the shipment of Brazilian gold to Portugal. Tiradentes was quartered. Nine years later, in Bahia, there was a conspiracy of Jacobin mulattoes, who fought for a "free and independent republican government, with unlimited access to all public posts for Mulattoes and Negroes." Four of the conspirators were quartered. Between 1807 and 1835, the Males (Negro Mohammedans) of Bahia mutinied seven times in attempting to establish a government under the protection of Allah. The rebellion of Manuel Balaio, in 1839—in which white liberals joined—was suppressed with the utmost harshness.

It could be said that the Indian peasant and the Negro slave initiated the struggle for independence almost as soon as the colonies had been established. But their rebellions had chance of success only when they coincided with the rebellions of the white bourgeoisie, the people of the cities.

The Creole Rebellions

A Creole is a person of Iberian (or French) descent born in America. The Creole of colonial times felt that he was a Spaniard, or Portuguese, because of his background and because this gave him prestige and privileges. But he also felt that he was an American, because he had been born in the New World and because his interests were bound to the colony and not to the motherland.

Like the *encomendero* and the Indian, the Creole resented

the taxes imposed by the Crown. But most of all, the Creole resented the fact that high posts in the colonial administration were not open to him but only to officials sent from Spain.* The Creole participated in government only at the municipal level. Thus his rebellions were not so much for the purpose of maintaining privileges (as were those of the *encomenderos*) as to preserve and enlarge municipal forms of government.

Most of the Creole rebellions began in the same way: a *cabildo,* upon receiving an order from the viceregal authorities, considered it contrary to the common interest and had recourse to the formula "respected but not complied with." If the royal official tried to enforce the order, the *cabildo,* assuming prerogatives not its own, discharged him from office or even deported him, and the rebellion was on. Because of the distance from Spain, many of these rebellions attained their object—at least de facto.

In 1624, Creoles in Mexico rose in protest against the monopoly on cereal grains enjoyed by a friend of the viceroy. During the same period, there were conflicts in Buenos Aires, Tucumán, Santa Fé, Asunción, and Santiago, all arising from dissatisfaction with officials sent from Spain. In 1717, Cuban planters rebelled against the attempt to establish a monopoly on tobacco; they arrested the governor and shipped him off to Spain. In 1749, there was a major rebellion in Venezuela against the Guipuzcoana company; the victorious authorities later annulled the concessions made to the rebels in order to restore peace.

Taxes were a frequent cause of Creole rebellions. The *cabildo* of Quito opposed a tax rise as early as 1591, and another in 1795. The captain general of New Granada was forced to flee when he tried to impose new taxes in 1630.

Asunción was a center of Creole resistance. Several times, when the appointment of a new governor was announced, the Asunceños elected a Creole governor, arrested the royal ap-

---

* The Mexican historian Lucas Alamán, a conservative but a Creole, calculated that throughout the whole colonial period, only four viceroys had been born in the Indies, and these four were the sons of Spaniards; of 602 captains general, heads of courts of appeals, and governors, only fourteen were Creoles; and of the archbishops and bishops, 601, or almost three-fourths, were born on the Peninsula.

pointee when he arrived, and sent him back to Spain. In 1721, the Creole governor José Antequera was beheaded; this did not prevent Fernando Mompó from heading a new rebellion, in 1730. Mompó said that "the power of the community (the *pueblo*) is greater than that of the king himself." When the governor from Spain tried to talk to the people, one of them shouted: "What's the meaning of *vox populi, vox Dei?* Your Grace may say what he likes, but we can tell him it is the Commune." Mompó's daring cost him his life.

The most far-reaching Creole rebellion, because it occurred at the same time as that of Tupac Amaru in Peru and was joined by Negroes and Indians, was that of the people of the commune in the province of Socorro, Colombia. In 1780, the Crown raised taxes; the brutal manner of their collection brought on the rebellion of Tupac Amaru; the disinclination to pay them, that of Socorro. One Sunday, the people coming out of church after mass gathered before the house of the mayor, while a woman, Manuela Beltrán, tore up the proclamation of taxes with the traditional cry of "Long Live the King! Down with Bad Government!" The people chose several notables as their leaders; the latter, frightened, hastened to the notary to declare that they were forced to act against their will. But the revolt spread to Venezuela and Ecuador. A people's army began a march on Bogotá. The archbishop, Antonio Caballero y Góngora, came out to meet them, negotiated with the *comuneros,* and agreed to reduce the taxes. An agreement between the archbishop and the rebels was signed in the church. The trusting people's army disbanded, but the archbishop sent troops to arrest the leaders, saying that the agreement had been signed under duress. Meanwhile, a mule driver and former student for the priesthood, Antonio Galán, organized a group of *llaneros,* defeated the viceroy's forces, and freed the slaves in the mines and the Indians in the workshops. The Indians proclaimed their own king, Antonio Pisco. In the end, the two leaders were taken prisoner. Pisco died in prison and Galán was hanged in Bogotá. But the viceroy had had a close look at defeat when Creoles, Negroes, and Indians united. The generals who fought for independence did not fail to benefit by the lesson.

The British, French, and Dutch in America

Although the Spanish and Portuguese tried to prevent all foreign influence in the New World, Latin America was never the exclusive dominion of Spain and Portugal.

Toward the end of the sixteenth century, British, French, and Dutch pirates settled in some islands of the Caribbean and from there attacked both merchant ships and the mainland coasts. The ships that joined the motherland to the colony had to travel in convoy, protected by galleons and frigates of the royal navy, which had frequent encounters and naval battles with both pirates and smugglers. Sometimes the pirates took refuge in a bay or on an island, and there were small local wars.

There were other incursions into South America. In 1621, the Dutch organized a West India Company which occupied several islands in the Caribbean; these were used as bases for expeditions against both the Atlantic and Pacific coasts of Latin America. In 1698, the Scotsman William Paterson tried to establish a colony in Panama. The French—in addition to encouraging piracy—tried to settle Florida, attacked the Pacific coastal regions, and, after acquiring Haiti, in 1795, tried to occupy the eastern end of Hispaniola (what is now the Dominican Republic).

As a result of these wars and incursions, many coastal cities were forced to fortify themselves or to relocate in the interior: for example, Mérida, in Yucatán, which kept Progreso as its port. Sometimes, when their cities were attacked, the Creoles would meet in open assembly and assume the defense of their city in the name of the Crown. In this way, they at once affirmed their loyalty to the king and their municipal autonomy. They did this when the British attacked Cartagena in 1740 and Havana in 1762; when the Dutch landed in the south of Chile in the seventeenth century; and when the British attacked the Río de la Plata area in 1806 and 1807.

The greatest opportunities for foreign intervention were in Brazil, where the population was smaller and the military less well organized than in the Spanish colonies. The English attacked the Brazilian coast only during the period 1580–1640, when Spain and Portugal were briefly united under the same crown. But one of the chief objects of the Dutch West India Company was the conquest of Brazil. In 1624, a Dutch squadron seized Bahia, and in 1630 another seized Pernambuco. Until 1654, the Dutch governed various provinces in the Brazilian Northeast, which they called New Holland; the capital was Recife (which the Dutch called Mauriciopolis). They were finally driven out by the Brazilian colonists, who fought them unaided by Portugal.

France had a special interest in Brazil, for in Paris it was considered that the French were the discoverers of the Brazilian coast. As early as 1556, a band of Huguenots built a fort on the site of present-day Rio de Janeiro; they called the region Antarctic France, but they were driven out eleven years later. The French seized Rio de Janeiro in 1710, but lost it immediately. After the loss of its North American territories, France made new attempts on Brazil, but finally had to be content with the territory of French Guiana, which it had occupied since 1626. Similarly, the Dutch were finally forced to be content with Surinam and Curação, and the English with the Caribbean territories originally occupied by British pirates, the most important of which were Jamaica, Trinidad, British Guiana, and Belize (British Honduras).

There were other changes of territory resulting from treaties between the European powers. The western end of Hispaniola (present-day Haiti) was ceded to France in 1795, and later the rest of the island. Florida was ceded to Britain in 1765; it was recovered in 1783 and sold to the United States in 1819. Louisiana was ceded by France to Spain in 1763, returned to France in 1800, and in 1803 sold to the United States by Napoleon, who had his hands full with the uprising in Haiti.

And thus begins the story of the struggle for independence in Latin America.

Independence

As the years passed, the interests of Spain and the American colonies became diametrically opposed. America was, for the motherland, the source of precious metals, exotic products, and taxes, as well as a market for the faltering handicraft and manufacturing industries of the Peninsula. As trade increased and more goods were manufactured in America, the American merchants sought permission to extend their markets beyond the Peninsula and to build up trade with other countries as well as with Spain. The Court obstinately refused. It went so far as to forbid cultivation of olives and grapes to prevent competition with Spain. Taxes and shipping costs raised prices and the cost of living in America, where many products were needed. But the Americans had to sell cheap, for since Spain was the only market, it fixed the prices of what it bought (and fixed them low), and being the only source of supply also fixed the prices of what it sold (and fixed them high).

The situation was no better in Brazil, where the Portuguese Court established monopolies on tobacco, salt, and sugar cane. Queen Maria I (1734–1816) ordered the closing of all Brazilian workshops in order to keep them from competing with the Portuguese ones. The situation finally became so unbearable that pirates earned more by smuggling contraband into Brazil than they did by capturing ships.

Charles III, the enlightened despot who ruled Spain from 1759 to 1788, tried to modernize America. He sent out investigators to the New World, created new viceroyalties (in Bogotá and Buenos Aires), expelled the Jesuits, and restrained the expansion of the temporal power of the Church. He abolished the *encomienda,* which had been legally suppressed two centuries earlier, and sent deputies to America to bring charges against those who maltreated the Indians. One of these, Victorián de Villava, wrote in 1797: "The names of things have been changed but not their substance." The ban on immigration of Catalans was rescinded, and many of them hastened to America, taking with them their experience in trade and manufacture. Venezuela and the region around Buenos Aires made rapid progress. The trade monopoly was modified and more ports were opened. Cultivation of grapes and olives, until then forbidden, were permitted. The Court considered admitting Creoles to administrative posts; it made a start by creating an American army, led by Creoles educated in Spain, in place of the traditional army from the

Peninsula. In 1783, the Count of Aranda proposed to Charles III that an American kingdom be established for each of the monarch's sons, which with Spain would constitute a dynastic community; this plan was never put into effect. Although the reforms ended when the enlightened ministry was replaced by traditionalist ones, the Spanish colonies had entered upon a period of prosperity that reflected the general prosperity of Europe at the time.

In Brazil, there was also what seemed like a progressive movement, headed by Prime Minister Pombal, who in effect ruled Portugal from 1751 to 1777. Pombal promoted education, industry, and agriculture in Brazil. He took away much of the powers of the Church and of the Jesuits (whom he banished in 1759), and theoretically, at least, ended Indian slavery. In 1763, the capital of the colony was moved from Bahia to Rio de Janeiro, a sign of increased government interest in lands that until then had been neglected.

These reforms were not enough to satisfy the Creoles. On the contrary, prosperity brought more discontent, encouraged the colonists' aspirations, and created conditions in which the former could be expressed and the latter fulfilled. This happens in all prerevolutionary epochs: the urge for great changes never arises out of poverty and desperation—which at best produce only mutiny and rebellion—but out of prosperity and hope, which, in societies with important segments frustrated in their desire for power, lead to revolution.

In Latin America, in addition to a long tradition of protest and rebellion in all sectors of the population, there was a certain tradition of independence. In 1659, a Frenchman, Guillen Lombart, forged the nomination of a viceroy in his own favor in order to proclaim the independence of New Spain; he ended up at the stake. In 1700, two Frenchmen living in Chile, Bernay and Grammusset, conspired to separate that colony from Spain. In 1765, in Quito, there was an attempt to crown the Count of Vega Florida king, and in 1780 there was another attempt to establish a kingdom extending from Quito to Patagonia. In 1785, a group of Mexicans negotiated with the English for help in achieving independence for their country; they did not obtain it. Again in Quito, in 1795, the Indian physician Francisco Eugenio de Santa Cruz Espejo (1747–95) plotted for independence; he died in prison.

His conspiracy is the first that can be properly considered as American and as showing the aspirations and influences that characterize the later independence movements.

It was at about this time, in Bogotá, that Antonio Nariño (1765–1823) translated and published the Declaration of the Rights of Man, which was then circulated throughout much of Latin America. For this he was tried and condemned; he escaped from the prison in Cádiz to which he had been taken, went to France, where he found no support, and then to England. Lord Liverpool offered British aid on the condition that the Spanish colonies, once they were liberated, would accept British sovereignty; Nariño refused. But then the war with Spain broke out, and London gave arms and money unconditionally. Nariño landed in New Granada in 1796, found little backing among the former *comuneros,* surrendered to the viceroy, with his liberty guaranteed by the archbishop, and was immediately imprisoned. He later held high office in Colombia.

In Venezuela, José María España (d. 1799) and Manuel Gual (d. 1800) organized a conspiracy, together with three Spaniards with republican sympathies. The plot was discovered and a total of eighty men were arrested and sentenced. A few years later, Francisco de Miranda (1750–1816), a romantic character who was a Jacobin general, a lover of Empress Catherine of Russia, and a visionary, obtained money in London, arms in Philadelphia, and men in Trinidad; in 1806, he landed on the Venezuelan coast. His attempt to overthrow the colonial administration failed. Three months later, he tried again and again failed.

There was some foreign influence—chiefly North American and French—behind the independence movements. The Jesuit influence was also important; after their expulsion from America, the Jesuits devoted themselves to study and in their historical works created the doctrinal basis of independence. The Enlightenment had the greatest effect on the sons of Creoles who had gone to Spain to study or to fight in the French revolutionary army, and on some abbés, physicians, and scientists in America. There were also Creoles who visited the new United States of America and studied its political system; this was later reflected in the drawing-up of the Latin American constitutions.

The masses, however, knew nothing of the American and French revolutions and did not read the writings of their principal actors. And among the great majority of Creoles—who were generally very Catholic—the idea prevailed that the revolutionaries of North America and France were heretics; the small amount of material aid the independence movements received from them confirmed this opinion.

The first Latin American colony to gain its independence was Haiti. As soon as the ideas of the French Revolution began to reach the island, followed by the Convention's first envoys, the slaves rebelled. Pierre Dominique Toussaint L'Ouverture (c. 1744–1803), a self-educated slave, led them, and despite the occupation of several coastal cities by the English fleet, conquered the entire island. The troops sent by Napoleon reached a peaceful accord with him, but then Toussaint was captured; he died in jail in France. Jean Jacques Dessalines (c. 1758–1806) kept up the fight and after proclaiming Haiti's independence, in 1804, had himself crowned emperor; he was later slain by an assassin. The slaves divided the land (the population growth later gave rise to the grave problem of minifundism, because the lots given to each family were not large enough for subsistence). The country underwent a series of civil wars, and in 1825 succeeded in getting France to recognize its independence.

If the French Revolution was directly responsible for the independence of Haiti, it was indirectly responsible for that of Brazil. When Napoleon's armies invaded Portugal, in 1807, the royal family fled aboard a British ship and took refuge in Brazil. In 1815, Brazil was put on an equal footing with Portugal. In 1821, the Portuguese ruler, João VI (1769–1826), returned to Lisbon, leaving his son Pedro (1798–1834) as regent in Brazil. But the independence movement in Brazil grew rapidly; it was led by José Bonifácio de Andrada e Silva (1765–1838), a tough aristocratic monarchist. The prince agreed to become Emperor Pedro I. By the so-called Cry of Ypiranga ("Independence or Death!," although in reality there was little danger of death), the country was declared independent, in September, 1822. In contrast to the other American countries, it was established as an empire. Portugal, weakened by war, offered no opposition.

But in the Spanish colonies, independence was not attained without war. Here, too, the impetus to the rebellion came as the result of Napoleon's occupation of Spain and his sequestration of King Ferdinand VII (1784–1833). At this point, many of the more conservative Creoles joined the independence movement because they did not want to be governed from Madrid by a court they considered revolutionary, heretical, and illegitimate. Many colonists regarded the first steps toward independence as a way of saving the colonies for Ferdinand VII, the "true king" who was confined in Bayonne. In many cases, the *cabildos* became the new powers, deposing viceroys and captains general who refused to accept their authority.

In Spain, the central junta, which had assumed power, was desirous of ensuring colonial aid in its struggle against Napoleon. Spanish liberals also favored reforming the colonial system. There was even a Creole, Miguel Lardizábal (1744–1823), of New Spain, on the central junta. In 1809, the junta proclaimed equal rights for Americans and Spaniards and ordered the viceroys to appoint representatives to the Spanish Cortes, which met at Cádiz in 1810. America sent twenty-seven deputies to Cádiz. The Cortes declared that the lands in America were not colonies but "an essential and integral part of the Spanish monarchy." And the junta told the Americans: "Your destinies do not depend on the ministers or on the viceroys or on the governors. They are in your hands." The Cortes twice confirmed the equality of rights between Spain and America. In 1811, it prohibited maltreatment of the Indians, decreed freedom of cultivation and economic activity, and freed Indians and mestizos from paying tribute. The Cortes also established freedom of trade, although the city of Cádiz managed to have the measure annulled.

In America, at this time, there were two well-defined groups: those who wanted to maintain the old colonial order and to ignore the decisions of the liberal Cortes of Cádiz, and those who wanted to establish a new political order. The latter group justified its desire for independence on the basis of the theory of the pact, saying that America was breaking her pact with Spain because it was to her advantage to do so. The Spanish liberals, for their part, said that the pact should be continued because Spain had as much desire for liberty as America and that together they would be able to obtain and maintain it. But their very fear of Spanish liberalism inclined many Creoles to the side of those who favored independence. Thus Jacobins and traditionalists found themselves united: the former sought to separate from a still traditional Spain, the latter to be separated from a Spain that was beginning to be liberal.

In 1814, Ferdinand VII, whom the people called "El Deseado" ("the Desired One") but who proved to be one of the most tyrannical rulers in the history of Spain, returned from Bayonne, recovered the throne, and began to persecute the liberals in Spain and the revolutionaries in America. In 1820, he organized a fairly large army to crush the American rebels. But the army, while waiting for embarkation to America, turned against him and forced him to swear to the liberal constitution of 1812.

With this, the mass of Creoles swung into action. They proclaimed independence in the *cabildos,* and organized armies with Indians from the haciendas, slaves from the mines, and mestizos from the cities. The bishops sided with the viceroys and the parish priests and educated abbés with the Creoles. The Negroes in general fought with the armies of independence and the Indians with those of the viceroys. There were even Spaniards in Spain who enlisted with the revolutionaries. Generally speaking, the aristocratic Creoles held the highest army posts, but a few men of the people rose to high positions and became popular heroes. Tributes were levied on cities and foreign loans were sought. British help was now more plentiful than in the conspiratorial period. The United States government sent money and arms to the rebels, but not very much and not steadily. The most important aid was that given to Bolívar by independent Haiti: soldiers with which to continue his fight.

What had begun as an activity of visionaries became a movement of the popular masses. At this point, two tendencies arose in the independence movement. The Creoles wanted a political revolution to separate the colonies from Spain and to give themselves power; they also wanted free trade. The mass of the people wanted a social revolution: freedom for the slaves, emancipation of the Indians, equality for the mestizos. Most of all, they wanted land. The struggle between the two tendencies did not emerge until independence was achieved; it has lasted until today.

The war for independence was in reality a series of local wars and long, fantastic marches over the Andes. These wars were fought with small, mobile armies of picturesque diversity. Cruelty was common on both sides. Bolívar proclaimed: "Spaniards, expect death, even if you remain neutral."

Many of the colonies achieved independence as a consequence of the struggle carried on chiefly by three: Venezuela, Argentina, and Mexico.

In Venezuela, there had been, as we have seen, several attempts to win independence. The fiction of "loyalty to the legitimate king" did not satisfy many Venezuelans, who had a particular grievance against Spain because of the presence in the colony of the Guipuzcoana company. The man who reflected and channeled this discontent was Simón Bolívar (1783–1830), whom Latin Americans call "El Libertador" ("the Liberator"). Bolívar had traveled in Europe and had attended the lectures of a Venezuelan teacher who was an encyclopedist. In 1810, he took part in a revolt by the people of Caracas, which was defeated by the royal troops. He went into exile in Jamaica, from which he wrote a long letter in 1815 that well expressed the frustrations felt by the Creoles:

> We have been harassed by a conduct which has not only deprived us of our rights but has kept us in a sort of permanent infancy with regards to public affairs. . . . We were never viceroys or governors, save in the rarest of instances; seldom archbishop and bishops; diplomats never; as military men, only subordinates; as nobles, without real privileges. In brief, we were neither magistrates nor financiers and seldom merchants.

After failing in several expeditions to Venezuela, Bolívar went to Colombia and there, with a hastily recruited army, won the battle of Boyacá, in 1819. This triumph made it possible to effect the independence of Venezuela, Colombia,* and Ecuador. Bolívar succeeded in uniting the three former colonies into a single, short-lived nation: Gran Colombia. He then advanced on Peru, which was being approached from the south by troops led by another of the liberators, General

---

* In 1806, the province of New Granada took the name Colombia, suggested by Miranda. It thus deprived the United States of a name proposed for that country, which until then had not been christened—nor has it up to now, the term "United States" being merely the description of a political system.

San Martín. In 1822, the two leaders met in Guayaquil and San Martín left the field free to Bolívar. Bolívar went on to defeat the Spaniards at Junín (1823) and Ayacucho (1824) and to found Bolivia, of which he became the first president.

Bolívar devoted the last years of his life to the attempt to organize the new countries of the northern part of South America, and to form a confederation of the former colonies; he failed in both attempts. The son of aristocrats, he was more idealist than politician. His failures made him foresee that Latin America was going to enter a period of dictatorships and tyranny and to feel that, in his own phrase, "Those who have served the revolution have plowed the sea."

No more fortunate was José de San Martín (1778–1850), who was born in an Argentine Jesuit mission, studied in Madrid, and enlisted in the Spanish army. He returned to Buenos Aires to offer his services to the independence junta established in that city, which until 1816 maintained the fiction of "loyalty to Ferdinand VII." In 1814, an army was organized to free Alto Perú, as what is now Bolivia was called. But San Martín realized that it was more important to liberate Chile and Peru first. He crossed the Andes, defeated the royal army at Maipú (1818), and helped Bernardo O'Higgins (1778–1842), since 1810 leader of the independence movement in Chile. In 1821, San Martín entered Lima and in 1822 met with Bolívar in Guayaquil. He loathed politics and, disheartened by factional struggles, went into exile in France, where he died.

Paraguay won independence without a struggle and fell under the dominion of an astonishing dictator, José Gaspar Rodríguez de Francia (1760–1840). Uruguay had to fight against both Brazil and Argentina, which tried to seize it; thanks to British mediation and the activity of José Gervasio Artigas (1764–1850), Uruguay obtained independence in 1830. Artigas was a former cattleman, of populist leanings, whose slogan was "the most unfortunate shall be the most privileged" and who distributed land among the peasants. This caused the Argentine government, fearful of such radical tendencies, to resist him unceasingly; independence became possible only when Artigas went into exile in Paraguay and it was clear that the independent regime would not be a revolutionary one.

In New Spain, there had been various Creole conspiracies,

and in 1810 the *gachupines* deposed the viceroy. In September of that year, a village priest, Miguel Hidalgo (1753–1811), rose up and to the cry "Death to the *gachupines!* Long Live the Virgin of Guadalupe!," began to free the Indians and give them land. He was defeated, condemned by the Inquisition, and executed. But another priest, José María Morelos (1765–1815), continued the fight. A congress of insurgents met to draft a constitution, but in 1818 the *gachupines* seemed to hold the winning hand, as there remained only small rebel groups, headed by Vicente Guerrero (1783–1831). The leader of the royalist forces, Agustín de Itúrbide (1773–1824), fearful of the liberal tendencies beginning to predominate in Spain, negotiated with Guerrero, signed a pact between the two groups (called the Iguala Plan), and effected independence in 1821. Itúrbide had himself proclaimed emperor, was routed, fled, returned, and was shot, in 1823.

In 1821, the eastern part of Hispaniola, which the Spaniards had reconquered in 1806, declared itself independent, with the name of the Dominican Republic; the following year, it was conquered by Haiti; the Haitian occupation lasted until 1844, when the Dominican Republic recovered its independence.

In Central America, conspirators had been active since 1810, but without success. In 1821, Guatemala took the lead in proclaiming the independence of Central America. But in 1822, Emperor Itúrbide, at the head of an army, forced the Central American states into a union with Mexico. When Itúrbide was overthrown, in 1823, the United Provinces of Central America proclaimed their independence from Mexico. All that was left of the Spanish empire were Cuba and Puerto Rico in America and the Philippine Islands in Asia. Cuba carried on a ten-year war with Spain, in 1868–78, and finally won independence in 1898; Puerto Rico was then acquired by the United States, with which it is still associated.

Independence was thus established, but order was not. There were struggles between those who, like San Martín, wanted a monarchy because the new nations "were not mature enough to be given too much freedom," and those who, like Bolívar, wanted well-regulated republics. All, however, let the landholders retain their privileges and respected the aristocracy of Spanish origin. In Peru, San Martín enriched the coats of arms of the nobles with a sun, thus legitimizing them, and sent delegates to fetch a European prince to rule the country—but none wanted such an unstable throne.

Local authorities attacked, ousted, and banished one another; upstart caudillos launched offensives against cities; constitutions were drafted in a few weeks and altered in a few hours. Bolívar complained: "There are no legal elections anywhere, nowhere does anyone succeed to office according to law." Bolívar himself was nearly assassinated in Bogotá by a group of conspirators who were his friends.

When Gran Colombia broke up into three countries, in 1830, Bolívar concluded: "From one end to the other, the New World seems an abyss of abomination. . . . There is no good faith in America, nor among the nations of America. Treaties are scraps of paper; constitutions, printed matter; elections, battles; freedom, anarchy; and life, a torment." And he demanded "a stable government, consistent with our present situation, befitting the temper of the people, and, especially, one that will remove us from this ferocious hydra of anarchic discord."

What Bolívar considered anarchy was the product of two historical circumstances: one was that under the colonial regime, the Creoles had been unable to gain any experience in government, had not formed political parties or developed ideologies; the other was that political change was not accompanied by social change, for the feudal relation of landowner and peasant persisted after independence and became even more marked, to the point at which possession of the land gave de facto possession of political power.

We shall see that these same circumstances have marked the entire history of Latin America, down to the present: inexperience resulting from dictatorships, and the absence of any social change among the many political changes. The colonies were succeeded by countries; the professional government sent by Spain gave way to makeshift governments designated by the great landholders; the ruling class of bureaucratic *gachupines* was succeeded by a new ruling class of landholding Creoles. After independence, the mass of the people remained dependent.

CHAPTER IV

Why Has Latin America Not Changed?

The history of Latin America in the nineteenth century is the history of attempts to create modern states without creating modern societies. The obvious impossibility of succeeding in an undertaking so absurd from the sociological point of view resulted in Latin America's being, at the end of a century and a half of independence, fundamentally similar to the Latin America of 1810–20: that is to say, nothing had substantially changed.

In the independence movement, as we have said, there were two camps: the most powerful desired a political revolution; the less influential desired, in a vague and obscure way, social change. The first tendency prevailed but the second persisted, because it answered a need. And because this need could not be satisfied through normal means, it resulted in constant social ferment that has expressed itself in political strife. Hence the great Latin American political questions have been, in reality, disguises of a profounder underlying social question.

From the beginnings of Latin American independence, we

find a characteristic situation that has lasted until the present: that attempts to resolve political problems without changing the social order, without modernizing the social structure, have always led to an aggravation of the situation.

We find the first instance of this in one of Bolívar's decisions. In 1824, the Liberator decreed that to spur progress in agriculture, all surplus lands in Bolivia—that is, lands that had belonged to the Crown and were now owned by the state—should be sold for one-third of their assessed taxable value. He also ordered that the Indians' ownership of their own lands should be recognized, and that they should have the right to sell them. The result of this was that Creoles who already owned large tracts of land—the only ones, together with a few merchants, who had large amounts of ready cash at their disposal—acquired the state's lands for low prices and made shrift to get hold of most of the Indians' lands by purchase or despoliation. Similar methods were adopted in all the former colonies.

In addition to the economic power that possession of the land gave them, the Creoles emerged from the war for independence with political power. The landholders—swiftly reduced to a few dozens or hundreds of families in each country—felt that they had the right of veto over government decisions. The tradition of government by Creoles was rapidly established, and this in time led to the formation of an oligarchic society in which ownership of land gave the right to hold power. The masses accepted this, and it became a mental conditioning. This situation, as we shall see, has not changed, except in a few countries.

Political life, over more than a century, developed exclusively in the middle class and in the nuclei of the oligarchy. When independence was attained, there were about 20 million inhabitants in Latin America, half of them in Mexico and Central America, 2.5 million in Gran Colombia, 3 million in Peru, and the remainder in the rest of the countries. Brazil numbered 2.5 million inhabitants. The Creoles probably formed 1–5 per cent of the population, depending on the country, and the middle class (mestizos, in many places), 10–15 per cent. Less than one-fifth of the inhabitants of Latin America were eligible to participate in political life (in reality, probably no more than 5 per cent did).

For a time after independence, there were no political parties. In many countries, Freemasonary grew rapidly, and when it was divided into the two rites most popular in Europe and the United States, these formed the nuclei of what were to be the two chief parties of the nineteenth century: the liberals and the conservatives. These parties frequently had odd names. The Mexican conservatives were called Yorkinos (because they had originated from masonic lodges of the Yorkist rite, whereas the liberals had proceeded from those of the Scottish rite); the conservatives of Venezuela were called Mantuanos, or Godos; in Central America, the conservatives were called Serviles and the liberals Fiebres; in Chile, Pelucones and Pipiolos, respectively; in Uruguay, Blancos and Colorados. But these parties were very slack; they functioned only at election time or in periods of military coups, centered around outstanding personalities, and attracted only Creole elements or sectors of the middle class (professionals, merchants, intellectuals). They never reached the mass of the peasants or even the artisans—whose guilds, in accordance with the liberal dogmas of the period, were dissolved by law.

Those who desired social change found an outlet only by the path of rebellion. A number of military men, who had emerged from among the people and won honors and fame in the wars for independence, felt that they were representatives of the people. They pushed themselves forward, exerted pressure, brought about coups. Thus there arose the paradox of Latin American militarism's having its origin in a popular desire for social change. But these men were either thoroughly beaten or thoroughly seduced by the Creole oligarchy, which patronized and used them. Moreover, the military men of later generations were not popular heroes but professional soldiers, simple servants of the state who intervened in public affairs to mediate between rival factions of the oligarchy, to satisfy personal ambitions or, in certain cases, to prevent attempts at social change. It became generally accepted that the military had the right to interfere in politics and to hold power. Out of this tradition came the figure of the caudillo, which we shall discuss later.

Organization of the States

The first problem that presented itself to the men of independence—since they were not interested in changing a social structure that was to their advantage—was that of organizing the colonies into countries. In general, the new countries were formed with the same administrative boundaries as the former colonies.

There were some attempts at unifying the different countries, but they swiftly failed. Gran Colombia, founded in 1821, broke up in 1830. The United Provinces of Central America, organized in 1823, lasted only until 1838, and its short lifetime was marred by civil wars and rivalries. In 1842–44, a new union, called the Central American Confederation, was formed of three states, but broke up when El Salvador and Honduras attacked Nicaragua.

The boundaries of the new countries were not always clearly defined, and boundary disputes soon arose among them. In 1826, Bolívar convoked a congress in Panama, to which ten countries sent delegates (and which Washington viewed with skepticism). The congress approved two principles: territorial integrity and compulsory arbitration of boundary disputes. But this remained a treaty that was never put into effect. Some of the boundary disputes turned into wars; others have continued to the present. (These will be examined in Chapter VII.) But the only important territorial change—apart from Bolivia's loss of its seacoast, in a war with Chile—was the formation of a new country, Panama, out of a former province of Colombia that had always been autonomist. With United States support, Panama declared its independence in 1903, to permit (on conditions very favorable to Washington) the immediate construction of an interoceanic canal.

A second aspect of the organization of the new states concerned their form of government. The monarchist tradition, of course, was strong. There were attempts to establish a monarchy in Peru and to give Bolívar a crown (which he refused). Agustín de Itúrbide founded an empire in Mexico and Central America that lasted less than a year. Later, in Mexico, French intervention in collaboration with internal groups seated Emperor Maximilian of Habsburg (1832–67) on a makeshift throne that crumbled after three years of civil war and the execution of the imported monarch. In Haiti, there were also two short-lived empires (that of Jean Jacques Dessalines in 1804–06, and of Faustin Soulouque in 1849–59). In Brazil, independence was proclaimed by the son of the king of Portugal, and the empire then established lasted until 1889. In the end, however, the example of the United States and of France made most of the insurgents lean toward a republican form of government.

A more important problem concerned the relations between the various regions of each country. Nearly all the new states included areas that were geographically, culturally, and economically unequal. The example of the United States —which carried much weight at the time the Latin American constitutions were drafted—seemed to offer a solution to the problem of creating national unity out of regional diversity: federalism. There were long struggles between the advocates of a federal form of government and those who wanted a centralist one. We may say, in broad terms, that the liberals were federalists because they were generally stronger in the provinces, whereas the conservatives favored centralism because it allowed a small group to control the entire country from the capital. But in some places the conservatives were federalists and the liberals were centralists.* There were bloody battles and even civil wars over this question in Venezuela, Colombia, Mexico, and Argentina.

The precolonial and colonial centralist tradition proved more powerful than the desire to imitate the United States, and although some countries adopted federal constitutions, the practise in all of them was strictly centralist. This included countries such as Argentina and Mexico, in which the governors and legislative bodies of the provinces were pop-

---

* A federalist leader in Venezuela, Antonio Leocadio Guzmán (1801–84), stated: "I do not know why they think that the people of Venezuela are so fond of federation, when they do not even know what the word means. The idea came to me and to others, when we said to one another: assuming that every revolution needs a banner, and since the convention did not choose to baptize the constitution with the name federal, let us invoke the idea; but if our opponents had said 'federation,' we should have said 'centralism.' "

ularly elected, and even those that adopted the expression "United States" in the country's official name: the United States of Mexico, the United States of Brazil.*

Another question that was debated was whether the new republics were to have a presidential system, like that of the United States, or a parliamentary one, in the European style. Presidentialism prevailed everywhere except in Peru, where at the side of a strong president there has traditionally been an equally strong legislature; in Uruguay; in Chile, where parliamentarianism prevailed in its struggle with President José María Balmaceda (1842–91), who committed suicide when he found he could not limit the power of the congress; and, for some periods, in Argentina. However, the tendency toward personal power—legitimate or not—has a long tradition, and in all Latin American countries political life has revolved around the president.

The organization of the new states was purely an administrative matter, since the political leaders were concerned only with how the state would best function, not with who would govern it. Centralist or federalist, the state was in the hands of a very small minority; the mass of the people were aware of its existence only when the private quarrels of this minority were aired in public, and even then only a small part of the people were affected, for the armies that took part in the civil wars never exceeded a few thousand men, and many of these had no knowledge of the cause for which they were being made to fight.

But the problem over which the active minority in Latin America was most aroused was the question around which virtually all political life in Latin America revolved: the problem of the Church. And beneath this purely political question lurked something much more serious: the question of what was to be the structure of Latin American society.

The Church and the Land

When independence became a reality, the Creoles were the only group left with any preparation for governing; they were also the sole private owners of what was then the chief

---

* By a law passed in May, 1968, Brazil became the Federative Republic of Brazil.

source of wealth: the land. Such land as was not in the hands of the Creoles belonged to the Church, which had acquired it through donations, legacies, and the like.

The Church was the major property owner in each of the new countries, not only in rural areas but also in the cities: a good part of the city dwellers paid rent to the Church. These were particularly city-dwelling mestizos, people who owned no land, were not part of the Creole group, and had no share in the exercise of political power. The urban mestizos (who lived chiefly in the provincial cities, whereas the Creoles tended to live in the capital) were artisans, teachers, professional men; some owned small farms worked by Indians, while others remained in the army, in which they had enlisted during the wars of independence.

The Industrial Revolution was only just beginning in Europe, hence Latin America could not rely upon industry to add to its wealth. The members of the mestizo middle class who wanted to improve their position could aspire only to ownership of the land. But the mestizos—by their very conditioning—were unable to conceive of taking land away from the Creoles. Moreover, to attack the property of the Creoles would have been to jeopardize their own position once they had acquired land. The only lands to which they could aspire, therefore, were those of the Church. The influence of the United States and of France, and of the liberals in Spain, made of the politically active mestizo minority a liberal minority, which in Latin American context meant anticlerical, although not necessarily anti-Catholic. The liberals did not bring into question the oligarchic system—they simply wanted to become a part of that system; for this purpose, in accordance with the liberal concept that all property should be private, they argued that the property of the Church should pass into private hands.

The struggles between liberals and conservatives over the question of the Church—which combined at times with those over federalism and centralism—lasted over most of the nineteenth century. The lines were clearly drawn: on one side were the conservative Creoles, the great landholders, and the Church; on the other were the liberal mestizos.

The conservatives wanted the new countries to be continuations of the colonies; they were proud of their Spanish heritage and adhered to the still powerful Spanish cultural influence. The liberals wanted to wipe out the memory of the colonies; they exalted the precolonial past and preferred the influence of France in philosophy, of England in economics, and of the United States in politics. The conservatives wanted strong governments and restricted suffrage (or no suffrage), whereas the liberals were democrats, who favored a gradual increase of suffrage and of individual liberties. Neither side questioned the social system; what was at issue was whether the Church or the middle class was to form part of the ruling group. Thus the social question underlying this struggle was rarely well-defined, because it was obscured by the rivalry between whites and mestizos, between believers and rationalists, between centralists and federalists, and between pro-Spaniards and anti-Spaniards.

The people and the army were the instruments of the struggle between liberals and conservatives. At times, the conservatives, through the Church, won over or neutralized the people and used the army to halt the advances of the liberals. At other times, the liberals mobilized the people against the Church and won over the army. In this way, the army became, in a sense, the arbiter between conservatives and liberals, between Creoles and mestizos, between the oligarchy and the middle class.

The struggles between liberals and conservatives were especially bitter when one side found a caudillo with popular appeal. At times, the army itself was divided and there was civil war. In Mexico, for example, in the mid-nineteenth century, there were two civil wars, one between liberals and conservatives over the so-called Reform Laws, and another against the conservatives who had put Emperor Maximilian on the country's throne. Civil wars broke out in Colombia and in Venezuela. The wars that bloodied Central America —which had as immediate cause the desire of some to maintain federation and of others to destroy it—were struggles between conservatives and liberals. In Argentina, the long dictatorship of Juan Manuel de Rosas was the result of the same situation, although there the existence of vast areas of unclaimed land in the pampas made it possible for the Church to sidetrack liberal pressure and to channel the desire for land into wars against the Indians. In Ecuador, the problem of the Church appeared very clearly when president Gabriel García Moreno dedicated the country to the Sacred Heart of Jesus. In Brazil, the struggle took on a different aspect: there, more than against the riches of the Church, the liberals fought against slavery, because they thought that its disappearance would allow the middle class to share power.

All these struggles led, in the majority of the Latin American countries, to the separation—on paper, at least, though not always in fact—of Church and state. In some countries, this separation was accompanied by expropriation of the Church's houses and lands; this had a consequence that was not precisely the one the liberals desired. The expropriated property was put up for sale, and was acquired either by well-to-do city dwellers or by the landholding Creoles, who in this way increased their possessions. Although the Church excommunicated all those who acquired its property, it later lifted this excommunication for those who made donations to the Church, so that the Creoles, a small part of the middle class, and not a few foreigners kept both their lands and their hopes of heaven.

To expropriate Church property, the liberals had adduced the principle that all property should be private; to be consistent, they also had to apply this principle to other cases of collective property, like that of the native communes—the *ejidos* in Mexico, for example. They divided such village properties and distributed the land among the residents. But the latter had never owned property and knew nothing about the laws of the marketplace. The result was that in little more than a generation, most of the Indians had sold their lands for pitiful sums or had been despoiled of them by caciques in the service of the Creoles or by the lawyers of greedy new landowners. The landholding Creoles allied with the Church increased their property, and this group was augmented by the mestizos who had lately become landholders, or by foreigners (chiefly Spanish immigrants). This happened in a number of ways.

In 1872, the Bolivian dictator Mariano Melgarejo (1818– 71) ordered the sale at auction of the Indian communal lands. Another Bolivian president, the liberal Ismael Montes, arranged to have the entire Tarco peninsula—including its Indian inhabitants—sold to him. In Venezuela, there was no president who did not provide himself with a hacienda, and Juan Vicente Gómez gave land to each of the members of his grasping family. In Argentina, in the so-called desert campaigns of 1832, the lands in the pampas were conquered from the Indians and then sold cheaply. In Brazil, the so-called Canudos wars of the 1890's, fought against the small farm owners of the *sertão* (the interior highlands)—on the pretext that they were being led by a religious zealot—gave the great landowners many hundreds of thousands of acres. In Mexico, after the defeat of Emperor Maximilian, the dictatorship of Porfirio Díaz consolidated the hacienda system and divided hundreds of thousands of acres among Díaz's political supporters.

The result of the laws against the Church's mixing in politics, then, was the intensification of latifundism: in the nineteenth century, the latifundists acquired as much territory as they had won in three centuries under colonial rule. The oligarchic system persisted, although it was slightly more independent with respect to the Church.

Thus, the liberals' dogmatic insistence upon private ownership led them to adopt measures that, in the long run, caused the fossilizing of the Latin American social structure. For many of the characteristics of this latifundist society have remained essentially unchanged from the nineteenth century to the present. Without an understanding of latifundism, it is impossible to understand the political, economic, or even the cultural life of the Latin American countries.

Latifundism

Despite the enormous size of Latin America, scarcely one-third of its surface is arable; mountains, jungles, and deserts take up the rest. Of this third, only one-half is under cultivation today (one-fourth of this is used for pasture), and the proportion was even smaller in the nineteenth century.

This cultivated land is in the hands of five classes of owners: (1) the state, which owns enormous expanses; in general this land is poor or not arable; (2) the latifundists—or great landholders—who have managers to run their undertakings, which account for the bulk of products for export (cattle, coffee, bananas, etc.): in some countries, the latifundists include powerful foreign companies;* (3) the ranchers or small landholders, who cultivate the soil with the aid of their families or a few wage-earning peons; (4) the peasants, who own tiny lots inadequate to support their families (many of them own no land at all), and who are often forced into servitude or sharecropping on the great estates; (5) the Indian communes—especially important, in the past, in Peru, Bolivia, and Mexico—which were greatly mistreated in the nineteenth century and which have recovered some strength in the present one; until recently, these communes were subject, through the local authorities, to the administrators of the great estates.

But the bulk of cultivated land is in the hands of the second class of owners. In Chile, 1 per cent of the population owns 52 per cent of the land; about 600 families own more than 40,000 acres each. In Argentina, 2,000 families (chiefly absentee cattlemen) own more than one-fifth of the country; a single family is the owner of 750,000 acres in Buenos Aires province; four companies own 625,000 acres in Tierra del Fuego. In Mexico, before the revolution of 1910–17, 1 per cent of the population owned 85 per cent of the arable land. In Brazil, 64,000 landowners own 210 million acres, or more than 3,250 acres each. In Bolivia—before the revolution of 1952—500 families owned the richest valleys in the country. In Venezuela—before the agrarian reform of 1961—85 per cent of the land was divided into ranches of more than 5,000 acres each. In Paraguay, there are 3,000 latifundios of more than 2,000 acres each.

In Latin America as a whole, farms of more than 2,500 acres make up 15 per cent of the total number of landholdings and include 64.9 per cent of the cultivated land. Properties of 250,000 acres or more constitute 7.9 per cent of all agricultural properties and 23 per cent of the cultivated land. But 90.6 per cent of all farms are under 250 acres; these farms make up 12.1 per cent of the total cultivated land.

The typical latifundist lives in the large cities or abroad (in the nineteenth century, Paris was the fashionable city) and many times has not even visited the lands from which he

---

* In most Latin American countries, large landholdings are called latifundios. But they are known as haciendas in Mexico, as estancias in Argentina, and as fazendas in Brazil.

derives his income. He is not interested in modernizing his plantation or in increasing its yield, since this is already sufficient to permit him to live royally and even to invest abroad. He prefers to buy more land rather than increase the output of what he already has. Thus only 2.6 per cent of the arable surface of Brazil is under cultivation; of Venezuela's 175 million arable acres, only 1.8 million acres are under cultivation; only 65 million of the 215 million acres suitable for agriculture in Argentina are being utilized.

Latifundism has also tended to foster one-crop farming, which is simpler and more profitable. This has exposed the country's economy to the price fluctuations of raw materials on the world market and has limited cultivation of foodstuffs to the lands near the cities and to small individual lots. The result is an unbalanced diet, a high percentage of family expenditure for food, and virtually nonexistent savings for the common people. By leaving many peasants with very small farms, it has also encouraged minifundism, a source of poverty, submission, and low productivity. Finally, latifundism has deprived the countries of capital, and thus obliged them to accept foreign capital in order to create industries and public services.

Economically, then, latifundism has been paralyzing. Politically, it has retarded the development of democratic social forms, since it has kept the great rural masses—the majority of the population—on the fringes of the national cultural, economic, and political life. This is the result of the systems of servitude, purely feudal in character, into which the landholding Creoles transformed what survived of the customs of the *encomienda*. In some countries, these systems of servitude have been kept alive by tradition; in others (Ecuador, and Bolivia before 1952), they have even been sanctioned by law.

These systems have prevailed in countries with a large Indian population. But they have also existed in other countries, disguised as tenant farming. Latin American sharecropping often includes furnishing labor as part of the rental, the rest of which is paid by a percentage of the harvest. In this way, the tenant farmer is obliged to work the latifundist's lands, just as in the Middle Ages he would have had to work on the lands of his lord. It is not unusual, when a latifundio is sold, for the peasants who work on it, and their cattle, to be transferred also. There are places in which the peasant's second name is that of the landowner.

The systems of servitude can be put into three broad categories:

1. The systems deriving from the *encomienda*, that is, which consist in the peasant's duty to give the landowner a share of his labor and of his harvest. This system has various names, according to country: *pongueaje, huasicamia,* etc.

2. The forced labor systems, in which in order to gain permission to work the land, the peasant must work for the owner. In this group are the *yanaconazgo, mita, shirongaje, marronaje, concertaje,* and *acasillaje.*

3. The systems in which the peasant has to labor on public works, that is, on works that are profitable to the latifundio owners, since the latter wholly control the local authorities. In this group are systems like *tequio, faena, minga,* and *chunca.* Even when these works benefit the community, the poor alone pay for them with their labor; they are not financed by taxes, whose payment would fall in greater proportion on the landholders.

An idea of how these systems have oppressed the peasant may be gained from the following facts: In *huasicamia* (a Quechua word meaning "housework"), the peasant and the members of his family have to furnish free domestic service to the owner of the latifundio in Peru, Ecuador, and Bolivia (before 1952); to conceal the servile character of this institution, the landowner often legally adopts peasant children to work in his house in the city.

In Colombia, under the system of *porambia,* the cane worker must work 144 days a year for the owner in return for the right to cultivate his plot of ground.

In Guatemala, under the *colono* system, the landowner gives a lot to the peasant, but sets the value of the harvest he expects; if the harvest is less than this, the *colono* has to pay the landowner—which makes him a feudal serf through the accumulation of debts; if the value of the harvest is greater than that estimated, the *colono* turns over to the landowner half of his harvest.

In Venezuela (before 1961), under the *conuco* system, poor-quality land on the latifundio was turned over to the peasants, who then worked for the owner for an infinitesimal wage. Nor was the peasant able to produce enough on his bit of land to support his family.

Under the *concertaje,* in Ecuador, a loan is "concerted" between owner and peasant, which the latter must pay for with his labor; this is in effect a sale of the peasant's person, since he cannot leave the land until he has paid his debts, which rarely happens; if it does, another loan is arranged.

Under the *yanaconazgo* system (in Peru, Colombia, and Ecuador), groups of peasants—forcibly brought from the mountains to the coast—arrange with the plantation owner a collective loan payable with their labor: a form of group slavery. This system made possible the modernization and mechanization of the sugar, cotton, and rice plantations in these three countries.

Under the *shirongaje,* companies that obtain concessions to extract rubber and oil-seed from the jungles of Brazil, Peru, Ecuador, Colombia, and Venezuela, parcel out lots to the *shiringuero,* who is obliged to sell to the owner, for a price set by the latter, the product obtained from the trees. The owner sells the *shiringuero* food, tools, and so forth, and through the debts incurred assures the permanency of the *shiringuero's* stay on his lands. If the latter dies before liquidating his debts, the debts are assumed by the eldest son.

Under the *acasillaje,* in northern Argentina and Paraguay, the peasant receives a small farm on a partnership basis and the owner sells him all he needs, by which means he is compelled to stay, since he can never finish paying off his debts.

Most of these systems have a collective aspect, for, within the vast landholdings, entire villages of peasants are subject to them. They are a tradition, they are accepted by all, and the courts see that they are respected. It is not unusual for a latifundist to have his own police force, or, since it is cheaper, to employ the local police.

Because the Indians—the great majority of the peasantry in most countries—have never in their history owned their own land, they do not exert any pressure for its distribution among them, but only hope to better the conditions under which they are exploited. In a few countries (Guatemala,

Mexico, Peru), a minority of Indians were allowed to possess communal lands and this appeased them, at least until the liberals gave them the lands—and by so doing put them in a position to lose them (as happened in Mexico and parts of Guatemala). In the nineteenth century, there were some local peasant rebellions when exploitation became unbearable. At the end of the century, Argentine sharecroppers, urged on by the socialists, organized and called strikes. In Brazil, the religious *sertão* movements were really peasant rebellions. In all cases, they were brutally suppressed.

The explanation of the peasants' resignation in this situation is not so much fear of reprisal as their isolation from the rest of society, which has kept them from acquiring any idea that it is possible to change their living conditions. There is also an abundance of landless peons willing to take their place.*

But these conditions of virtual servitude cannot be called slavery, for that was legally abolished.

The Abolition of Slavery

During the wars of independence, the liberators declared the emancipation of the slaves, as José María Morelos (1765–1815) in Mexico and José Antonio Galán in Colombia had already done. But the measure was enforced only when there was a need for soldiers, and many landowners ignored it. As late as 1810, the independence junta of Buenos Aires earmarked a port for the delivery of slaves and fixed their price in order to prevent speculation.

After independence, however, the caudillos often abolished slavery, and where they did not, the middle class and the liberals campaigned for its abolition. This was proclaimed in 1811 in Chile, in 1813 in Argentina, in 1824 in Central America, in 1825 in Bolivia, in 1828 in Mexico, in 1842 in Uruguay, in 1844 in Paraguay, in 1851 in Colombia, in 1852 in Ecuador, in 1856 in Peru, and in 1858 in Venezuela. In

---

* The number of landless agricultural workers is considerable: in Ecuador, more than 58 per cent of the total agricultural population; in the Dominican Republic, 68 per cent of it; in Nicaragua, 71 per cent; in Chile, 74 per cent; in Venezuela, 71 per cent; in Argentina, 74 per cent; in Uruguay, 78 per cent; in Colombia, 79 per cent; in Guatemala, 80 per cent; in Peru, 86 per cent; in Panama, 94 per cent; in Bolivia (before 1952), 95 per cent; and in Mexico (before 1917), 96 per cent.

1873, emancipation was declared in Puerto Rico, still a Spanish colony, and in 1886 it was decreed in the other Spanish colony, Cuba. Haiti had abolished slavery in 1794. Abolition came to the British colonies in the Antilles in 1835, although a clandestine slave traffic lasted for another thirty years.

Brazil was the last country to abolish slavery, in 1888, for there, because of the vast plantation system and the scarcity of Indian labor, slavery continued to be profitable when it had generally ceased to be so on the rest of the continent. But there was a strong abolitionist movement, led by the former slave Luiz da Gama, the Baron of Rio Branco (1847–1912), the poet Antônio de Castro Alves (1847–71), and the orator Joaquím Nabuco (1840–1910). In 1871, the Brazilian congress passed the so-called Law of Free Birth (Rio Branco Law), by which the children of slave mothers were declared free. In 1885, all Brazilian slaves over sixty years of age were freed by decree, and in 1888, the congress, after three days of impassioned debate, passed a law, consisting of a single article, that abolished slavery. The abolitionists covered the benches in congress with roses, and the United States ambassador commented, "What took a civil war in my country is ended here by roses." A year and a half later, the republic was proclaimed, for abolition had created a situation in which everyone was discontented: the landowners because they had lost their slaves; the slaves because they could not find work; and the middle class because, having won one victory, it wanted more power.

The abolition of slavery came close to destroying the system of great landholdings in Brazil. But the oligarchy came right back. Even before abolition, it imported Chinese coolies, but there was much protest and congress forbade this. Then the immigration of European peasants was encouraged; they became sharecroppers. The attempt was also made, with some success, to attract Indian laborers. Former slaves were engaged as sharecroppers or as paid workers—for an infinitesimal wage. The Negroes, most of whom lacked any trade or skills, were unemployed and abandoned. Many thousands went to the interior or to the jungle and subsisted by tilling small lots as squatters. Others, upon leaving the *senzalas* (the slave quarters at the fazenda), rushed to the cities, where they lived in squalor in the newly created slums (*favelas*).

Gradually, they either returned to the fazendas or found work in the new industries, and were changed into urban workers.

In Spanish America, where the percentage of slaves was smaller than in Brazil, the transition to freedom was made without any great disturbances. The Negroes continued to work, for very low wages, in the homes of the rich and on the plantations. To earn the extra income needed to pay the wages of the ex-slaves, the plantation owners on the coasts were forced to modernize their methods. This gradually created a difference in attitude between the owners of coastal plantations and the owners of latifundios in the interior. The former acquired a more modern point of view, deposited their money in banks, and even invested in the new industries, thus linking the budding capitalism with the oligarchy.

Toward the end of the nineteenth century, Latin America also began to feel the effects of the Industrial Revolution, which had transformed European society and was altering that of the United States. The Industrial Revolution created the conditions for the appearance of a new social group that was not connected with the oligarchy.

Industrialism and the Middle Class

The technological progress of colonial Latin America followed closely upon that of Europe; in 1590, for example, Buenos Aires already had water mills, and two centuries later, Mexico had one of the world's most advanced schools of mining. But after independence, owing to the indifference of the ruling groups, Latin America became sluggish and this caused a delay of thirty to forty years in its participation in the benefits of the Industrial Revolution. Buenos Aires, for example, did not have its first steam engine until 1845.

Latin American peasants wove their own cloth, made their own furniture, molded their own clay dishes, cut leather for their shoes and harnesses, and even produced their own farming implements, which were often made entirely of wood. Only city people needed manufactured goods, and these could easily be imported, thanks to the export of raw materials and agricultural products; hence the governments did not seek to promote industrialization, nor did private individuals invest in industry. There were a few farsighted men: the Mexican conservative Lucas Alamán (1792–1853), who founded a bank and encouraged the building of textile mills; and Irineu Evangelista de Souza (1813–1889), Viscount Mauá, who tried to establish an iron industry and the first railroads in Brazil, but who ended in bankruptcy. When, in the second third of the century, it appeared that some industrialists might at last come forward, the development of coffee planting, with its growing world market, sidetracked the greater part of investments in Brazil, Colombia, and Central America.

Cuba, where Spain concentrated what energy it had left over after the loss of its other American colonies, was the first region to become industrialized, although in very modest degree. In 1823, the island had three steamers; in 1836, a steamship line was established between Havana and New Orleans, and in 1845, between Cuba and Spain. Cuba, moreover, became adapted before the rest of Latin America to the production of coffee, tobacco, and sugar, for which there was a growing demand in the Old World, and this furnished the country with the means for importing machinery.

Brazil had experienced a first period of industrialization in the mid-nineteenth century, centering around a number of captains of industry; when the industrializing fever subsided, following the bankruptcy of the entrepreneurs, traditional methods of agriculture returned in force. The *garimpeiros* (the prospectors for gold and precious stones) returned to agriculture, and many cities were abandoned. (All this frustrated the abolitionist efforts for several decades.)

But in 1875, the first sugar refineries were built, Swiss colonists built New Freiburg and Petropolis, and in São Paulo, to attract European immigrants, a system of compulsory profit-sharing was established. The Amazon basin was thrown open to all nations for exploration and exploitation, although this succeeded only in arousing interest in rubber and in creating an agricultural proletariat of white foremen and Indian peons, who were to all intents and purposes serfs. The rubber boom soon ended—when rubber was smuggled out of Brazil and taken to Southeast Asia—but it was the basis of great fortunes. It even led to the building of an opera house in Manaus, a faithful copy of the Paris Opera that was soon abandoned. Many of those who made money during this boom period, instead of buying land, invested their capital in the cities. The collapse of the rubber boom was followed by the spread of coffee planting. Coffee became the new basis of the country's economy, and the coffee planters formed, within the oligarchy, a more modern branch that invested in the building industries. All this gave nineteenth-century Brazil a modern air.

But only in Argentina and, to a lesser extent, in Mexico were modern and lasting industries begun—and none employed more than a thousand workers. Only in mining, as in colonial times, was there investment. Thus the opportunity furnished by the abolition of slavery, which had made available a considerable number of paid workers—that is, people who needed to buy products—was wasted. The immigrants were the ones who gave impetus to the mechanization of industry, especially in the Plata region and in Brazil. But the artisan group survived for decades, since it was adequate to supply the limited urban groups who were economically able to buy manufactured products.

Communications, so necessary in the vast stretches of Latin America, progressed slowly. Roads were bad and poorly maintained. The spread of railroads was very slow. In 1855, there were only about 30 miles of railroads in Mexico, 120 in Brazil, 160 in Chile, and 145 in Colombia; the other countries had none. By 1875, all the countries had railroads, although the mileage was limited.

To understand the slow pace of industrialization in Latin America, we must take into account the fact that for almost thirty years after independence there were no governmental budgets—Peru had the first, in 1845; one of the measures advocated by the liberals was the regular making of budgets. The economy was directed by the oligarchic group in each country. Protectionism was sovereign, not so much to foster a scarcely existent industry as to amass funds; since there were hardly any direct taxes, the only sources of government income were the customs and indirect taxes on consumer goods. Moreover, customs constituted the best—virtually the only, in fact—guarantee the governments could offer when they sought loans abroad or issued bonds on the London market (which was the most favorable), or those of Paris and New York. As we shall see, one of the most frequent causes of conflict with the big powers at the time was intervention by the latter in order to collect debts.

After 1870, industrialization was accelerated, although always on a moderate scale and concentrated in a few regions and cities: São Paulo in Brazil, Puebla in Mexico. Buenos Aires was the center of greatest industrialization. In 1853, it had 76,000 inhabitants, of whom 1,500 were industrial workers; by 1887, there were 42,000 workers among the 500,000 inhabitants, and by 1915 the number had grown to 146,000 out of 1.5 million. Nevertheless, in 1900 Latin America was still predominantly agricultural; the percentage of the population living directly off the land was 80 per cent in Mexico and Venezuela, 52 per cent in Peru, and 47 per cent in Argentina. In Bolivia and Chile, mining absorbed a large part of the labor force—14 and 11 per cent of the population, respectively.

As a result of the rather modest first wave of industrialization and the growth of cities, new social groups began to emerge during the second half of the nineteenth century. The most profound changes took place in the middle sectors.

The mestizos had entered this sector as merchants, professional men, small landowners, owners of small industries, and the number of people engaged in these activities had grown steadily. The formation of regular armies attracted many of these men to military careers.

The establishment of industries also brought the emergence of an industrial working class, which grew slowly. Although very close to the rural class, since most of its members came from the villages (and often returned there when they could not find work), it was acquiring city ways.

In Europe and the United States, there was a yeomanry of comparatively prosperous and independent small- and large-sized farmers, and the proletariat therefore could not consider itself part of the middle class. But in Latin America, the bottom layer of society was composed not of factory workers but of agricultural workers (who, in reality, were often serfs) and the bulk of the peasantry. The working class, although subject to extreme exploitation—as it has been in all countries in the first stages of industrialization—occupied a relatively privileged position in comparison with that of the peasantry. This had important social consequences once the proletariat won its first advances, which emphasized its economic and cultural separation from the peasantry.

The middle class began to intervene in politics, usually on the side of the liberals, for which, to a certain extent, it furnished the activists in both elections and civil wars. But the only people who voted were those with regular incomes and the ability to read and write, that is, a very small minority of those of voting age. Women, of course, had no vote. In these minority groups, political passion was considerable, especially in the question of Church-state relations. Later, the middle class would be interested in a special way in a problem whose cause emerged in the last third of the nineteenth century: foreign capital.

Foreign Investment

The immigrants, for the most part, became members of the middle class. When they were successful, they invested within their new countries. But with this exception, there was very little investment in industry in nineteenth-century Latin America. The landholders tended to acquire more land or to send their profits abroad; there were some native capitalists, but they were few in number. Public services and, especially, modern industry, were the creation of foreign capital.

Great Britain was the first foreign country to invest in Latin America, and the first important bankers in Latin America were of English origin. In 1880, there was scarcely £2.5 million invested in Latin America. By 1891, there was £167 million invested, especially in refrigeration plants in Argentina and Uruguay—England was the chief buyer of meat and wool from those countries—and in Chilean nitrate. British firms also developed the exploitation of Mexican oil, although American capital invested in it, too. English, and later Canadian and Belgian, companies invested in public utilities, streetcar lines, and railroads in various countries.

European capital, in the last third of the nineteenth century, was generally invested not in the development of local industry but in public services and mining. In this way (and without planning), it may be said to have contributed decisively to producing a crude version of what is now called the infrastructure of development. Although these investments indirectly encouraged the creation of local industries, their fundamental objective was to take advantage of the low cost of labor and the slow growth of the world market. The Latin American governments, in this period, looked favorably upon foreign investments. They granted concessions and tax exemptions, and instituted virtually no checks or controls. There was no mistrust of European capital.

Westward expansion did not leave the United States with a surplus of capital to invest abroad, and so until that movement was over we do not find American capital in Latin America. As a result of just this movement, however, between 1848 and 1855, there was built, with American capital and a mighty effort on the part of the Latin Americans, a forty-seven-mile long railway across the Isthmus of Panama, for the many thousands who did not want to risk the route through the Middle West, and who could afford the boat passage to California via Panama. But when the rush to the West slackened, this railroad fell into disuse.

With the end of the Spanish-American War, American capitalists began to discover Latin America. They were especially interested in the mines, whose crude products they needed for industry. They met in the field not only Englishmen, but also French, Belgians, Spaniards, Canadians, and Germans. Later, Japanese capital entered into the competition.

With the entry of American capital upon the scene there began a period of competition between foreign investors that reached its peak between the two world wars. At that time, the United States and Great Britain accounted for 92 per cent of foreign capital investment in Latin America, and for nearly half of all investments, national and foreign. There then began a period of impassioned debate over the question of foreign capital, which will be discussed in later chapters.

Traditionally, the capital of certain countries had inclined toward certain fields: Spanish investments were in the food industry, those of France in the great department stores. The Germans were attracted to coffee planting, the Canadians to electrical services. Only American and British capital (which was invested chiefly in Argentina and Uruguay) was distributed in all fields.

Foreign investments made a decisive contribution to the creation of a limited and timid capitalistic system. But it was of a very special character, since it was geared not so much to the needs of the Latin American countries—as it would have been had it arisen directly from them—as to the needs of the investing countries, which were interested in raw materials: minerals, meats, hides, etc. This, combined with the weakness of internal investment, gave the foreign investors a disproportionate influence over the internal affairs of each country. It also created conditions favorable to the appearance and growth of anti-imperialist sentiment, which soon became, for reasons to be explained later, essentially anti-American.

In addition to foreign capital invested in Latin America, there were frequent foreign loans. The independent Latin American governments were in constant need of money, especially to maintain their armies. Great Britain was the leading loan market, followed by France and, later, the United States. In general, these loans were rather one-sided affairs; since security was minimal, the interest rate was very high and was discounted immediately; land and, even more frequently, the income from the customs served as collateral. There were cases in which, to protect their investment, the lending nations named an administrator of the customs, and others in which the creditor countries sent their warships to blockade ports to enforce the payment of debts. By 1920, 61 per cent of the total public debt of Brazil was owed abroad, and interest payments absorbed 34 per cent of the national budget. Fifty-one per cent of Argentina's debt was to foreign investors. To cancel its debt to English banks, Peru, in 1886, made over its railroads to them for sixty-six years. In general, despite pressure, contracts, and high interest rates, the creditor countries did not make too large a profit, for delays and arrears were frequent. But the loans made possible the building of highways and railways—as well as the carrying on of absurd wars and the maintainance of large armies.

The economic vacuum created by the oligarchy, then, was filled by foreign investments, which hampered economic modernization. But the oligarchy was also responsible for a political vacuum: this was filled by the caudillos, who hobbled the possibilities of political modernization.

The Caudillos

The great mass of the population—the peasants—had no political status. But there were urban masses, in the capital and in the provinces, who formed no part either of the oligarchy or of the more prosperous sectors of the middle class. These masses had aspirations—they wanted more power, a better life—and since there were no political parties to represent them, they inclined, in moments of political tension or excitement, toward figures who dazzled them and gave the impression (although it was a false one) that they had influence in the country. These figures, who knew how to attract the masses and to create the illusion that they represented them, were the caudillos.

In the early days of independence, the caudillo was a man who issued from the people, distinguished himself in the army by his bravery and boldness, won high rank, and, when the fighting was over, used his popularity and the troops under his command to try to express the wishes of the people —and to impose them by force, when no other way was open. In this sense, it can be said that Latin American militarism, the custom of military interference in politics, had a popular origin. But the caudillo was always "seduced," so to speak, by the oligarchy, which tamed him by inviting him into its drawing rooms. With the death of the heroes of the struggle for independence, the military became professional and bureaucratic. The oligarchy used it in times of popular tension, and it became accustomed to assuming the role of "savior" and arbiter in the rivalries between different groups of the oligarchy. Only toward the end of the century did it become what it is now: the police force of the oligarchic system.

The caudillo was usually a mestizo, wherever the middle sectors were predominantly mestizos. The caudillo had in him the ambivalence and, also, the ambition and boldness, that characterized the mestizo—the only human type that can be considered truly Latin American.

We may distinguish four stages in the life story of every caudillo: (1) he adopts the aspirations of the people and wins over the masses; (2) he comes to power, now allying himself with one of the groups of the oligarchy, now arbitrating between the groups, now displacing them all; (3) he exercises power, trying in part to satisfy the masses by giving them the impression that they are governing through him (but not by granting them genuine rights); little by little, he allows himself to be seduced by the oligarchy, becomes moderate, and withdraws from the people; and (4) he falls, having isolated himself from the source of his power (the people) and being no longer useful either to them or to the oligarchic faction that used him.

The caudillo was nearly always a member of the military. He came to power sometimes through elections, sometimes by a military coup (and he was often a minister in the government he overthrew). Although there were liberal and conservative caudillos, many caudillos did not belong to any party; sometimes, they created their own party. But above all, the caudillo did not feel bound by the political process; once in power, he ignored the laws.

The caudillo did not hesitate to use brutal methods to keep himself in office. The caudillo put on a show; he organized parades, set off local wars, had "his" constitution ratified, decorated and promoted himself, gave himself impressive titles: "His Most Serene Highness," "Benefactor of the Fatherland," "Defender of Christianity," "Hero of the Desert." It was this melodramatic side to his personality that has given Latin American history its picturesque—and grotesque—aspects. A caudillo would sometimes try to promote progress, but he contributed nothing to the fundamental need of all the Latin American countries: greater popular participation in government, so that the people might learn to govern themselves. This is what made the caudillo a negative figure in comparison with what he might have been.

Bolívar had written shortly before his death: "I regard the present state of Latin America as comparable to the state of Europe following the collapse of the Roman Empire, when each dismembered part established a political system according to its interests and situation, or following the personal ambition of some leaders, families, or groups." The caudillos were the product of this situation.

The history taught in Latin American schools is the history of these caudillos. Schoolchildren learn, for example, that José Gaspar Rodríguez de Francia (1760–1840), of Paraguay, proclaimed independence and governed for nearly thirty years; that he kept the country isolated and closed to immigration; that he dissolved the religious orders, forbade religious processions, founded a Paraguayan Church, to which he appointed priests, and had himself called "El Supremo"; that he divided the former Jesuit mission lands among the Guaranís, encouraged skilled labor, and tried to form an equalitarian and autarchic society. He was succeeded by his nephew, Carlos Antonio López (1790–1862), who built the country's first railroad, established its first newspaper, installed the telegraph, initiated factories and river-shipping, and in general tried to open the country to the world. Children are taught that his son, Francisco Solano López (1827–70), continued his father's policies to the point of provoking a long war with Brazil, Argentina, and Uruguay, which decimated the population and ended with his death in battle. Since then, Paraguay has alternated between false democracy and authentic dictatorship, existing virtually outside the modern world and economically subjected to the Argentine landholders who, after the end of the war in 1870, bought up the country's best lands for a trifle.

In Argentina, there was a long period of violent struggle before the establishment of a system democratic in appearance, with rigged but regular elections. President Bernardino Rivadavia (1780–1845) founded the stock exchange, the national bank, the university, and the patent office, and signed a commercial treaty with Great Britain, which initiated the influence of that power in the Plata region. He also opened the door to immigration for the first time, nationalized Church property, and tried to found an Argentine Church. He found an opponent in Facundo Quiroga (1794–1835), a gaucho soldier whom the people called "The Tiger of the Llanos." To the battle cry "Religion and *Fueros*" (that is, the special judicial exemptions that put priests and soldiers outside civil law), Rivadavia was overthrown. This opened the way for the caudillo par excellence, Juan Manuel de Rosas (1793–1877). The owner of great ranches and the partisan of the predominance of Buenos Aires over the rest of the country, Rosas ruled Argentina from 1829 to 1852, with the help of the *mazorca,* a peasant terrorist organization. He provoked two small wars—with France and with England—to keep himself in office, until he was finally overthrown in battle by his adversaries.

In Uruguay, Fructuoso Rivera (1778–1854) was the leader of the liberal Colorados (or "Savages," as they were called by their opponents), and Manuel Oribe (1792–1857) of the conservative Blancos ("Executioners," as they were known by theirs). The Blancos were the allies of Rosas, who aided their attempt to take power by force of arms. Although Uruguay enjoyed social reforms of some importance, the domination of the wealthy cattlemen never disappeared.

In Chile, the oligarchy governed through the very powerful senate and with the support of a strong Church. The conservatives (Pelucones) were passionate advocates of the parliamentary system, which they always managed to control. They were led by Diego Portales (1793–1837), who was assassinated by the military. The liberals tried to strengthen the presidency; a liberal president, José María Balmaceda (1842–91), committed suicide when he failed in his attempt to dominate the congress, which had opposed his policy of separation of Church and state.

In Peru, the conservatives were nearly always dominant, especially under Ramón Castilla (1797–1867), who came to power in 1845 as a leader of a rebellion against slavery; Castilla proclaimed himself Grand Marshal and held power for fifteen years. The only Peruvian liberal of importance was the moderate Nicolás de Piérola (1839–1913), who reformed the national treasury, was dictator during the war with Chile (1879–83), and founded a Democratic Party that never fought the oligarchic system. The Peruvian army was so prone to intervene in political affairs that even a conservative like Manuel Pardo (1834–78) thought it necessary to found a Civilian Party, whose sole program was to assure government by nonmilitary men. Pardo was elected president, but was then assassinated by a sergeant.

In Colombia, there is a saying that the difference between a liberal and a conservative is that the former goes to mass at ten o'clock and the latter at twelve; but it was not always so, and at one time the two groups—both oligarchic—carried on impassioned and bloody struggles. The liberals—who managed to abolish the death penalty and even academic titles

—fought for strong municipal government and a weak executive branch. They wrote all this into the constitution of 1853, by which they thought they had changed the country. But the conservatives rose, seized power in the provinces in 1858, and annulled the federal constitution by means of the state constitutions. The constitution of 1858 established an official religion and defended the caste system through the creation of an all-powerful executive. Despite their profound differences, both liberals and conservatives in Colombia always defended the oligarchy. Tomás Cipriano de Mosquera (1798–1878), a conservative who went over to the liberals, was president for three terms, separated Church and state, created a national church, unseated bishops, and expropriated Church property. But then Rafael Núñez (1825–94), who switched from the liberals to the conservatives, and who was also president for three terms, drew up a new constitution in 1886; it established a centralist government, Catholic education, and strengthened the executive power.

The Venezuelan people had formed many illusions during the war for independence. After the death of Bolívar, they rose up against the conservative Godos ("Goths)," the large landowners. General José Antonio Páez (1790–1873) crushed mass revolts several times during his two terms as president, as did his conservative successor, General José Tadeo Monagas (1784–1868). The liberals, who had popular support, were not anti-oligarchic, although their leader, Antonio Leocadio Guzmán (1801–84), promised the abolition of slavery and the division of lands. Monagas banished him, but popular pressure was so great that the conservatives split; their moderate wing succeeded in getting a new constitution ratified in 1861. A liberal caudillo, Antonio Guzmán Blanco (1829–99), took advantage of this to establish a dictatorship that lasted from 1864 to 1887, in the course of which he attempted to found a national church, entered upon a controversy with the Pope, and nationalized the property of the religious orders, which he suppressed; but he did not effect the agrarian reform the people hoped for.

Central America was troubled by civil wars and even by foreign invasion, for the centrifugal tendency of the conservatives did not slacken until they had destroyed the five little countries joined in the United Provinces of Central America. The federal constitution of 1824 gave the congress more power than the executive branch. Congress suppressed the convents, permitted priests to marry, and proclaimed religious freedom. A dictator of El Salvador, José Matías Delgado (1768–1833), who was a priest and the president of the National Assembly, independently established a bishopric and named himself head of it. But in 1840, the conservatives, led by the Guatemalan General Rafael Carrera (1814–64), defeated the liberal El Salvadorean Francisco Morazán (1792–1842), president of the federation. Two years earlier, the congress had voted to dissolve the federation. In 1842, El Salvador, Honduras, and Nicaragua reorganized the union under the name the Central American Confederation, but it came to an end in 1844, when the first two countries declared war on Nicaragua.

In Guatemala, the liberals succeeded in replacing Carrera with Justo Rufino Barrios (1835–85), who built the first railroad in his country and nationalized Church property. Barrios governed as dictator for twelve years, until he was killed in the war against El Salvador while attempting to re-create the union. In 1897, Manuel Estrada Cabrera (1857–1925) succeeded to the presidency when the liberal president, who had proclaimed himself dictator, was assassinated. Cabrera ruled with an iron hand for twenty-two years.

There were many dictatorships in the other Central American countries, but they were shorter lived and did not involve persons of such importance. Only Costa Rica enjoyed a degree of stability without dictatorship, for the country was so poor and so thinly populated that it did not arouse the ambitions of the caudillos.

The American dramatist Eugene O'Neill was inspired to write his *Emperor Jones* by the life of Henri Christophe (1767–1820), who killed the Haitian "emperor," Jean Jacques Dessalines (1758–1806), and had himself proclaimed king. Christophe ruled for eight years in the north of Haiti and invaded what is now the Dominican Republic but was then still a Spanish colony. There, the caudillo Pedro Santana (1801–64) served five times as president; in 1861, Spanish dominion was re-established, at the invitation of Santana, who remained as governor. In 1871, Colonel Buenaventura Báez (1808–84), who also served five times as president, proposed the annexation of the country by the United States, but the American senate rejected the offer. General Ulises Heureaux (1846–99) was elected president and governed for seventeen years by means of terrorism and foreign loans, until he was assassinated.

In Brazil, there were both liberals and conservatives, but the "moderating" power was in the hands of Emperor Pedro I. Opposition to Pedro's Portuguese sympathies led to his abdication in 1831. Ten years later, his son, Pedro II, ascended the throne, with the support and backing of the liberals. But republican sympathies grew during his reign, and a year after the abolition of slavery, and under pressure from the army, Pedro II abdicated and the republic was proclaimed. On the whole, the nineteenth century was more tranquil in Brazil than in Spanish America, not only because of the existence of an imperial system—which acted as moderator and arbiter in the struggles between factions of the oligarchy—but also because there were several periods of economic progress: the rush for gold and precious stones, a wave of industrialization, and the growth of coffee planting.

The two clearest and most dramatic examples of the struggles between liberals and conservatives, and of the caudillist form they took, are found in Ecuador and Mexico. In Ecuador, the conservative dictator Juan José Flores (1801–64) tried to re-establish Spanish colonial rule in 1846, when the liberals seemed to be gaining strength. He failed, but the conservatives finally raised to power Gabriel García Moreno (1821–75), whose long residence in Paris had not dimmed his mystical and theocratic leanings. Upon assuming power, García Moreno consecrated the country to the Sacred Heart of Jesus; in 1862, he signed a concordat with the Pope giving the Church control of all education, and established a special code of exemptions for the clergy. Only Catholics were allowed political rights; so that everyone should be Catholic, he founded a great number of schools and made education compulsory. He defeated several attempted coups by liberal elements of the military. The liberal polemicist Juan Montalvo (1833–89) agitated against García Moreno in writing until he was exiled. In 1875, García Moreno was assassinated by conspirators at the gate of the presidential palace; he exclaimed, before dying: "God does not die." Montalvo, when he heard the news, said: "My pen killed him." In 1895, the liberal Eloy Alfaro (1842–1912) was elected president and dominated the life of the country for seventeen years. The liberals instituted divorce, secularized marriage and cemeteries, and forbade the entry of foreign clergy. But after Alfaro's assassination, many of the liberal measures were annulled.

In Mexico, the conservatives, led by Lucas Alamán (1792–1853), tried to encourage industry and investments, and also established a credit bank. But in 1830, a general whom they had appeased, Antonio López de Santa Anna (1795–1876), allied himself with the liberals and seized power. The liberals, in power from 1832 to 1836 under Valentín Gómez Farías (1781–1858), tried to separate Church and state. But then Santa Anna went over to the conservatives and seized power again. He failed to prevent either the secession of Texas or the U.S. invasion of Mexico, in 1847. Santa Anna was a megalomaniacal and crafty dictator who had himself called "Most Serene Highness" and who ordered a solemn official burial of his leg when it was amputated as a result of a wound suffered in battle. In 1855, he was finally deposed and exiled in the United States, where he popularized the use of chicle gum.

The liberals then seized power under the leadership of Benito Juárez (1806–72), drew up a new constitution, and enacted the so-called Reform Laws, which separated Church and state, expropriated Church property, and distributed among the Indians their communal lands (*ejidos*). This was followed by three years of civil war with the conservatives, who opposed these laws. When the liberals triumphed, the archbishop of Mexico, together with some conservatives, went to Europe, persuaded Archduke Maximilian (1832–67) of the house of Habsburg to accept the throne of Mexico, and persuaded Emperor Napoleon III to support him. There was another civil war, between the republican government of Juárez, who wandered about in the provinces, and the French and Mexican conservative forces who supported Maximilian. But Maximilian turned out to be more liberal than his backers had expected; he tried to protect the Indians and little by little lost the support of the conservatives. He was eventually abandoned by Paris, defeated, captured, and executed in Querétaro in 1867. The Reform Laws were then applied, but when Juárez died there was a struggle for the succession. Finally, in 1876, one of Juárez's generals, Porfirio Díaz (1830–1915), took power. He held it for thirty years, during which time he smoothed relations with the Church, attracted foreign capital, fought social movements, encouraged latifundism, and brought stability to the country and a degree of prosperity to its middle and upper classes. This prosperity, as we shall see, created conditions favorable to the Mexican Revolution of 1910–17.

Santa Anna was not the only caudillo with traits that seem absurd to us but were politically tragic. Guzmán Blanco of Venezuela boasted: "I have never listened to anybody's ideas." The Guatemalan Estrada Cabrera, when he named a minister (without consulting him), would say: "You can choose between the ministry and the jail." Mariano Melgarejo (1818–71), of Bolivia (who held power several times and was assassinated by his son-in-law), was a great admirer of Napoleon; when the Franco-Prussian War broke out, he wanted to declare war on Germany; when he learned that the French emperor was not Napoleon I but his nephew, he declared Bolivia neutral. Melgarejo once had the English consul lashed to the back of a donkey and taken through the streets of La Paz. When Queen Victoria heard of this, she asked for a map of South America, had the location of Bolivia pointed out to her, and running a pen through the outline of the country, declared: "Bolivia has ceased to exist." But Melgarejo continued to exist for the Bolivians.

What distinguished the caudillo from the dictator was that he established a relationship with the common people that gave them the illusion he was protecting them. The people approved the brutality, the excesses, the immorality of the caudillo because they identified with him and because he did what the man in the street would have done had he been in power. At least at the beginning of his regime, the caudillo governed with popular support—"popular" here refers to that part of the people who were interested in politics. The caudillo sometimes appeared anti-oligarchic and was sometimes sincere in this, even trying to adopt some measures unfavorable to the rich. But before long the oligarchic system, the bureaucracy, and his own army restrained him and obliged him to renounce all anti-oligarchic decisions—although, to conceal this renunciation, he continued to use the popular revolutionary vocabulary and often even the accent, idioms, and manners of the people.

Perhaps more than being anti-oligarchic (a concept not yet general in the nineteenth century), the caudillo was anti-aristocratic—and this was exactly what attracted the public. Frequently, his caprices won sympathy. Rosas, for example, was fond of the color red; during his regime, all the houses in Buenos Aires had red borders around their façades. By the end of his regime, Rosas' picture was on all church altars.

What was the cause of caudillism? There are many possible explanations, but the most accurate, or the one corresponding to the greatest number of cases, seems to be that in any society in which the people find the legal and peaceful road to power closed off, conditions are favorable to the appearance of strong, demagogic personalities who give the public a vicarious sense of power and who, in some degree, avenge the oppression and isolation to which the people have been subjected.

Caudillism would not have been possible if the Latin American armies had not adopted, at the time they were first organized, the practice of intervening in politics. The caudillo in reality always relied on the army, or at least a part of it, or forced the army to follow him, threatening it with arousal of the masses it had misled. In this sense, caudillism was a result, as well as a promoter, of Latin American militarism.

Similarly, it would not have been possible for a phenomenon typical of politically immature countries to have lasted into the late nineteenth century—in some countries, until the present—and to have been revived again in other forms,* had there not been constant collaboration between the caudillos and foreign capital. For nineteenth-century foreign investors, interested only in immediate results, the caudillo represented a kind of insurance of public order favorable to business and the collection of debts. For their part, the caudillos favored foreign capital, not only because in this way

---

* In the twentieth century, Juan Perón in Argentina, Getúlio Vargas in Brazil, and Fidel Castro in Cuba may be said to have exhibited certain characteristics of the nineteenth-century caudillo.

they gained support for their regimes, but because with foreign capital they succeeded in producing a sense (at times justified) of prosperity, although this rarely did the mass of the people any good.

The situation began to change, however, with industrialization, the formation of the labor movement, the growth of the middle class, and the appearance of political parties that did not accept the oligarchic system but wanted to modify or even abolish it. In some countries, this happened toward the end of the nineteenth century and the beginning of the twentieth; in others, between the two world wars; in others, it is just beginning to happen.

CHAPTER V

What Do Latin Americans Want?

By the end of the nineteenth century, the political problems that had agitated the early part of the century were at last dying out. The form of government in every country had been consolidated, and Church and state had found a modus vivendi. One political problem still remained to be solved, that of representative democracy. Although all the Latin American constitutions were democratic, in practise only small minorities participated in political life.

Moreover, the Latin American countries were still not politically stable, but were marked by constant changes of governments and constitutions. Ecuador, in 135 years of independence, had thirty-one constitutional presidents, fifteen interim presidents, thirty-nine dictators (or "supreme leaders"), and five military juntas; it had fourteen constitutions. In Paraguay, there were twenty-two presidents in thirty-one years; they served an average term of nineteen months (though one governed only twenty-one days and another fifty-three). In El Salvador, there were 117 military coups in 138 years.

In all Latin America, since the beginning of independence, there have been more than 1,000 attempts—failures and triumphs—to overthrow governments, whether constitutional, dictatorial, or provisional. Weariness with this constant coming and going has led some to say that Latin Americans are ungovernable, that Latin America is not ready for democracy, and that there can be no progress as long as there is no stability.

The history of the period that extends from the late nineteenth century to the end of World War II shows, rather, that there cannot be stability until there is progress, or real democratization without modernization of the Latin American social structure. These statements, which seem so obvious today, are the result of more than half a century of struggle, discussion, and analysis of the realities of Latin American life.

In its first hundred years of independence, Latin America sought a form for its states without calling its society into question; in the last half-century, Latin America has been in quest of a form of society, without concerning itself with the state. Just as the nineteenth century was primarily political in its orientation—because its fundamental problems assumed political forms and its struggles centered around political questions—so the first half of the twentieth was fundamentally social, since its problems were posed in terms of the social structure.

The experiences of the first century of independence finally brought realization of the fact that the essential thing was not the form but the content of the state, that the content was the social structure, and that as long as the social structure was oligarchic, Latin America would be stagnant, with small possibility of progress for the new social forces that had emerged in the nineteenth century: professionals, industrialists, merchants, workers, and, later, the technologists characteristic of all industrialized societies, or those on the way to becoming so.

During the nineteenth century, the different political tendencies followed imported ideologies. The liberals imitated the United States and tried to apply the principles of Manchesterism; the conservatives were inspired by Spain and applied the principles of the most traditional elements of the Catholic Church. Though in tactical matters they yielded to Latin American realities, especially in their acceptance and utilization of caudillos and caciques, in the field of thought and legislation they tried to be very European or American; the nineteenth-century Latin American constitutions might have been drafted by jurists in Paris, Washington, or Madrid. Of course, these paper constitutions and laws were not obeyed, because they did not reflect reality but were imposed upon it. Not until the twentieth century did there emerge thinkers and then politicians who tried to view things with Latin American eyes and to propose solutions in keeping with the real conditions. In this sense, only in the twentieth century do we begin to find any self-confidence among Latin Americans, and that only among certain groups: not those who governed in the past century but those who aspire to govern in the present one.

The Composition of Society

Latin American society may be represented graphically by a rectangle divided into three layers. In the top layer, we should place the oligarchy: the great landowners and their flunkeys, the politicians; the high military command; bankers. This layer contains, according to country, from 1 to 5 per cent of the population, and receives about 30 per cent of the total Latin American income. This layer includes the group that holds power, that either directs the government or exercises an unwritten veto power over government decisions. This "right" is not only the product of the economic power derived from possession of the land and ownership of the greater part of exportable crops and livestock, the basis of nearly every country's economy. It is also the product of tradition, of the mental habits of the people, who are accustomed to the fact that this group makes the major decisions, and who neither do nor suggest anything that they know beforehand will not be tolerated by the oligarchy.

"Oligarchy" is not an abstract concept in Latin America. In every country, the people know which families belong to it and which club is frequented by its most active members. If one looks over the lists of ruling officials and "distinguished families" of Chile—or of Colombia, Peru, Ecuador, or Panama—he will find the same names repeated through a century and a half. In other countries—Argentina, Brazil, Venezuela, Central America, the Caribbean nations, and Mexico (before the revolution of 1910)—this repetition is found not among the politicians but only among the families of high society. Sometimes, the oligarchy is divided into two groups: one that we may call traditional, composed of hacienda owners, and one with a more modern outlook, composed of owners of more or less mechanized plantations, who invest in industries and especially in banks. Politically, the oligarchy may be conservative or liberal; the conservatives have influence among the peasants and the Church, the liberals among the urban population and a part of the intellectuals and middle class. The number of people in this oligarchic group is virtually not subject to change, and its share of the national wealth has not varied greatly in the last half-century.

The same cannot be said of the layer below this, which we may call that of public opinion, and which includes, generally speaking, all those who read the newspapers (a practice still not very widespread in Latin America). These are the people who are interested in politics, who are more or less informed about what is happening in their country and in the rest of the world, who have ideological concepts, vague though they may be, a degree of education, definite aspirations, and the certainty that they can fight to satisfy them. Within this layer are very diverse groups, but they have a common denominator: they do not form part of the oligarchy and their interests are not in maintaining the status quo but in enlarging the possibilities for social change—at least among themselves.

This layer includes from 5 to 25 and even 30 per cent of the population, depending on the country. Just as the oligarchy in general is white, the public-opinion layer is mestizo or mulatto (except in countries without an Indian population, where, of course, it is also white). It includes industrialists, merchants, professionals, some members of the clergy, intellectuals, the bureaucracy (including army officers), small farmers (where there are any), petty merchants and artisans, skilled workers, and organized labor. From this layer come the intellectuals and students, the technicians, the officials, and the young businessmen—the most evident segments of contemporary Latin American society. This layer is the most active politically, the one that sustains cultural life and tries to analyze and influence the realities of Latin America. It is the only socially and economically active sector of Latin American society.

This group has been growing and improving its living standards throughout the nineteenth century and especially in the twentieth. Its share of the national wealth has been increasing, but this does not satisfy its members because they feel that they produce *all* the national wealth. At the same time, little by little they are obtaining a greater share of power—although not so much in decision-making as in the privileges of power. This group receives about 50 per cent of the total Latin American income.*

Twenty per cent of the total income, what remains after the needs of the oligarchic and public-opinion strata have been satisfied, serves to maintain the third layer of Latin American society. This layer, which forms the vast majority of the population—65 to 90 per cent, depending on the country—may be called the submerged mass. In this layer are the unskilled or unorganized workers (or certain groups of organized workers without any voice in the organizations), the peasants (including farm workers, sharecroppers, virtual serfs, members of Indian communes), petty merchants and village artisans, and the inhabitants of the big city slums—uprooted peasants whose number grows year by year, who are without a trade and often without a regular source of income. Most of the members of this submerged mass are Indians and Negroes, or mestizos and mulattoes who live like Indians or Negroes (except, again, in countries of almost entirely white population, where the submerged mass, although generally much smaller, is also white).

---

* There are, of course, no precise statistics. What statistics there are do not separate the group I have called public opinion from the oligarchy, in itself a revelation of the bias of those who prepare these statistics. According to one survey, the two groups ("middle- and upper-occupational strata") constitute 35.9 per cent of the population in Argentina, 33 per cent in Uruguay, 22.3 per cent in Costa Rica, 21.9 per cent in Colombia, 21.7 per cent in Cuba (before 1959), 18.2 per cent in Venezuela, 16.9 per cent in Mexico, 15.2 per cent in Brazil, 15.2 per cent in Panama, 14.2 per cent in Paraguay, 10.5 per cent in Ecuador and El Salvador, 7.7 per cent in Bolivia and Guatemala, 4.5 per cent in Honduras, and 3.0 per cent in Haiti. Roger Vekemans, S.J., and J. L. Segundo, S.J., *Tipología Socieconómica de los países latinoamericanos* (Washington, D.C., 1963), p. 145.

It is in the submerged mass that we find traditional—what the tourists call "picturesque"—survivals: greater irresponsibility on the part of fathers of families, common-law marriage, and the two extremes of blind clinging to tradition and native place, and total rootlessness. In the same family may be found children who remain permanently in the *pueblo* in which generations of their family have lived, and others who do not stay a year in the same city, in the same job, or with the same woman. In certain countries, a part of the submerged mass does not speak Spanish but only native languages. Illiteracy is general. The percentage of alcoholism is high (although this is not lacking in either the oligarchy or the public-opinion group, in the latter with more discretion and in the former with more freedom). The use of locally available drugs is also widespread (coca in the Andes, marijuana in Mexico and Central America); this is often not so much for escape as to supplement an inadequate diet. A significant part goes barefoot. Its children have the highest infant mortality in the hemisphere.

This submerged mass does not have any interest in politics (unless some collective emotional situation arises), it has no cultural life (outside the films and radio, and only a part has that), it has no consciousness of the fact that its needs may mount or that it has the right to fight to satisfy them. It is an enormous, indifferent, passive mass.

This is the picture of our own times. There are no statistics to enable us to draw it exactly for earlier times. But it may be stated that there has been no substantial change from independence to the present. The only thing that changes is the public-opinion layer—the number of its members and the share of the national income it produces and consumes. Latin American society may be called static.

The history of the first half of the twentieth century centered around the efforts of the groups forming the public-opinion layer to attain political power, displace the oligarchy, and draw the submerged mass into the political and economic life of the nation. There were two clearly defined stages in this struggle. In the first, political parties and class organizations sought to modify the social structure in order to give power to their own class; this was the period in which the labor movement (political and unionist) was formed and in which were created the characteristic parties of the middle class, usually called the radicals. In the second stage, a series of movements emerged: they have been called the democratic left, or national revolutionaries, but they may best be defined as populist. The populist movement seeks to unite various classes, to awaken the submerged masses, and with them to win power for all the people. The oligarchy has opposed these attempts through various tactics: sometimes by military coups and traditional dictatorships; at other times by means of demagogues of more or less fascist coloring; finally, by tacit alliances with the Communist and extreme nationalist elements. Since the situation in Latin America today is the direct result of these struggles, and since the clichés about them in the United States do not serve to make them understood, it may be useful to explain them in some detail.

The Labor Movement

The term labor movement, when used in reference to Latin America, has the same meaning that it does in Europe, that is, it includes not only the trade unions but also the parties and groups that consider themselves, in their makeup and objectives, as proletarians: socialists, anarchists, anarchosyndicalists,* and Communists.

There had been guilds during the colonial period, which took an active part in the fight for independence, but they were subsequently dissolved, in accordance with the liberal thinking of the period. The artisans promptly formed mutual aid associations, which, in time, became unions.

The first union in Latin America was founded in Buenos Aires in 1857. It was a printers union, following the tradition that printers begin the union movement, since they have a trade that requires them to know how to read and are therefore better informed. (In Cuba, the first unionists were cigarmakers; it was their custom to pay someone to read aloud to them, as they worked, books about social problems.) The first strike of importance was called in 1867 by the weavers

---

* Although both anarchism and anarchosyndicalism are apolitical, or antipolitical, anarchism is terroristic and individualistic in the extreme; anarchosyndicalism is collectivistic and organized for mass action.

in Mexico City, who demanded a twelve-hour day for women "to give them time to attend to their homes." The normal working day at that time was from fourteen to sixteen hours; women and children worked the same hours as men, but for lower wages. One of the most frequent demands was for payment of wages in gold; this was either to prevent payment in scrip, which was exchanged for goods at the company store, thus enabling the company to exploit the workers twice, or to prevent payment in paper currency that rapidly lost value.

The greatest impetus to the labor movement came from the European immigrants, especially those who arrived in Latin America after the failure of the 1848 revolutions and the overthrow of the Paris Commune, in 1871. Many of these immigrants had belonged to workers' organizations in the Old World. Once in the New, they formed their own societies, known as German, French, Spanish, Italian, etc., sections of the International. This was, of course, the First International, founded in London in 1864, in which there was a struggle between the authoritarian tendencies of Karl Marx and the anti-authoritarian ones of Mikhail Bakunin. The immigrants took the initiative in organizing national labor federations in various countries, uniting in them the already existent local unions.

The European immigrants also brought with them socialist and anarchist ideas, which had already reached America, but were known to only small nuclei of intellectuals. Thus, for example, the Argentine Esteban Echeverría (1805–51), one of the founders of the May Association society, published a work on "socialist dogma" in the 1830's. In 1850, in Chile, Francisco Bilbao (1823–60) and Santiago Arcos Arlegui (1822–74) founded the Society for Equality. In the 1840's, in Uruguay, the Frenchman Eugène Taudonnet published various socialist materials and in Mexico, in the 1860's, a Greek tailor, Polonio C. Rhodakanaty, did the same. In some places, phalansteries were founded, according to the concepts of the French utopian socialist Charles Fourier; all of them were failures.

It was the immigrants who organized the first socialist parties and anarchist groups, notably in Argentina, Uruguay, and Brazil. The socialists, who were partisans of political action, had as their first problem the ensuring of honest elections. But even when the elections were dirty, the socialists succeeded, at the beginning of the century, in electing deputies and senators in Argentina, Chile, and Uruguay. In Mexico, various radical elements of the Liberal Party considered themselves socialists. The anarchists, on the other hand, who were advocates of direct action and enemies of the state and of the political process, encountered rigorous legal repression, especially in the laws for the deportation of immigrant "agitators."

Socialists and anarchists fought among themselves for control of the unions, and each group frequently formed its own parent union. In Brazil, Peru, Mexico, Cuba, and Bolivia, the anarchists were the founders of the labor movements. (In a number of countries, however—the Dominican Republic, Haiti, Venezuela, Ecuador, Central America—because of industrial backwardness or ruthless dictatorships, the first unions did not appear until well after 1918.)

Until World War I, the labor movement was characterized by frequent and bloody strikes, persecution, terrorism, deportation, and assassination, and by the struggle between the socialists and the anarchists. The passage of the first social legislation (shorter working hours, the prohibition of night work for women and children) was obtained not only through the parliamentary activity of the socialists but also thanks to the psychological pressure of direct action, often terrorist, of the anarchist groups. After World War I, the latter lost influence and today have virtually disappeared.

But a new element appeared at that time: the Communist movement. The Communist parties were formed, like those in the rest of the world, by splinters of the socialist parties and in one case, that of Brazil, by a schism in the anarchist movement. But if the Communists won immediate sympathy among intellectuals and the middle class—who were dazzled by the Russian Revolution—they gained little power in the union movement. Communist theorists had never paid much attention to Latin America. Marx spoke of it only twice: to call Simón Bolívar a "dictator" and a "scoundrel," and to approve the United States' annexation of Texas as a "progressive" action. Lenin briefly referred to the continent in his study of imperialism. The leaders of the Communist International included Latin America in the category of "semicolonial" countries, and the Communist parties had to apply mechanically the theses of the International on the subject of "anti-imperialism," although these did not fit the Latin American picture. The result was the isolation of the Communists. They were to emerge from it during World War II, as we shall see.

Meanwhile, in a few countries (Argentina, Chile, Mexico), members of the middle class came into power and they quickly passed legislation to protect the workers—legislation that was rarely put into effect and that did not put the oligarchic system into any danger, but which rather effected a partial change in the labor movement. Eventually, unions won legal recognition and the right to strike was established everywhere.

Latin American social legislation has had two common characteristics: it is paternalistic (that is, it offers protection to the workers without giving them any participation in the very machinery that protects them, which remains entirely in the hands of the state), and it is dominant (that is, it subjects the unions to state control). This is effected by means of state intervention in union affairs, by the establishment of requirements with which unions must comply if they want legal recognition (without which they could not take part in collective bargaining), and through the establishment generally of compulsory arbitration by the state in labor conflicts, which, by definition, falsifies the nature of collective bargaining and converts it into a judicial process.

Moreover, this very legislation has tended to divide the union movement, for example, by forbidding the formation of national confederations, as in Brazil, or by giving the right to bargain only to craft unions but not to those of an industry or a region. A similar object was attained, in many countries, when the first social security systems were established, a little before World War II. These were generally not unified national systems (except in Mexico) but pension funds for each trade, which led to economic rivalry among the different trades.

In Brazil, the dictatorship of Getúlio Vargas suppressed the existing unions and created a union system that was virtually governmental, rigidly regulated by the state. It was maintained by succeeding regimes. In Argentina, the government of General Juan Domingo Perón intervened in the unions, which were passing through a leadership crisis; it put military officers and then Peronists into control, and used the unions as political shock troops. In return, as we shall see, it gave them a certain participation, never really authentic, in the regime and thus won over a large part of the working class.

Although there was momentary satisfaction over the recognition and respectability attained by the union movement, the union members soon began to want greater independence. One reason for this was the appearance of the populist movement, which many union leaders joined; this gave the union movement a political character, not so much in the sense of being identified with a party as of having a populist ideology. The old struggle between socialists and anarchists in the union movement was succeeded by the struggle between populists and Communists, when the latter, in the heat of the popular-front tactics, finally attained considerable, if short-lived, influence in the unions immediately before, during, and after World War II. The populists triumphed in this struggle about 1950.

The Latin American labor unions have made a number of attempts to form a continent-wide organization. In 1919, through the initiative of the American Federation of Labor (AFL) and the Mexican Regional Federation of Labor (CROM), there was formed a Pan-American Federation of Labor (COPA). It united only unions of the Caribbean countries, and after the death of its moving spirit, the American labor leader Samuel Gompers, it rapidly crumbled. In 1929, the Communists organized a Confederation of Latin American Unions (CSLA), which did nothing of importance and in 1938 disappeared, giving way to a new organization, the Confederation of Latin American Workers (CTAL). In a short time, the CTAL united nearly all the Latin American unions and encouraged their creation in countries that had none.

The CTAL made a great contribution to extending the union movement, especially in the less industrialized countries. But after the Nazi-Soviet pact, it opposed all workers' demands and even the struggle against European dictatorships, for fear this would endanger Allied aid to the Soviet Union. This attitude shows the degree to which the CTAL was controlled by the Communists and their fellow travelers, under the direction of the Mexican Vicente Lombardo Toledano (1894–1968). But the CTAL had the support of European unions and of the American Congress of Industrial Organizations (CIO), although not of the AFL. After 1946, the AFL supported the democratic elements in the CTAL, which, believing that reform was impossible, decided in 1948 to create the Inter-American Workers Federation (CIT), which included many Latin American unions as well as the AFL. Just as the CTAL was affiliated with the Communist-dominated World Federation of Trade Unions (WFTU), the CIT was affiliated with the International Confederation of Free Trade Unions (ICFTU), founded in 1949. In 1951, the CIT became the Inter-American Regional Workers' Organization (ORIT), the American branch of the ICFTU, which the CIO also joined; within a few years, the ORIT had drained the CTAL of its members.

The only important labor organization outside the ORIT was the General Labor Federation (CGT) of Argentina; it was dominated by Peronists, who created the doctrine of a "third position" (neither capitalist nor Communist) called *justicialismo,* and who tried to found a Latin American parent union, the Association of Latin American Union Workers (ATLAS), which collapsed with Perón in 1955. In 1954, a Christian Democratic organization, the Latin American Confederation of Christian Trade Unionists (CLASC), was formed; it is aggressively anti-American, but so far it has had little influence.

The union movement emerged from these struggles larger in numbers but greatly bureaucratized. It faced new challenges: the need to struggle against both the traditional dictatorships and the militaristic demagogues who were trying to attract the workers; the wish to participate in decisions regarding industrialization, so that the workers should receive the largest possible share of its benefits; accelerated urbanization, which was changing great masses of peasants into members of the working class; the necessity of taking a stand in the conflicts of the cold war; the need to be free of all direct or indirect governmental control, and to have unions independent of political parties, although not of populist or other ideas. It should be said that, to the present, the unions have not faced up to most of these challenges.

The Communist loss of influence in the union movement was due in great part to the activity of elements that had become attached to a new movement: populism.

Radicals and Populists

By the end of the nineteenth century, the pressure of labor agitation, the influx of socialist ideas, and the growth of the middle class had created divisions within the liberal parties. The radical parties were the product of this division.

The adjective "radical" is to be understood in the French sense and not the Anglo-Saxon, that is, the radical parties were moderate, left of center, middle class, and anticlerical. The radical parties sought social legislation that would appease the workers, favored electoral reforms that would guarantee fair elections, and in a few cases dared to fight for moderate agrarian reforms. The most important radical party was that of Argentina, where, during the presidency of Roque Sáenz Peña (1851–1914), it got a law passed incorporating great masses of the people into political life. The Argentine Radicals won power in 1916 and again in 1928 under Hipólito Irigoyen (1852–1933), who effected considerable political reforms but who was deposed by the military in 1930. The Radical Party then split into a moderate and a leftist group.

In Chile, there was also a Radical Party, which after years of electoral struggle came into power in a coalition government in 1938. The man who enacted the role the Radicals had played in Argentina was Arturo Alessandri (1868–1950), leader of a dissident wing of the Liberal Party, who was twice elected president, in 1920 and 1932, and who brought about the country's first social legislation. In Uruguay, the liberals (Colorados) became the party of the middle class under José Batlle y Ordóñez (1854–1929), elected president in 1903 and again in 1911. He was the author of reforms that converted the country into a vast bureaucracy.

In the other Latin American countries, the middle class was smaller, and it either did not create its own party or did not do so until after the fall of the dictators who dominated those countries. In Mexico, as we shall see, the situation was very different because of the revolution of 1910. But the radicals, although they appeased the workers—recognizing their unions at the same time that they were putting them under state control—did not manage to confront the deep-rooted cause of Latin America's backwardness: the oligarchic system. The result was that the military destroyed their governments or that the conservatives capitalized on the disillusionment of the public-opinion groups. The radicals were important, however, because they reflected the desire of the middle class to hold power and because they brought into question the "right" of the landholding oligarchy to monopolize it. The hits and misses of the radicals prepared the field for populism.

Populism was important because it represented the first attempt to interpret Latin American realities in Latin American terms. All previous political movements had been based, as we have said, on ideologies that were the product of European and American conditions. When Argentine socialists tried to formulate a theory of land ownership, they turned to the doctrines of the American Henry George, and their chief theorist, Juan B. Justo (1865–1928), formulated a biological interpretation of history that bore little relation to the realities of Latin American life. The few Marxists in the hemisphere confined themselves to repeating the formulas then in use. An exception was the Peruvian José Carlos Mariátegui (1895–1930), one of the few to attempt to adapt Marxism to the realities of Latin America; he founded the Socialist (Communist) Party in his country, but was accused of heresy by Moscow. The populists saw that no small part of the ineffectual and transitory nature of these movements could be attributed to their lack of roots in Latin American society. They wanted to look with fresh eyes at what was going on in their countries.

About 1924, the Peruvian Víctor Raúl Haya de la Torre (b. 1895) formulated the doctrine that, with adaptations and modifications, was to be the basis of populism. Today, the majority of anti-oligarchic democratic parties of Latin America may be considered populist: the American Revolutionary Popular Alliance (APRA) of Peru; the Democratic Action party (AD) in Venezuela; the Nationalist Revolutionary Movement (MNR) of Bolivia; Febrerismo in Paraguay; the Dominican Revolutionary Party (PRD) of the Dominican Republic; the National Liberation Party (PLN) of Costa Rica; the Auténticos and Ortodoxos in Cuba (before 1959); the Institutional Revolutionary Party (PRI) of Mexico; and, in some degree, the Christian Democratic movement.

The fundamental points of populism may be summed up thus: Contrary to Lenin's view that imperialism is the final stage of capitalism, imperialism in Latin America is the *first* stage of capitalism. The struggle against imperialism is not the task of the working class alone but must unite in a single movement *all* the people (hence the name populism), starting with the peasants and workers and moving up through the middle sectors to the industrialists. In order to establish democratic regimes, it is necessary to awaken the people and mobilize them ("go to the people," as the nineteenth-century Russian populists said). The struggle against imperialism should seek the support of liberal and labor elements in the United States and must consist, first of all, in the struggle against the oligarchy, without which there would be no imperialism and no threat to national independence from foreign investment. Finally, the solutions to Latin America's problems can only be found through the union of all the Latin American countries into a supranational organization.

The populists understood—perhaps, without being entirely conscious of it—that the Latin American countries were not yet real nations. To attain nationhood, it would be necessary to unify the entire population, end the caste (oligarchic) system, and unite all the Latin American countries so that they would be in a better bargaining position vis-à-vis the United States. Only then, they said, would it be possible to accept foreign capital without endangering national independence, and only then would anti-American sentiment disappear. The populists wanted to reach an understanding with the United States that would be neither disguised surrender nor impotent resignation. In this sense, precisely because of their nationalism, they have always been more aware of the inevitability of relationships with the United States than have the other Latin American political movements.

The strength of the populist forces came from the middle class and the organized workers. The populists were soon leading the union movement in various countries (Peru, Venezuela, Bolivia); they captured a portion of the youth, offering them a sense of mission they had previously found only in Communism; and, as we shall see, after World War II won elections and power in various countries (in Paraguay, even a bit earlier, for a brief period).

The radicals had enlarged the number of voters, but even so great masses remained outside the electorate. In many countries, the vote is still refused to the illiterate, a normal situation in countries where the vast majority are able to read and write and where there are schools for all, but undemocratic in countries where the majority are illiterate and where there are schools for only a tiny proportion of the children. In Bolivia, for example, with more than 3 million inhabitants, it was common, before 1952, for no more than 45,000 votes to be cast in a presidential election; there was one case of a deputy's being elected although he received only 17 votes.

For the populists, this presented a major problem, since a great part of their support came from illiterates; the voting limitation faced them with the dilemma of putting up candidates without hope of electoral victory, since the majority of their potential electors were eliminated by law, or to profit by the awakening of the masses to launch them into violent struggle. In general, the populists favored gradual change; they seldom resorted to violence, and only when backed into a corner.

Populist concepts had considerable influence in Latin America. It was populist propaganda that brought about widespread acceptance of the concepts of agrarian reform, social reform, and Latin American integration, which, until that time, no one had dared discuss. It may also be said that the original concept of the Alliance for Progress was inspired by populist ideas.

But populism also aroused profound hatreds.

Although there are Marxist influences in populism, its tactics immediately aroused the opposition of the Communists, who saw in it a dangerous rival and attacked it with the same fury with which they assailed the socialists in Europe. It can be said that in countries where there has been a powerful populist movement, the Communists have not made much progress.

In addition to the Communist opposition, there was that of the rightist and militarist elements, which three times effected coups to keep Haya de la Torre from becoming president of Peru, and effected coups in several other countries to oust populist governments elected by vote of the people. Where there were radical parties or their quasi-radical equivalent, as in Argentina and Chile, populism made even less progress, and it had no success in Brazil.

But the partnership of the Communist and oligarchic groups would not have been sufficient to keep populism from victory in the majority of Latin American countries had the military not been there to block its road. This gave the militarists a new "function" and provided a new rostrum for Latin American militarism.

Militarism

Latin America, together with Spain, has been a region of barrack-room coups and *pronunciamientos,* to the point that this word has become a part of other languages.*

It is possible to distinguish several stages in Latin American militarism. In the early days of independence, there was the populist militarism of the popular caudillos. At that time, military pressure was the only means by which the people could express their wishes.

Later, there was the militarism of the caudillos, which was

---

* It should be said that what Latin Americans call a military coup is sometimes described as a "revolution" in the United States. The North American tends to regard all violent seizure of power as a revolution, whereas for the Latin American, a revolution is only the seizure of power by popular or civilian forces. Thus, the American will speak of the "Ecuadorian revolution" of 1963, which in Latin American eyes had nothing revolutionary about it but was simply a military *pronunciamiento*. The Latin American, on the other hand, will speak of the 1958 Venezuelan "revolution" to overthrow the dictatorship, with its two days of street fighting; the American would call this "mob action" or "mob violence." This semantic difference should always be kept in mind while reading Latin American historical works or the Latin American press.

at times liberal and popular, at times conservative, but always within the oligarchic system. During this period, the armed forces rarely took the initiative but followed one or another caudillo. In some cases, the army itself was divided and there were civil wars.

By the twentieth century, the armed forces had become a mere police force at the service of the oligarchy for preventing, by means of military coups, any advance by democratic forces that advocated social change. This police-state militarism flourished until World War II, and still survives in some countries. In others, as we shall see, it has taken on a new character.

The 1930's saw a series of military coups in Latin America. In Argentina, after more than a century of civilian government, the army staged a coup in 1930, overthrowing the Radical regime of President Hipólito Irigoyen; since that time, directly or indirectly, it has governed the country and may be considered responsible for whatever has happened there. In Cuba, in 1933, Sergeant Fulgencio Batista took advantage of the climate of unrest following the overthrow of the dictator Gerardo Machado to install himself as president; he ruled until 1944. In 1952, he staged another coup to seize power from a popularly elected president and held power until 1959.

In Peru, Augusto Leguía (1863-1932), a businessman and politician, had served two terms as president with army support. But in 1930, he was deposed by a military coup. Since that time, Peru has lived under more military regimes than civilian ones.

In Venezuela, Vice President Juan Vicente Gómez had seized power in 1908 while the president was on a trip to Europe. He dominated his country's life until his death in 1935. He was succeeded by two generals: Eleazar López Contreras and Isaías Medina Angarita, who governed until 1945.

In El Salvador, in 1931, vice president General Maximiliano Hernández Martínez (1882-1966) overthrew the elected president and governed for fourteen years. In Guatemala, General Jorge Ubico (1878-1946) was elected president in 1931; in 1935, he organized a plebiscite to remain in power without re-election and governed until 1944. In Nicaragua, General Anastasio Somoza (1896-1956) took power in 1936 and governed for twenty years until he was assasinated by a student; he was succeeded by his son Luis, and then by a second son, Anastasio Somoza, Jr.

In the Dominican Republic, General Rafael Leónidas Trujillo (1891–1961), who had served with the American occupation forces in the country, seized power in 1930 and then had himself elected president; he ruled, directly and through presidents he designated, for thirty years. In Honduras, General Tiburcio Carías (b. 1876) was elected president in 1933 and governed the county for sixteen years.

In Bolivia, following the Chaco War, there were three military governments with socialist tendencies. In Paraguay, victorious in the Chaco War, there were several military governments; that country had seen nothing but dictatorial government for half a century. In Haiti, the army set up and deposed presidents at its fancy until 1957, when a civilian dictator François Duvalier (b. 1907) seized power. In Ecuador, dictators were changed every two or three years (sometimes every two or three months).

Even in Chile, which is considered very democratic, the military (led by the navy) engineered several coups against the Radical government of Arturo Alessandri in 1925, and from 1927 to 1931 was in power under Colonel Carlos Ibáñez del Campo (1877–1960). In Uruguay, also considered democratic, Gabriel Terra (1873–1942), although a civilian, governed dictatorially with the support of the army in 1931–38. In Brazil, the military had played an active political role since the founding of the republic, although it did not hold power but simply exercised a right of veto which no one disputed; the military helped to install Getúlio Vargas as president in 1930, and he governed with its support until 1946.

In most of these cases, the military entered the political arena to prevent social change, or the possible formation of a party advocating social change. It is not that the coups are ordered by the oligarchy—although it is not unheard of that the president of a constitutional government, seeing himself unable to withstand the pressure for change, organizes, sub rosa, the coup that deposes him. It is simply that the military has become so accustomed to considering itself the preserver of "order" and of "Christian civilization," and to identifying these two values with the continuance of the oligarchic system, that whenever it believes the system is in danger, someone—more daring, more ambitious, or more reactionary than the rest—gets the idea of staging a coup.

These coups are not very dangerous affairs. What usually happens is that the ambitious military personage telephones or wires the minister of defense, informing him that he is in revolt and that he has at his disposal so many men and such-and-such weapons; the minister informs him, in turn, of the forces at *his* disposal. After a comparison of both sides, the general and the defense minister—who is also usually a military man—decide the winner and the loser takes asylum in an embassy or abroad. Rarely is there serious opposition to the coup; civilians protest in manifestoes or in published articles; some are exiled, others are jailed. The unions almost never attempt a general strike against the new dictatorship, which usually receives the benediction of the Church.

But as time goes on, when it is perceived that the dictatorship is not solving any of the problems that served as its pretext for taking power, when it is proved that there is not less corruption but more, nor less administrative disorder but more, then a certain inquietude begins to show itself in political circles. Manifestoes appear and demonstrations are organized. This is followed by martial law, repression, the assassination of opponents by government forces. Then the military—often with Church backing—decides that it would be dangerous to permit civilians to seize the initiative in the struggle against the dictatorship, advises the dictator that it would be best if he got out—and if he does not listen, makes a *pronunciamiento* to "re-establish the constitutional regime." Since the dictator has often had a new constitution ratified, and even had himself elected, the new civil regime restores the earlier constitution and calls for the election of a constitutional assembly. The constitutions do not greatly differ from one another, and neither do the governments, civilian or military, although the former are generally less rigid in maintaining public order and allow the citizens to enjoy (without overdoing it) the basic human rights.

If the dictatorship has not been of long duration, there are no great political problems, for the old governing personnel return to power and know how to exercise it. But if the dictatorship has lasted for years (and in Latin America, dictatorships of twenty and even thirty years are not rarities), the new generation has not been able to acquire any political experience; the political problems become more acute; and it is discovered that the dictatorship, instead of solving problems, has tabled them or even made them worse.

The military men of the twentieth century do not possess the picturesque traits of the nineteenth-century caudillos, but are fatuous, greedy, and indifferent to the national interest. When in power, they organize collective corruption in government, give juicy appointments to other military men, and create an atmosphere of fear and indifference.

Often, they turn the country into a virtual family business, for nepotism is a characteristic of these modern dictators. During the "reign" of Juan Vicente Gómez in Venezuela, hundreds of his relatives took possession of most of the country; the one exception was the oil industry, in which concessions were granted to foreign investors. At the time Trujillo was assassinated, his family owned more than one-third of the resources of the Dominican Republic.

The dictatorships also grant privileges to military officers. The Military Club of Caracas, built by a dictator, is one of the most luxurious buildings in the world. The Peruvian dictator General Manuel Odría, when he came into power in 1948, established a state monopoly on the sale of coca (the plant from which cocaine is made, which the Indians chew as a drug) and decreed that the profits from the legalized sale of the drug should be used to improve the living conditions of the officers. In the Dominican Republic, the military dictatorship of 1963–65 gave officers the right to import all goods duty free, and they thus became the legal smugglers of refrigerators, radios, and machinery, to the great indignation of the country's merchants. The only article they were not permitted to import was automobiles, because the head of the dictatorship owned an agency that sold American cars.

The military dictatorships are, however, great friends of public works, which pay commissions and disguise the true condition of the country. It is also not exceptional for a military regime to pass laws that are apparently progressive (for example, the military promulgated the first labor code in Chile, in 1931). But these laws never endanger the system; they are, rather, attempts to incorporate adverse forces into it, which will serve at the same time to present the dictatorship in a "popular" or "progressive" light.

In recent years, police-state militarism has been modified by two new forms of militarism: fascist militarism, and a "technocratic" militarism that even effects a "revolutionary" appearance.

Fascist militarism dates from the 1930's, and reflects the influence of European fascism. There were fascist influences in some Bolivian military lodges, which supported the reformist governments that followed the Chaco War. The fascist-type government of Getúlio Vargas (1883–1954), who dominated Brazilian politics from 1930 to 1954, encouraged this outlook in the army. But the fascist influence was most clearly shown in Argentina. There, the officers who formed the Group of United Officers (GOU)—or, when that sounded better, "Government, Order, Unity"—made open fascist (even imperialistic) propaganda in the armed forces, for they saw Argentina as destined to dominate in South America. General Perón belonged to the GOU and had its support; when he came into power, in 1944, he opened the doors of the country to Nazi capitalists fleeing Germany and to crypto-Nazis. Argentine military fascism was never "pure," however, for it was always blended with caudillo or police-state elements.

In the second half of the twentieth century, a new type of technocratic militarism arose. This is sometimes called "Nasserism" because its adherents aspire to do what Nasser has done in Egypt. These young officers, many of whom have been educated in the United States, believe that democracy has failed in Latin America (although there has never been any real democracy there). They believe that social change is necessary, and they hope to realize it by forming alliances with younger elements of the business world. This group seeks to establish a paternalistic dictatorship with an extreme nationalist character. It is also very prone to form alliances with the Communists, if the latter support it, as they have supported other dictatorships in the past. (This technocratic militarism will be examined in greater detail in subsequent chapters.)

To understand the role of the military in Latin America, we must take into account the fact that Latin American armies have seen very little military activity. Since the wars between the Latin American countries that took place in the first three-quarters of the nineteenth century, they have had no occasion to exercise their intended function of national defense, with the exception of the Chaco War between Bolivia and Paraguay in 1932–35. Promotions, medals, and honors have been won in the *salons* by political maneuvering, or in the streets, in action against civilians.

Latin American armies did not intervene in any way in World War I. In World War II, Brazil sent an expeditionary corps to Italy, and Mexico sent an air escadrille to the Pacific. In the 1950's, Colombia and Brazil sent small forces to Korea. But Latin American armies have caused more casualties in our time than they would have by participating in all the major international wars. It has been estimated that between 1900 and 1966, more than 100,000 Latin Americans were killed by military action in demonstrations, strikes, guerrilla fighting, and encounters with insurgent forces. In some cases, the army has executed massacres, like that of the Haitian laborers in the Dominican Republic in 1937, and that of the peasants of El Salvador in 1932; in each of these instances, more than 10,000 peasants were killed. (On the other hand, the army was unable to prevent mutual killing by liberals and conservatives in Colombia, in 1950–60, in which it has been estimated that 200,000 persons perished; nor did it succeed in crushing the rebellion of Fidel Castro in Cuba in 1956, when his forces consisted of a dozen poorly armed youths.)

The consistently antidemocratic attitude of the Latin American armed forces in the last half century has cost them prestige in their own countries. But their feelings of isolation and social ostracism have only aggravated their tendency to dominate. Moreover, the armed forces have managed to capture foreign support, notably that of the United States.

It has been customary to accuse the United States of supporting military coups through its military attachés and through the sale of American arms to the Latin American armies. In some Central American countries, the army has been considered a mere instrument of the large American firms. At any rate, the Latin American armies have never opposed armed U.S. intervention (as in Nicaragua, Haiti, and the Dominican Republic), and at least since World War II there has been close cooperation between the Latin American armies and the United States military in professional training, maneuvers, equipment, and planning.

Most Latin American arms are bought from the United States. But they are also purchased from France, Great Britain, Italy, Switzerland. Since World War II, a genuine arms race has developed among the Latin American countries, especially among Argentina, Brazil, Chile, and Peru. When Argentina buys a submarine, the Brazilians buy two; when Peru acquires more planes, Chile does the same. U.S. diplomats try to prevent this, but the Pentagon encourages it, in order to comply with the congressional demands for the sale of obsolete arms. These arms, of course, are never used for national defense, nor even in military coups, which, as we have mentioned, are virtually bloodless.

The Pentagon has recently encouraged "civilian action" programs in the armed forces, by which the military undertakes such tasks as the construction of highways and bridges, sanitary campaigns, and so on. It was asserted that in this way the army would cease to be militaristic. In 1964, the Bolivian army proved the falsity of this assumption, for although one of the few dedicated completely to "civilian action," it did not hesitate to rise up and seize power when conditions were favorable for a coup.

(In reality, the military has always assumed civil functions in Latin America. In Argentina, for example, the military took the initiative in creating a metallurgical complex in the city of Córdoba. The Brazilian army for years shouldered the task of protecting and civilizing the Indian tribes of the interior. In Brazil, too, the military school was for a long time the only place where one could study engineering. In most Latin American countries, the army was the only organization with abundant means of communication and the only one that could transmit government orders to distant parts of the country. Exploration, surveying, cartography, even public works were the task of the military.)

The Latin American armed forces as a whole number about 600,000 men, of whom 400,000 are from the nine largest countries. The largest forces are those of Argentina (107,000 in the army, 21,500 in the navy, 19,000 in the air force) and Brazil (90,000, 8,000, and 9,200, respectively). Also important are the armed forces of Cuba after 1960 (79,000 men) and of Mexico, Chile, and Peru (40,000 to 50,000). However, there are countries with a small population and armed forces that are proportionately very large: the Dominican Republic (17,000), Venezuela and Colombia (22,000 each), and Ecuador and Uruguay (13,000 each).

Only two countries have no armed forces: Panama and Costa Rica. Costa Rica disbanded its armed forces in 1948. Panama, however, maintains a national guard that has effected coups more than once.

Although the proportion of the national budget earmarked for the armed forces varies greatly, it is below 5 per cent in only three countries: Costa Rica, Mexico, and Uruguay; in two countries, Honduras and Venezuela, it is 5–10 per cent; in the others, 10–20 per cent (13.2 per cent in Argentina, 18 per cent in Peru and Chile); and in Haiti and the Dominican Republic, it is above 20 per cent.*

There are small armies that receive a significant share of the gross national product: Paraguay (4.5 per cent), the Dominican Republic (3.2 per cent), Peru (3 per cent), Haiti 2.9 per cent), Chile, Nicaragua (where the armed forces are known as the national guard), Argentina, Venezuela, and Brazil (2.5–2.8 per cent). Mexico's armed forces receive less than 1 per cent of the gross national product.

Latin American militarism is clearly different from the European type, which tends to dominate (without seizing power) in international political matters; and from that of the Arab, African, and Asian countries, which presents itself as reformist or modernizing (although such tendencies are cropping up in Latin American armies). Latin American militarism resembles only that of Spain, and it is likely that both have a common historical cause: the initial absence of means of political expression for the people and the enthronement of a landholding oligarchy that has employed the army to protect the social system, sometimes by diverting the people with caudillism, at others with police-style coups. The basis of Latin American militarism is a political system that does not allow popular participation and a social system

---

* Irving Louis Horowitz, "The Military Elites," in Seymour Martin Lipset and Aldo Solari (eds.), *Elites in Latin America* (New York, 1967), pp. 154–56.

in which a tiny minority protects its interests against those of an immense majority. The future of Latin American militarism, therefore, is conditioned by the social structure. We shall find an example of this in the Mexican Revolution.

The Mexican Revolution

The Mexican Revolution is of special interest because it was, in a sense, the culmination, in one country, of the historical, political, and social factors that have formed the woof of Latin American life since the arrival of the Spaniards, and because it shows that what appear to be characteristics of Latin America are merely characteristics of a social structure that change when the structure is changed. The Mexican Revolution was also the first revolution of the twentieth century, antedating the Russian and the Chinese, and it found solutions for problems that other parts of the world were facing in the same period. For these reasons, it must be discussed in some detail.

The history of post-independence Mexico is a deeply troubled one: three civil wars; wars with the United States and France; the loss of more than half its territory (acquired or conquered by the United States); two invasions; two empires that ended with the execution of the emperors; seventy-two governments in one hundred years, only twelve of them wholly legal in origin; expropriation of Church property; division of the Indians' communal lands; the increase of latifundism.

In November, 1876, a liberal general, Porfirio Díaz (1830–1915), staged a coup and seized power, which he held, directly or through presidential henchmen, for the next thirty years. His slogan was "Administer and Modernize." Foreign capital flowed in, and railroads, highways, and factories were built. But Díaz's government encouraged latifundism at the same time that it sought foreign capital to industrialize the country. By the end of the nineteenth century, there were 500 haciendas of more than 25,000 acres, eleven of more than 250,000, and seven of more than 625,000. A large number of the *hacendados* were foreigners, chiefly Spaniards. There was a shortage of trained labor for the new industries, since the peasants were virtually tied to the haciendas. But foreign investors wanted quick profits and opposed all social change

—although this would have made possible a balanced industrialization by creating a rural market. The buying power of the peasants was one-fourth of what it had been before independence, since they were obliged to buy in the company stores of the haciendas. In spite of the caciques and a rural guard, organized by Díaz with outlaws taken from the jails, peasant rebellions were frequent.

Toward the end of the century, there assembled around Díaz a group of politicians, educated in French and English positivism, who advocated industrialization; the public ironically called them the "scientists." But for all their sociological training, they did not see that Mexican society was paralyzed by what could, without exaggeration, be called agrarian feudalism.

A Mexican poet of the period, Guillermo Prieto (1818–97), recognized the dominant social reality: "Since independence we have become the *gachupines* of the Indians," he said. And where the Mayas had a ruling class who called themselves *holac huinic* ("the only true men"), the Mexican landholders and the *nouveaux-riches* of Díaz's time, with the "scientists" at their head, considered themselves the elite and regarded the people as an infantile mass—disorderly, irresponsible, and in need of constant supervision and guidance.

Socialist and anarchist groups had been formed in the 1870's, but protest against Díaz did not find an organized outlet until 1906, when Ricardo Flores Magón (1873–1922), from exile in St. Louis, Mo., founded the so-called Mexican Liberal Party; this party promptly founded centers in the factories and even in the *pueblos*. Two major strikes in 1906, one in the textile city of Rio Blanco and the other in the mining city of Cananea—both of which were violently suppressed, the latter by American goons who came into the country with Díaz's permission—and several peasant uprisings gave the Liberal Party great prestige.

Meanwhile, the middle-class elements wanted to end the perpetual incumbency of Díaz, who was already very old. In 1910, a *hacendado* from the north, Francisco I. Madero (1873–1913), published a book against re-election. He was nominated to oppose Díaz, lost the election, fled to the United States, returned to his country, and proclaimed himself president. A number of guerrillas, rising up in the north, supported him, and in the south, near Cuernavaca, a peasant, Emiliano Zapata (1883–1919), headed a rising of peons and burned haciendas; his slogan was "Land and Liberty."

In May, 1911, Díaz stepped down and went into exile, and Madero entered the capital in triumph. Zapata refused to lay down his arms; Flores Magón, in Lower California, distrusting Madero, proclaimed a Socialist Republic with the help of members of the American IWW (International Workers of the World, a union organization with anarchist tendencies). In the elections held soon afterward, Madero won an enormous majority. But he did not dare to effect agrarian reform, and he sent the army—the same one that had supported Díaz—against Zapata and Flores Magón. The latter, crushed, fled to the United States, where years later, blind, he died in the Fort Leavenworth prison. But Zapata continued fighting.

Madero did not satisfy the social aspirations of the people or succeed in pacifying the *hacendados* but contented himself with effecting the modest political revolution he had aspired to: the establishment of representative democracy. Taking advantage of the discontent this aroused, a general whom he trusted, Victoriano Huerta (1845–1916), staged a coup in February, 1913, assassinated Madero and his vice president, and had himself proclaimed president. To celebrate, the U.S. ambassador to Mexico, Henry Lane Wilson, arranged a great fiesta on the night of Madero's assassination, something the Mexicans have not yet forgotten.

But the country had had a glimpse of democracy and did not want to give it up. A governor from the north, Venustiano Carranza (1859–1920), refused to recognize Huerta, gathered other governors, some military men, and a few young intellectuals, and began a fight against him. The guerrillas who had welcomed Madero three years before were the shock troops of this coalition, which called itself the Constitutionalists. They were led by a daring and picturesque peasant, Francisco (Pancho) Villa (1877–1923).

In 1914, Huerta was forced to relinquish power and exiled. The Constitutionalist forces faced the problem of what to do with their victory: some of their numbers wanted a truly revolutionary government, while others simply wanted representative democracy. Villa broke with Carranza and began to distribute land among the peasants in the north.

Villa and Zapata became allies and occupied the capital. A constitutional convention was set up with a government opposed to Carranza's moderate regime, and there was a long factional struggle, finally won by the Constitutionalists. Zapata, however, was treacherously assassinated in April, 1919; Villa was assassinated a few years later.

The workers, organized in the so-called *Casa del Obrero Mundial* (World Workers' House), had not intervened in these struggles; influenced by anarchist ideology, they considered the revolution merely a struggle between "bourgeois factions." They thus wasted the opportunity to ally themselves with Zapata and Villa and to control the revolution. Finally, in 1915, General Alvaro Obregón (1880–1928), a small planter from the north who had become the strategist of the Constitutionalists, persuaded the leaders of the *Casa del Obrero Mundial* to form "red battalions," which were used against the still rebellious peasants, thereby separating the labor movement from the rural masses. Shortly afterwards, Carranza disbanded the "red battalions" and harassed the unions. The attitude of the workers prevented them from presenting their bill to the revolution, so to speak, and changed the revolution into a system for protecting the people rather than a system of popular participation in government.

Zapata had won the military victory for the revolution, as Huerta did not venture to use all his forces against Carranza for fear Zapata would take the capital. Zapata was also the cause of the revolution's being social as well as political and nationalistic, for without the pressure of the southern peasants there would have been no distribution of land or breaking up of the haciendas. These objectives of the revolution, which emerged in the course of the struggle, were expressed in the constitution ratified by the constitutional congress that met in 1917 in Querétaro, the city in which, half a century earlier, the Emperor Maximilian had been executed. This constitution is still in force and is one of the longest-lived of all Latin American constitutions.

There are three essential articles in the Mexican Constitution of 1917: Article 3, which makes all government schools sectarian and forbids schools owned by religious orders; Article 27, which declares the lands, the waters, and the subsoil national property and gives guarantees to small property owners and to the *ejidos;* and Article 123, which guarantees workers the right to organize and establishes minimum conditions for their protection.

The history of Mexico since 1917 has been the history of the slow, hesitant, application of these articles to Mexican life. Three stages in that history may be singled out: in the first, Carranza was deposed and assassinated, and was succeeded by General Obregón. The latter was succeeded by the politician who probably had the best understanding of the revolution, a schoolteacher turned general, Plutarco Elías Calles (1877–1945). Calles was succeeded by three presidents who were largely under his control. During this period, agrarian reform was carried out according to the aspirations of the peasants, that is, by giving them lands and considering the *ejido* a transitory institution, a school of ownership for peasants who had never owned land, either before the Conquest or after independence. The revolutionary government was solidified. The party that was to call itself official—the National Revolutionary Party (it later adopted the names Party of the Mexican Revolution and Institutional Revolutionary Party)—was created. From 1928 to 1931, it carried on a long struggle with the Church, which was opposed to secular education; the party organized not only strikes of the priests in the churches but even guerrilla movements. The army was disciplined, after a series of unsuccessful coup attempts, and there was collaboration with the union movement to establish, in practice, the constitutional guarantees of Article 123.

The second stage is that of the government of General Lázaro Cárdenas (b. 1895), who was elected president in 1934. Cárdenas freed himself of the influence of Calles and, in order to gain support, tamed congress, until then very independent. He also tamed the union movement, accustoming it to winning victories through the influence of the government rather than by strikes. Cárdenas also modified the agrarian policy, making the *ejido* a permanent institution of a collectivist character and creating around it an extensive bureaucracy.

Cárdenas is famous chiefly for having nationalized the oil industry, in 1938, after the foreign companies that owned the oil fields (mostly British, a few American) refused to honor a judgment of the Mexican supreme court validating the government's arbitration in ending a long strike by the oil workers.

There was great protest over the nationalization of oil. (Cárdenas had earlier nationalized the railroads, but no one protested, because the railways were losing money.) Diplomatic relations with Great Britain were broken off and were renewed only during World War II. The Franklin D. Roosevelt administration backed the foreign companies in their claims for indemnity, but did not exert any pressure against nationalization itself, despite an intense campaign in the American press, which accused Cárdenas of being a Communist. In 1941, after long negotiations, the amount of the indemnity was established, and this was completely paid by 1960. The oil industry was administered by an autonomous governmental agency, which has increased production and kept prices low.

Cárdenas was succeeded by General Manuel Avila Camacho (1897–1955), who calmly carried out a rather moderate policy.

Mexico then entered a new stage, that of the present, in which all the presidents have been civilians. In order not to alarm the partisans of Cárdenas or the *ejido* bureaucracy, agrarian reforms have been discreetly modified by amortizing the *ejidos* (which are economically unprofitable and do not furnish enough land to the constantly growing number of peasants and by encouraging small and middle-sized agrarian ownership.* Most important, industrialization has been promoted through the creation of institutions for public investment. These have transformed the Mexican economy into a mixed type of capitalism: private investment combined with "Mexicanization" of mining and of certain enterprises of public character (electricity, telephones), through purchase by the government and by Mexican capitalist groups of the stocks of foreign enterprises.

* The distribution of land followed an ever more rapid rhythm: Carranza distributed 437,000 acres; Obregón, 3 million; Calles, 11 million; and Cárdenas, 62 million. Later, there were further distributions, some latifundios were expropriated, and permission was given to establish large landholdings that could not be profitably worked on a small scale, and which were exploited by typically capitalistic methods. The important point is that, since the revolution, the possession of land has not automatically guaranteed a share of political power.

Throughout the fifty years since 1917, the Mexican government—with the aid of the "official" party, which is not the only party but which wins most of the elections—has succeeded in maintaining an independent international position. It has opposed all intervention by one country in the affairs of another: for example, it has refused to recognize General Francisco Franco's Spanish regime, which it considers a product of German and Italian intervention in the Civil War of 1936-39, and it has refused to break off relations with Fidel Castro's regime in Cuba.

Mexico has also maintained a genuine independence with respect to the United States. At the same time, it maintains friendly relations with this "neighbor to the north," whose investments in Mexico are constantly growing—without endangering that independence—precisely because they are subject to national laws and because the government is strong enough to insist that those laws be respected.

The Mexican regime is essentially tutelary (owing, primarily, to the lack of union participation in the revolution), with a type of paternalistic democracy that successive governments have attempted slowly and cautiously to extend, giving women the vote (1953), supporting the presence of a parliamentary opposition (1964), and respecting the fundamental freedoms, a matter of exceptional significance in Latin America. Despite the fact that the Mexican president has more de facto powers than the head of any other modern state, there have been no important cases of violation of human rights. (In 1968, however, the army was called out against restless students and behaved brutally, killing scores of protesters.)

Mexico's rate of economic growth has been one of the most rapid and regular in the world. However, the revolution has not abolished poverty; Mexico is still a land of great contrasts in living and cultural standards, a condition aggravated, in recent years, by a class of *nouveaux-riches* risen out of industry. Nor has the government been able to reduce the country's birth rate.

But, on the whole, it may be said that even with mistakes, delays, and corruption, Mexico has made greater progress toward general well-being than any other country in Latin America and has achieved a political stability unmatched elsewhere on the continent. This stability has permitted gradual enlargement of the degree of popular participation in government and the reforming of reforms to adapt them to new conditions. On the long road from colony to nation, Mexico, of all the Latin American countries, has come closest to establishing nationhood.

In short, it may be said that although the Mexican Revolution did not solve any problems—nor does any revolution, anywhere, have for its object the presentation of solutions but only the destruction of obstacles to the search for and application of solutions—by abolishing the oligarchic system, it created conditions under which it would be possible to propose solutions to the fundamental problems facing the country. The fact that various remedies have been tried, and without great upsets or crises, shows that the Mexican Revolution did attain its objectives.

The Mexican Revolution was a nationalistic one, fought to guarantee the independence of the country on both the economic and the diplomatic levels. It was also an agrarian one, fought to destroy the landholding oligarchy and distribute land to the people. Finally, it was a revolution of the middle class, to establish a democratic regime suited to the capacities of the country, and a capitalistic system that would at the same time recognize the rights of the workers and the advantages of state intervention in economic affairs: all with the aim of encouraging social development, that is, ensuring that all groups of society should benefit.

Why did revolution break out in Mexico before any other Latin American country? To find the answer, we must take into account Mexico's nearness to the United States, which imposed upon the Mexicans an attitude of mistrust (justified by their early relations with that country) and a constant need to affirm their own worth. The fact of having had to struggle against American invasions and French interference helped to give the Mexicans a sense of owning their country, a sense that does not exist elsewhere in Latin America. In this sense, the revolution was the result of the desire to give legal and political form to this citizen-ownership of the nation.

Moreover, Mexico, thanks to its considerable natural resources, was able to begin industrialization relatively early and to attract abundant investments before the end of the century. The most important Spanish American colony, and the one with the most intense cultural life, Mexico was also the one in which the mixture of Indian and white had been most extensive. All this contributed, even in the nineteenth century, to the creation of an urban mass of mestizos with aspirations to power, which they achieved under the liberals, and which the revolution consolidated.

The Mexican Revolution has had no direct effect upon Latin America. It had no immediate imitators, and the Mexicans did not trouble to carry the revolution to other countries. But the Mexican Revolution did constitute proof that the oligarchic system was not untouchable. The success of the Mexican Revolution—however qualified it may have been—demonstrated that it would be possible to attempt solutions outside the oligarchic system.

The aspirations that led to the Mexican Revolution were the same as those of Latin Americans in other countries. In some countries, these aspirations did lead to revolution; in others, they have led to economic policies designed to prevent revolution, as we will see in the following chapter.

CHAPTER VI

Where Is Latin America Going?

The nineteenth century in Latin America was essentially a time of political preoccupations. The first half of the twentieth century was agitated by social questions. The second half of our century is a period of obsession with economics. Just as, in the nineteenth century, social questions were often disguised as religious ones, today they appear as problems connected with what is called economic development.

It is customary to class Latin America among the underdeveloped regions of the world. This may be convenient, but it does not reflect reality. For although it is true that Latin America is much less developed than the United States or Europe, it is much more so than Africa or Asia, and its economic and social problems are very different from the problems facing those two continents. It does not, for example, have Africa's characteristic problems of transition from a tribal to an industrial society, nor those of Asia in what may be called an oligarchy of usurers. Latin America's problems are those peculiar to a society with feudal traits that wants to become capitalist. Several of its countries, at different times in their history, have been close to the take-off stage of development, and a few—Argentina, Mexico, Venezuela—have attained it. The degree of industrialization is also greater in Latin America than in Africa or Asia. The statistics themselves (however little representative they may be) show that the living standards of the Latin American countries fall somewhere between those of Africa and Asia and those of the industrialized countries. Finally, Latin America has had the experience of 150 years of independence, lacking in the majority of African and Asian countries, and it also has states of a Western type.

It is often forgotten that Latin America is—in its culture, history, and society—a part of the Western world, although it is a part that lags behind chronologically. Latin America's population has lived for more than four centuries in contact with Western civilization and so is much more susceptible to Western influence than are the people of underdeveloped countries in the rest of the world. Latin America is not so much an underdeveloped region as a Western region whose development has been retarded.

Obviously, then, the solutions that may be suggested for the development of Latin America must be different from those proposed for the development of Asia or Africa. In one respect, however, the three continents are similar: in the enormous variations in living standards among their inhabitants, and the indifference of the ruling groups to the living conditions of the mass of the people.

Standard of Living

In examining economic questions, it is essential to bear in mind that Latin American statistics, whether prepared by government bureaus or international organizations, afford only a vague reflection of actual conditions and never permit us to get to the bottom of the problem, that is, to know how the national income is distributed. There are plenty of figures (often contradictory) relative to the gross national product and the rate of economic growth, but there are few reliable studies to tell us what part of the national income goes to the submerged masses, what part to the middle sectors, and what part to the oligarchic stratum. Since without knowing this distribution it is impossible to understand the structure of a society, it is necessary to rely on personal experience and direct observation in order to correct and complete the statistical data.

The impression gained by every traveler in Latin America is one of poverty and of great contrasts, not only in the standards but in the ways of living. Alongside skyscrapers we find huts; alongside automobiles of the latest model, carts drawn by animals; by the side of hospitals with all the newest equipment, village medicine men; next to residential areas with every convenience, slums without paving, sewers, electricity, or running water; alongside superhighways, vast areas without communication of any kind. There are powerful tractors and wooden plows; blast furnaces and village smithies; haciendas the size of states and plots of land the size of suburban gardens. There are modern newspapers and great masses who do not read at all; peasants submissive to the hacienda overseer and the flames of haciendas set afire by peasants in rebellion; universities equipped with cyclotrons and rural schools without desks or a blackboard; expensive foreign schools and children who sell newspapers and sleep in the street.

In a region with such vast differences, statistics mean little. But they can be useful in helping us to understand the extent of Latin American poverty if we agree that each figure is only an average, and bear in mind that more than 50 per cent of the total income is absorbed by 5–10 per cent of the population and the rest by 90–95 per cent of the population.

The figure most often used to define the living standard of Latin America is the per capita income. The per capita income is highest in Argentina ($830 per annum, in 1965) and Venezuela ($734). Countries in which it is more than $400 are Uruguay ($597), Panama ($475), Mexico ($402), Chile ($479), and Costa Rica ($450); from $300 to $400 a year: Colombia ($339), Brazil ($334), El Salvador ($314), and Guatemala ($307); under $300: Nicaragua ($298), Ecuador ($286), Peru ($265), Dominican Republic ($218), Honduras ($201), Paraguay ($196), and Bolivia ($126). Haiti, for which no figures are available, is probably about the same as Bolivia.*

---

* All figures cited in this part of the chapter are from Inter-American Development Bank, *Social Progress Trust Fund* (Washington, D.C., 1966); and DESAL, *America Latina y desarrollo social* (Santiago, 1966).

The countries with a per capita income of more than $400 a year include 16 per cent of the population of Latin America, whereas the countries with a per capita income of $300–$400 a year account for 65 per cent. There are, of course, considerable differences within each country: Mexico City and the southern part of the country, for example, seem like two different worlds, as do the industrial region of São Paulo and the Brazilian Northeast, or Buenos Aires and the northern Argentine pampas. The differences between the various social groups are still greater.

Although statistics on per capita income seldom show the distribution by social groups, a few figures are available to give an indication of the real situation. In Peru, for example, where the per capita income in 1965 was $265, 0.1 per cent of the population—about 8,700 families—received 35 per cent of the national income. This means that 99.9 per cent received 65 per cent of the national income, so that for the vast majority of the population the per capita income was not $265, but much less. We should have to know what share went to the middle sectors in order to know how much was actually received by the Peruvian peasant or slum dweller; probably, it was no more than $50 per year.

In general, it may be said that 80 per cent of the population of Latin America receives an income below the country's annual per capita figure.*

In Brazil, workers, peasants, slum dwellers, who constitute 70 per cent of the population, had an annual per capita income in 1965 of $71 (or 19 cents per day), or a per family income of $355 per year (or 95 cents per day); in Chile, the figures for this group were $95 per capita, or $475 per family; in Ecuador, $98 and $490; in El Salvador, $57 and $285; in Venezuela, $222 and $1,110. The corresponding figures in the United States were $1,030 and $5,150. Thus the poor of Venezuela, who had the highest income of the poor in Latin America, still received an income only about one-fifth that of the poor in the United States.

The latest income statistics of the Economic Commission

---

* The United Nations made an attempt to study the distribution of income by social strata, and came up with these figures: the poorest (50 per cent of the population) received 16 per cent of the income; the nearly poor (45 per cent) received 51 per cent of the income; the nearly rich (3 per cent), 14 per cent; and the rich (2 per cent), 19 per cent. United Nations, *El desarrollo económico de América Latina en la Postguerra* (New York, 1963), p. 68.

for Latin America (ECLA) indicate that the annual rate of increase in actual income for 1960–66 was 4.2 for the total, and 1.2 for each inhabitant. But in several countries, individual income declined (Honduras, Nicaragua, Paraguay, Haiti, Dominican Republic, Uruguay, Venezuela), although total income did not. In the years 1960–65, per capita income increased 35 per cent in Latin America, but the world increase was 42 per cent; it was 52 per cent in industrialized countries, whose inhabitants earned $175 more per year in 1965 than in 1950, whereas Latin Americans earned only $40 more.

Let us look at a few other statistics in order to see how Latin Americans live. It is well known that the higher the percentage of the family budget set aside for the purchase of food, the lower the standard of living. In Latin America, nearly always more than half the family expenditures are for food (55.6 per cent in Peru, 52.2 per cent in Colombia, 51.2 per cent in Haiti, 46.9 per cent in Guatemala, compared to 32.9 per cent in the United States). About one-quarter of the family budget—even less in some countries—is allotted for shelter, against one-third in the United States. Ten to twenty per cent of expenses are for clothing (against 6.6 in the United States). All this leaves very little left over for education, amusement, travel, health.

The high percentage of the budget allocated to food does not mean that the Latin American has an adequate diet. The Planning Commission of the Central American Common Market has estimated that the per capita income in the Central American countries is $43; the Central American Institute for Nutrition estimates that on the Isthmus an adequate diet costs $125 a year. In Brazil, farm workers earned a daily wage of 20–30 cruzeiros in 1966; an adequate meal for a peasant family cost 25 cruzeiros. In Peru, 60.7 per cent of the mountain population, 19.8 per cent of the coastal population, and 26.2 per cent of the urban population have a calorie intake of less than 75 per cent of the minimum requirement.*

---

* In the United States, the per capita annual consumption of cereals is 148 pounds; it is 231 pounds in Argentina, 200 pounds in Brazil, and 172 pounds in Venezuela. The consumption of sugar is 90 pounds annually per capita in the United States, 70.4 pounds in Argentina, 63.8 pounds in Brazil, and 68.2 pounds in Venezuela. Americans eat 198 pounds of meat per year, the Argentines (great enthusiasts of their chief national export), 268.4 pounds, the

It is estimated that of the 237 million inhabitants of Latin America in 1966, 190 million suffered from malnutrition. They were also badly housed.

In Honduras, 90 per cent of all dwellings—rural and urban—have floors of beaten earth, as have 83 per cent in Venezuela, and 66.7 per cent in Colombia. The roofs are of thatch in 60 per cent of the dwellings in Colombia, in 58 per cent of those in Panama, 78 per cent of those in Paraguay, and 67 per cent in Venezuela.

Only a small proportion of dwellings have running water: 7.4 per cent in Colombia, 4.5 per cent in Chile, 9.7 per cent in Panama, 61 per cent in Venezuela, as compared to 83.9 per cent in the United States.

Only 4.2 per cent of all dwellings in Colombia have electricity; of those in Chile, 14.5 per cent; in Honduras, 1.3 per cent; and in Venezuela, 9.1 per cent—compared to 92.1 per cent in the United States.

Plumbing is very scarce: it is found in only 11.3 per cent of Colombian dwellings, in 35.2 per cent of those in Panama, 12.9 per cent of those in Venezuela. The situation may be said to be the same in the other Latin American countries.

An increasing part of the submerged masses lives in slums in the big cities, under conditions worse than any found in slums in the United States. These slums have a characteristic name in each country: in the *favelas* of Rio de Janeiro, for instance, live 38 per cent of the city's inhabitants; in Lima's *barriadas*, 21 per cent; in the *colonias proletarias* of Mexico City, 25 per cent; in the *ranchitos* of Caracas, 38.5 per cent; in the *villas miseria* of Buenos Aires, 20 per cent; in the *callampas* of Santiago, 31 per cent.

The Inter-American Development Bank has calculated that there is a total deficit of nearly 7 million living units in the cities of Latin America, and nearly 8 million in the rural areas. It would be necessary to build 910,000 urban units and 440,000 rural units every year just to take care of the population increase. But in both these sectors, an average of only 423,000 units is being built per year.

Brazilians 63.8 pounds, and the Venezuelans 50.6 pounds. The consumption of fats and oils is 46.2 pounds per capita in the United States, 30.8 pounds in Argentina, 15.4 pounds in Brazil, and 17.6 pounds in Venezuela. It should be remembered that Argentina and Venezuela are the most prosperous countries in Latin America.

Sanitary conditions have improved somewhat in the last thirty years, and this is one cause of the population increase. But the infant mortality rate is still very high: in Paraguay, it exceeds 100 out of every 1,000; in Haiti it is 171 per 1,000; in Chile, 111. Only in Uruguay, Panama, and Honduras is it under 50 per 1,000. More than half of the deaths are of children under five. Life expectancy, which has risen steadily in the last half century, is still only forty-three years for men and forty-nine years for women. Major causes of death include gastrointestinal illness (from bad food and water), and pneumonia and respiratory diseases (from insufficient clothing and poor housing).

The people are badly cared for. There are about 114,000 physicians in all Latin America, or 5.5 for each 10,000 persons. There are great differences among the countries: in Argentina, there are 13 physicians per 10,000 persons, but in the Dominican Republic, there are 1.5 (in the United States, the figure is 13.2 per 10,000). The distribution of physicians is very uneven; at least half practice in the large cities. The number of nurses and midwives is also inadequate (1.8 nurses per 10,000 persons, against 28.9 in the United States), and 0.5 midwives per 10,000. Altogether, there are 627,000 beds in the hospitals, or 3.1 beds per 1,000 persons. Although there are modern hospitals in the capitals, some owned by foreign companies, many hospitals are antiquated and poorly staffed.

With the growth of the population, and the small amount of attention paid by the governments of most countries to these problems, the situation, instead of improving, is becoming worse. We need only glance at the percentages of governmental budgets earmarked for social welfare to be aware of this lack of state aid: in basically agricultural countries, the average budget allows 4–5 per cent for agriculture; for housing, from 0.3 to 2.1 per cent (and in many countries, nothing); for health, from 2.3 to 9.5 per cent (in two countries, El Salvador and Panama, more than 10 per cent). The allotment for education varies from 1.3 per cent to 28.7 per cent, but in most countries it is about 15 per cent.

It has been estimated that about 40 million Latin Americans are affected by unemployment; seasonal unemployment is common among agricultural workers and big-city slum dwellers. The economically active population varies from approximately 45 per cent (Peru) to 53 per cent (Argentina) of the population of working age. Two out of every five economically active persons are under twenty years of age. Two out of every five over sixty-five continue to be economically active.

The percentage of the national income that went to pay wages and salaries in Latin America was 50–55 per cent in 1960 (the last year for which such figures are available). In the United States, the percentage was 71. To have an idea of how low these wages are, one only has to convert them into dollars.

In Argentina, where living costs for the middle class are about the same as those in a large American city, the hourly wage in industry, in 1962, was 33 cents. In Mexico City, where the middle class has monthly expenditures about equal to those of the middle class living in an American small town, the hourly wage was 38 cents. In Colombia and Brazil, where living costs are lower, it was 19 cents. In 1962, the hourly wage in the United States was $2.39.

The constant inflation in many countries has meant a lower living standard for wage-earning groups. In Argentina, for example, the buying power of industrial wages in 1963 was half of what was considered the bare minimum five years earlier.

The existence of a legal minimum wage in most countries does not constitute a guarantee, both because this wage is often far below the minimum necessary for decent existence and because the law is often flouted. Moreover, in many countries the minimum wage applies only to industrial workers, and not to agricultural workers or government employees.

The worker has certain other guarantees, although in all cases it must be remembered that there is a considerable difference between the law and its enforcement, and that social legislation usually does not apply to peasants, to domestic workers, and in many cases to civil servants.

In most Latin American countries, there is a forty-eight hour work week—it is forty-four in some countries—although this regulation is often flouted, especially in rural areas. Paid vacations are required by law in all Latin American countries, usually two weeks per year. At Christmas, there is a bonus of two weeks' or a month's pay. A few constitutions (in Chile, Mexico, Argentina, Brazil, Ecuador, and Venezuela) establish the workers' right to profit-sharing, but this has been enforced only in Mexico (and only since 1964).

Women workers usually have more rights in Latin America than in the United States, for example, during the pre- and post-natal periods, when they do not work but continue to receive their wages. Although the work of minors is regulated, in reality many children do a full day's work; in every Latin American city, children may be seen selling newspapers and shining shoes in the street.

Although in recent decades the attitude of businessmen toward unions has become more cooperative, rejection of unions by employers is still quite general, as is the use of administrative maneuvers and even bribery to violate labor laws. It is not unusual to hear firms accused of paying their employees less than the legal rate, of requiring them to work longer hours than the law permits and under unhealthful conditions. Although it is forbidden by law, it is still customary in rural areas for the employer or firm to sell necessities to the workers, deducting the cost from their wages; this is especially frequent among rubber workers, plantation employees, miners, chicle workers in Guatemala and Belize, yerba maté pickers in Paraguay, or gatherers of carnauba wax in northeast Brazil.

There is no state unemployment insurance, and most workers are unable to afford private insurance. The insurance companies aim their propaganda at the middle class, the only ones able to pay the premiums, which are usually higher than in industrial countries. Industrial safety is, generally, so much wet paper, for lack of inspectors to see that the regulations are enforced or because of the venality of the existing ones. Industrial accidents are frequent.

All the Latin American countries, however, have social security systems. These are older than the social security system of the United States, although the rate of compensation is much lower. The retirement age is also low: at sixty years of age, or after twenty-five years of work. In all countries, social security is tripartite, with contributions by the worker, the employee, and the state, but its administration is usually the task of government officials, and the unions and employers' organizations are granted only a consultative role. In some countries, social security is organized by trades, not as a single system including all industrial employees. And except in Mexico, there is no social security for the peasants. But, in general, it may be said that the worker receives better treatment and protection when he stops working than when he is working. What he receives for an accident or disablement does not usually constitute a living, but what he receives as a pension permits him to live better—with the aid of another job.

To sum up: it may be said that the poor of Latin America live in much greater poverty than those of the United States; they have very little chance of ever owning a refrigerator or a bicycle, not to mention a television set. The living conditions of the peasants, in particular, are greatly inferior to those of any social group in the United States (with the possible exception of migrant workers).

Industrial workers live, more or less, like the inhabitants of American slums in the matter of food and housing, worse in the matter of education and entertainment, but better in the area of economic security. There are some groups, however—the specialized and white-collar workers—who live like the middle class of their respective countries.

The Latin American middle class lives under conditions comparable to similar groups in poorer sections of the United States. An average lawyer in Lima, for instance, will live like an average lawyer in Alabama; a successful merchant from Managua will live like a merchant in a small town in Tennessee.

Government employees, although considered part of the middle class, have income and working conditions greatly inferior to those of American civil servants. Many countries do not offer an administrative career or job security; when the government changes, not only high officials but many humbler ones, too, are replaced. However, there is a growing tendency to grant job tenure to government employees. In a few countries, they are allowed to organize unions but in none are they permitted to strike.

Intellectuals, who enjoy considerable social prestige, are economically worse off than their American counterparts, although their living conditions have improved somewhat in recent years; university professors, for example, seldom have full-time employment and have to perform other professional duties and even hold down a government job in order to be able to lead a modest, middle-class life.

It might be said that the same difference that obtains between the poor of the United States and of Latin America is found—but in reverse—between the rich. Those Latin Americans who can consider themselves well off—the latifundists, big industrialists, bankers, highly successful professional men, leaders in the bureaucracy and the army—live much better than the rich American, although their actual income and capital may be smaller. The rich Latin American pays fewer taxes, to begin with; he owns palatial residences within and outside his country; he has many servants; he travels a good deal. His living conditions, which would be considered luxurious anywhere, become in his own country, by comparison with those of the rest of the population, fabulously sumptuous. The rich North American cannot be distinguished in the street, at table, in many ways, from the rest of his compatriots; the rich Latin American is in every way (often even in the color of his skin) a different kind of being, identifiable at first glance. The rich American is accustomed to working and to not showing off his wealth; the rich Latin American often lives abroad, without doing anything, and likes to show his wealth in an extravagant fashion: the most spectacular parties in Europe and the United States are usually given by Latin Americans, and in films, in fiction, and in life the idle, rich Latin American—playboy, spendthrift, insolent, boorish —has become a tradition.

It is against this background, then, that Latin American economic thought and policies must be viewed.

Economic Thought

Since the mid-nineteenth century, Latin American economic thought has revolved around the problem of accelerating development (or, as it was called until about twenty years ago, "progress"). Because this problem has political, sociological, and cultural ramifications, it has been discussed not only by economists but also by politicians, sociologists, and even novelists. In reality, there were scarcely any economists in Latin America until after World War I; or, better said, any politician, sociologist, or lawyer who possessed a certain amount of information was considered qualified to theorize about economic questions.*

During the nineteenth century, the cause of failure to progress was sought not in the social structure but in the collective psychology. In nearly every country, there were writers who attributed the lack of progress to the laziness, individualism, or even the racial mixture of the Latin Americans. The Chilean historian Francisco Encina (b. 1874), in his book *Nuestra inferioridad económica (Our Economic Inferiority)*, imputed Latin America's backwardness to lack of initiative, perseverance, and morale, the result of inheritance and bad training. Agreeing with him were the Argentine Octavio Bunge (1875–1918), in *Nuestra América (Our America);* the Bolivian Alcides Arguedas (1879–1946), in *Pueblo enfermo (A Sick People);* and the Brazilian Euclides da Cunha (1866–1909), in *Os Sertões* (translated into English as *Rebellion in the Backlands*). The recommended remedy was generally imitation of the United States, through an act of will, a collective effort, or by the "elites." The idea of elites was widespread among the positivists, who at that time dominated Latin American intellectual life.

After World War I, economic thinking changed direction. Latin Americans were no longer held responsible for their own backwardness. Instead, their failure to progress was attributed to foreign influence, to imperialism. Only the populists, with Haya de la Torre at their head, tried to see the cause of backwardness in the social structure. Haya pointed out that the "feudal governments, vassals of imperialism" proclaimed that any capital was good, whereas the "passionate radicals" said "we don't need capital." For him, "the capitalist stage should emerge under the direction of the anti-imperialistic state." The populists wanted to make use of the old Indian communalism as one of the bases for the economic future.

* In this résumé of Latin American thought, I have followed Albert O. Hirschman, "Ideologies of Economic Development in Latin America," in Hirschman (ed.), *Latin American Issues* (New York, 1961).

Serious analysis of the Latin American economy did not begin until after World War II. This analysis was undertaken by a group of U.S.- and European-trained economists associated with the United Nations Economic Commission for Latin America (ECLA), established in 1948 with its seat at Santiago; from 1950 until 1962, it was under the direction of the Argentine economist Raúl Prebisch (b. 1901).

The ECLA economists—whose work was considered "radical" and viewed with distrust in the United States—attacked the old theory of the international division of labor, according to which Latin America was supposed to produce raw materials and buy manufactured goods.* World War II, the ECLA economists said, had given Latin America the opportunity to industrialize; in order to profit by this opportunity, it was necessary to modify the international terms of trade. There is a twofold imbalance, according to the ECLA, between the "center"—the industrial countries, and especially the United States—and the "periphery"—the countries producing raw materials. It consists, on the one hand, in the declining prices of raw materials and agricultural products and the rising prices of manufactured goods; and, on the other, in the decreasing demand for food and raw materials and the increasing demand for industrial products. The peripheral countries need protection for the development of industry, as well as control of imports and a plan for their substitution. In short, the ECLA blamed the international trade system for the backwardness of Latin America. In 1954, the ECLA suggested that international aid, amounting to at least $1 billion per year for ten years, be extended to the Latin American countries (these figures were later used in the plans of the Alliance for Progress).

Until 1959, the ECLA occupied itself chiefly with studies of foreign trade; after that year, it began to urge economic integration and the formation of a Latin American common market. It was the ECLA that advised the experts who founded the Central American Common Market. Not until 1961 did the ECLA begin to interest itself (and with little

---

* It is interesting that this idea was also put forth at the time when, in Communist countries, a "Marxist" theory of the division of labor was being promulgated, one which attributed to the Soviet Union the role of industrial exporter.

enthusiasm) in the economic consequences of the social structure, particularly the landholding system, despite the fact that within the United Nations there had been talk of agrarian reform since 1955.

The thinking of the ECLA, which placed responsibility for the backwardness of Latin America on external causes, but which also demanded that Latin Americans make decisions and efforts in their own behalf, exerted considerable influence, particularly among nationalist and populist elements. In showing itself an advocate of planning, the ECLA was responding to both Latin American tradition and the populist outlook; in a sense, it united the psychological pessimism of the thinkers of the nineteenth century with the nationalism of those of the twentieth. The Latin American governments agreed, without enthusiasm, to let the ECLA make studies of economic planning in their countries.

The ECLA found many opponents. Businessmen were pleased by the criticism of the trade system but mistrusted the tendency to planning, for they regarded the state as inept and passive. This was a result not only of their own experience, but also of the endless propaganda in favor of "free enterprise"—issuing from North American business firms, government organizations, academic bodies, and even labor unions—that for decades, particularly after World War II, flooded Latin America.

What may be considered the traditionalist view of economic development in Latin America is represented by the Brazilian economist Roberto de Oliveira Campos (b. 1908). Campos has attacked certain common beliefs in Latin America: that inflation can be an instrument in the formation of capital, that nationalization creates new resources, that wealth can be redistributed without increasing production, that industrialization and the creation of capital are more important than the development of agriculture and the investment in education. Campos—together with many of the economists who have held government posts in various Latin American countries in recent years—believes that there can be no development without a healthy financial situation; the fight against inflation is fundamental.

Among economists who do not belong to either of these

two camps—in general, academic economists without direct influence on government decisions—there is a predominant blend of Keynesism and Marxism that may be called nationalist *dirigismo,* the "directed economy." There are also the "pure" economists, usually educated in universities in the United States, whose influence is minimal. Finally, there are the economists we may call analysts, who view the Latin American economy as a product of social and historical factors, and who try to find both an applicable economic policy and general principles for giving it direction. Notable among the latter are the Mexican Víctor Urquidi (b. 1919) and the Brazilian Celso Furtado (b. 1918). Few economists, however, have attempted to formulate a theory of Latin American development, despite the fact that there are today examples of countries in a state of accelerated development (Mexico), of countries whose development has been paralyzed by political causes (Argentina), or by financial ones (Chile), or of others which have experienced a purely regional development accompanied by great inflation (Brazil).

The majority of Latin American economists regard development as a means not merely to raise the living standards of the people, but also to bring about a more equitable distribution of the national income and to move Latin America from the economic periphery to the economic center, that is, from a position of dependence on other countries to one of independence. In Mexico, for example, it is usually considered that development was made possible by an agrarian reform and a revolution that encouraged social mobility. Furtado attributes the development of Brazil to the fact that the country "conquered centers of decision" that were previously located abroad. A subject that has not lost interest is whether agrarian reform should be considered a prerequisite of development—as Mexican and some other economists maintain—or if, on the contrary, the existence of a feudal agrarian economy aids development because it permits forced accumulation of capital.

Latin American economists, obviously, are highly ideological; this distinguishes them from the pragmatic North Americans, which gives rise to not a few misunderstandings. But if Latin American economic theory is ideological, economic practice is just the opposite.

Economic Policy

Latin American economic policy has always had to answer the question, What is its object: to reinforce the social structure and the political institutions derived from it, which retard or impede economic development, or to modify that structure and its institutions and thus encourage economic development? Except for a few cases—which we call revolutions—Latin American economic policy has answered that its function was to preserve the social structure and to try to produce, within it, the greatest possible economic growth.

The mercantilism of the Spaniards and Portuguese impeded the development of the American colonies and was of little help in adapting the Indian masses to the new social reality. But at the same time, it encouraged certain technical advances—mining, navigation, the training of native artisans —and in this way developed limited sectors of the economy. But it also impeded development of other branches—notably industry—that might have offered competition to the motherland. In the eighteenth century, when it became apparent that this system was functioning badly, an attempt was made to modernize it: more industries were authorized, there was liberalization of trade. But the system, although modified, remained essentially unchanged.

Nor did it change after independence. But there had to be further modifications, since industrialization, the development of communications, and mass immigration added greatly to the complexity of economic life. After the 1850's, it was no longer possible to maintain exclusively agricultural and latifundist societies. To preserve the oligarchic system, it became necessary to add to it certain features proper to an industrial society. These were modeled on those of Europe and, later, on those of the United States: outwardly democratic political institutions, annual government budgets, banking systems, systematization of taxes. These measures encouraged the building of railways, the creation of industries, and attracted foreign capital.

But, in effect, the mercantile economy was continued. For example, at the close of the nineteenth century, two inventions made possible the development of the Argentine and

Uruguayan economies. One was refrigeration, which made it possible to ship meat instead of live cattle to Europe; the second was barbed wire, which made it possible to enclose pastures and thus gave unity and shape to the latifundios. But the oligarchic character of Argentine society prevented the country from profiting by the economic bonanza produced by the export of meat and wheat. In fact, the governments saw to it that there would not be any large-scale industrialization, for fear that Great Britain—the principal buyer of meat and grain and the chief seller of industrial products—might decide to reduce its purchases if Argentina developed industries that would narrow the market for British goods. Only during the two world wars, when England could not export goods to Argentina, were local industries able to start and grow.

Those who were concerned with the economy did not think of themselves as mercantilists but as free traders. But as new industries were formed, protection was sought for them. And since tariffs were the state's chief source of income, and also served as collateral for foreign loans, free-trade theory never reached the stage of practice.

At the same time, the liberals, for political reasons, favored private ownership. Whenever they came into power, they abolished the two forms of collective property: those of the Church and of the Indian communes. The result (as we have seen) was the opposite of what the liberals intended, since it encouraged latifundism and made the Indians, more than ever, into serfs; and if the Church lost economic power, it gained considerable influence among the new latifundists, who obeyed its behests in exchange for forgiveness for having acquired Church lands. All of this discouraged industrialization. Similarly, at the time of independence, the liberals, in abolishing the guilds established in colonial times, had thought they were encouraging social mobility and aiding the labor force; in reality they were leaving the artisan class without protection against the early industrialists, who found in the artisans a low-paid work force the new industries needed.

During all this period, economic policy was influential only among the urban minority and the latifundists; it only very indirectly affected the rural masses, who went on living as before—in a subsistence economy as consumers, on a supply-and-demand basis as producers—no matter what measures the government adopted.

In the last third of the nineteenth century, under the influence of positivism, there began a period of imitation of Europe and the United States. (It was even proposed that wheat replace corn in the diet of the people.) It was thought, for example, that the building of railroads would have the same effect it had in the American West: but it was not realized that in the United States the railroad extended the "homestead" because it advanced through unoccupied land. In Mexico, Argentina, and Brazil, the railroad crossed great latifundios and hence did nothing to develop the rural regions, since there was no available land, but was useful only to the cities.

One aspect of the imitation of Europe was industrialization. which required capital and labor. Since the great landholders invested either in more lands or abroad, foreign investment was encouraged; since there was no skilled working force, immigration was sought. Immigrants received land, foreign capital received privileges. But in the twentieth century, as the national enterprises began to acquire some importance, nationalist sentiment began to arise. From that time on, the rivalry between foreign and native capital has never ceased.

At first, native capital showed itself favorable to certain changes in the social structure that were being effected by the first wave of industrialization. The oligarchic strata were uneasy. Thinking that a greater influx of foreign capital would strengthen their position, they made ever greater concessions in its favor: concessions to mines, lands, and public services were granted almost without guarantees and on extremely favorable terms. This gave foreign capital an advantage over native capital and increased nationalist sentiment. But native capital was still small, hesitant, and timid, and at the first pressure of the labor movement, and later of the populists, native capitalists, instead of heading the movement for social reform, went over to the side of the oligarchy and of foreign capital. Thus Latin American capitalism, originated by foreign investment, never developed enough force and personality to displace the oligarchic groups: it preferred collaborating with them to superseding them.

All of this was translated into a government economic policy that at first encouraged a moderate degree of industrialization and foreign investment and then subsidized, directly or indirectly, investors and exporters of raw materials. The governments also allowed public utilities to charge high rates. These actions hindered the very industrialization they were trying to promote.

In nearly all Latin American countries, congressional control of the budget has been a constitutional myth without reality. The Latin American governments have prepared and administered the budgets as they have seen fit, and in them the shares for the armed forces, the diplomatic corps, and the bureaucracy have much greater importance than those for education and agriculture. The tax systems have also continued to be substantially the same as they were a century ago. Nor did the governments do very much to create the infrastructure of a modern economy.*

This picture was not altered with the establishment of corporate regimes, like those of Getúlio Vargas in Brazil and Juan Perón in Argentina. The corporate state existed more on paper than in reality. The Vargas and Perón regimes constructed public works and subsidized new industries, but did not modify the social structure, as witness the fact that when Vargas and Perón fell, the oligarchic system continued to function as before.

The result of this economic policy—a direct consequence of the essential preoccupation of all Latin American governments with maintaining the social status quo—is an economy very difficult to describe. It is not strictly feudal, since along with latifundism and serfdom there are modern industries, labor unions, and technological progress, and along with an antiquated banking system there are very modern methods of marketing. Neither is it a typically capitalistic economy, since private and public investment coexist in it, as do private initiative and free enterprise, government planning

* In 1966, there were only about 650,000 miles of roads in Latin America, and many of these were unpaved. There were about 500,000 miles of railroads, and rail service is poor: trains often arrive twenty-four hours late. In 1966, there were about 1.4 million telephones in Latin America (compared with 58 million in the United States); telephones are generally installed as the result of "pull," bribery, or the purchase of telephone stock. Mail service is undependable; even today, the United States Post Office will not accept registered or insured parcels destined for some Latin American countries.

and intervention; and since by the side of capitalistic institutions we find feudal survivals so powerful that they have the virtual right of veto over government decisions. It is not an agrarian economy, for industrialization and urbanization are rapidly increasing, but neither is it an industrial economy, since there is not a significant rural market, nor is the bulk of income derived from industry. It is not strictly a market economy, because in the majority of countries the mass of the people are not consumers of industrial products; but it is not strictly a subsistence economy, since this same mass of people performs an economic activity linked to the market.

Perhaps the most fitting description would be that in Latin America, except in a few countries, there is a caste economy in a society in which castes are disappearing. This is most plainly revealed by examining the principal features of Latin American economic life.

The Business World

The first thing that impresses the foreigner about the Latin American business world is the way in which the Latin American, businessman or man in the street, relies on the state to solve his problems, at the same time that he mistrusts and is unhappy with the state.

Latin Americans have one of the worst bureaucracies in the world: inefficient, indifferent, presumptuous, corrupt, slow, extremely complicated. Yet they accept government interference with business, which submits the economy to this bureaucracy, and see no contradiction—as would be the case in the United States—in the government's being both the owner of enterprises and the regulator of economic life.

In reality, the Latin American has never known a true system of free enterprise; it is foreign to his history and mentality. Before colonization, the economy was directed and controlled by the priest-kings. During colonial times, it was controlled and directed by the Spanish or Portuguese authorities (in greater degree by the former). After independence, although the official doctrine was one of the *laissez faire,* the oligarchic groups exercised indirect but constant control over economic decisions, and the lack of income taxes made it essential to maintain a rigorous (though frequently violated) tariff system. Today, the tendency to state planning is very powerful in nearly all countries, in many of which it is looked upon as a panacea for economic problems.

Official economic activity takes many forms. The state often subsidizes exports of raw materials when prices go down on the world market; or it fixes a special dollar exchange for them; or it exempts certain imports from the customs. Often, the state subsidizes certain foodstuffs, with the end of keeping their price low in times of shortage. Frequently, it freezes the cost of public services, in order to preserve the impression that living costs are not rising. In countries where private cultural patronage is almost completely lacking, the state gives commissions to artists and jobs to writers. This government aid to certain economic groups is tutelary, because the beneficiaries of the assistance never play any part in making decisions respecting it; the state decides who is to receive assistance, grants it, and administers it.

The government does not always take advantage of its opportunities for planning, however. For example, government permission is required to open a new business, but the government rarely makes use of this authority as an indirect means of planning, or to guide investment.

Moreover, many regulations governing the business world are not enforced, or it is possible to get around them through personal influence. Businessmen in most countries know that there are laws against monopoly, but they also know that these laws are rarely enforced and that executives never go to prison for establishing monopolies. Similarly, there are controls forbidding the export of hard money without government permission, and limiting the import of luxury articles; but these are nearly always much more theoretical than real. There are ways of flouting these controls, and there is plenty of smuggling, both organized and sporadic, whose chief effect is to raise prices but rarely to diminish the flight of dollars or the entry of cameras, medicines, and nylons. Only in the import of such goods as automobiles, tractors, and machinery is it possible to make the controls work, and even here the use of influence makes it easy to obtain permits or exemptions.

Political influence—sometimes through friendship, at other

times through bribery—is an important fact of Latin American economic life. It is taken for granted that the friend of a minister, the mistress of a general, or the nephew of a deputy should manage to obtain what an ordinary merchant cannot. The fact that government officials become rich while they are in power is considered normal in the majority of Latin American countries (although in a few there are strict standards of administrative honesty), and no one criticizes a dictator or president for leaving his post a rich man, although he is frowned upon if his enrichment is showy or excessive.*

This government interference must be constantly borne in mind in examining Latin American economic life.

There are 2.5 million businesses in Latin America, of all sizes, employing 25 million persons (in trade, services, and industry, excluding agriculture). More than half of these businesses are devoted to trade, and only 20 per cent to manufacture. Many agricultural enterprises and retail businesses and a good part of the small industries are individually or family owned. Only the larger sales organizations and important industries are stock companies, although the number of these is increasing.

Following the Roman system, the law permits a great variety of company forms: sleeping partnerships (in which some partners contribute capital and others experience); simple partnerships; limited companies (a form unknown in the United States, in which partners are liable only for the amount of capital they contribute); corporations, which, unlike those in the United States, are formed by contract and not by charter; and the cooperative, which has had relatively little development.† Finally, there is the mixed company in

---

* There are many slang expressions for government employment and also for the bribe. Government employment is called *cambús* in Venezuela; *corbata* (necktie) in Colombia; *estar en el dulce,* or *en la onda* (to be in the sugar, or on the wave) in Uruguay; *tanga* in Argentina; *pega* in Ecuador, Bolivia, and Chile; *mamata* in Brazil; *chamba* in Mexico; *botella* (bottle) in Cuba. The bribe is called *mordida* (bite) in Mexico; *coima* in Argentina, Chile, and Uruguay; *grasa* (grease) in Bolivia and Venezuela; *tajada* (cut) in Honduras, *serrucho* (handsaw) in Colombia, *engracada chola* in Brazil; *picada* (bite) in Cuba. The general idea is one of oiling, of smoothing the operation of the administrative machinery.

† In 1966, there were 3,161 consumers' cooperatives in Latin America, with 1,831,000 members; there were 3,966 agricultural cooperatives, with 942,888 members; 678 housing cooperatives, with 90,940 members; 1,508 credit cooperatives, with 1,055,890 members; 568 electrical cooperatives, with 494,536

which, along with private funds, there is capital from public funds.

Despite the laws against it, monopoly is a frequent feature of the economy in many Latin American countries, where often only one firm produces a certain product. Oligopoly is also very widespread. Approximately 2 per cent of Latin American enterprises employ about 60 per cent of the industrial labor force. The largest firm in Latin America, SIAM di Tella, in Argentina, does a business of about $128 million a year, and the F. Matarazzo United Industries of Brazil yield almost $100 million a year. In Mexico, a group of nine banks controls more than three hundred enterprises, which form the bulk of the nation's industry. The result of this situation is price-fixing by the firms and not by the market, the refusal of credit for the establishment of competitive firms, and the restriction of production to keep profits high. This, in turn, raises the cost of living for the consumer and makes it almost impossible for national products to compete in the foreign market, because of their poor quality and high cost. The public is vaguely opposed to monopoly, but the monopolists themselves often take advantage of the nationalistic atmosphere to direct these feelings against foreign firms and divert them from their own. The economists—most of whom are employed in government institutions or in private firms—have scarcely examined this phenomenon.

Although Latin Americans boast of attaching greater importance to "spiritual" motives than to material ones, there has been a general interest in making money—at least among the economically active groups of the society—and the crudest and most direct methods of accomplishing this have always been accepted without censure.

No business is worth starting if it is not to return a 25–40 per cent profit, as compared with a normal profit of 10–15 per cent in the United States; profits of 70 and even 100 per cent are considered normal in everyday trade.

The middlemen between producer and consumer are numerous and abuse their function, especially in the agri-

---

members; a total of 4,903,303 persons belonging to the 10,998 cooperatives of different classes. The cooperative is most highly developed in Argentina, Chile, and Brazil, where 4–9 per cent of the population belongs to a cooperative; in the remaining countries, less than one per cent belongs.

cultural market. The small and medium-sized farmer is a persistent victim of these middlemen, who buy his standing crop at a wretched price, taking advantage of his lack of cash and of credit. The frequency with which governments fix maximum prices for staple products makes it possible for middlemen to impose low prices, but they rarely pay any attention to those prices when they sell to the public. The Mexican system of establishing purchasing agencies for necessities, which are sold directly to the public at cost, so far seems to be the only effective method of price control. Of course, this method can be applied only to widely used products: rice, sugar, cereals, detergents. For superior quality products, the prices are virtually unregulated, and subject to speculation. But the middlemen tend to distribute high-quality goods only in wealthy neighborhoods (not necessarily at higher prices) as a way of pacifying the community's influential elements; the best products are usually exported.

The differential between the price paid the producer and the price charged the consumer is also much greater in Latin American than in industrialized countries because it is not unusual for a single distributor, or a cartel of distributors, to have a monopoly on the sale of a certain product in a city or region. This happens especially in the case of milk, meat, and cereals. Sometimes the monopoly is enjoyed by the relative of a dictator; Trujillo's family, for instance, had a monopoly on the sale of milk in the entire Dominican Republic.

Latin America's commercial habits reveal a curious relation with those that might have been necessary in the past, when there were few means of distribution. Although in the cities there are great department stores, specialty shops, supermarket chains, etc., the small merchants and even peddlers are the chief means of distribution for most of the people, especially in rural areas. In the villages, barter is still common and prices are often fixed for reasons that have nothing to do with the law of supply and demand; foreigners, for example, are charged less (or more, depending on the place) than local residents; more is paid per piece if all the pieces are the same than would be paid if they were all different (in reality, a premium is paid on the monotony of the work, which is psychologically not illogical). In the cities, especially in slum areas, there are many street booths, improvised markets on which no watch is kept, and along the highways it is common to see peasants selling fruits and vegetables to travelers.

Haggling is an attraction for tourists from industrialized countries. The buyer is sure that the seller is trying to get more than the proper amount and considers it essential to obtain a reduction. For his part, the seller knows that he will not sell unless he lowers the price, and this induces him to jack up the price beforehand.

An interesting and little studied phenomenon is the variation of prices during the day. As afternoon draws on, the peasants tend to lower their prices in the market, since their produce will be ruined if it is not sold. But the shopkeeper from whom they buy thread, pins, and cloth does not reduce his prices. Thus the peasant finds himself subject to the same difference in price between what he sells and what he buys that the Latin American countries have to suffer between what they export and what they import (to loud lamentation by their governments).

There are in Latin America, as elsewhere, many business associations. There are chambers of commerce and associations of industrialists, miners, bankers, landowners in nearly all the countries. These associations often have representative functions established by law; in all cases, they are very active and influential, sometimes undertaking campaigns to "educate" the public on economic questions. (It is significant that these organizations are allowed to participate in drawing up development plans, although unions and peasants' organizations are not.) They serve, moreover, as a channel of communication between the government and the business world. It is not unusual for a Latin American government, before licensing the establishment of a new firm or industry, to consult the existing firms, to avoid what is called "unfair competition." Since in Latin America there are no enforced legal restrictions on conflict of interest—nor do the Latin American congresses generally hold investigations into the various interest groups—it is not unusual for industrialists to be members of the government, or for politicians to be openly interested in industry.

All this is the result not only of underdevelopment but also, as has been said, of the age-long tradition of the directed economy, which is not, in the eyes of the average businessman, an attack upon his freedom but is on the contrary regarded as a help to his prosperity, since he plays such an important part in its direction.

The Mixed Economy

In recent years, it has begun to be understood that the so-called mixed economy that predominates in most Latin American countries is not disguised or "creeping" socialism but the form capitalism has adopted within the historical, social, and international framework characteristic of Latin America. Most Latin American business enterprises are in private hands, although they are subject to some degree of government control. But the government—directly or, more often, through autonomous government agencies—is also the owner of firms. Moreover, a number of companies are the joint property of government and private capital, and private investment and government funds often collaborate to create new industries. This interlacing of public and private interests is what is called the mixed economy.

Latin American governments—both colonial and independent—have traditionally had a monopoly on the exploitation or importation and sale of certain products: salt, explosives, matches, even playing cards. Some of these monopolies are curious: Peru has a monopoly on *guano,* Colombia on emeralds. These monopolies are conceded to private firms or are administered directly by the governments. Often a monopoly contributes a large income to the national budget; if the product is (as is usual) one for general consumption, the monopoly constitutes a disguised method of indirect taxation.

Following the Spanish tradition, the state always exerts control over minerals and the subsoil. In nearly all countries, the state is considered the owner of the subsoil, which is exploited through governmental concessions. The concession may be paid for in the form of a simple rental, or by a percentage of the value of the minerals extracted (the latter procedure is followed primarily in the exploitation of oil). Sometimes a government administers a mining industry directly, as in the case of Mexico, after the nationalization of oil in 1938, or in that of the Bolivian tin mines, nationalized in 1952. In other cases, official agencies are entrusted with the discovery and exploitation of oil, sometimes exclusively, sometimes in competition or in collaboration with private enterprise.

Rarely has an official monopoly been used to force prices down, or to distribute a product to the public at cost. Except when there is political pressure, official monopolies are administered from the standpoint of a private enterprise and not to satisfy the needs of the public.

The latter is usually attempted by governments through public investment, that is, by competing with private firms. This has happened with electric power and with the purchase and sale of essential foodstuffs. Sometimes the government assumes administration of a bankrupt firm whose closing might leave the country dependent on the importation of a product, or cause unemployment in a particularly sensitive spot. At other times, a government will establish firms for the exploitation of oil (Venezuela, Argentina) as an example to and guide for foreign firms. Or it will finance a new enterprise and then concede its exploitation to private interests (especially in the case of hotels for the promotion of tourism). And in the nineteenth century, it was common for governments to subsidize the building of railways by foreign firms.

Today, railroads, some steamship lines (in Brazil, Colombia, Ecuador, Argentina, Chile, and Mexico) and some airlines are government property. But the majority of the airlines, and some railroads and shipping lines, belong to foreign (especially American) companies; sometimes they are subsidiaries, like the railroads and shipping lines that belong to the fruit companies in Central America.

Many large enterprises (the blast furnaces in Mexico, Argentina, and Colombia) are the result of a combination of private and public capital. In these cases, the government retains the majority of stock, or, once the company is in operation, sells it to the public.

There are several reasons for government investment in

industry. One is that private capital rarely risks originating large enterprises in Latin America, and so public capital must do it. In some cases, it is necessary to maintain low costs for services, in order to encourage development (or not to increase economic inequalities).

Then, too, in Latin America, where industrialization is still in its first stage, the creation of certain large enterprises could put into a few hands an economic power without counterpoise in the rest of the economy, one that could be a threat to other industries and even to the government. The classic example is that of the fruit industry in the Central American republics. In Honduras, Guatemala, Panama, Costa Rica, two American firms virtually monopolize the market and are deciding factors in the economic life of these countries; when it has suited their purpose, they have not hesitated to use the army to overthrow governments. Thus the tendency to create industries with government participation, so that they will always be subject to official control.

We have spoken about nationalization, but it is important to give an exact definition of this word. Contrary to the general impression in the United States, nationalization is not a socialistic measure, since it does not give the ownership of an industry or source of wealth (land, mines, oil) to the people, or even necessarily to the state. It is a nationalistic measure, which gives ownership to native capitalists or to the state. In short, nationalization is simply the passing of an enterprise or source of wealth from foreign hands to national ones. Except in the case of agrarian reforms, and in Cuba since 1959, there have been no nationalizations of property belonging to nationals but only to foreigners. And nationalized property has passed either directly into the hands of nationals (in the case of land and of some enterprises whose stocks have been put on sale) or into those of the state, but never into those of the unions, the cooperatives, or other organizations of a popular character. Mexico is the only country that has ever tried to put the unions in charge of administering nationalized property—the railroads, in 1935—and it abandoned the attempt within a few months.

Nationalization has been effected by force (distribution of land in Mexico in 1917) and by law (Mexican oil in 1938,

Bolivian tin in 1952, Argentine telephones in 1947). It has also been effected by the purchase of stocks of foreign enterprises: in some cases by national capitalistic groups (Mexican telephones, 1955), in others by the state (the Argentine railroads in 1947, Mexican electricity, 1962), in still others by the creation of new stocks which are handed over to the state (Chilean copper, 1964). There has also been nationalization through the seizure of property accumulated by deposed dictators (Gómez in Venezuela and Trujillo in the Dominican Republic). The effects of nationalization have been neither as bad as its adversaries predicted nor as good as its advocates promised. In general, they may be considered no worse—frequently they are better—than those brought about by the former owners.

The existence of nationalized enterprises and others with public capital poses a problem both for the labor movement and for the governments concerned. In most countries, the law forbids unions and strikes by civil servants. The question is whether workers in nationalized or publicly owned companies should be considered as government employees. There have been cases in which strikes by workers in nationalized industries have been ruled illegal, and others in which their conflicts have been negotiated in accordance with labor laws applying to nongovernment workers. There are no uniform criteria, and the government's action depends on its character: if it is rightist or a dictatorship, it forbids strikes in nationalized industries; if it is leftist, it tolerates them.

Finance

Latin America's financial system—money, banking, taxes, budgets—is an anachronism that has undergone no important modification in this century, although there have been some changes in detail. It may be considered the product of the prevailing social structure, the colonial tradition, and foreign influence, which is very powerful in this area.

Until the early twentieth century, bimetallism prevailed, to such an extent that there were frequent strikes to obtain wages in gold. Gold or silver coins circulated, depending on the market price of the metal. Although bills were issued after independence (because the departing *gachupines* took with them most of the hard money), they were not general until the end of the century; bills were generally issued by commercial banks, except in a few cases in which they were issued by the government.

Today, the Latin American currencies have different names (and values): peso in Mexico, Argentina, Colombia, Cuba, the Dominican Republic, and Uruguay; quetzal in Guatemala; sol in Peru; lempira in Honduras; gourde in Haiti; escudo in Chile; bolívar in Venezuela; boliviano in Bolivia; cruzeiro in Brazil; colón in El Salvador and Costa Rica; sucre in Ecuador; guarani in Paraguay; córdoba in Nicaragua; balboa in Panama. In general, these bills are not redeemable, although the governments hold in reserve guarantees in an amount equivalent to about 25 per cent of the total bills in circulation.

After the economic crisis of 1929, the pound sterling and the dollar were accepted as reserve along with gold; today, the bulk of the reserves of Latin American countries is in dollars. Except for a few countries with free exchange (Mexico, Panama), the majority have kept control of the exchange, prohibiting the export of gold, etc., since 1930.

Large foreign-exchange reserves were accumulated during World War II, but after the war, when the United States resumed its exporting, most of them were rapidly exhausted, not in the purchase of capital goods (such as machinery and tractors) but for luxury items (such as automobiles). From January to May of 1948, a period in which trade with the industrial countries was normalized, Latin America's reserves fell by $2.6 billion. The situation was so serious that nearly all the countries imposed controls on imports and stiffened those on exchange.

The Latin American countries are members of the International Monetary Fund (IMF) and abide by its rules to fix the rate of exchange of their currencies. Only the Mexican peso has been considered by the Fund as support money (since 1965). For modifications in the rate of exchange above 10 per cent, the consent of the Fund is required. Devaluations are frequent, since the market quotation on the national currency is often different—nearly always lower—from the official rate, and there comes a moment at which it is necessary to close the gap in order to discourage the black market in foreign exchange. This market flourishes in all countries that have control of the exchange and especially in those that suffer from persistent inflation (Chile, Brazil, Bolivia, Argentina).

In these countries, as in some that have balance-of-trade problems, the control of exchange is also used to regulate foreign trade, especially to reduce imports. With this end in view, extremely complicated systems with different rates of exchange were established, according to the end for which the foreign money was intended: high rates for the purchase of luxury goods, lower for necessity items. There was a special rate for the purchase of books, etc. This, of course, left room for an active market in influence, and not a little corruption. This system is tending to disappear, owing to the influence of the International Monetary Fund.

The banking system has made little contribution to economic development in Latin America. The first bank in Latin America was the Monte de Piedad, established in Mexico in 1775 for the pawning of articles, but the first with the true functions of a bank was the Bank of Brazil, founded in 1807. Banks did not become general until the second half of the nineteenth century, when various foreign banks—especially British ones—began to open branches in Latin American cities, chiefly for the use of foreign investors. Eventually, banks were established by the Americans, Canadians, Germans, French, and Italians, as well. These banks were founded mostly with native capital, because in many countries landowners who were unwilling to invest in industry were ready to enter the banking business. This gave banking certain characteristics of the oligarchy; even today, it is helpful in obtaining a bank loan to be a personal friend of the director, to be a member of the same club, or to have a prestigious name.

Most banks are of the commercial type, designed to accept savings and charge accounts and to make short-term loans—at high interest rates (8–12 per cent). But the scarcity of savings, and the fact that checks are not used to pay small bills—many shops refuse to accept checks and, to cash one, identification is required—mean that only the well-to-do have regular accounts.

Commercial banks—unlike those in the United States—may

also make long-term loans and even facilitate operations of a monopolistic type ("cornering" the market). But they tend to extend credit to persons and institutions that have already obtained it, or who have some prestige, rather than to those who can offer only new ideas and the ability to realize them. Very little industrial activity is initiated with bank funds. Often, a bank will be associated with certain activities: extending credit for sugar industries, for example, or fishing interests.

Central banks were established very late: the first, in Uruguay, dates from 1896. Now all the countries, except Brazil and Panama, have them; the majority were founded about 1920. A central bank is directly controlled by the government, which owns it in concert with other banks and with public shareholders. Although they usually accept general banking business, their principal functions are to issue money, administer the gold reserve and foreign exchange, fix interest rates, and accept the deposits of private banks, which the law usually demands as a guarantee for current accounts. In many places, these deposits are used to direct credit toward certain economic activities. On the other hand, rediscounting is unusual. Finally, the central bank receives the deposits which, in many countries, importers are required to make to guarantee payment of the hard money with which they will pay for their purchases abroad; commercial banks usually give credit for these deposits.

The inadequacy of the banking system has produced a series of special financing institutions, such as mortgage banks for building, for investment in new industries (Nacional Financiera of Mexico, Corporación de Fomento of Venezuela and Chile), for agriculture (Banco de Crédito Ejidal of Mexico), for mining (the Banco Minero of Bolivia), and even for unions (the Banco Obrero of Argentina, Honduras, and Venezuela, with capital from union funds). There are also banks for cooperatives, which began to be general about 1960.

All these institutions depend upon government funds and the income from the issue of bonds backed by the government. Since the stock exchanges have a very limited importance in Latin America, these bonds are almost the only means by which the public can participate in the financing of the economy.

The Treasury

Until World War II, Latin American budgets were very small. At the beginning of the century, the largest budget, drawn up by Mexican president Porfirio Díaz, was about $40 million. It should be realized that spending for the economic infrastructure and for public services is very recent in Latin America. Except for the schools and a few hospitals and mental institutions, which were receiving government funds by the second half of the nineteenth century, the governments did not begin to undertake this kind of activity until after World War II.

The share of the national income absorbed by governments for their operation is higher in Latin America than in the industrialized countries. The average is 25 per cent (as against 17 per cent in the United States), although a few countries have a much lower percentage (Argentina, 11.1; Brazil, 10.1; Mexico, 8.1).

If we divide government expenditures into three main groups—social services (public works, education, health, etc.); administrative (courts, presidency, legislature, police, etc.); and military (pay of officers and soldiers, arms, etc.)—it can be said that there is a tendency for the first group to increase slowly, and for the other two groups to increase even more slowly. Of course, the high administrative costs do not signify high salaries for government employees, or even for the military; the bureaucracy is ill paid, bureaucrats frequently hold several posts, and administrative immorality is not uncommon; but for these very reasons, the bureaucracy is inefficient and therefore its numbers are considerable and constantly growing.

The small amount of expenditures for social welfare explains the relatively low government debt. On average, the debt reaches about 20 per cent of the national income. The most backward countries have the smallest debt, because with an antiquated fiscal policy and a low level of productivity, they find it difficult to obtain loans. In the last thirty years, Latin American governments have been abandoning the custom, popular in the past century, of issuing bonds on the foreign market, and the greater part of the debt is internal.

Mexico, however, thanks to its exceptional solvency, resumed issuing bonds abroad in 1964.

Although the states (or provinces) and the municipalities have their own finances, in reality they depend in great measure on subsidies from the central government; sometimes, the latter assumes the collection of local taxes, which are later turned over to the city, not always in money but often in services.

The chief source of government income in Latin America is indirect taxes. In Latin America as a whole, indirect taxes contribute 61.8 per cent of the total (compared with 35 per cent in the United States), direct taxes 31.6 per cent, social-security payments about 6 per cent.*

The indirect tax is, then, in its various forms—customs, sales tax, official monopoly—the principal source of government income. Among other sources of income are the profits from nationalized enterprises; the profits (when they are not losses) from operations carried on by the government in the exchange market (usually in Brazil and Argentina); also, at times, the difference between the price paid by the government to producers and the price obtained on the world market, when a monopoly is established on the export of certain products (as with wheat in Argentina under Perón). The national lotteries also contribute funds (generally, not more than 10 per cent of the total spent on them), which are normally used to finance welfare and educational activities.

Income taxes are in existence almost everywhere, although in most countries they have been in effect only a few years. Direct taxes on land are provided by law in some countries, but they are very low; in most countries, they either do not exist or are not collected.

Indirect taxes, of course, affect the poor and middle-income groups much more than the rich. It is estimated that the poorest 50 per cent of the Latin American population pay 13

* In Ecuador, indirect taxes contribute 76 per cent of the government's income, direct taxes 14 per cent; the rest comes from various sources. In Colombia, Honduras, Guatemala, and Nicaragua, indirect taxes account for more than 80 per cent of the budgetary income; in El Salvador, 71 per cent; in Costa Rica, 60 per cent; in Bolivia, 72 per cent. In Venezuela and Peru, indirect taxes contribute slightly more than 30 per cent; this does not mean that direct taxes are higher than indirect, but only that the government collects a higher percentage of its income from other sources.

per cent of their income in taxes; the 45 per cent whom we could classify as the middle sectors pay 20 per cent; whereas the richest 3 per cent pay 17 per cent, and the very richest 2 per cent pay 20 per cent. This means that for the lowest income groups the tax system is retrogressive, and that for the highest income groups it is only moderately progressive. (In the United States, the counterpart of the richest group pays about 55 per cent.)

In recent years, as the result of some fiscal reforms, there has been an increase in the income from direct taxes and a small decrease in the income from indirect taxes. But resistance to authentic fiscal reform or truly progressive taxation is so great that many economists have suggested that funds be obtained by such indirect means as taxes on luxury items.

To some extent, fiscal policy has been used as an instrument for guiding the economy. This is done especially by means of tax exemptions for new industries in fields considered profitable to the country, or by exemptions on the import of capital goods or raw materials. Exemptions have also been granted on profits that were reinvested. At times, exemptions have been granted to encourage development in certain sections of the country, for example, the Amazonian jungles of Peru, where new enterprises have not paid customs duties or taxes of any kind. This system lends itself to injustices and favoritism, as well as lamentations by industrialists when the moment comes for them to pay taxes. But it seems to have had favorable results.

For a time, it was believed that agrarian reform could be realized by levying heavy taxes on land—especially idle land—since the owners would prefer getting rid of their lands to paying high taxes on them; but the lack of statistical data on the size of estates, and the deficiencies of fiscal administration, nullified the effect of the laws in those cases in which they were made and their enforcement attempted.

Inflation

The financial problem that harasses many Latin American governments, and for which no solution has yet been found, is inflation.

A few countries have experienced accelerated development without significant inflation (Mexico and Venezuela); a few have experienced slow growth accompanied by inflation (Argentina, Bolivia, and Chile); still others have experienced both rapid development and considerable inflation (Brazil). In the period 1945–60, Argentina had an annual economic growth rate of about 2.6 per cent and an average annual increase in the cost of living of 185; Chile, with a growth rate of 3.1, had an increase in living costs of 340; Brazil, with a growth rate of 5.4, had an increase of living cost of 57 (much more in recent years). In Bolivia, the rate of growth was 1.1 and the rise in living costs, 1,250.

Depreciation of the currency is general: the annual rate of depreciation, in the decade 1955–1965, was 29.7 in Brazil, 23.4 in Argentina, 22.5 in Chile, 21.1 in Bolivia, 9.8 in Colombia, 8.1 in Peru, 3.7 in Mexico, 1.2 in Venezuela.*

In a few countries—Bolivia, Chile, Brazil—new bills have been issued (the boliviano in Bolivia, escudo in Chile, nuevo cruzeiro in Brazil). These are generally composed of 1,000 of the old units. It was believed that the new currency would have a beneficial psychological effect, although everyone continued to calculate by the old; but at least it saved time in banks and shops in counting change, and made it possible to carry about smaller bundles of bills. (In Brazil, at a time when a streetcar ride cost 100 cruzeiros, five-cruzeiro bills, worth no more than one-quarter of a cent, were still in circulation.)

There are several schools of thought on the problem of inflation. What we might call the traditionalist school—which in Latin America is called "monetarist"—has for its chief exponents the International Monetary Fund and the Brazilian economist Roberto Campos. This school holds that inflation—which is a product of bad fiscal policies, deficit financing, and an increase in the amount of money in circulation—is always harmful. This school maintains that inflation prohibits economic development. The IMF has come to make anti-inflation plans a condition of application for its aid. As

* The American dollar was worth the following in 1950 and 1965:

	1950	1965
Argentine peso	14.0	250
Brazilian cruzeiro	19.7	1,850
Chilean peso	72.5	3,800
Colombian peso	3.0	20
Mexican peso	8.64	12.50
Peruvian sol	14.95	26.82
Venezuelan bolívar	3.35	4.50

a result of this, Peru, Bolivia, Chile, Argentina, Brazil, and Colombia drew up stabilization plans; in general, these were not successful. The plans usually put the burden of the austerity policy on salaries—which are more easily controlled than prices and profits—and this has lead to accusations (when the limitations are enforced) that the government is acting for the benefit of business. The existence of the IMF is very useful to government officials who are trying to enforce an austerity policy, since they can answer protesters that the fault lies with the Fund, which, in the public eye, is identified with the United States.

The second school of thought on inflation, known as the structuralist, is supported by economists of the ECLA. This school views inflation as a phenomenon to be expected—though not always to be desired—in every stage of development, since it is caused by the interrelation of the different economic sectors. Business, instead of absorbing salary increases, social-security premiums, and the like, passes them on to the consumer in price rises, causing an expansion of credit which, in turn, brings new rises in wages and prices. The chief victims of inflation are the peasants who, as a consequence of inflation, reduce their crop output, which in turn produces new price rises. And so we have the spiral of prices and wages. At the same time there appear inflation and an unsold surplus of goods. This, say the structuralists, can be explained only by the fact that money—that is, buying power —is in the hands of a small group in each county. There are structuralists who maintain that inflation actually fosters development—since, when more money is available, it is invested—provided inflation is kept under control. In the struggle against excessive inflation, the structuralists prefer a policy that limits profits and prices rather than wages. Up to now, this policy has rarely been put into effect.

In view of the practical ineffectiveness of the two positions described above, a third position arose: the institutionalist, which holds that inflation is largely the product of institutional decisions and can be combated by institutional decisions. The latter should be exercised, particularly, in the form of qualitive controls of credit. But if this has produced some results in cases of occasional or limited inflation, it does not appear to have combated important inflations.

It should not be forgotten, however, that prices in Latin

America have never been stable, nor has the value of money; and that money has always been regarded as a simple medium of exchange, never as something that should be accumulated —perhaps, as a consequence of the instability of prices. Saving, until very recently, has usually taken the form of buying land. This leads us to another aspect of the Latin American economy: financing.

Financing

The fundamental element in all development is capital formation. Its importance will be clear if one realizes that to create a new job it is necessary to invest $5,000, and that every year nearly 1 million persons enter the Latin American labor market as a result of the population growth.

Development may be financed either by making the rich pay (by investment, reinvestment, taxes, etc.), or by making the poor pay (by underconsumption and unpaid labor), or by a combination of both. In the nineteenth century, development in Latin America was financed by foreign investment and by underconsumption on the part of rural and lower-income urban groups. Local investment and reinvestment were very low; the greater part of the income of high-income groups was spent for luxury goods, deposits abroad, or the acquisition of more land. Later, domestic investment began to develop and underconsumption, especially by the urban groups, began to lessen though not to disappear. The middle class, as its living conditions improved, began to save, although in a limited degree; at the same time, there was an increase in private foreign investment, to which, after World War II, was added international public investment (by international or national organizations).

But all these methods of capital accumulation have not been sufficient to give Latin America the mass of capital it needs for rapid and balanced development. This has led to the formation of limited areas of industrialization—the São Paulo region in Brazil, Buenos Aires in Argentina, Mexico City and Monterrey in Mexico, Santiago and Concepción in Chile, Lima in Peru; to the growth of industries that are directed toward the only existent market, that of the upper- and middle-income urban groups; and to a general stagnation in agriculture.

The economic habits of the Latin Americans, the structure of Latin American industry, and the policies of the governments do not appear suited to stimulating the accumulation of surpluses. Here, too, tradition is important. Before the Spaniards came, saving consisted in the accumulation of immovable capital, like jewels and plumes; during colonial times, in the accumulation of lands which, since they were only partially cultivated, represented another way of immobilizing capital. During the colonial period, Latin America was in fact an exporter of capital—in the form of gold and silver—and the Spaniards who returned to Spain after independence took with them almost all their capital. Only the Church and the great landholders had money available; they used it to buy more land, which drove the price up and converted it into a form of sterilized capital.

The great landholders have generally not invested within their countries but instead try to send as much of their money as possible abroad. It has been estimated that the amount of capital in flight from Latin America each year exceeds all that is received in various forms of aid. Personal savings are very low, partly because of the low income of most of the population and partly because of the ostentatious habits of the well-to-do.

Business enterprises, many of which belong to an individual, a family, or a small group, tend to distribute high dividends rather than reinvest them. The average of reinvestment is less than 25 per cent of profits (as compared to about 50 per cent in the United States). The insurance companies are not very powerful financially (since their market is relatively limited), and the law generally allows them to invest abroad, which they do not fail to do. The limited development of the stock corporations and investments banks and the scarcity of credit available to small and medium-sized business (which could be a source of reinvestment) are other causes of the low rate of accumulation. The stock exchanges are small and without economic influence.

The Latin American governments—the dictatorial ones, especially—have devoted a great part of their surplus to erecting public monuments. Another part is sent abroad. Finally, one share (not very large, to be sure) has been spent on caring for a population whose life span was short and therefore did not return the investment made in its education, health, and welfare.

Finally, private foreign capital, by seeking exemptions and privileges, has aggravated the situation and made its solution more difficult.

Various proposals have been made to deal with the problem of lack of capital. A study prepared by the ECLA revealed that the 5 per cent of the population with the highest income consumes 15 times more per family than the 50 per cent of the population with the lowest income; if this difference were reduced to eleven times, and the amount saved were invested, the rate of increase in per capita investment would rise 1–3 per cent; if the difference were reduced to nine times, the rate of increase would rise by 4 per cent.

Few economists acknowledge publicly that corruption, especially in upper government echelons, has created considerable fortunes and can be a factor in capital formation. It is not the most honorable way, but undoubtedly no worse than encouraging underconsumption—and it achieves quicker results.

One remedy to the problem of lack of capital has been the creation of so-called financing institutions to channel existent savings into investments. To attract capital, these financing institutions pay a high interest rate—as much as 12 per cent a year—and they are pledged to redeem on sight the bonds they issue, which makes money still dearer. The governments have also tried to improve the situation through official financing companies; public investment; the issuance of bonds whose proceeds are intended for industrial promotion; guaranteeing—for instance, with government bonds—the credit operations of commercial banks; and even guaranteeing certain foreign investments.

In recent years, there has been an increase in investment.*

---

* In Ecuador, for example, investment amounted to 12.6 of the total GNP in the five-year period 1945–49 (none of it public investment); these figures had risen to 17.0 per cent in the five-year period 1960–65 (30 per cent of this investment was public). In El Salvador, the 9 per cent of the five-year period 1945–49 rose to 12 in the last five years (19 per cent of this public). In Bolivia, the increase was from 16.3 in 1945–49 to 34 in the last five years (32 per cent of this public). In Venezuela, owing to a drop in oil investments and the flight of capital because of fiscal reform, investment fell from 30.1 per cent of the GNP in 1945–49 to 18 per cent in 1964 (50 per cent of this was public). The proportion is comparable in other countries. Charles W. Anderson, *Politics and Economic Change in Latin America* (Princeton, N.J., 1967), p. 324.

But it has not been sufficient and, furthermore, is not a result of any diminishing difference of incomes between the two poles of society. From 1960 to 1965, investment increased by 3.3 per cent a year; but if the population increase is taken into account, it will be seen that little more than 0.5 per cent a year was added to Latin American capital.

Production of Goods

It is generally believed that Latin America is an immensely rich continent. The reality does not bear this out. The wealth that has been exploited is probably only a small part of that still undiscovered, but much of this wealth belongs to categories that are losing their economic usefulness because they are being replaced by synthetics. Moreover, raw materials are so widely dispersed that it is often difficult and costly to exploit them. Finally, the fact that the bulk of Latin American wealth derives from raw materials subjects the countries to dependence upon the world market, in which the prices of these raw materials tend to fall. In view of this, Latin America cannot be regarded as "immensely rich," although certainly if its riches were exploited in a rational manner, and not by merely adhering to traditional forms and the interests of small groups, the living standards of Latin Americans would be higher and the prospects of progress greater.

More than 50 per cent of the Latin American labor force is employed in agriculture; industry absorbs somewhat more than 15 per cent; mining, 4 per cent; and services (transportation, distribution, banks, bureaucracy, army, etc.), 25 per cent. But only 20 per cent of the gross national product is derived from agriculture; 24 per cent is derived from industry, 6 per cent from mining, 3 per cent from construction, and 47 per cent from services.*

Moreover, although industrial production increased by 97 per cent in the decade 1951–60, agricultural production increased by only 42 per cent in the same period. (In this same period, cattle-raising increased by not quite 15 per cent.)

---

* The statistics in this section are taken from the *Boletín Estadístico de América Latina,* prepared by the Economic Commission for Latin America (New York, 1966). Because figures change rapidly, owing to technical progress and population growth, those cited should be taken chiefly as indications of predominant trends in the Latin American economy.

Only in a few countries—Ecuador, El Salvador, Mexico, Peru, Venezuela, and parts of Brazil—has agricultural production surpassed the growth of population, and in several cases this increase has been in products for export and not for domestic consumption.

It is significant that agricultural products whose production has increased most rapidly are those intended for export (coffee, cotton) and that those whose production has increased most slowly are staples, such as wheat and corn. In Central America, for example, agricultural production increased by nearly 50 per cent between 1952 and 1965; but in the same period, production of foodstuffs decreased by 15 per cent. Many Latin American countries have to import foodstuffs: Cuba, Chile, Bolivia, and Venezuela import more than 25 per cent of their foodstuffs; only Argentina, Mexico, Guatemala, and Haiti produce more than 95 per cent of the food consumed in the country.

Low agricultural production keeps the Latin American gross product low, even when production rises in other branches. It produces an imbalance between urban and rural standards, as well as an inadequate development of the rural market, which in turn limits the possibilities of industrial expansion and has caused an exodus to the cities that has had serious consequences. Finally, it is the determining factor in causing malnutrition and in the waste of trade balances in the importation of foodstuffs—or in both at once.

Of course, agricultural production is low not because the peasants are lazy but because the system of landowning— latifundism and minifundism—and the scarcity of modern mechanized cultivation result in underproduction; because of lack of interest on the part of owners and peasants in increasing productivity; and because of concentration on a few crops in each country (monocultivation).

The indifference toward technical progress in agriculture is shown in many ways. In many places in Latin America, wooden plows are still used, and human beings do the pulling. Latin America has only 6 per cent of the world's tractors (about 500,000 units), an average of one for every 578 acres under cultivation (as against one for every 102 acres in the United States). U.S. factories for producing tractors and tools have been established in Brazil (with a production of 15,000 tractors a year), Mexico (7,500 units a year), and Argentina (10,000 units), but these factories work at only one-third of capacity.

There is also little use of fertilizers: only 2.4 pounds are used per acre in Latin America, as against 56.5 pounds per acre in Japan, 22.6 in the European countries, and 11.8 in the United States.

Irrigation, although it is increasing, is not sufficient to combat either the frequent floods or the droughts. There are regions, like the Brazilian Northeast, that have been devastated by droughts that have caused the death of half a million people; this is in a region in which half of the land belongs to 3 per cent of the owners, and 80 per cent of the population owns no land at all and is thus unable to accumulate reserves of food or money against periods of drought. Only Mexico has a systematic irrigation policy, with great systems of the type of the Tennessee Valley Authority, as well as ditches dug with pick and shovel.

Because hillsides are generally cultivated without terracing, there has been extensive erosion. There has also been considerable deforestation, caused by the lack of coal, gas, and electricity in rural regions; it is necessary to go deeper and deeper into the forests to find good wood. Reforestation policies are very feeble; the lumber companies are often more powerful than the organizations responsible for the protection of the forests.

Unfortunately, none of this induces students to dedicate themselves to the study of agriculture, which is taught in old and antiquated schools; agricultural extension services are small and often inadequate; agricultural credit services are rudimentary; and the encouragement of agricultural cooperatives is a bureaucratic function undertaken without enthusiasm and opposed by the landowners.

In the past, there was significant foreign investment in agriculture; before 1960, investment in agriculture accounted for half the U.S. investment in Latin America. (The fact that this investment did not transform agriculture, except in a few cases, shows both how great is the need for capital and how little influence foreign capital has had on the over-all Latin American economic picture.) But foreign investment decreased sharply after the expropriations effected by the

Castro government in 1960. In 1965, investment in agriculture was not quite 10 per cent of total investment in Latin America. It has been estimated that to increase agricultural production by 5 per cent annually (which would raise the annual per capita income of the rural population from $50 to $60) would require a supplementary investment of from 60 to 100 per cent of today's total within ten years.

Fishing is little developed, perhaps because Latin Americans (like the Spaniards, Aztecs, and Incas) are not a seafaring people. Only in Peru has an important fishing industry developed, and its sailors are mostly Basques from Spain.

There has been a significant increase in mineral production, however. The extraction of iron ore has increased five and one-half times in the last fifteen years, that of copper 39 per cent, and that of zinc, 34 per cent. Sulphur, formerly negligible, is now important. The production of oil has increased 81 per cent (with Venezuela producing 80 per cent of the total in Latin America). In Bolivia, Chile, Peru, and Venezuela, mining is the basic export activity, although most of the mines belong to foreign companies.

Industrial growth has been generally important, and in a few places—Mexico and parts of Brazil—spectacular.* But still more interesting is the fact that the industrial structure has changed at the same time. From 1955 to 1965, light industry's share of total industrial production fell from 60 to 51 per cent, and heavy industry's share rose from 40 to 49 per cent. The production of steel, for example, has increased to three times the 1950 figure; that of cement and paper has more than doubled; that of chemical and petroleum products is 130 times what it was in 1950. The iron-and-steel industry can now satisfy 75 per cent of Latin America's demand.† But the per capita consumption of steel is still low: 49.5 kilos per year, against 29.3 kilos in 1952 (300 in the United States and 132 as an average world figure). It is estimated that by 1975, the total steel production will be 27.9 million tons

---

* Industry accounts for 27 per cent of the gross national product in Mexico; for 26 per cent in Brazil; 21 per cent in Argentina; 17 per cent in Chile and Peru; and 16 per cent in Colombia.

† Brazil produces 35 per cent of Latin America's steel; Mexico, 27 per cent; Argentina, 21 per cent; Chile, 7 per cent; Venezuela, 4 per cent; Colombia, 3 per cent; and Peru and Uruguay, 2 per cent each.

(it was 11.5 million in 1964), if this is preceded by an investment of about $5 billion.

Latin American nations have also begun to manufacture machinery and automobiles. In 1960, Argentina, Brazil, and Mexico—the only automobile-producing countries—turned out 222,000 vehicles; in 1965, they produced 504,000. Nearly all imported automobiles are assembled within the various other countries, and production of parts for them has begun. Assemblage of cars amounted to 287,000 in 1960 and 574,000 in 1965. Three-fifths of these were passenger cars, two-fifths commercial vehicles. Yet in 1966, there were still only about 6.3 million motor vehicles in all of Latin America.

But there is not enough growth of light industry, which produces articles for everyday use. Textile production, for example, has remained stationary. It is the lower-income groups that suffer from this, since the well-to-do tend to use imported fabrics. The phenomenon is similar—although less acute and for different reasons—to that which prevailed in the Soviet Union during the Stalin regime.

Economists are beginning to predict that industrial growth cannot continue indefinitely as long as Latin America does not have available domestic markets able to absorb its industrial production, at the same time that it is unable, for reasons of technique and transportation, to compete with the industrial countries. Technological progress has been considerable in recent years—especially since 1955—but only in the few industries that employ computers and are planning automation. Only 10 per cent of the economically active population is employed in enterprises making use of advanced techniques, which is one reason why the average production of the Latin American worker is only 15–30 per cent that of the European or American worker.

Many Latin American industries work at half or less of capacity, and additional ones cannot be created because there would be no market for their products. Hence, if industrialization is to continue, there must be a better distribution of income, and the entry into the economics of consumption of the great masses of the Latin American population, who now are only an element in production.

Thus there are two fundamental economic problems in

Latin America today, and like all Latin American problems they are not purely economic but social and political: the problem of the agrarian structure, which must be solved by agrarian reform; and the problem of the commercial structure, which must be solved domestically by economic integration, and abroad through new international terms of trade.

Foreign Capital

Between the two world wars, Great Britain and the United States, together, accounted for 92 per cent of the foreign capital invested in Latin America, and foreign capital accounted for nearly half of all investments, national and foreign.

Moreover, foreign enterprises—sometimes a single one— often controlled production of the basic export of a country. Thus (until 1964), Chile's copper was controlled almost entirely by two American firms, Anaconda and Kennecott; Bolivian tin (until 1952), by three firms: Aramayo, Hoschild, and Patiño (these were exceptional in not being originally foreign). Mexico's oil (until 1938) was in British, and, in lesser degree, U.S. hands; Venezuela's, to the present day, is chiefly American-owned. The minerals produced in Peru, in Cuba (until 1959), and a large part of those of Mexico were controlled by foreign firms.

In Central America, Colombia, Ecuador, and the Antilles, three U.S. companies—United Fruit, Standard, and Grace—still control the export of fruit, and foreign firms control cotton exports in Mexico and Central America. (Owing to the sugar-quota system, the United States has also played a decisive role in the economy of lands whose major export crop is sugar: the Dominican Republic and pre-Castro Cuba.)

World War II caused a rapid loss of the power of British capital in Latin America and the temporary disappearance of Japanese, Italian, and German investments, which almost everywhere were attached by the governments. American capital became dominant, although after about 1955 Italian, Japanese, French, and German investments rose again.

In recent years, however, there has been a relative decline in U.S. investments. In 1950, U.S. world investments reached $11.8 billion, of which $4.4 billion was invested in Latin

America. In 1965, these figures had risen, respectively, to $49.2 billion and $9.3 billion; in other words, although American world investments had more than quadrupled, those in Latin America had barely doubled.* The relative decline in U.S. investments was partly due to restrictions placed upon foreign capital.

During World War II, the Latin American countries were left without many products that had issued from the belligerents. This led to the rapid creation and improvisation of local industries. When the war was over, the local industries found themselves at a disadvantage in competition with American and, later, with European and Japanese industries. The native industrialists were desirous of official protection and resentful of the privileges earlier conceded to foreign capital, which the latter refused to surrender. This gave rise to rivalry between national and foreign industry, with considerable political and economic implications.

It is often said—in the United States as well as in Latin America—that foreign investors earn larger profits than national ones. The statistics do not confirm this. The profits of foreign firms are not, in general, higher than those of similar national firms, although they were in certain periods and in certain fields during the nineteenth century. But some of the practices of foreign firms have afforded a basis for hostility to foreign capital, even though often only a minority of foreign firms are guilty of these practices. For example, foreign firms will sell low-cost medicines at high prices, introduce as "new" products for which there is no longer an American market, or use equipment that has been discarded as obsolete in the United States.

Another criticism of foreign companies is that they export raw materials to subsidiary enterprises at a price below the market price in order to lower their taxes. In Venezuela, when the dictatorship of Pérez Jiménez fell in 1959, an investigation was opened into iron-mining companies, which

---

* Of the direct U.S. investment in Latin America in 1965, $3 billion was in oil, $1.9 billion in manufacturing, $1.1 billion in mining, $839 million in trade, $709 million in public utilities, and the remainder in agriculture and other activities. The country that has received the most American capital is Venezuela ($2.8 billion); it is followed by Brazil ($1.1 billion); Mexico ($873 million); Argentina ($797 million); and Chile ($768 million). The others have received less than $500 million each; at the bottom of the list are Uruguay with $53 million and Bolivia with $32 million.

were selling ore to their American parent firms below the market price.

Another objectionable trait imputed to foreign capital—and with justice, although native capital is almost equally guilty—is that it is invested in enterprises yielding the quickest profit, although they may not be those most necessary to the progress of the country. It is also criticized for adjusting production in accordance with the interests of the country in which the capital originated, or of the parent firm, without considering the needs of the host country.

Another custom that exasperates Latin American businessmen is the tendency of American businessmen to invest private American capital in national enterprises that are already flourishing—thus eliminating the risk entailed in investing in a new enterprise.

Mining interests are rightfully reproached for exporting raw ore instead of building refining plants in the host country, which would provide income and jobs to nationals.

Foreign firms are also blamed for the intolerable living conditions of certain workers (rubber, chicle, etc.), who are victims not only of the climate but of the greed of the middlemen, the only ones with whom the companies deal in buying raw materials.

The result of this mixture of emotional attitudes and justified criticism has been a series of measures, in nearly every country, designed to bring foreign capital under control. Because foreign capital, during the nineteenth century, considered itself entitled to special treatment, most of these measures have taken the form of requiring foreign investors to submit to the laws of the host country and to renounce the protection of their own country in the case of a dispute.

Although regulations vary from country to country, they are usually directed toward preventing foreign companies from having an advantage over national ones, or from being in a position to influence the country's internal affairs. Generally, the foreign investor is considered a national in business matters, in both his obligations and his rights. Mexico permits the conduct of business only by foreigners whose countries allow Mexicans the same privilege. Panama limits the opening of shops to citizens of countries whose firms in Panama extend job equality to Panamanians. Haiti forbids trade (not industry) and ownership of land by foreigners. In nearly every country, foreigners are forbidden to own property along the frontiers or coastlines. Corporations are sometimes subject to special taxes (in Brazil, a surtax of 15 per cent if profits are sent out of the country). Some countries require that a percentage of the capital of a firm must be national (Mexico requires 51 per cent).

One of the most strictly regulated aspects of foreign investment is that of personnel, for it irritates Latin Americans that the best posts in foreign firms are held by foreigners. There are laws that require that 80–95 per cent of the personnel of a foreign firm be citizens of the host country, or that nationals are to receive a certain percentage of the payroll, or that a foreigner may not be hired if a qualified national is available.

Regulations on the mining industry are similar in all countries. Very large firms are sometimes required to pay a heavy tax on production as a condition of the concession (in Venezuela, this tax is now 60 per cent in the oil industry).

The costs of services have also been made subject to regulation. At times, these have been prejudicial to the public utilities, which until shortly before World War II never paid the taxes stipulated in their concessions. For political reasons, governments have nearly always refused to allow price increases, and the companies, in turn, have restricted their services, with the result that the public has been the loser.

Some countries require government permission for the investment of foreign capital, or place restrictions on the sending abroad of profits and of the capital itself. Other countries have signed agreements with the United States to compensate investors if their property is confiscated or if it is impossible to transfer their profits abroad. In some foreign-aid agreements, the U.S. government gives guarantees to investors in the country it is aiding.

Some Latin American governments, especially the dictatorships, offer privileges and exemptions to foreign capital because they expect foreign capitalists, in turn, to exert pressure on Washington to support a government that guarantees such privileges. With their usual lack of foresight, foreign investors prefer such governments to democratic regimes that will not grant privileges but whose reforms will broaden the market and, in the end, create a climate as advantageous to foreign as to native capital.

Opinions differ about the true value of U.S. investment to Latin America. American businessmen point out that in 1962, for instance, U.S. investments added $1.5 billion to the Latin American gross national product (or 94 per cent of the increase of the GNP for that year). But some economists have pointed out that from 1946 to 1964, debt service took $13.6 billion out of Latin America, so that, in that period, the proceeds from investment returned to the United States more money than it invested. Even if we subtract the amount of American aid in the same period, we still find that $1.4 billion went from Latin America to the United States.*

Obviously, there are contradictory views on the role of foreign investment in Latin America. At best, the feeling toward it is ambivalent, and the tendency today is to prefer foreign public investment to private investment.

Foreign Trade

Exports constitute about 16 per cent of the gross national product of Latin America as a whole (as compared to 4 per cent in the United States). Raw materials account for 91 per cent of all Latin American exports. Manufactured goods account for 73 per cent of all imports; the rest are semifinished products and some raw materials (especially hydrocarbon combustibles).

For a long time, Europe was the outlet for Latin American exports. At first, these were precious metals; when the Industrial Revolution opened up markets for other raw materials, the products of farm and ranch were exported. When the United States entered the market, exports were diversified, but they lost that diversity when the United States became the chief buyer. Thus, Latin America's economy has depended not so much on fluctuations in the price of raw materials (as Latin Americans themselves generally contend)

---

* See J. Peter Grace, "Implications of Latin American Imports of Private Capital," in Norman A. Bailey (ed.), *Latin America: Politics, Economics, and Hemispheric Security* (New York, 1965), p. 101; and Wendell C. Gordon, *The Economy of Latin America* (New York, 1950), p. 241.

as on the general progress of the world economy and, especially, on the needs and even the fashions of the industrialized countries. When the latter began to buy from Latin America, manufactured articles were not produced there; the ease with which raw materials were sold and the oligarchic character of the society—which gave power precisely to the producers of raw materials—prevented large-scale and persistent promotion of industrialization, and condemned Latin America to the role of exporter of raw materials, with all the difficulties this involved.

Today, one-fourth of Latin American exports are accounted for by oil and its by-products, 18 per cent by coffee, 9 per cent by sugar, 4 per cent by cotton, 2.5 per cent by copper, and 2.4 per cent by iron. These six products among them account for nearly three-fifths of all Latin American exports.* Meats, leather, wood, cacao, corn, wheat, tobacco, quebracho bark, lead, tin, zinc, and saltpetre are also exported in quantity.

The prices of these products have decreased by 9 per cent since 1950—before the rise caused by the Korean War—and 16 per cent as compared to 1955 prices, that is, the prices fixed by the demand brought about by that war. Coffee, cotton, lead, and zinc have fallen as much as 25 per cent.

Nearly half of Latin America's exports go to the United States, especially oil, coffee, copper, iron, lead, and cacao. But since World War II, Latin American exports to the United States have fallen by 50 per cent. In 1967 alone, they decreased by $300 million.

One-third of Latin America's exports go to Europe. Trade with the countries of the European Common Market is important; 10.2 per cent of its imports came from Latin America in 1958, and 8.9 per cent in 1966; but the value of these sales has risen 65 per cent in the same period, whereas the value of Latin American purchases from the Common Market has risen only 19 per cent. Since the growth of European population is not rapid, trade between Latin America and

---

* The fourth most important source of foreign income—after oil, coffee, and sugar—is tourism. The income from tourism differs in each country, depending mainly on its distance from the United States: thus, of the $500 million annual tourist industry, more than half goes to Mexico, Central America, and the Antilles. Tourists from three countries—Brazil, Argentina, and Venezuela—actually spend more abroad than these countries receive from tourism. Tourism is one form of foreign income that is likely to increase.

the Old World will not increase much, except in the area of oil and minerals.

The balance of Latin America's exports go to Latin American countries, to the countries of Asia, Africa, Oceania, and the Soviet bloc, and to Japan. There is little likelihood of a significant increase of trade with the Soviet bloc—not for political reasons but because these countries do not constitute a market for Latin American products, even less so since they have been obliged to absorb a good part of Cuba's exports. Notwithstanding, Peru, in early 1969, signed a trade agreement with the Soviet Union. This was more for diplomatic than for political reasons, that is, to put pressure on the United States in the conflict over the American oil company expropriated by the military government. Brazil and Ecuador also negotiated trade agreements with the Soviet Union in 1969.

Trade with Communist China is limited, and the balance is favorable to Latin America. In 1957, exports to China were worth $3.9 million and imports worth $1.3 million; in 1963, these figures had fallen to $3.4 million and $1.2 million, respectively.

From 1950 to 1965, the total of Latin American exports rose from $6.8 billion to $10.4 billion, an increase of 46 per cent. In the decade 1956–65, according to the Inter-American Development Bank, the value of Latin American exports increased on an average of 3.9 per cent a year; but that of the industrial countries increased by 10 per cent, of the Asian countries by 5.4 per cent, of the African countries by 15.2 per cent, and that of the world as a whole by 7.7 per cent.

An inevitable result of the downward trend of exports and their value was a very slow rise in imports, which increased, in the same decade, on an average of only 2.2 per cent a year. (The total value of imports rose from $6.874 billion in 1955 to $8.856 billion in 1965.) This was due in part to the increase in domestic production of manufactured articles, but in great part it is attributable to unfavorable trade balances.

Most of Latin America's imports are of industrial products. Consumer goods account for between one-fourth and one-third of the imports of each country, with perishables predominating. The remainder is divided between raw materials (especially metals) and machinery. Some countries also have to import building materials and food.

Nearly half of the imports come from the United States and Canada, with a tendency to decline; 29.2 per cent come from Western Europe and the Soviet Union; 14 per cent from other Latin American countries; 4.2 per cent from Japan; and the rest from Africa, Asia, and Oceania.

In general, Latin America has a favorable balance of payments vis-à-vis the countries of Western Europe, Asia, and Africa, and unfavorable vis-à-vis the countries of Eastern Europe. The balance with the United States has varied from year to year; since 1964, it has been unfavorable.

In general, it may be said that Latin America has not benefited from the vigorous growth of world trade. Since 1962, Latin America's share in world trade has dropped from 6.5 per cent to 5.4 per cent.

One reason for this is that a large share of Latin America's exports consists of foodstuffs, whose consumption varies little with changes in income; the increase of income in Europe did not increase the purchase of Latin American foods, and the United States imports hardly any Latin American foodstuffs except coffee, bananas, and sugar. Cereal and meat exports from Latin America have been especially affected. Cotton and tobacco have gained, but the exportation of Argentine and Uruguayan wool has dried up. A few countries have succeeded in manufacturing cottons for export, particularly to Africa and Asia, where there is a market for very cheap goods, which the more industrialized countries, with their well-paid labor, are not interested in producing.

Latin America has made considerable advances in the sale of minerals; the sale of iron has risen greatly, as has that of copper, since the iron reserves in Europe have begun to be exhausted and there are none of copper. Mexican lead has displaced Spanish, and Mexican and Peruvian zinc have replaced that of Australia in the world market. Bolivian tin, however, has slumped. Oil production and exportation, especially in Venezuela, has risen steadily, although that country is losing its world market because of the higher sulphur content of its oil, which makes it a source of air pollution. It would be necessary to submit it to a costly process to get rid of this handicap.

Many industrial countries find themselves at a disadvantage in Latin America because they are not markets for Latin American products. Switzerland, Holland, Belgium, and Japan, for example, can offer many articles to Latin America, but can buy relatively few goods—chiefly coffee, cotton, and tropical fruits. The larger countries, on the other hand—the United States, Great Britain, Italy, France, and West Germany—are at once buyers and sellers. The Latin American countries naturally tend to buy from those countries that buy from them—chiefly the United States, not only because of its proximity but because the economic ties are closer and the market more stable. However, some attempts are being made to diversify sales as well as purchases.

Clearly, Latin America's foreign trade cannot compensate for the instability and imbalance of its economy. If foreign trade does not increase, the situation of the mass of the people will deteriorate, for the ruling classes will not sacrifice their incomes but will compel the subordinate groups to accept sacrifices to make up for the lower profitability of exports.

Foreign Aid

To relieve its unfavorable trade balance, Latin American governments rely in no small measure on foreign aid.

Until President Truman put forth his Point Four program, Latin America had not received any foreign aid, with the exception of some credits extended by the Export-Import Bank to Brazil (to build blast furnaces) and to Chile (for a program of industrialization). When the Marshall Plan went into effect, some Latin American economists spoke of the usefulness of a similar program for their own countries. At the Inter-American Conference in Bogotá, in 1948, the Latin American countries proposed the establishment of an Inter-American Development Bank, but the United States curtly opposed this. (This Bank was eventually established in 1961.) The United States did help Latin American governments in several specific fields—sanitation and public health, for example—and the United Nations extended technical aid in cultural, agricultural, and sanitation fields; but foreign aid did not become important until 1956.

The volume of foreign aid has increased from an annual

average of $570 million in the period 1956–60 to $1.2 billion in the period 1961–65 (although when the amortization payment is discounted, these sums are reduced to a net disbursement of $360 million and $760 million a year, respectively).

The United States is the principal source of aid, either directly or through contributions to multilateral organizations and the United Nations. American aid is extended through various organizations: the Export-Import Bank, the senior organization in this field; the programs of the Alliance for Progress (which are administered through the Agency for International Development); and military aid. From 1945 to 1963, American aid of all kinds reached $5.1 billion, of which $802 million was for military aid and the rest for economic aid and technical-assistance programs. Of this, $1.2 billion was in grants and $2.8 billion in credits. Sometimes, a part of the American aid is intended to cover the budgetary deficits of a government, in order to prevent the political and social disturbances arising from the bankruptcy of a government. The greater part of nonmilitary aid, however, goes to the formation of the infrastructure and to the building of hospitals, schools, and other services that normally should be provided by local governments.

In addition to furnishing funds, the United States also furnishes technical assistance, aid to schools and universities, scholarships, and exchange programs for students and professors. There were also 8,500 Peace Corps volunteers in Latin America in 1961–66. Despite its missionary air, the Peace Corps is probably the most effective aid program, since it is the only one that does not go through government channels but directly to the people.

American critics never weary of pointing out that the greater part of U.S. aid never reaches the masses, since between the use of funds by governments in a way that will favor the oligarchy, and the cases of outright corruption, most of the aid stays on the upper echelons of society.

On the other hand, U.S. aid programs have not escaped criticism from Latin Americans. The most frequent is that military aid is absolutely useless, since it contributes nothing to the defense of the continent, encourages military coups, and burdens the country with debts for nonproductive expenses. Critics also say that aid is utilized for diplomatic ends:

for instance, it is suspended when there is a military coup or when a government refuses to put exploitation of a product (usually oil) on a private basis. The so-called Hickenlooper Amendment to the Foreign Assistance Act of 1962 prohibits American aid (and preferential trade agreements) to any country that expropriates American property without adequate compensation.

Criticism is not limited to the purposes of aid, but also to the form in which it is extended. An increasing percentage of American aid is in the form not of grants but of loans, half the products involved in the aid programs have to be shipped in American vessels, and a certain percentage of these products has to be bought, on not always advantageous terms, from American firms.

It has also been pointed out that a great part of the income considered as aid is offset by what the recipient country loses, either through a drop in prices of the raw materials it exports or because of the tariff barriers these products encounter in the American market. Quotas on textile imports, for instance, virtually prohibit the export of Latin American textiles to the United States.

In view of this situation, the Latin American governments have put forth three demands they consider essential: better prices for their raw-material exports, better terms for their semi-manufactured exports in the American market, and freedom to buy (and to transport what they buy) with aid funds. So far, however, they have not been successful in their demands,* although the coffee countries got a certain amount of satisfaction when the United States, in 1965, adhered to the International Coffee Agreement.†

Aid received from countries other than the United States is very small. The Common Market countries have earmarked for Latin America 3 per cent of the total sums al-

---

* In June, 1969, however, the United States ended its restriction that required recipient countries to spend most of their aid funds in the United States.

† International commodity agreements represent an indirect form of aid; for Latin America, the most important are those applying to coffee, cotton, wool, and cacao. The Latin American countries use ingenious methods for flouting these agreements when it suits them, however. Brazil, for instance, in accordance with the Coffee Agreement, was supposed to uproot more than one and one-half billion coffee trees; it did so, but without cutting production, since the coffee bushes pulled up were in marginal zones often attacked by frost.

lotted to foreign aid; the bulk of this contribution has been in refinancing operations or the consolidation of pending obligations. Spain has offered credit toward the purchase of Spanish materials. Canada has contributed $100 million, Japan $175 million. Israel has offered technical assistance. The Soviet Union and Communist China have sent aid missions to a few countries (Bolivia, Brazil), but up to now nothing concrete has been accomplished; however, since 1960 the Soviet Union, the countries of Eastern Europe, and China have furnished considerable aid to Cuba in the form of sugar purchases and credits for foodstuffs and capital goods.

Aid from multilateral organizations has been rising; it accounted for 31 per cent of the total aid in 1956–60, and 61 per cent in 1961–65. The multilateral organizations that make loans to Latin America are the International Bank for Reconstruction and Development (World Bank) and the Inter-American Development Bank (IDB). In recent years, Latin America has become the best "client" of the World Bank, receiving 44.6 per cent of the loans made by the Bank in 1966. (On the other hand, the International Development Association, an affiliate of the World Bank, loaned only 2.6 per cent of its total in 1966 to Latin American enterprises.)

The Inter-American Development Bank, founded in 1961 with United States and Latin American capital, and directed by the Chilean Felipe Herrera (b. 1921), has made loans in the amount of $1.9 billion (to 1966). About $20 million of this amount went to the Central American Bank for Economic Integration (BCIE), which lent them in turn. Loans have been made in the fields of industry and mining, electric power, sanitation, housing, education, and cultural affairs. The IDB has also administered contributions from the governments of Canada, Great Britain, the German Federal Republic, Switzerland, the Netherlands, and Spain.

The debt created by foreign aid has begun to worry economists. Amortization of the foreign debt rose to $1.3 billion in 1967, compared with an annual average of $340 million in the period 1956–60. Since a large share of aid is not devoted to profitable projects but goes to defray military costs, or to balance the budget, economists fear that the benefits derived from foreign aid may not keep pace with the increasing payments for amortization of the foreign debt. One-sixth of the value of Latin American exports is absorbed by foreign debt service. This means that in future there will be less available every year for reinvestment and the acquisition of capital goods, unless foreign aid is redirected exclusively toward projects that are profitable and of direct benefit to the people.

Economic Integration

A possible remedy for the shortcomings of the Latin American economy has recently been sought in the economic integration of the various countries.

Latin Americans, like most other peoples, are fond of panaceas. In every period of their history they have sought a universal remedy for their problems: first it was independence, then the separation of Church and state, industrialization, agrarian reform. Today, economic integration is offered as the solution to Latin America's difficulties.

The aggregate gross product of the Latin American republics is about $90 billion, which constitutes a market of appreciable size (one that would be much greater if the mass of the people were made part of the market economy). But as long as this market is fragmented and closed by national frontiers, industrialization remains unbalanced and expensive.

Often, a single country does not have sufficient capital to develop large industries. A plant that produces 100,000 tons a year of laminated steel needs an investment of $700 per ton; for a plant producing 1.5 million tons, this figure is reduced to $300 per ton; but such a plant can be built only with contributions of capital from several countries and with a market that takes in several countries.

For the small countries, a customs union would not only open up a larger market for their industrial goods, but would also make it impossible for a single industry to win the entire national market and establish a monopoly. For medium-sized and large countries, too, the national market is too limited for low-cost production. In Buenos Aires and São Paulo, for example, there are elevator factories that could operate much more cheaply if confined to one of those cities. Chile produces a vast amount of cheap paper but cannot sell it in Argentina; Chile also has several car-assembly plants, and, to protect them, does not permit entry of cars produced in Argentina. Chile subsidizes its beet producers to obtain sugar at three times what it would cost if imported from Peru. In Brazil, subsidized wheat costs $120 a ton, whereas Argentine wheat is sold for $70 a ton.

A proposal for a customs union for the entire hemisphere was made as early as 1889, at the first Pan-American Conference. This attempt did not succeed, nor did other attempts to form customs unions in certain areas (Gran Colombia, the Caribbean, and the Plata region). The United States opposed these efforts, as it did all others until about 1960.

But in February, 1960, the Treaty of Montevideo was signed, establishing the Latin American Free Trade Association (LAFTA). Argentina, Brazil, Chile, Colombia, Ecuador, Mexico, Paraguay, Peru, and Uruguay were charter members. Later additions were Bolivia (under special conditions, because of its low income level) and Venezuela.

The LAFTA is an organization devoted solely to lowering tariff barriers between its members. The Treaty of Montevideo provides for a gradual tariff reduction over a period of twelve years. The LAFTA has carried out long and not always successful negotiations, although it has succeeded in reducing the tariff on 9,500 products. Although the member countries of LAFTA account for about 90 per cent of the gross product of Latin America, the gains have not been spectacular, because the trade among member countries is only about 15 per cent of the total Latin American trade. But between 1960 and 1965, trade between the LAFTA members rose 86 per cent, to a value of $1.4 billion.

The Central American Common Market (CACM) has had greater success, both because it is more ambitious and comprehensive and because its member countries are more homogeneous from the point of view of their economic development and institutions. The Common Market was created in 1960, following ten years of negotiations, which led in 1952 to the formation of the Organization of Central American States and to various educational, statistical, and other activities in common. In 1963, the Central American Bank for Economic Integration (BCIE) was founded to finance projects of the Common Market.

The Common Market is composed of the five countries of Central America, which have a gross product of about $4 billion dollars a year. Both Panama and the Dominican Republic have also expressed a desire to become members. Trade among the Common Market countries rose 300 per cent between 1960 and 1965; in the latter year, it amounted to $136 million.

The Central American Common Market is more than a tariff union, for it initiates action in other fields: it established a Central American school of public administration, and has tried to unify the university system, to facilitate transfers of the labor force, and to guide investment in such a way as to avoid duplication of industries, all things the LAFTA has not done.

The end goal of the Common Market is to achieve political unity on the Isthmus, an idea that has regularly been rejected by the member governments of the LAFTA. But in 1965, President Eduardo Frei of Chile asked four leading Latin American economic experts to explore the possibilities of overcoming the limitations of the LAFTA. These experts advised the formation of a Latin American common market. After much negotiation and discussion a meeting was held at Punta del Este in April, 1967; it was attended by all the Latin American presidents except the Cuban, because the country was outside the inter-American system, and the Bolivian, as a protest against the decision not to discuss the question of a seaport for the country. President Lyndon B. Johnson of the United States also attended.

The conference proposed the formation, by 1970, of a Latin American common market, which would be in "substantial operation" by 1985. The United States pledged $300 million annually to aid in the preparation of the common market. It was also agreed to foster projects of mutual concern and to encourage cooperation between the LAFTA and the CACM. Under the auspices of the Treaty of Montevideo, Argentina, Bolivia, Brazil, Paraguay, and Uruguay signed an agreement to develop the Río de la Plata basin. Bolivia, Chile, Colombia, Ecuador, and Peru have signed an agreement establishing an Andean common market. However, the Latin American common market is still largely in the blueprint stage—that it has reached this stage is due to the efforts of the democratic governments of Venezuela and Chile, and the diplomatic pressure exerted by the United States.

It should be pointed out that the conference did not discuss the social ends of the common market, nor, for example, the question of labor participation in the common market, although the problems of the labor force and its mobility are basic in an undertaking of this sort. At bottom, the question is whether the purely economic integration of countries that are still socially unintegrated makes much sense—even if it is possible.

Populism has always maintained the need for Latin American unity—political as well as economic—both because it considers that problems shared by all the countries of the continent can best be solved in common, and because it sees in unity the means of achieving a better position from which to deal with the United States. But populist propaganda for political unity did not achieve any success until 1964, when the Peruvian parliament, which had a strong Aprista minority, convoked the parliaments of the different countries to form a Latin American Parliament; its first meeting took place that year in Lima, and it has continued to meet, though it has no effective power and has achieved no noticeable results.

Political unity is obviously still a long way off, as is the adoption of mutual means that may be really decisive in economic development: for example, continental planning for industrialization and the enforcement of an internationally financed plan for agrarian reform.

In sum, it may be seen that all Latin American problems—and economic ones in particular—are constantly taking on a more continental and international aspect.

CHAPTER VII

Is Latin America in the World?

It is a characteristic of underdeveloped countries that the question of power is posed for only a small part of the population. In Latin America, during the colonial period, there was a struggle for power between the conquistadors and the Creoles, on one side, and the representatives of the Crown on the other; after independence, the struggle was between different factions of the oligarchic group, with occasional intrusions by the small middle class of the period. By the nineteenth century, the number of aspirants to power had been enlarged by the middle-class parties and the socialists (where there were any). But the great mass of the people, who supplied the fighters in the violent struggles, had no share of power, although at times their aspirations found support among the liberals and, later, among the radicals and populists.

Even before independence, these struggling factions sought foreign support. Great Britain and the United States helped some of the revolutionaries. Later, foreign interests—British and, especially, American—became virtual allies of the more conservative elements. But foreign "influence" also took other forms. For decades, there was fear of a Spanish attempt to recover its colonies. Mexico had to fight against the United States in defense of its territory, and against France in defense of its republican regime. Later, European nations and the United States intervened in various countries to collect debts, maintain privileges, and even create new countries (Cuba, Panama). In the end, this not unjustified fear of foreign interference took the form of anti-imperialism: anti-British for a time, then anti-American and, later, although in much less degree, anti-Soviet.

It is logical, then, since the majority of the people enjoy no participation in the exercise of power, and since there is frequent foreign intervention, that Latin Americans should have come to ask themselves: Who really is master in Latin America? The answers vary, but all agree that the people of Latin America do not rule. Some think the oligarchic groups rule, with the aid of foreign business interests. Others assert that the foreign interests are the real rulers, through the agency of the military and the oligarchy. Others think that although political power is in national hands, it is subject to control by the foreign interests. In short, Latin Americans feel that their ownership of Latin America is mortgaged.

For this reason, political disputes, social struggles, economic measures, and even intellectual activities have always been closely intertwined with international questions and the role that Latin America plays—or does not play—in the world.

The Aspiration to Isolation

The international tendencies of the Latin American countries may be said to reflect an unending contradiction between the desire for isolation and dependence on international trade.

In a sense, the first attempt at the isolation of Latin America is found in the treaty of 1750 between Spain and Portugal, by the terms of which each country promised mutual aid to prevent its ports, in the motherland or in America, from being used by the enemies of the other; it was also agreed, in the event of war between Spain and Portugal, not to extend the conflict to the colonies. This treaty was, in a sense, a prefiguration of the Monroe Doctrine, in that it tended to keep America out of the conflicts of the Old World.

From the beginnings of independence, the Latin American countries were aware of their weakness vis-à-vis the countries of Europe, and Bolívar also feared the United States. During the nineteenth century, beginning with the congress convoked by Bolívar in Panama in 1826, meetings of various Latin American countries were held for the purpose of defending themselves against outside interference or seeking arbitration in conflicts; none of these conferences, however, addressed itself to world problems or to extracontinental ones. It was as if, looking at the map of the world, the diplomats came to the conclusion that Latin America could exist apart from the other continents, diplomatically as well as geographically.

The tendency to isolation was especially noticeable during the two world wars. In 1917, eight countries (Cuba, Panama, Brazil, Nicaragua, Guatemala, Costa Rica, Haiti, and Honduras) declared war on the Central Powers—that is, at the time the United States did and under pressure from Washington. Five countries broke off diplomatic relations with the Central Powers. Argentina and Mexico remained neutral. No country, however, sent any forces to the front, although Brazil was preparing to do so when the war ended.

In World War II, public opinion was sharply divided, since Nazi Germany found many admirers among the people and the military. Only when the United States entered the conflict, in 1941, did several Latin American countries take an official position: Mexico (which sent an aerial escadrille to the Pacific), and Brazil (which sent an expeditionary force to Italy). The Central American and Caribbean countries declared war on the Axis Powers, and the other countries broke off relations with them, Peru and Colombia declaring themselves belligerents. At the time, many Latin American governments were in the hands of dictators, but this did not prevent their declaring themselves democratic and antifascist and signing the Atlantic Charter—and did not prevent the Allies from accepting them as members.

Eventually, all the Latin American countries declared war

on the Axis, although Chile declared war on Japan alone and Brazil only on Germany, both for internal political reasons arising from the existence of large German and Japanese colonies in their territories. Argentina did not declare war on the Axis until March, 1945; it did so in order to be able to participate in the San Francisco Conference establishing the United Nations. Nearly all the countries froze the assets of citizens from Axis countries, and several allowed the United States to establish military bases within their borders. (It was during World War II that the United States began to sell arms to Latin America and to train Latin American officers in American military schools.)

But even though many countries managed to sidestep them, the two world wars affected Latin America's political life, as did the world economic crisis of 1929, the Korean War of 1950, and the cold war. Latin America's economy was closely bound to that of Europe and the United States. Isolation was simply impossible, as it had been for the United States. In any event, foreign countries would have gone about putting an end to it.

European Interventions

A Mexican politician has said, "between the weak and the strong, the desert," and for many years that part of Mexico bordering on the United States was virtually abandoned.

But Latin America could not surround itself with deserts, and precisely because Latin American countries have been politically and socially weak, they have invited intervention; in fact, ever since its independence, Latin America has lived in fear of foreign intervention.

Spain for many years refused to recognize the new independent republics. In 1823, Spain called upon the Holy Alliance, which it hoped would assist it in reconquering America. In 1864, Spain made another attempt to regain its colonies. At that time, Spain attacked Peru from the sea; when Chile supported Peru, Spanish ships shelled Valparaíso.

But after Cuba won its independence, in 1898, better ties were established with the former mother country, which many Spanish Americans still call "the motherland." The proclamation of the Republic, in 1931, deepened the existing sympathy, but the Spanish Civil War of 1936–39 divided Latin Americans, as it did people everywhere. However, exiled Spanish republicans were welcomed in all Latin American countries, even in the dictatorships; a few countries broke off relations with Franco Spain for several years after World War II. Mexico has never recognized the Franco regime, considering it the product of foreign intervention, and since 1946 has recognized a Spanish government-in-exile. With these exceptions, present-day relations with Spain are very cordial and the ideological undertone has disappeared from them. Even Castro's Cuba maintains friendly relations with Spain.

Brazil, for its part, never had any serious problems with Portugal, although Brazilians in general are patronizing toward the mother country because of its backwardness and long period of dictatorship.

British intervention in Latin America has a long history. In colonial times, British pirates attacked the coastal cities of the viceroyalties. In 1806, an English expedition took Buenos Aires, but lost it when the Creoles rose against the British. A year later, the same thing happened to an expedition that had occupied Montevideo. London supported the independence movements, although always secretly, and gave immediate recognition to the new republican governments. After independence, Britain began to extend its influence in Latin America.

In 1833, Britain occupied the Falkland Islands and expelled the Argentine garrison. Between 1830 and 1841, taking advantage of the political disorganization on the Isthmus, Great Britain extended the borders of Belize (British Honduras) and occupied the port of San Juan in Nicaragua, under the pretext of establishing a protectorate over the coast of Mosquito Gulf, which lasted until 1860. Britain kept an armed squadron in the Caribbean and another along the South American coast to protect its trade—it must not be forgotten that the period was one in which there were still pirates and slave traffic. But London wanted not only to protect its trade but to prevent the extension of United States influence and to maintain a degree of control over the Isthmus of Panama, where there was talk of opening a canal. In fact, there came to be a kind of Anglo-American condominium in the Caribbean, in which Disraeli, speaking in 1856, recognized American "special interests." In Brazil, Britain profited from its alliance with the Portuguese royal house to obtain preferential treatment until 1844. In the rest of Latin America, its shipping gave it a de facto preference.

Considerable British capital was also invested in Latin America. By the mid-nineteenth century, Great Britain's investments in Latin America amounted to about £2.5 million; more than half of this was in stocks and the rest in government bonds. To protect these investments, which were enormous for that time, London had no need to intervene in the internal affairs of the Latin American countries, for no government, liberal or conservative, would have dreamed of attacking British interests. There was also a certain sympathy for the country that had supported Latin American independence when it saw that its plan to replace Spain in America could not succeed. In general, it may be said that although there was some anti-imperialist agitation against Great Britain, especially in the Plata region, where British interests were greatest, it was never as intense as that later directed against the United States.

However, Britain did not hesitate to send ships to collect debts from dilatory governments, and it occasionally allied itself with other powers. France managed to enlist the aid of Britain, and also of Spain, in the expedition that set Maximilian on the throne of Mexico, although both countries drew back when they realized that there was an archduke behind the debts that had served as the pretext for the intervention.

In the late nineteenth century, Venezuela succeeded Mexico as the scene of European intervention. In 1895, Great Britain broke off diplomatic relations with Venezuela over the old dispute about the British Guiana border. Caracas asked American aid, and Secretary of State Richard Olney invoked the Monroe Doctrine, proclaiming: "Today the United States is practically sovereign on this continent, and its fiat is law upon the subjects to which it confines its interposition." A year later, London agreed to arbitration with Venezuela. In 1902, Great Britain, Germany, and Italy—after obtaining Washington's consent—blockaded the coast of

Venezuela to compel the government to compensate or pay debts to their citizens. This matter was also submitted to arbitration after President Theodore Roosevelt told the German ambassador that the United States would not permit Venezuela to become "another Egypt" (a country occupied at the time by the English and French for the collection of debts). In 1903, England dismantled its naval bases in the Caribbean and accepted the formation of the new state of Panama. British influence in the Caribbean had been replaced by that of the United States.

France, which managed to penetrate Mexico under England's nose, was unsuccessful in its other attempts to establish itself in Latin America. France supported Spain in the Holy Alliance of 1823. In 1838, to recover indemnities for some French citizens whose pastry shops had been destroyed in a riot, France sent its fleet to Veracruz and landed in that port, initiating what was humorously known as the "Pastry War." Also in 1838, French ships blockaded the Río de la Plata to protest the Argentine law that required French citizens living in Argentina to serve in the military. In 1840, an agreement between the two countries was reached and a pact of friendship signed. But five years later, in 1845, France and England again blockaded the Río de la Plata to keep Argentine troops from annexing Uruguay, in which both countries had interests. Rosas, the Argentine dictator, asked the United States for help, but Washington replied that the Monroe Doctrine did not encompass any promise by the United States to aid the countries of Latin America but was solely for the purpose of defending North American interests in the hemisphere.

Then, for five years (1862–67), French armies supported Emperor Maximilian on the throne of Mexico. But today there is no anti-French feeling in Latin America, not even in Mexico, possibly because French investments were widely distributed and concentrated more on trade than on industry. Moreover, at least until World War II, the strongest cultural influence was that of France.

Germany invested a good deal in Latin America before World War I, and before the war many Latin American armies sent their officers to German schools (just as naval officers were sent to British ones). German political influence was considerable, particularly after the rise of Hitler in 1933, although not lasting: German immigrants, who were numerous in Argentina, Chile, and Brazil, organized themselves Nazi fashion and tried to influence the internal life of those countries. German cultural influence, however, has been small.

A more subtle form of European intervention, accepted by virtually everyone, was the formulation of historical doctrines intended to attract Latin American countries into the cultural, diplomatic, and possibly the economic spheres of the European countries, especially of Spain and France. It was Spanish intellectuals who first began to talk of Hispano-Americanism, following the Spanish loss of Cuba and the Philippines, in 1898. The dictator Primo de Rivera, who ruled Spain in the 1920's, tried to capitalize on Spain's cultural influence; he even organized a Hispano-American Exposition in Seville in 1929. Later, the regime of General Franco launched the doctrine of "Hispanidad," which found support in more conservative groups but did not attain any important influence. Nor did the doctrine of "Latinism," launched by some French intellectuals in the 1920's, which held that Latin America was a child of the French Revolution. These points of view were so far removed from Latin American reality that they were not even used to counterbalance American influence.

Relations with the United States

But intervention by the United States has been of much greater importance and has been much more deeply resented than European interference. Most Americans are aware of perhaps four or five such cases of intervention, but in the fifty years before 1933 there were no fewer than sixty, nearly always for the protection of citizens or interests of the United States. As early as 1811, congress agreed that, although the United States saw nothing objectionable in Spain's keeping its possessions in this hemisphere, it would oppose the transfer to a third country of possessions adjacent to the United States. The independence juntas were not recognized by the

United States government, but no obstacle was put in the way of their purchases, their agents, or their business. At the time, the United States was negotiating the purchase of Florida from Spain; in 1822, after the negotiations were completed, the United States recognized the government of Gran Colombia and shortly thereafter recognized the other new independent governments. Haiti, the first Latin American colony to proclaim its independence, was not recognized until 1862 because of the opposition of American slaveowners.

In its relations with Latin America, the United States has had two constant objectives: to prevent the influence, or at least the presence, of extracontinental powers in the Western Hemisphere—Spain, England, and France in the nineteenth century, the Soviet Union in the twentieth—and to exercise the greatest power possible in the hemisphere, primarily through investment but also through diplomatic and military activity. The idea that Latin America is the "backyard" of the United States dates from the mid-nineteenth century.

The Latin American countries, all less powerful than the United States, have had a double objective in their relations with the "Colossus of the North" (as the United States used to be called): to win its collaboration in opposing the presence of extracontinental powers, even more disturbing to the Latin American countries than to the United States, since this presence was often manifested by occupation of their territories; and at the same time to avoid a unique or too dominant American influence. Hence they have tried to counterbalance American influence by giving a degree of influence to European powers, and also by trying to unite among themselves with the object of presenting a strong united front capable of negotiating with Washington.

The objectives of both the United States and the Latin American countries have remained constant, although they have appeared in various forms and nearly always hidden under a diplomatic rhetoric that has tried to disguise divergence of interests under such phrases as "continental solidarity," "Good Neighbor Policy," and so on.

But it is only if we see and accept the fact that the interests of a powerful country and those of weak countries close to it cannot regularly coincide—although they may be identical on certain issues—that we can understand the true meaning of relations between the United States and Latin America. The history of these relations may be divided into several stages, all determined by the attitude of the more powerful party, the United States.

1. *A Self-Serving Doctrine.* On December 2, 1823, President James Monroe, in a message to congress, declared that the United States would avoid involvement in European affairs and would also oppose any attempt to extend alien European political systems to the Western Hemisphere. This did not mean that the United States would oppose the existing European colonies but that it would resist any new attempts at colonization.

There were three reasons for the declaration: to resist France's attempts to aid Spain in recovering its former colonies, through the Holy Alliance; to oppose the Tsar's ukase of 1821, which stated Russian claims to American territories on the Pacific Coast extending as far south as the 51st parallel; and to gain British support for the American position. In reality, the Monroe Doctrine did not represent a new position: the United States had always wanted to be isolated from world politics.

When they learned of this doctrine, several Latin American governments suggested to Washington that they sign mutual assistance pacts in the event of an attack by European powers. Washington rejected the suggestion, which shows that it viewed the Monroe Doctrine merely as a defensive element of its diplomacy and not as an instrument in its relations with Latin America. Nor was Washington represented at the Panama Conference convoked in 1826 by Bolívar, for the United States delegation was named so late that by the time it arrived the conference had ended. In any event, except in the case of Mexico, at the very gates of the United States, there is little Washington could have done to oppose European intervention. And in fact it did very little, as we have seen. It did act in a few instances, however. When the Civil War was over, the U.S. government exerted pressure in Paris to have French troops withdrawn from Mexico in exchange for official American neutrality between Juárez and Maximilian. This withdrawal, like the United States' opposition to the sending of Austrian troops to help the archduke, contributed to the victory of the Mexican republic. Indirectly, Washington aided Juárez, allowing him to buy arms and in general lending him discreet support. Later, when the Dominicans rebelled against Spain, Washington brought pressure on Madrid and the Spanish Cortes annulled the annexation.

But, in general, the Monroe Doctrine may be said to have been more a justification held in reserve than an instrument of active diplomacy.

2. *Expansion to the East and West.* The expansion of the United States to the west, and later to the east, led it to change into an interventionist power in Latin America. Beginning in 1836, Washington had to face the problem of Texas, a Mexican state that first proclaimed its independence and then joined the Union, to which it was annexed by an Act of Congress in 1845. This was the cause of a war with Mexico and of the invasion by American troops of its southern neighbor in 1847. The war took place during the presidency of James K. Polk; it was opposed by Lincoln and the Whigs. In the peace negotiations that followed (which resulted in the Treaty of Guadalupe Hidalgo), Mexico lost half of its territory: the present states of California, New Mexico, Arizona, Nevada, Utah, and part of Colorado. It lost additional territory through the Gadsden Purchase of 1853.

The South pressed for the acquisition of more territory. President Thomas Jefferson had shown interest in Cuba, and several filibustering expeditions against the island were organized during his administration. In 1845, the American ministers in Paris, London, and Madrid joined in declaring that if Spain refused to sell Cuba to the United States, that country should take possession of the island; Madrid was intransigent, and Washington repudiated the declaration of its diplomats. But President Polk made a declaration—known as the Polk Corollary to the Monroe Doctrine—to the effect that the United States had special interests in the Caribbean and would oppose the replacement of one European power by another, should any of the islands declare its independence.

The filibustering expeditions to the Caribbean and to Central America increased. Washington began to take an interest in Central America, urged by the need for a less arduous route to the West. In 1846, the Bidlack Treaty with Colombia was signed. By its terms, that country was granted U.S. protection and the recognition of the integrity of the Isthmus of Panama, in exchange for the right of passage via the Isthmus. In 1850, the Clayton-Bulwer Treaty with Great Britain was signed; the two countries agreed to exploit in common any interoceanic canal that might be built. William Walker's filibustering expedition to Nicaragua in 1855 was also connected with the plan to open a canal through that country.*

Outside Central America and the Caribbean, however, the United States was very cautious. In 1840, Yucatán, dissatisfied with the situation in Mexico, proposed annexation to the United States; the proposal was rejected. In 1871, a treaty annexing the Dominican Republic was signed when proposed by a group of oligarchs of that country, but the U.S. senate rejected the treaty.

With the end of the Civil War, the United States began to pay more attention to Latin America. In 1880, President Rutherford B. Hayes sent a message to congress in which he stated that the interests of the United States demanded that it have sole control over any interoceanic canal. This was in direct opposition to the Clayton-Bulwer Treaty, which in 1901 was superceded by the Hay-Pauncefote Treaty, providing for the construction and exploitation of a canal by the United States alone.

The theorist of American naval power, Admiral Alfred T. Mahan, had wanted the Caribbean to become "the Mediterranean of the United States," and after the opening of the Panama Canal, order—at least external order—in the Caribbean islands was a constant preoccupation of American diplomacy, and even of its armed forces.

3. *Intervention*. Westward expansion had led to the war with Mexico. Eastward expansion led to a series of interventions in the Caribbean, the details of which will be discussed further on. This stage lasted until Franklin D. Roosevelt's time, although it was prolonged, in a sense, intermittently

* In 1855, an American adventurer, William Walker (1824–60), who had already failed in his attempt to proclaim an independent state in northeastern Mexico, landed in Nicaragua, overthrew the government, and had proclaimed a president who then appointed him chief of staff of the army. The countries of the Isthmus united against Walker and overthrew him in 1857; in 1860, he returned to Honduras, made a similar attempt at conquest, was captured, and executed.

and in different form, during the following stage: in the interventions in Guatemala (1954), Cuba (1961), and the Dominican Republic (1965).

4. *Continentalization.* After Roosevelt and his Good Neighbor Policy, the United States was deeply involved in Latin American politics, as much because of the problems of World War II and the cold war as through the growing American investments in Latin America. Although bilateral relations, agreements, and pressures continued, U.S. policy increasingly tended to regard Latin American affairs from a global, and continental, point of view. This was shown, especially, in the Alliance for Progress and in the Cuban problem. Since World War II, it may be said that U.S. relations with Latin America have been so close, and the interaction of the two parties so constant, that even the internal problems of the Latin American countries have become international problems. This holds as much for the Latin Americans, who cannot attempt to solve their problems without taking into account their position vis-à-vis the United States, as for the North Americans, who cannot avoid taking into consideration the effects on their own national interest of the solutions the Latin Americans find for their problems.

United States Interventions

In December, 1904, President Theodore Roosevelt stated that the United States had the right to exercise "an international police power" in the Western Hemisphere for the protection of the American nations and to prevent disorder. This was known as the Roosevelt Corollary to the Monroe Doctrine; popularly, it was known as the Big Stick Policy. Even earlier, Roosevelt, as under secretary of the navy, had proposed a similar doctrine with respect to Cuba. The United States never opposed Spanish dominion over the island, for it was thought that Spain was too weak to be dangerous, although it did prevent an intervention by Mexico and Colombia, in 1825. When the Cubans revolted against Spain, in the long war of 1868–78, President Grant affirmed the right of the United States to intervene but made no attempt to do so. But some years later, following another rebellion, President William McKinley stated that the United States could intervene, for humanitarian reasons, to protect the interests of American citizens on the island, to prevent the destruction of property, and to restore order. In early 1898, President McKinley sent the battleship *Maine* to Cuba. But on February 15, the warship was blown up in Havana harbor—it is still not known by whom. A few months later, the United States intervened with armed force against Spain. When the war was over, the United States, although it had announced that it had no annexationist plans, annexed Puerto Rico (which had obtained its autonomy from Spain shortly before) and the Philippine Islands (where the guerrilla forces of Emilio Aguinaldo resisted for three years).

In Cuba, Washington succeeded in having introduced into the new country's constitution an amendment, approved in advance by the U.S. congress, by which Cuba recognized the right of the United States to intervene in the island to maintain its independence, support a competent government, and enforce fulfillment of international obligations. The Platt Amendment, as it was called, was introduced into the Cuban constitution only after the United States announced that its military forces would not leave the island until its demands were complied with. This amendment had important consequences, for the Cubans formed the habit of seeing the United States as the final arbiter of their destiny. (It was later to influence the passivity of the Cuban people in the face of Fidel Castro's changes of policy, since everyone believed that the United States would prevent any handing over of the island to the Communists.)

Washington intervened militarily several times in Cuba: in 1906, upon the petition by the island's president to crush a revolt of his opponents; in 1912, to help suppress a rebellion of Negro workers; and in 1917, to keep the elected government in office. But in 1933, when the dictator Gerardo Machado (1862–1940) faced a popular rebellion, Washington refused to intervene with armed force, although it did exert some diplomatic pressure against the dictatorship in its last moments. When Machado fell, President Roosevelt declared that the United States would not exercise the right of intervention; but he did not recognize the revolutionary government—moderate democratic, in reality—that succeeded the dictator and was quickly overthrown by a military coup. The following year, however, the Platt Amendment was abrogated.

The case of Cuba proved that intervention for the purpose of maintaining an elected government in power in fact abets the transformation into a dictatorship of that government (which has generally been elected by fraudulent proceedings), since the dictator is confident that the U.S. marines will prevent any popular attempt to overthrow him.

Shortly after the Platt Amendment had been imposed on Cuba, the United States acted as midwife to a new American state: Panama. As with Cuba, the price of independence was the establishment of a virtual U.S. protectorate over the new country. Panama, a province of Colombia, had won autonomy in 1851. In January, 1903, after Ferdinand de Lesseps' French company discontinued its attempt to build a canal across the Isthmus, Colombia and the United States negotiated the Hay-Herrán Treaty, granting the United States virtual sovereignty over a ten-kilometer strip of land across the Isthmus. The Colombian congress refused to ratify the treaty; there was a rebellion in Panama, and Washington sent ships to prevent the Colombian forces from going into Panama and strangling the rebellion. In November, 1903, the province declared its independence. Washington immediately recognized the new state, despite the fact that the Bidlack Treaty of 1846 had recognized Colombia's sovereignty over the Isthmus. Theodore Roosevelt himself declared that he had taken the Canal Zone and left the debate to congress, and that "while the debate goes on the canal does also."

A convention between the United States and the new government of Panama was immediately negotiated and was signed exactly fifteen days after Panama declared its independence. The convention granted the United States the right to intervene to maintain public order in the cities of Panama and Colón, as well as to construct a canal and to establish facilities in a zone the length of the canal, ceded in perpetuity in exchange for an immediate payment of $10 million and an annual payment of $250,000, annuity that has subsequently been increased several times.

The United States intervened several times in Panama (in 1908, 1912, and 1918) and developed the doctrine of the right to intervene not only in that country but in any part of the Caribbean to protect the canal. The right of intervention in Panama was annulled in a new treaty negotiated in 1936 and ratified by the U.S. senate in 1939. But the problem of sovereignty over the Canal Zone still persists; Panama maintains that this territory, although ceded for usufruct to the United States, continues to be Panamanian territory, and demands that the flag of Panama shall fly over it, that Panamanian laws shall apply there, and that working conditions and wages shall be equal for all persons working in the Canal Zone, regardless of national origin. The American labor unions representing workers in the Canal Zone were long opposed to this equality, until the AFL-CIO persuaded them to accept it after World War II.

A new treaty was negotiated in 1967 after major riots had occurred in Panama in 1964. This treaty recognized Panama's sovereignty over the Canal Zone and provided for that country's participation in its administration and for equality of treatment and wages between Americans and Panamanians. The same conditions were agreed upon for a new sea-level canal, in the event that the United States should decide to build one on the Isthmus. This treaty has still not been ratified by either of the parties.

The Panama Canal question has been a constant source of agitation in Latin America; the populist movements have favored continentalization of the canal, and the Panamanians have talked of nationalizing it; in the United States, certain powerful interests have opposed any change in the situation.

The United States had opposed the use of force by European powers to collect debts. But it did not renounce its own right to use force or to interfere in various Caribbean countries. In 1912, Washington sent the marines to Nicaragua, where they remained as a garrison. In 1914, the marines went ashore in the Mexican port of Veracruz, where revolution was in full swing; they met with resistance, and finally withdrew what was called a "punitive expedition" over an incident that had occurred, not in Veracruz but in the port of Tampico. The real purpose of the intervention was to weaken the Huerta dictatorship, but this did not lead the revolutionaries to view the landing favorably, and they too resisted it. In 1916, forces commanded by General Pershing crossed the Mexican border in pursuit of the revolutionary guerrillas of Pancho Villa, who had attacked the American border town of Columbus. U.S. troops occupied Haiti in 1915, following widespread disorder in the capital. The United States signed an agreement establishing a virtual U.S. protectorate over the country, which lasted until 1935. From 1917 to 1920, there were also American troops in Cuba, and from 1916 to 1924 troops were garrisoned in the Dominican Republic, where some of the officers discovered Rafael Leónidas Trujillo (1891–1961) and groomed him to become head of the army—a post from which he elevated himself to the presidency.

In 1924, the marines occupied Nicaragua, following a dispute over the Bryan-Chamorro Treaty, which gave the United States the right to construct a canal through the country. The marines were accustomed to being welcomed everywhere by "distinguished" people, met with hostility by the middle class, and received with indifference by the masses. But this time they met with unexpected resistance. An officer who had been a mine worker and farmer, Augusto César Sandino (1893–1934), rebelled against the foreign occupation, organized a guerrilla band in the mountains, and from 1927 to 1934 fought both the marines and the Nicaraguan national guard. At first, the Communists supported Sandino, but they abandoned him when he refused to go along with their idea that the anti-imperialist struggle should be directed by the working class (virtually nonexistent in Nicaragua at the time). When President Roosevelt ordered the marines to withdraw, Sandino laid down his arms; he was invited to a meeting with the Nicaraguan president and upon leaving the presidential palace was slain by the national guard, commanded by Anastasio Somoza (1896–1956), who shortly thereafter seized the presidency. Sandino enjoyed enormous popular sympathy throughout Latin America, where he is still a legendary hero.

The pretext, and in many cases the true reason, for the U.S. interventions was the desire to collect debts, especially through the administration of the customs, and to "restore order." The point of departure was the hypothesis that if a social and political system was not capable of establishing order, that system should not be changed for a more effective one but should be maintained by force of arms and those who wanted to change it prevented from doing so. Thus American intervention was like a premium on incompetent government and dictatorship. This type of intervention ended with the Franklin D. Roosevelt administration. But there have been other cases of open intervention, although based on another point of view.

In 1912, a Japanese fishing company tried to lease a Mexican port for its fleet; whereupon Senator Henry Cabot Lodge added a new corollary to the Monroe Doctrine when he stated, in a speech before congress, that the United States would oppose any attempt by extracontinental powers to establish naval or military bases in the Western Hemisphere. It should be said that, at the time, the powerful German colonies in southern Brazil and in Chile, and the plans of the German navy to obtain bases in the Dutch Caribbean colonies, presented Washington with the threat of a German expansion more dangerous than the one that served as the pretext for Lodge's speech. The Lodge Corollary provided a basis for American diplomacy during World War II and particularly during the cold war, when the Soviet Union, if it did not go so far as to try to install bases in Latin America, at least attempted to put at the service of Soviet diplomacy the influence the Communists had won there.

The first intervention of this type took place in Guatemala in 1954. A long-lived dictatorship had been replaced in 1944 by a democratic government. The Communists, taking advantage of the political inexperience produced by the dictatorship, made themselves influential in the labor unions, in a few political parties, and in the government headed by Colonel Jacobo Arbenz (b. 1914), which had succeeded the democratic regime of Juan José Arévalo (b. 1904). The Communists made use of a moderate agrarian reform law to create a conflict with the United Fruit Company, which owned great plantations in the country; the Communists had arms bought from Czechoslovakia and, in general, through their propaganda and their influence in the government, alarmed Washington.

Washington therefore encouraged Colonel Carlos Castillo Armas (1914–57) to organize an invasion of the country, by way of Honduras; the army did not fight, the people did not defend the regime, Arbenz fled, and Castillo became president. The Communists accomplished what they had set out to do: to create a platform for anti-American propaganda—at that time the fundamental objective of Soviet diplomacy in Latin America—and to destroy the still-existent image of Roosevelt's Good Neighbor Policy. There was widespread indignation throughout Latin America over the U.S. intervention in Guatemala.

The second case of this type of intervention failed. Early in 1959, the Cuban dictatorship of General Fulgencio Batista (b. 1901) was overthrown by a popular movement. One of the movement's leaders, Fidel Castro (b. 1927), seized power and established another dictatorship (whose history and characteristics are analyzed in Chapter VIII). Castro gave the Communists increasing influence and, while he attacked the United States he strengthened Cuba's ties with the Soviet Union. The U.S. government felt that there was a danger that the Soviets would get a military foothold in Cuba (as they actually did try to do a year later) and organized groups of Cuban exiles to overthrow the Castro regime. On April 17, 1961, these exile groups landed at the Bay of Pigs—and were routed. President Kennedy, who had inherited the operation from his predecessor but who permitted it to be carried out, acknowledged full responsibility. In this case, as in that of Guatemala seven years earlier, the organizers of the intervention were agents of the Central Intelligence Agency (CIA).

The third intervention of this sort was open and of a military character. It took place in April, 1965, in the Dominican Republic. In 1961, the dictator Trujillo was assassinated, and after a period of unrest, elections were held in early 1963. The winners were Juan Bosch (b. 1909) and his Dominican Revolutionary Party (PRD). Seven months later, in September, 1963, a military coup, urged on by the oligarchic groups, overthrew Bosch and exiled him. But in April, 1965, there was another coup against the civilian dictators who had succeeded Bosch, and a part of the army, desirous of wiping out the past, took advantage of the coup to proclaim a return to the constitutional regime. The U.S. ambassador in Santo Domingo refused to mediate when asked to do so by the

Constitutionalist faction. The Constitutionalists armed the people, singling out members of the PRD and, no doubt, some members of the three Communist groups in the country as well.

From the information supplied by its embassy in Santo Domingo, Washington concluded that the Constitutionalist movement had been taken over by the Communists (a conclusion quickly proved erroneous by events, for the democratic elements had never lost control). The White House immediately ordered the marines to land in Santo Domingo, saying first that this was to protect American lives and then that it was for the purpose of avoiding a "second Cuba." There followed a period of struggle between the two factions, with Washington supporting the dictatorial group. There were protests from all over the world—including, and especially, the United States. Following diplomatic negotiations, Washington finally asked to have its unilateral intervention transformed into an intervention by the Organization of American States, which Washington had not consulted before sending in the marines. After several weeks of negotiations, a committee of the OAS persuaded both factions to accept a provisional government, which held elections in June, 1966. The interventionist forces of the OAS—which were 98 per cent American, and to which only four dictatorships and one conservative constitutional government furnished soldiers—withdrew.

The Dominican intervention left a feeling of profound resentment against the United States, as much among those of the right, who would have liked unconditional support from Washington, as among those of the left, who felt that the marines had kept them from re-establishing a constitutional regime. It was plain that there had been no danger of a Communist coup, and in all Latin America the Dominican intervention restored the image of the United States that had existed before Franklin Roosevelt and which the policies of President Kennedy (as we shall see later) had profoundly altered.

In addition to these cases of armed intervention—from that in Mexico in 1847 to that in the Dominican Republic in 1965—there have been interventions by other less dramatic and, to a certain degree, more normal means. Latin Americans—who despite their fondness for rhetoric are very realistic in political matters—know that the influence of the rich and powerful United States must inevitably make itself felt in their countries, and they know that they cannot dispense with American goods, the American market, or American aid. They also know that this influence must necessarily manifest itself in pressure for the adoption of measures that are important to the national or economic interests of the United States. A certain degree of discreet intervention, then, is inevitable, however disagreeable it may be. What irritates Latin Americans is that the intervention is often so crude, that it is carried out not by the American government but by a private enterprise, or that it is openly undertaken in favor of private interests and not in what might seem the obvious national interests of the United States. In short, Latin Americans, without saying so, accept as a fact of life their dependency, in some measure, on the United States. But they do not accept having this dependency confused with submission or servility, or used to prejudice the interests of their countries. (On this point, obviously, Washington faces the problem of the different interpretations of the "national interest" made by the various social groups in each country. For example, the oligarchic groups consider it against the national interest to limit the sale of arms, to refuse to buy the country's raw materials at special prices, or to press for fiscal and agrarian reforms; the populists consider it against the national interest to furnish weapons to the military, to support American companies that refuse to accept agrarian reform, or to label as "Communist" every attempt at social change.)

Nonmilitary U.S. intervention, permanent and disguised, is exercised in different forms. It suffices here to point out the most frequent types, since all have considerable influence on the working out and application of the Latin American policy of the United States and the international policy of the Latin American countries.

First of all, we must distinguish a current form of diplomatic intervention that is used throughout the world but that takes on special significance in Latin America: recognition. Since military coups and unconstitutional changes of government are frequent in that continent, the question for the United States has been whether every regime should be recognized, no matter what its origin, or if only constitutional or popularly elected regimes should be recognized. Until the time of President Kennedy, the policy of the United States was extremely pragmatic. Recognition was granted to all regimes that were in power, regardless of their origins—except in the case of Mexico, whose revolutionary government was not recognized until 1923, precisely because it was revolutionary. But President Kennedy refused recognition, for several months, to military regimes in Peru, in 1962, and in the Dominican Republic, in 1963. This did not overthrow the military juntas, but it undoubtedly helped to prevent harsh reprisals against the democratic elements. This nonrecognition was accompanied by the suspension of aid; sometimes, aid was suspended without the withdrawal of recognition (in Haiti, after 1962, for instance). But it should be noted that although before World War II, U.S. diplomatic pressure and the withdrawal of recognition could have been enough to overthrow a dictatorship, since the war the situation has changed all over the world: Albania can thumb its nose at Moscow and Haiti at Washington, and the lack of recognition is irritating but not decisive.

We must also note a paradox: Latin American opinion has invariably reproached the United States for hasty recognition of dictatorial regimes, but it has never brought pressure on its own governments to refuse recognition. As a matter of fact, dictatorships have always been recognized by Latin American governments, including the two mentioned above from which American recognition was withheld.* Thus, at the Inter-American Conference at Caracas, the United States was attacked for decorating the Venezuelan dictator Pérez Jiménez; but no one mentioned that all the Latin American governments present did the same thing, and for the same reason: that they were the guests of the Venezuelan government. (When, in 1963, the American courts, for the first time in the history of that country, allowed the extradition of Pérez

---

* Two exceptions should be noted, however: Mexico, which did not recognize the Dominican junta of 1963, and Venezuela, which from 1960 to 1969 did not recognize any government resulting from a coup.

Jiménez, accused of corruption by his country, the United States was accused of not respecting the right of asylum.)

A second form of indirect intervention is that of the Pentagon. The U.S. military has its own Latin American policy, which does not always coincide with the official policy of the United States. The military considers public order fundamental, and believes that regimes originating in force are better at maintaining order than are democratic ones. The activity of the Pentagon takes several forms: education of Latin American officers in the United States; training of military forces in guerrilla warfare, in a special school in Panama; training of Latin American police in riot control; studies of political motivation in different countries; joint planning with Latin American armies in the Inter-American Defense Board in Washington; the sale and standardization of arms; combined military maneuvers, and so on.

The results of this what we may call "technical" intervention have been mediocre. Most of the military coups of recent years have been staged by alumni of American military schools, which proves either that no attempt has been made to convince them the armed forces should be apolitical, or that these attempts have not been successful. Military action against guerrillas—where there have been any—has had little success. Joint planning has been unrealistic; at the time of the Cuban missile crisis in 1962, no Latin American army had a plan for evacuating civilian city-dwellers or even members of the government. The discovery of the motivation studies commissioned by the Pentagon in several American universities provoked a scandal, as well as embarrassing bona fide American investigators. This was particularly true of the "Camelot" plan for studying the possibilities of revolution in Chile, in 1965; the "Simpático" plan for studying the motivation of Latin Americans; and the "Rex Americana" plan for analyzing the means of maintaining American hegemony. Because of the protests aroused by these studies, President Johnson decreed that no government agency was to make any study abroad without first obtaining permission from the State Department.

But the most frequent form of Pentagon intervention in Latin American affairs has consisted in giving the "green light" to military coups. Rarely does the military of a Latin American country plan a coup without first consulting the American military attaché. Sometimes, the latter advises the military to be patient and abandon the coup. At other times, he informs the U.S. ambassador, who in turn advises the local military against a coup or informs the menaced president. But at other times, if the Pentagon (or simply the military attaché) has a point of view different from that of the State Department, it gives the plotters to understand that although there may be a suspension of aid and relations may be broken off, this will only be temporary—and the coup is staged. It can be said that the Pentagon does not really organize military coups, but it can also be stated that there are almost no military coups that have not received a green light from the Pentagon or the American military attachés.

It is possible that the United States' most difficult problem in its Latin American policy is that of imposing the official policy—that of the State Department—on the military attachés and the Pentagon. To a lesser degree, and less frequently, a similar duality is found between official activity and that of the Central Intelligence Agency, complicated, in this case, by the fact that different sections of the CIA carry out different policies; for example, the regional section generally supports reactionary elements whereas the special-operations section supports democratic leftist elements. Under such conditions, the U.S. ambassador often appears to be more the victim of conflicting policies than the representative of a great power.

A third group that also exerts influence and that does not hesitate to resort to intervention consists of the great American economic interests. On the one hand, the economic interests see to it that foreign aid is utilized to protect private interests; for instance, in 1964–65, that part of American aid to Argentina and Peru that was of greatest benefit to the people (such as community development) was suspended in order to bring pressure on the governments of those countries to adopt more conciliatory positions in the current negotiations, or disputes, they were maintaining with the American oil companies. On the other hand, private interests have intervened in the formulation of important operations set on foot for political reasons (such as the fear that the Communists would take over a government); for example, in 1965, private interests contributed no little to having Washington falsely informed that there was a Communist threat in the Dominican Republic.

But intervention by private interests is often direct and outside official diplomatic channels; only when their activities lead them into dangerous waters do they hasten to obtain diplomatic protection, and by so doing embarrass the United States and provide fuel for anti-American propaganda. There was a period, between the two world wars, in which the power of a few fruit companies in the Central American countries led to the latters' being called "banana republics," because their governments were changed at the pleasure of the directors of these companies and according to the concessions they granted or refused. This period passed, as did the period after World War II in which the large American firms preferred to recognize unions controlled by Communists rather than democratic labor unions, because the former, in exchange for recognition, were less exigent in their demands.

But we are still at the stage in which the big firms try to obtain concessions and privileges from the governments, getting themselves supported now by diplomats, now by financial pressure from other firms. Of course, when there is a military overthrow of government and the new regime concedes oil rights (as the Argentine military government did in 1965) or port privileges (as the Brazilian military government did in 1964) that had been refused by the earlier civilian governments, Latin Americans conclude that the great companies had a hand in preparing the military coup and that the military took power, among other reasons, in order to grant the concessions the foreign companies wanted. From there it is only a step to accusing the United States of inspiring military coups for the benefit of American firms.

There is no doubt that the big firms do exert pressure on the State Department against governments that seem unsympathetic to their interests and in favor of those that grant them privileges. There is no doubt, either, that the constant American advice to Latin American governments against nationalizing industries (even with compensation), and against those governments' investing in firms or becoming owners of them, is a form of economic intervention. Often, it is not just a matter of advice: in 1950, the U.S. Secretary of State informed the Brazilian government that the United States did not approve of that government's being the owner of the oil industry and that, consequently, all financial support would be withdrawn. In 1963, a committee headed by General Lucius Clay recommended that no American loans be extended to nationalized or government-owned industries. Of course, the United States, like any country, may lend money as it pleases; but to Latin Americans this "argument" looks like intervention in the domestic affairs of their countries.

The large American firms also benefit when an international organization with a conservative outlook exerts pressure on a government to adopt certain economic measures. This has frequently happened with the International Monetary Fund (IMF), which will help governments in financial difficulties only if they adopt the anti-inflationary measures the Fund supports; in general, these consist in an austerity policy at the expense of the poorest sector of the population, and the encouragement of private foreign investment.

Perhaps what has most hurt American capital's image in Latin America is the pressure it has systematically exerted on Washington to oppose attempts at change in Latin America. For this reason, Latin Americans hold American capital responsible for their countries' backwardness, for dictatorships, and for social injustice; they try to convince themselves that had it not been for the alliance between foreign capital and the oligarchy, Latin America would be different. This is an exaggeration, for foreign capital was unable to prevent the Mexican Revolution, or the Bolivian, or the democratization of Venezuela, or Castro's revolution in Cuba—all of which it opposed. But a scapegoat is convenient and American capital, by its very attitude, has willingly offered itself for this role.

In reality, American capital has behaved in Latin America no differently from the way it has behaved in other places, nor unlike capital from other sources; it could even be said that it has behaved no differently from local capital. Foreign companies have had a tendency toward monopoly, price manipulation, and the corruption of governments for the sake of obtaining privileges; they have tended to favor a policy of social immobility; they have favored rejection of free unions and encouragement of company unions, initial harsh treatment of workers, and then paternalism to wean them away from the unions. But all these things could also be said of local enterprises. It could even be said that, in recent years, foreign firms have treated their workers better than have domestic ones, thus arousing the resentment of local firms. But what is tolerable on the part of domestic firms becomes an unbearable abuse on the part of foreign ones; the nationalists call it "colonialism" or "imperialism."

It should be noted that in countries like Argentina and Uruguay, where British investment was predominant, opposition to British capital was never as strong as that directed against American capital. Possibly this is because British investments were made in a less nationalistic period, one in which the general attitude was favorable to foreign investment. American investment, on the other hand, began to be important in a period of rising nationalism, in which United States diplomacy was expressed in terms of armed intervention. If we remember that the United States has been the chief market for Latin American products, the principal supplier of goods, the principal investor, and, in recent years, the chief source of foreign aid, it is not surprising that Latin Americans have the sensation of being totally dependent on the United States economy and that in the last thirty or forty years private American investment has been regarded with a great deal of mistrust.

Obviously, the situation is a transitory one. When Latin America has changed its social structure and transformed itself into a capitalistic society with sufficient domestic investment to speed up its development, foreign capital will no longer represent a threat to national capitalism, its attempts at intervention will not succeed, and it will be accepted (or possibly its existence will be forgotten), as happens in any capitalistic country. For just this reason, the position of American investors is difficult to explain except as the result of the shortsightedness of American businessmen, who steadfastly oppose all social change and reforms capable of creating conditions that would give them respectability in the eyes of Latin Americans.

Naturally, the latter are angry when they see announcements in the United States proposing investments in Latin American countries and offering, among other inducements, low wages and almost nonexistent taxes. It is difficult to make them understand that these are the facts of life and that they are not just characteristics of American capital but of capital in general. To Latin Americans, foreign capital is American capital—and that is that.

Latin American Interventions

In addition to interventions in the Latin American countries by European nations and the United States, there have also been cases of intervention by the Latin American nations themselves.

The three major wars in Latin American history were the War of the Triple Alliance (1864–70), between Paraguay and the "triple alliance" of Argentina, Brazil, and Uruguay, in which Paraguay was defeated and lost a large percentage of its male population; the Pacific War (1879–83), between Chile on one side and Peru and Bolivia on the other, in which Chile was victorious, Bolivia lost its territories on the Pacific, and Peru lost territories rich in nitrates; and the Chaco War (1932–35), between Bolivia and Paraguay for control of lands rich in oil, which ended in Paraguay's victory and international mediation.

In addition to these three major conflicts, there have been frontier wars or incidents between Bolivia and Brazil, Peru and Brazil, Ecuador and Peru, Colombia and Peru, Brazil and Colombia, Argentina and Chile, Nicaragua and Honduras. There are still disagreements over the borders between Argentina and Uruguay, Colombia and Venezuela, Honduras and Guatemala, Costa Rica and Panama. These disputes have sometimes been settled by mediation, several times by Spain, at other times by Great Britain or the United States. (A long-standing conflict over the Mexican-United States border was settled in 1964, when the tiny Chamizal region was returned to Mexico.)

There have also been disputes over colonial territories. Mexico and Guatemala disputed Belize (British Honduras); Venezuela claimed part of British Guiana (now Guyana);

Argentina has claimed the Falkland Islands; Honduras, Swan Island. Chile and Argentina have quarrelled over territories in the Antarctic.

Despite these wars and disputes, it may be said that for a century and a half—from independence to the present—Latin America, of all the regions of the world, has enjoyed the longest periods of peace. This was true in the colonial era as well, for the various rebellions were not very bloody ones. With the exception of the wars for independence and the Mexican Revolution, the armed conflicts that have taken place cannot be compared, in violence and destructiveness, with those on other continents.

In addition to military interventions, there have also been cases of political intervention by one Latin American country in the affairs of another. These were nearly always for ideological reasons. When a conservative government rose to power in a country whose neighbor had a liberal government, it would occasionally attempt to overthrow the latter, sometimes by encouraging the neighbor's army, at other times by joining in conspiracies. Similarly, a liberal government would sometimes attempt to overthrow its conservative neighbors. An instance of this occurred when the Peruvians, through the Chilean Church, tried to intervene in Chilean politics; this led to the breaking off of diplomatic relations between the two countries in 1910. This kind of political interventionism was especially frequent in Central America.

There has also been a certain amount of economic intervention by the larger, more prosperous Latin American states in the affairs of the less powerful ones. Argentina and Brazil play toward Paraguay and Bolivia, and Mexico toward Central America, roles that are basically no different (if less overpowering) than that played by the United States toward the Latin American countries.

Latin American Diplomacy

Bolívar's international policy, as we have said, was an attempt to isolate Latin America from the rest of the world and to find points of interest that would unite the Latin American countries. In a sense, it may be said that Latin American diplomacy has stirred into activity only when there was a need to maintain the de facto isolation of the continent. The Latin American nations have attempted to do this by forming a general union, or partial unions, that would permit Latin America to present a front that would be respected, and thus to isolate themselves from the rest of the world.*

In 1826, Simón Bolívar convoked a congress in Panama to which all the new countries except Chile and Argentina sent delegates. The United States—whose presence Bolívar opposed—was invited by the president of Mexico, but its delegates did not arrive until after the meetings were over. The congress approved a treaty of "perpetual union, league, and confederation." Bolívar proposed that Great Britain be asked to join the confederation as a check upon the United States. But the confederation was never organized.

Mexico made several attempts to convene other congresses, but none of them was successful. In 1847, delegates of Bolivia, Chile, Ecuador, Colombia, and Peru met at Lima and signed a treaty of union and confederation that was aimed not only against the European powers but also against those of the hemisphere. In 1856, at the time of Walker's expedition to Nicaragua, representatives of Chile, Ecuador, and Peru convened to sign a continental treaty of alliance and mutual assistance. That same year, the ambassadors of Mexico, Peru, Costa Rica, Guatemala, Colombia, Venezuela, and El Salvador signed a similar treaty at a meeting held, paradoxically, in Washington.

Seeing that their plans for confederation were having no result, the diplomats agreed on the formula "family of nations"; this emerged from a meeting held in Lima in 1864 to study the problems posed for Latin America by the American Civil War. After this time, the idea of confederation was abandoned, and such agreements as were adopted from then on dealt with lesser, more specific matters.

All these meetings emphasized several ideas derived from the Congress of Panama: an assembly of representatives of the various countries to guide the proposed confederations; arbi-

---

* In some countries, the tendency to isolationism has gone so far as to include isolation from Latin America. The Mexicans and the Argentines do not feel that they are Latin Americans; this may partially explain the slight effect on the hemisphere of the Mexican Revolution, and it is the reason for the constant affirmation by the Argentines—at least by the people of Buenos Aires —that their country is more European than Latin American.

tration by this assembly to resolve conflicts between the member countries; full use in common of military forces; and refusal to accept the intervention of outside powers in the internal affairs of the Latin American countries. This last point—which was the most urgent—was expressed in diplomatic terms in the declaration of the Argentine Foreign Minister Luis María Drago (1859–1912), who was sent to Washington in 1903, when England, Germany, and Italy tried to intervene militarily in Venezuela to collect debts. Drago stated that the public debt could not be the occasion for armed intervention or the occupation of the territory of the American nations by a European power. This thesis, which was accepted by the second International Peace Conference at the Hague, in 1907, has become known as the Drago Doctrine, although in reality it was the work of the Argentine jurist Carlos Calvo.

But there are several Latin American diplomatic customs that are peculiar to the continent and are not accepted by the United States and Europe. The chief ones are automatic recognition and the right of asylum.

Most Latin American governments automatically recognize any government in power, regardless of its origins. Mexico follows the so-called Estrada Doctrine, named after Mexican Foreign Minister Genaro Estrada (1887–1937). The Estrada Doctrine was formulated in order to avoid the necessity of having to give specific recognition to every change of regime. Diplomatic relations are to be automatically continued with whatever government is in power, unless this contravenes Mexico's national interest. The Estrada Doctrine was designed to prevent the kind of indirect intervention caused by the granting or withholding of diplomatic recognition.

The right of asylum assures any person who considers himself the victim of political persecution the right to seek asylum in the embassy of any Latin American country. His government must then guarantee him safe conduct if he wants to leave his own country. The right of asylum was recognized in 1954 in a convention signed by all the Latin American countries, and it has been respected by all of them, even by the Castro regime in Cuba. The right of asylum has saved the lives of many opponents of the regime; it has also saved the lives of fallen dictators, of aspirants to power whose coups have failed, and of presidents deposed by military coups.*

Over the years, rivalries have sprung up among the Latin American countries for leadership in inter-American affairs. The struggle for supremacy has not always been peaceful, but no country has ever attained continental leadership. Chile attained first place in the Pacific region, after the war in which it defeated Peru and Bolivia; on the Atlantic coast, Argentina and Brazil contested for leadership. Mexico was at one point leader in the Caribbean, after it annexed Central America in 1821; but it lost this two years later, when Itúrbide's empire fell and Mexico's plans for invading Cuba and other Caribbean islands still under Spanish dominion were unsuccessful. The Mexican Revolution of 1910–17, which accomplished many of the things desired by the populist movements in other countries, did not give that country a position of leadership, even among the more or less revolutionary forces; there was sympathy for the Mexican Revolution but no solidarity with it, or, on its part, with revolutionary movements in other countries.

Until World War II, there was talk in diplomatic circles of the ABC countries (Argentina, Brazil, and Chile), which generally consulted with one another over important problems, tried to mediate in disputes with other countries, and even held meetings to discuss restrictions on naval armaments (at Valparaíso, in 1923).

After World War II, General Perón tried to establish Argentine supremacy on the continent, basing his claim on the doctrines of the Peronist movement; this attempt had little success. Brazil, under President Juscelino Kubitschek (b. 1902), tried to achieve the supremacy to which Perón had aspired, particularly with a series of economic proposals made in 1958, which were influential in the U.S. State Department.

The government of Fidel Castro in Cuba came close to assuming this leadership role, as much by the sympathy it

* In 1949, the dictatorship of Peru refused to recognize the right of asylum when the Aprista leader Víctor Raúl Haya de la Torre took asylum in the Colombian embassy, where he remained for five years. The International Court of Justice settled the matter by ordering the Peruvian government to give Haya safe conduct.

first aroused as by the aid it gave some guerrilla movements. But this influence waned after the 1962 missile crisis.

In recent years, the Latin American nations have divided into three blocs, especially on economic questions: the larger countries (Mexico, Argentina, Brazil) usually discreetly object to every attempt at common action, since each believes that, being the largest, it will get a bigger piece of the pie through bilateral action; the middle-sized countries (Chile, Venezuela, Colombia, and Peru), because they hope to have more influence in any continental grouping, prefer to act in concert; the small countries try to follow the American lead, in the hope that by so doing they will derive greater benefit than they could obtain merely on the basis of their individual importance.*

But in general, it may be said that the Latin American countries are almost as suspicious of one another as they are of the United States. Where the Latin American countries have acted in concert, at least since World War II, is in the international organizations.

Latin America in International Organizations

Mexico was the only Latin American state to take part in the first International Peace Conference at The Hague, in 1899. Mexico and Brazil attended the second conference, in 1907, which adopted the Drago Doctrine (in weakened form) as the Porter Doctrine.

Nine Latin American nations signed the Treaty of Versailles, and fifteen of them became charter members of the League of Nations that it established. But the amount of the assessed quotas, and, especially, the fact that the United States was not a member, lessened the enthusiasm of several countries, since Latin America did not anticipate conflicts with the countries of Europe but only with the United States. At one time, or another, however, all the Latin American countries were members of the League, although never all of them at the same time. By the time of the last meeting, in 1945, the number had fallen to ten.

* There have recently been a few signs of a tendency toward cooperation on economic matters. In June, 1969, the Inter-American Economic and Social Council of the OAS, meeting in Port of Spain, and a foreign ministers' meeting at Viña del Mar called for greater inter-American cooperation on economic matters and collective presentation of proposals and complaints to the United States.

Argentina withdrew from one session when its delegate was not elected president of the Assembly. Brazil withdrew in 1926 when it was not elected a permanent member of the Council; Costa Rica withdrew for budgetary reasons. Paraguay withdrew during the Chaco War in protest against the arms embargo. Mexico did not join the League until 1931, and withdrew for a brief period in 1933; nevertheless, it was the most active Latin American member, particularly in supporting the Spanish republican government during the Civil War. Both Mexico and Argentina were members with reservations, since they refused to recognize the Monroe Doctrine, which was included in Article 21 of the Convenant of the League.

The League intervened in Latin America on only two occasions: in 1932, in the dispute between Peru and Colombia over the Amazonian city of Leticia, which the League administered while an agreement was being negotiated; and, in the same year, in the Chaco War between Paraguay and Bolivia, which was finally settled in 1938, not by the efforts of the League but through arbitration by five South American presidents.

Their experience with the League of Nations made the Latin American nations view the United Nations with skepticism when it was organized in 1945. But the greater permanence and universality of the organization have worked to dissolve that skepticism, although the Latin American states have by no means succeeded in turning the United Nations into a counteracting force to the United States. Actually, in every attempt of this kind, they have had to avoid what is virtually unavoidable: that the Soviet bloc will turn to its own advantage any criticism whatever of the United States. In a certain measure, the cold war has sterilized the United Nations as far as Latin America is concerned.

The Latin American countries took an active part in the San Francisco Conference establishing the United Nations (where they unsuccessfully opposed the veto power), and all the Latin American countries are charter members of the organization, including Argentina, whose membership was opposed by the Soviet Union. Two nonpermanent posts on the Security Council are held by Latin American nations, and there is always a Latin vice president of the General Assembly, if not a president.

The Latin American countries generally vote as a bloc on the majority of economic and social problems, although less often in political matters. Since the Latin American delegates receive flexible instructions from their governments, the power of this bloc is considerable. In problems arising from the cold war, the Latin American countries have, in general, voted with the United States. In June, 1950, the votes of Cuba and Ecuador—which were at that time members of the Security Council—afforded the necessary majority for the Security Council to approve aid to the Republic of (South) Korea. Since 1959, of course, Cuba has been an exception; it has tended more and more to vote on the side of the Soviet Union and after 1960 ceased to form part of the Latin American bloc. It should also be noted that Mexico and Guatemala (at least until 1954) have always voted with greater independence than the other Latin American countries. Brazil has supported Portugal on colonial questions, but the rest of the Latin American countries—and Brazil also, when Portugal has not been concerned—have voted against any colonial position.

At the 1945 San Francisco Conference, the Latin American nations had sought to prevent the Security Council from intervening in inter-American conflicts. To this end, they supported the adoption of Article 52 of the U.N. Charter, which recommended that regional conflicts be referred first to regional organizations. At the time, the United States accepted Article 52 with the utmost unwillingness; but in fact the Latin American countries did the United States a great service, for it was thanks to this article that the United States was later able to organize, without contravening the Charter, the North Atlantic Treaty Organization (NATO), the Southeast Asia Treaty Organization (SEATO), and the Central Treaty Organization (CENTO).

The United States has become the most ardent defender of regional organizations, and it has consistently voted in the Security Council to have cases referred to that body by the Latin American countries put before the Organization of American States (OAS). The Soviet Union, for its part, has been eager for a chance to intervene in inter-American affairs, and has always vetoed recommendations for referral to the OAS. It has opposed the OAS even when this has meant opposing the condemnation of a dictatorship. Thus, in 1960, the Soviet delegation asked the Security Council to deny validity to the economic and diplomatic sanctions invoked by the OAS against the Trujillo regime, on the ground that these were measures that could not be enforced without the authorization of the Security Council. The council confined itself to "noting" the decision of the OAS.

Only three Latin American countries have appealed to the Security Council, where they hoped to have the support of the Soviet bloc, rather than to the OAS. These were Guatemala, in 1954, when a group of U.S.-supported Guatemalan rightists invaded the country; Cuba, in 1961, on the occasion of the unsuccessful Bay of Pigs invasion; and Uruguay, in 1965, on the question of the U.S. intervention in the Dominican Republic. The United Nations sent a representative to investigate the Dominican situation, who discovered numerous cases of assassination and torture perpetrated by the Dominican dictatorial military forces.

In 1962, in the crisis that arose over the placement of Soviet missiles in Cuba, the United States, which considered itself the victim of aggression, also appealed to the Security Council, and the U.N. Secretary General went to Havana. But Castro refused to permit international inspection of the withdrawal of the Soviet rockets, a decision that some interpreted as freeing the United States from its promise not to attempt to overthrow the Castro government if the rockets were withdrawn.

Latin Americans have played distinguished roles in U.N. peace missions, for example, Galo Plaza, the former president of Ecuador, in Cyprus in 1965. But with the exception of Brazil and Colombia, which contributed (virtually token) forces to the Korean War, the Latin American countries have not sent contingents to U.N. forces in countries where conflicts have broken out.

Within the United Nations' sphere of action, Mexico convoked a conference in 1963, with the support of Chile, Brazil, Bolivia, and Ecuador. These nations negotiated a treaty, signed in February, 1967, which declared Latin America a denuclearized zone, that is, a region in which atomic tests and nuclear arms were prohibited. The United States and most of the Latin American countries signed this treaty, although Cuba did not.

It is from the specialized agencies that the Latin American countries have derived most benefit from their U.N. membership. The Economic Commission for Latin America (ECLA), with headquarters in Santiago, Chile, has played a leading role in formulating development policies, in preparing plans for the economic integration of Central America and of all Latin America, and in protesting international trade terms. The World Health Organization (WHO) has continued the public-health program carried out for more than half a century by the Pan American Health Organization (PAHO). In Patzacuaro, Mexico, the United Nations Educational, Scientific, and Cultural Organization (UNESCO) has established a center for the training of specialists in basic education. UNESCO also collaborates with other international organizations, particularly the International Labor Organization (ILO), in planning for the education and relocation of Indian groups in Bolivia, Peru, and Ecuador.

Many Latin Americans hold high positions in these organizations (as well as in the United Nations Secretariat): the Mexican Jaime Torres Bodet was director general of UNESCO from 1948 to 1952 (he resigned when the funds requested by the organization were not approved); the Brazilian Marcolino G. Candau has been director general of the WHO since 1956.

From Pan-Americanism to Inter-Americanism

We have seen that the Latin American countries tried, shortly after independence, to establish machinery for alliance and arbitration that would protect them from external aggression and resolve problems that arose among themselves. But all these attempts, beginning with the Congress of Panama of 1826, failed, and after the Lima conference of 1864, the idea of confederation was abandoned. In reality, tendencies toward local nationalism were more powerful than those toward what may be called Latin American nationalism. Not until the United States decided to take part in the efforts toward continental cooperation were they successful.

In 1881, the U.S. Secretary of State, James G. Blaine, proposed to the Latin American countries the convocation of a conference in Washington "for the purpose of considering and discussing the methods of preventing war among the nations of America." But although Blaine gave assurances that Washington would act on a footing of absolute equality, his proposal did not win support until 1889, when the first International Conference of American States was held. All the countries of Latin America were represented at the meeting, except the Dominican Republic, which did not attend in protest against the United States' failure to ratify a commercial treaty signed five years earlier. The American press, following the fashion of a period in which there was talk of Pan-Slavism, Panhellenism, and so on, began to speak of Pan-Americanism, and the name stuck.

The conference was to discuss an arbitration treaty, a customs union, and various commercial matters. Before the meeting, all the delegates were taken on a railway tour of the United States, to impress them with its industrial potential; they were so deeply impressed that they did not try to reach any agreement on commercial matters, for fear of further encouraging the United States' economic superiority. The United States, for its part, opposed—in vain, since it had only one vote—a denunciation of the right of conquest and of intervention in defense of foreign interests. An arbitration plan, although approved, was never ratified by the various countries.

But the conference was successful in establishing the institutions that were the basis of the Pan-American system: an International Union of the American Republics, with a Commercial Office of the American Republics as its only arm. At a second conference, held in Mexico City in 1901–02, the adjective "commercial" was deleted and the office was given an executive council composed of the Latin American ambassadors to Washington and a representative of the United States. At the fourth conference, held in Buenos Aires in 1910, the name of the organization was changed to the Union of American Republics, and the secretariat was renamed the Pan American Union. At a conference held in Havana in 1928, the name of the organization was changed to the Union of American States. A convention was drafted to regulate the operation of the Pan-American system, but this was never ratified by a sufficient number of countries. At the eighth conference, held in Lima in 1938, a new arm was established, the Meeting of Consultation of Ministers of Foreign Affairs, to deal with urgent matters; two years later, it authorized the formation of an Inter-American Peace Committee.

In addition to changing names, these conferences occupied themselves chiefly with drafting agreements for the solution of conflicts between countries. These were climaxed by the adoption of a Treaty to Avoid or Prevent Conflicts Between the American States (the so-called Gondra Treaty), signed in Santiago in 1923 and ratified by all the countries except Argentina. It established two commissions of inquiry, one in Montevideo and one in Washington, to which all conflicts were to be submitted; if these conflicts were not resolved within eighteen months, the parties were free to settle the conflict as best they could, that is, by force. In 1928, a special Conference on Conciliation and Arbitration met in Washington and drafted a convention of conciliation, ratified by eighteen states, and a convention of arbitration, ratified by sixteen. Still two more treaties were signed with the purpose of avoiding conflicts: the Saavedra Lamas treaty of nonagression and conciliation, signed in Buenos Aires in 1933; and a treaty of good offices and mediation, prepared by the Inter-American Conference on the Maintenance of Peace, which met in Buenos Aires in 1936. It was ratified by fifteen states. At this last meeting, the formation of an Inter-American Court was suggested, an idea that has often been proposed but never carried out. Altogether, twelve treaties were signed, none of which provided a system of enforcement. Nevertheless, with the exception of the Chaco War, all conflicts that arose were resolved in accordance with these treaties.

The first Meeting of Consultation of Ministers of Foreign Affairs was held in Panama in 1939, at the beginning of World War II. A second meeting was held in Havana in 1940, after the fall of France; it declared that any aggression against an American state would be considered as aggression against all the American states. The third meeting took place in Rio de Janeiro in 1942, after the Japanese attack on Pearl Harbor. These meetings were called in accordance with a leisurely proceeding: a country suggested to the executive council in Washington that, in its opinion, the situation was grave; the council consulted the governments, and if the majority decided that the gravity of the situation was sufficient to justify a meeting, it was called.

Until the end of World War II, then, the Pan-American system was composed of a few organizations and treaties, and was particularly concerned with questions relating to conflicts between the American states. But at the beginning of 1945, an Inter-American Conference on the Problems of War and Peace was held in the Palace of Chapultepec in Mexico City. This was attended by all the countries of the Pan-American system except Argentina, which had not declared war on the Axis powers. The Latin American governments, fearful that the new United Nations organization would absorb all the functions of the Pan-American system, wanted the system strengthened. The Latin Americans won out, and the so-called Act of Chapultepec was drafted; it declared the juridical equality of all the American states and affirmed that an attack against any state would be regarded as an attack against all, which, after consultation, would then invoke sanctions against the aggressor. The conference also proposed the codification of the rules and procedures of the Pan-American system. This was done at several successive conferences: the Inter-American Conference for the Maintenance of Continental Peace and Security (Rio de Janeiro, 1947); and the Ninth International Conference of American States (Bogotá, 1948). It was at the Bogotá conference that the Charter of the Organization of American States (OAS) was signed.

The Organization of American States does not confine itself to political questions but also deals with economic, cultural, and scientific matters. Its members are assessed according to a system of quotas; the United States furnishes approximately 60 per cent of the OAS budget.

The highest authority of the OAS is the Inter-American Conference. Scheduled to meet every five years, it has in fact met only once, at Caracas, in 1954. In urgent cases, a Meeting of Consultation of Ministers of Foreign Affairs is convoked. The Meeting of Consultation is assisted by an Advisory Committee on Defense. The executive arm of the OAS is the Council (COAS), which is composed of member countries' ambassadors to the OAS. The Council has three specialized subdivisions: the Economic and Social Council, the Council of Jurists, and the Cultural Council.

There are also various specialized organizations of the OAS: the Inter-American Children's Institute (Montevideo), the Inter-American Commission of Women (Washington), the Inter-American Indian Institute (Mexico City), the Inter-American Institute of Agricultural Sciences (San José), the Pan American Health Organization (Washington), and the Pan American Institute of Geography and History (Mexico City). There are also several advisory institutions, with headquarters in Washington: the Inter-American Commission on Human Rights, the Inter-American Defense Board, the Inter-American Nuclear Energy Commission, the Inter-American Peace Committee, the Inter-American Statistical Institute, and the Special Consultative Committee on Security. With the creation of the Alliance for Progress, in 1961, new organizations were set up.

In 1967, a Special Inter-American Conference, meeting in Buenos Aires, made some changes in the structure of the OAS, but they were more of nomenclature than of substance. The Inter-American Conference was replaced by an annual General Assembly, the Council was made into a Permanent Council and the Pan American Union into a Secretariat General. The Inter-American Economic and Social Council and a new Inter-American Council for Education, Science, and Culture will have equal ranking with the Permanent Council and will be responsible to the General Assembly. The Secretary General will be appointed for five years instead of ten, and may be re-elected, but may not succeed a person from his own country.

But the really important thing is, clearly, the juridical foundation of the inter-American system. The Charter of the OAS affirms the equality of all member states and the principle of nonintervention of one state in the internal affairs of the others. Aggression against one member is considered as aggression against all. The Charter refuses to recognize territorial or other acquisitions obtained by force. All conflicts between the member states are to be resolved by means of direct negotiations, good offices, mediation, investigation and conciliation, arbitration, or judicial settlement. In emergencies, the president of the Council may convoke a Meeting of

Consultation and the Council of the OAS may act as a provisional Meeting of Consultation.

The two pillars of the inter-American system are the Inter-American Treaty of Reciprocal Assistance (Rio Treaty) and the American Treaty of Pacific Settlement (Pact of Bogotá). The Rio Treaty gives the OAS the means of enforcing its decisions. By its terms, member states may take immediate measures to aid a country that has been attacked, without waiting for consultation. If a situation arises that jeopardizes the peace or safety of the Americas—although without being one of armed aggression—the Meeting of Consultation of Ministers of Foreign Affairs is to convene. In the event of conflict between two or more American states, the Council of the OAS is to order a truce and restore the *status quo ante bellum*. The treaty provides for a series of measures or sanctions: withdrawal of ambassadors, breaking off of diplomatic relations, interruption of economic relations and of communications, and the use of armed force. The OAS may adopt these measures only by a two-thirds vote of its members, and, once adopted, the enforcement of any measure is obligatory (although no country may be compelled to use armed force without its consent).

The Treaty has been invoked in several cases which, altogether, have affected more than half the members of the OAS, and has served to prevent minor conflicts among American countries from developing into wars. Especially notable have been the aid to Costa Rica, when that country was invaded by way of Nicaragua in 1955; the sanctions against the Dominican Republic in 1960–61, after it had organized an attempt on the life of President Betancourt of Venezuela; and the solution of the boundary dispute between Honduras and Nicaragua in 1957.

Other events have shown that the Treaty has serious defects, however. The use of armed force is, in reality, limited to the United States, with some token forces from other countries, as in the case of the intervention in the Dominican Republic in 1965. Moreover, the majority of the Latin American countries tend to consider any collective use of armed force as military intervention. Thus in 1965, when the United States proposed the formation of a permanent Inter-American Peace Force, the majority of the Latin American countries opposed this, because they feared it would facilitate intervention. For example, in the event that a majority of the Latin American countries were under dictatorship, such a force could be used to protect the dictatorships from their domestic adversaries (who would always be labeled as Communists), or to support the enemies of democratic regimes. Significantly, the only countries that supported the idea of the Inter-American Peace Force were those under dictatorial regimes: Argentina, Paraguay, and Brazil. (The peace force should not be confused with the proposed Inter-American Army. This army would be charged with defending the Latin American countries against extracontinental interference. By replacing the national armies, it would, rather than encouraging coups, make them impossible.)

On the other hand, although the enforcement of sanctions invoked in accordance with the Rio Treaty is to be obligatory, there is no way of compelling this. When, in 1963, it was agreed to break off relations with Cuba, several countries took months to implement the decision and Mexico never did, despite diplomatic pressure from Washington. Of course, a treaty that is enforced only because of the insistence of one of its signatories is a treaty that has no value in itself but only serves as a pretext—and only to the extent to which one of the signatories can and wants to exert pressure for its enforcement. Just because of this, although there is much talk of the Rio Treaty in government circles in Latin America, the people as a whole have never taken it seriously and know very little about it.

The other pillar of the inter-American system is the Bogotá Pact. It must be pointed out that this pact has been ratified by only ten of the twenty-one American countries; the United States is among the countries that has not yet ratified it. The signatories of the pact have committed themselves to submit for peaceful solution all disputes and conflicts with other American states, before referring them to the United Nations. Should one of the parties fail to carry out the decision of the International Court of Justice or of an arbitral award, the other party may propose a Meeting of Consultation of Ministers of Foreign Affairs; in this sense, the Bogotá Pact is related to the Rio Treaty.

The Inter-American Peace Committee has been more effective than the Bogotá Pact. The committee, whose members are elected for five years by the Council of the OAS, is responsible only to a Meeting of Consultation, but it may not intervene unless requested to do so by the two parties to the dispute and within the limits established by the two parties themselves. Although the decisions of the committee are not compulsorily binding, it has succeeded in settling some disputes.

The inter-American system has functioned relatively well in what could be considered normal cases of conflict. But it has not worked so well in the unprecedented situations arising from the cold war and from the wish to accelerate development, characteristic of the present stage of relations between the United States and Latin America. In this stage bilateral relations have been losing importance because the problems have arisen on a continental scale and solutions have been sought for them on that scale. Thus present-day relations between the United States and Latin America must be viewed in relation to political developments in Latin America in the last quarter century.

CHAPTER VIII

Who Wants Social Change?

The present stage of Latin American history, which began with World War II, has been characterized by accelerating industrialization, development of the labor movement, the attempts of populist movements to effect social change, the relative success of revolutions in Venezuela and Bolivia, the appearance of new forms of militarism, the radicalization of nationalism, the establishment of a Communist regime in the hemisphere (Cuba), and, finally, the reinforcement of standpat and conservative tendencies.

The last thirty years have witnessed profound changes in the middle sectors of society and much smaller and by no means fundamental changes in the life of the submerged masses. This has brought consequent changes in the nature of political power and the growth of spectacular forms of political action: guerrilla warfare, student activism, militant anti-Americanism. But the problem that has concerned all groups is that of how to accelerate development.

The problems connected with development and social change came to the fore in 1960, thanks in large part to the

Alliance for Progress. If the Alliance, as we shall see, failed insofar as it was merely a plan for development, it exercised a considerable influence as an ideological program in which a maximum amount of pragmatism was mixed with a minimum dose of dogma.

The struggles over the problem of development—the solutions that will be proposed, the new thinking that will emerge—will no doubt determine the pattern of Latin American history and of the relations between Latin America and the United States in the decades to come.

The Isolated Revolutions

The repercussions of the 1929 world economic crisis, which limited the markets for Latin America's exports, and the rise of fascism in Europe, created the conditions for a series of governments by force in Latin America in the 1930's. In all South America, only Colombia, Uruguay, and Chile had democratically elected governments; in Central America, only Costa Rica.

But at the same time that this wave of dictatorships and semidictatorships was making itself felt, there was also a rise of democratic elements. The populist movements grew, new groups favoring social reform arose, and the previously scattered labor movement was unified under the impetus of the Confederation of Latin American Workers (CTAL), still not controlled by the Communists, although the latter were influential in it. In Bolivia and Paraguay, there were short-lived military governments supported by the populist movements. These democratic forces hoped that President Roosevelt's Good Neighbor Policy would mean American support for the forces of democratization in Latin America. But they were mistaken. Washington limited itself to trying to prevent Nazi infiltration of Latin America and to ensuring the collaboration of the Latin American governments in the event of war.

When the war broke out, the situation began to change. The Communists, as a consequence of the Nazi-Soviet pact of 1939, tried to organize strikes and to exert pressure on the governments to remain neutral. This put them back into the state of political isolation from which they had emerged through the popular-front tactics beginning in 1935. But the democratic and reformist elements became increasingly aggressive, for they were convinced that the United States would eventually enter the war and would then see the necessity of supporting their efforts to overthrow the dictatorships in Latin America as well as in Europe.

It did not happen in that way. When Germany attacked the Soviet Union, in 1941, the Latin American Communists emerged from their isolation and regained their influence. They won control of the labor movement in several countries, as well as the direction of the CTAL. Above all, they fought to abort the struggle against the Latin American dictatorships, for they believed that any change would endanger Allied aid to the Soviet Union. The Communists even supported dictatorial governments: they backed the Peruvian dictator Manuel Prado (b. 1889), whom they called the "Creole Stalin"; they supported Somoza of Nicaragua (1896–1956), describing him as a "fatherly" dictator; they agreed to organize a Communist Party in the Dominican Republic, so that the dictator Rafael Leónidas Trujillo might be presented as a "good democrat"; and they furnished several ministers to the dictatorial Batista regime in Cuba. Following the tactics of presenting themselves as "good democrats," the Communists changed the name of their party in several countries: they became the Popular Vanguard Party in Haiti and Costa Rica, the Popular Socialist Party in Cuba, Colombia, and the Dominican Republic. The Communists also characterized all anti-imperialist campaigns as "infantile." The dictators, for their part, declared themselves antifascist—even Vargas, who sent an expedition to fight with the Allied forces in Italy. Only the Argentine conservatives and military resisted pressure and remained neutral, turning their country into a refuge for Nazi capital and, later, for Nazi fugitives.

But none of this could prevent a wave of democratization following the end of the war. This was owed entirely to the populist movements and to popular pressure, for neither North American diplomacy nor the Latin American Communists (although the latter had no decisive strength anywhere) did anything in that direction. In some countries, the military assumed the task of overthrowing the dictatorship (Brazil); in others, the dictators called for elections and yielded their places (Peru, Ecuador, and Cuba); and in others, students, political groups, and small nuclei of young military men fought to overthrow dictatorships (Guatemala and Venezuela). But dictatorships remained in the Dominican Republic, Paraguay, Bolivia, Nicaragua, Honduras, El Salvador, and Argentina.

Mexico elected its first civilian president since the revolution, Miguel Alemán (b. 1902), in 1946. In Chile, the Radical Gabriel González Videla (b. 1898) became president in 1946 as head of the Popular Front. In Cuba, a democratic government, headed by Ramón Grau Sanmartín (b. 1887) and disposed to effect some reforms, was elected in 1944. In Guatemala, an exiled educator, Juan José Arévalo (b. 1904), was elected in 1945 and governed democratically, despite a score of attempted military coups against him.

In Costa Rica, an attempt by the government, in which the Communists had a great deal of influence, to annul the 1948 elections that had given the victory to a conservative candidate, provoked a rising of youth groups. After a brief civil war, a junta was set up, presided over by José Figueres (b. 1906), the founder of the new National Liberation Party. After nationalizing the banks and effecting some reforms, he turned over the government to the previously elected conservative candidate.

In Venezuela, the junta set up after the fall of the dictatorship of General Isaías Medina Angarita (1897–1953) drafted a new constitution, encouraged the organization of labor, and undertook a program of agrarian reform, all under the presidency of Rómulo Betancourt (b. 1908), founder of the new Democratic Action party (AD). The junta called elections in 1948, and the novelist Rómulo Gallegos (1884–1969) was elected president.

In Peru, the populist APRA movement supported the candidacy of Luis Bustamante Rivero (b. 1894) in the elections of 1945, won a great victory at the polls, was legalized, and furnished the government with several ministers, who tried to effect some moderate reforms. In Ecuador, a liberal, Galo Plaza (b. 1906), was elected president in 1948. In Brazil, General Eurico Gaspar Dutra (b. 1885) was elected president in late 1945 and governed constitutionally, although he did not modify any of the Vargas policies.

Political democratization was thus fairly extensive. And in certain key countries, like Venezuela and Peru, power was held by populist elements disposed to bring about social change. Latin America was going through a period exceptionally favorable for creating the conditions that would end its stagnation and make progress possible. The oligarchic groups and the armies were demoralized and therefore willing to make concessions for the social democratization of their countries. The forces of reform—the middle class, organized labor, intellectuals—were in the ascendancy, convinced that they should wait no longer for a just participation in government, and populist ideology had penetrated large segments of the population. The Latin American countries had available considerable cash reserves that had been accumulated during the war, and could be invested in capital goods. New industries had also been created during the war, and there was beginning to be a domestic market for Latin American products. Raw materials were still selling at high prices, for they were needed in the reconstruction of Europe and the conversion of American industry to peacetime use.

One single factor was lacking, which in Latin America at that time was considered indispensable because it had been so for so many decades: United States acquiescence in, and support of, social change. But Washington was unaware of the efforts the Latin American people were making for democratization and change, and of the fact that these changes would be in the national interest of the United States. Preoccupied with postwar Europe and the Soviet Union, the United States believed that only by encouraging order and immobility in Latin America would it be able to isolate the continent from the cold war and keep it from becoming another headache for American diplomacy. And because of this, the efforts for change were frustrated.

When the oligarchic forces saw that the United States would not actively support the populist elements, they recovered their aggressiveness. There followed a series of military coups that destroyed the populist governments. In Venezuela, the same military men who had helped to overthrow the dictatorship in 1945 seized power in 1948 and sent President Rómulo Gallegos into exile. Ten years of brutal and corrupt dictatorship followed, during which the Democratic

Action party, the labor unions, and later the new Christian Democratic party (COPEI) carried on an underground struggle against the regime of Colonel Marcos Pérez Jiménez (b. 1914). In Peru, President Bustamante Rivero, under pressure from the oligarchy, broke off his alliance with the APRA; he was thus left without a base of support and the military overthrew him in 1948, establishing a dictatorship under General Manuel Odría (b. 1897). During his eight years in power, Odría brutally persecuted the Apristas, accusing them of being Communists while accepting the support of the real Communists; he finally agreed to call elections in 1956.

In Cuba, General Batista took advantage of popular discontent with the corruption that had characterized the government of President Carlos Prío Socarrás (b. 1903), but which had not prevented it from being one of the most progressive and liberal regimes in the island's history. Batista seized power in 1952 and held it until 1959, when his regime collapsed more under the weight of its own corruption than because of the activity of Fidel Castro's guerrillas.

In Brazil, the former dictator Getúlio Vargas was elected president in 1951, and although this time he did not govern dictatorially, he maintained the social structure. He committed suicide in 1954, under pressure from the military. In Ecuador, in 1947, the military exiled President José María Velasco Ibarra (b. 1893), a demagogue who had himself elected again in 1952 and governed virtually as dictator.

Colombia had enjoyed nearly a century of civilian rule. In 1946, a conservative government succeeded a long series of liberal governments, and in 1950 the election was won by an extreme right-wing candidate, Laureano Gómez (1889–1965). Gómez massacred liberals in the villages and set off a long period of guerrilla warfare and terrorism, which in ten years cost the country several hundred thousand lives. In 1953, General Gustavo Rojas Pinilla (b. 1900) seized power, established a dictatorship, was unable to end the rural violence, and was finally deposed, in 1957, by a general strike of workers and tradesmen in which even the bankers joined.

In Paraguay, dictatorship followed dictatorship, until in 1954 General Alfredo Stroessner (b. 1912) consolidated his power; he has been at the head of the government ever since.

Even in Chile, with its democratic tradition, General Carlos Ibañez del Campo (1877–1960), who had been dictator a quarter of a century earlier, was elected president in 1952 with a demagogic program, and although he governed by constitutional means he set off an inflation that has paralyzed the country's progress for years. In the Dominican Republic and Haiti, the dictators who had survived the war stayed in power. In Nicaragua, Anastasio Somoza was shot to death by a student in 1956 and was succeeded by his son. In Honduras, Tiburcio Carías (b. 1876), who had governed the country as dictator since 1933, retired in 1949, but was succeeded by a series of his friends. In El Salvador, there was a series of military governments, more or less progressive and constitutional, which, however, did not alter the social structure or guarantee the basic human rights.

Only Mexico, Costa Rica, Uruguay, and Chile maintained uninterrupted constitutional government. The oligarchic system had recaptured the greater part of its positions. Only in three countries did it appear threatened: Bolivia, Guatemala, and Argentina.

In Bolivia, the Nationalist Revolutionary Movement (MNR), formed after the Chaco War by Víctor Paz Estenssoro (b. 1907), included some fascist elements in its ranks but was in fact populist. The MNR supported the colonels who seized power on three occasions between 1939 and 1946 and tried to effect moderate reforms. In 1951, the MNR won the elections. The incumbent president made a deal with the army, and a coup was staged to prevent Paz's inauguration. But the miners, organized into a powerful union by Juan Lechín (b. 1912), together with some groups in the MNR, fought the army and defeated it. In April, 1952, the MNR took over the government to which it had been elected.

Paz immediately nationalized the tin mines (all in the hands of Bolivian capitalists) and, a year later, instituted an agrarian reform. Bolivia entered upon a period of grave economic crisis, marked by inflation and a budget deficit. But the United States, when it saw that the Bolivian revolutionary government was not leaning toward the Soviet Union and that the Communists, although they were very active, were not assuming leadership of the revolution, began to aid the MNR government. Since that time, the United States has given extensive aid to Bolivia; more dollars per capita than to any other Latin American government.

The MNR government was able to carry out essential reforms because the army had been broken up in the struggles of 1952. But the miners, the revolutionary combat troops, won considerable privileges, which they refused to give up when requested to do so by the government in order to combat inflation. The 1956 elections were won by Hernán Siles Zuazo (b. 1914), whose term of office was marked by a constant struggle with the miners to impose a stabilization plan. When Paz was re-elected, in 1960, he succeeded in making the agrarian reform effective, and in 1964, for the first time in its history, Bolivia imported virtually no foodstuffs.

In that same year, the MNR, to prevent the election of Lechín (whose demagoguery it feared), amended the constitution with the object of permitting Paz's re-election. But shortly afterwards his vice president, General René Barrientos, allied himself with Lechín, the Communist students, and the rightist parties, and staged a coup. After a period of undisguised dictatorship, Barrientos had himself elected in 1966, without any real opposition, and then imposed on the miners restrictions more severe than those the MNR had asked. After a massacre of the miners, he virtually destroyed their union. In April, 1969, Barrientos was killed in an air accident; he was succeeded by his vice president, Luis Adolfo Síles Salinas, but this brought no change in the country's situation.

Barrientos' coup should be considered an accident within the framework of the revolution, for the fundamental elements—nationalization of tin, agrarian reform, and political integration of the masses—were respected, perhaps because it was literally impossible to revert to the pre-1952 situation. The Bolivian Revolution was tough and violent, and was not above corruption and injustice. It did not substantially improve the living standard of the average Bolivian, although it did considerably raise that of the peasants, and that of the miners even more. But it achieved something very important in a country that had previously had systems of serfdom in full flower and a long history of dictatorships: it changed the Indians into peasants, giving them a sense of dignity and participation in the nation's life, and for twelve years it gave the country constitutional government. It should be noted that the Bolivian Revolution no longer interests the "revolutionaries" in Latin America.

Another country in which it appeared that the oligarchic system was going to disappear was Guatemala. When the Ubico dictatorship was overthrown in 1944, no one in the country had any political experience. A dozen political parties and several union confederations were immediately formed; thanks to their better preparation, scattered Communist elements attained influential posts in one or the other of these groups. President Juan José Arévalo governed by balancing the different parties against one another instead of trying to fuse them into two or three solid ones.

In 1949, Colonel Francisco Arana, considered Arévalo's most likely successor, was assassinated, and in 1951 Colonel Jacobo Arbenz (b. 1914) was elected president. Congress passed a moderate agrarian reform law, whose enforcement remained wholly in the hands of Communist elements (the only ones with any clear ideas on the matter), who had already won direction of the unions. The Communists organized the peasants and finally presented themselves publicly under the name of the Guatemalan Workers' Party. Instead of giving land as property, they began to divide it on the basis of usufruct, which gave them a lever for pressuring the peasants, for the latter saw the Communists as those who could turn lands over to them—and could also take them away.

The United Fruit Company objected to the distribution of some of its lands, and a conflict ensued. But instead of negotiating and obtaining concessions, as the democratic government of Costa Rica was doing at that very moment, the Communist directors of the Institute of Agrarian Reform used the conflict to create a strong anti-American sentiment and to put themselves into key positions. The government bought arms from Czechoslovakia, adopted an international policy favorable to Soviet positions and, following the Party line, opposed Central American unification, which was beginning to be talked of.

The Communists in Guatemala had been able to make use

of the inexperience of the young politicians to create a situation which, although it in no way served the nation's interests, could be considered a provocation of the United States. That country—as we have seen—answered by ill-concealed support of an invasion headed by Colonel Carlos Castillo Armas (1914–57), which took place in 1954. The U.N. Security Council, to which Guatemala appealed, did nothing. Arbenz fled, his army did not put up a struggle, and neither did the militia organized by the Communists.

Castillo Armas annulled the agrarian reform and closed down the unions. There followed a long period of dictatorship and semidictatorship. The possibility of social change was thus frustrated by the Communists' wish to employ it as a trap for American diplomacy and by their utilization, to that end, of the general political inexperience that had resulted from many years of dictatorship.

In Argentina, after the military assumed power in 1930, all governments had in reality been controlled by the armed forces. In 1943, the military staged a coup against the conservative government, despite the fact that the latter had shown itself docile and had kept the country out of World War II. The people, however, soon grew tired of military rule. A young military lodge, the Group of United Officers (GOU), among them Colonel Juan Domingo Perón (b. 1895), Minister of Labor, decided to seek civilian support. The middle-class parties rejected them, and Perón began to work on the unions, taking advantage of the fact that many of their members were peasants who had only recently entered industry, during the war, when industry had grown and there was no possibility of immigration. These workers, whom he called *descamisados* (shirtless ones), formed the base of Perón's support. Perón established control of the military over the General Labor Confederation (CGT), which was passive and badly divided, and then made a bid for the direction of the unions and unionists he had drawn to his side. They organized a large demonstration when Perón was arrested—in fear of a coup—in October, 1945, and forced the authorities to release him. In February, 1946, Perón was elected president.

Perón encouraged industrialization, and in order to acquire capital goods exhausted nearly all the foreign-exchange reserves accumulated during the war. He also bought the British-owned railroads and the telephone system. To win over the Church, he established the teaching of Catholicism in the schools—which broke a long tradition of secular education in Argentina. To hold the loyalty of the trade unions, he promulgated laws for the protection of the workers (social security, organization of agricultural workers, vacations with pay) and enforced others that had been passed years earlier.

But, at the same time, Perón established an increasingly dictatorial regime; it was founded on a makeshift doctrine called *justicialisimo,* which claimed to be neither capitalist nor Communist and was in fact modeled on the fascist regime in Italy. Perón's wife, Eva (1919–52), united all of Argentina's charitable foundations into a single organization under her control, and by this means won enormous popularity and influence. The regime exiled opponents, some of whom, basing their charges on documents found in Germany, accused the Peróns of having been Nazi agents. At home, conservative, radical, and socialist opposition was energetic but weak. The government had recourse to violence and torture by the police and incited its partisan mobs to attack the socialist *Casa del Pueblo* and the oligarchic Jockey Club. Particularly harsh repressive measures were taken against the railway and maritime unions, which had refused to submit to Peronist control. Meanwhile, the government established a monopoly of foreign trade, buying from producers at low prices and selling abroad at high prices, for the purpose of making funds available for its social programs.

But with its systematic anti-Americanism and some efforts at modernization, the regime satisfied the national vanity of the Argentines. It also gave the workers and part of the peasantry, traditionally forgotten, the feeling that they were at last being taken into consideration and that they were the ones who really governed the country. Perón and his wife talked of the *descamisados,* created a populist folklore, and were very skillful in giving advantages and privileges to the unions without alienating the business world.

There were some attempts against the regime on the part of the more conservative generals, but the young army officers were Perón supporters. But in 1954, for reasons that are still obscure (apparently because the Church was trying to influence the unions), Perón attacked the Church and the strong reaction against him counterbalanced union support. In September, 1955, the navy and part of the army rebelled. Perón gave up without a struggle and fled to Paraguay, then to Venezuela, the Dominican Republic, and Spain.

Perón was much admired during his ten years in power. His propaganda—especially its anti-American features—found a response in Latin America, and Peronist parties and unions were founded in some countries, although they never achieved real influence. The Perón regime was incontestably demagogic, for it promised many things it did not produce. It mounted a constant verbal attack on the oligarchy, which it blamed for its inability to develop the country, but it never adopted any measures for reforming the basis of the oligarchic system, the country's agrarian structure. It was also extraordinarily corrupt.

But, in the context of Latin American politics, Perón effected an important innovation: he was the first chief executive to appeal to the masses and to give them the feeling that they had power, although in reality, political power was in the hands of the Peronist group and the military officers who supported it. The masses identified with Perón, and above all with Eva Perón. When Eva died, and it was learned that she had left millions of dollars' worth of jewels and clothing—at a time when meat had to be rationed in Argentina, the world's leading meat-producer—the Argentine women felt proud that "their" Eva had dressed and bedecked herself "like a lady." "That's what I would like for my wife. If she can't have it, I'm glad Evita could," the workers said. It is not surprising that, after Peron's fall, the Peronist masses—who amounted to more than 2 million voters—showed themselves homesick for the days in which they were cosseted, all the more because the Argentine employers hastened to try to take away from the workers the benefits Perón had given them. In the workers' eyes, the governments that succeeded Perón were identified with measures to lower their standard of living and to lessen the influence of the unions. This is why Perón continued to be very popular, at least until 1966, when his followers began to divide into "Peronists with Perón" and "Peronists without Perón."

Perón's fall marked the beginning of the end of the wave of postwar dictatorships. But for ten years, a large part of Latin America had lived under dictatorship—and precisely that part in which the populist social-reform movements had seemed closest to triumph. Profound changes had occurred during those ten years. The dictatorships especially benefited from the increasing industrialization and the rise in the price of raw materials caused by the Korean War. Upon this base were superimposed the plentiful public works that every dictatorship undertakes, and the general prosperity of the West in that period. The result was an accelerated growth in the size and prosperity of the middle sectors. The living style of these groups was rapidly Americanized. As new industries were created, a new type of businessman emerged. Unlike the traditional Latin American businessmen, who were attached to the oligarchic system because it guaranteed order, these new businessmen looked to the state less for police functions than for the promotion of industry and public works. The first crop of economists, engineers, and technicians educated after the war united with the middle class and began to work in industry alongside a new generation of workers who, since they had been educated under dictatorships, had no interest in a political life that had not existed or in ideologies no one had been able to discuss.

In short, there was increased prosperity for the entire society—except for the submerged masses. The consequence of this was that the middle sectors (or those we have called public opinion) changed their attitude. Without ceasing to talk of—or to desire—changes in the social structure, they began to think that such changes would come about automatically through a steady enlargement of the middle class. It was not necessary to resort to revolution or to destroy the oligarchic system, because this system would continue to be transformed by the effects of the economic revolution. In short, development would create the conditions for further development and would destroy the obstacles to it.

This integration into the system was not made by a decision from above or as a result of planning. It resulted from an increasing prosperity that occurred at a time when political and social change was impossible because there were dictatorships nearly everywhere. Of course, in joining the system—often without realizing that they were doing so—the middle sectors acquired certain characteristics of the system. They became "oligarchs," so to speak, in their way of acting and functioning; they did not abandon their conviction that it was necessary to "go to the people," but now they did so in a paternalistic way, as a new "elite," and accepted the idea, which they had previously rejected, of revolution from above.

At the same time, the growing U.S. investments in Latin America, the support of the dictatorships by the Eisenhower administration, the pressure of the State Department—which applied the epithet "Communist" to any reform group—and the case of Guatemala, all created a climate in which the germination of an aggressively anti-American nationalism was almost spontaneous. The Communists abetted this anti-Americanism—which joined such opposites as leftist students and businessmen resentful of American competition—but they did not create it. This nationalism gave the middle sectors an ideological "justification" for having abandoned their earlier revolutionary position and for having allowed themselves to be integrated, in some measure, into the oligarchic system.

The forces that might have counterbalanced this tendency to the acceptance of the oligarchic system were persecuted by the dictatorships; their leaders and militants were in exile, in jail, or in hiding, and many were assassinated—especially in Venezuela, Peru, and Cuba.

The dictatorships, however, found systematic support from the Church and from the Communist movement. The Communists presented an interesting phenomenon: in countries under dictatorships, the Communist parties divided; a small group joined the opposition and went into exile, while the cadres and a group of leaders collaborated with the dictatorships. Officially, the dictators were all extremely anti-Communist, and all passed laws to outlaw the Communist Party (although they never enforced these laws). Yet they left the field open to the Communists when their police forces eliminated the democratic union leaders, killing, exiling, or jailing them, and hindered the propaganda of the populist and democratic movements and the democratic education of the young. In this way, the Communists were able to seize the leadership of many unions, train new militants, and make propaganda, while the democratic groups were gagged and persecuted; in return, although tacitly, the Communists tried to prevent strikes and popular action against the dictatorships—though they did not always succeed.

But despite the support of the Church and the Communists, the dictatorships ended by arousing general opposition, since their excessive corruption disrupted the economy. The middle sectors, although they had become evolutionists, did not cease to desire a democratic political regime; the greater their prosperity, the more impatient they became for political power, something best achieved under a democratic government. Eventually, the younger elements in the Church and the army became disturbed by the loss of prestige of those institutions and it was these elements, impelled by the growing activity of the democratic opposition, that finally brought about the overthrow of the dictatorships.

The Church, alarmed by its experience in Argentina, which proved that a dictatorship was not always loyal to its ally, induced the hierarchy in many countries to draw away from the dictatorial regimes and to condemn them; the students, reflecting the sentiments of "public opinion," redoubled their protests. All this nearly always induced a military group (often the navy) to rise up against the dictatorship and administer the *coup de grâce*.

The fall of the dictatorships found a prosperous middle class impatient for power (or, at least, for participation in it) and extremely nationalistic; a body of youth without political experience (because a dictatorship had not let them acquire any) but accustomed to illegal and at times violent protest; and an oligarchy that had integrated its chief opponents into its economic system and was ready and disposed to integrate them into its political system.

This was the situation in Latin America at the time of the inauguration of John F. Kennedy, who appeared disposed to seek a new U.S. Latin American policy.

Bureaucratization of the Revolution

The word "revolution" has a different meaning in Latin America from that usually given to it in the United States.

In the United States, a revolution is thought of as a change of power brought about by force, or the inauguration of a socialist or Communist regime. But in Latin America, a revolution is seen as the destruction of obstacles to economic development and the establishment of democratic regimes.

The Truman and Eisenhower administrations were more impressed by the American meaning given to the word revolution than by the capitalistic content this term had in Latin America, and they rejected it. The Latin American revolutionary elements thus found themselves isolated. Eventually, as we have just seen, these revolutionary elements were absorbed into the very society they had wanted to alter. And it was then that Washington showed itself disposed to accept and support a revolution that the Latin American middle sectors had wanted almost twenty years earlier but that they did not really want any longer. The lack of synchronization between the dynamic sectors of Latin America and Washington isolated the possibilities of revolution after World War II; the same lack of synchronization bureaucratized them after John F. Kennedy's electoral victory in 1960.

Anti-Americanism, as we have said, was very strong among the middle sectors at this time, for they considered that Washington not only did not oppose the dictatorships but actually supported them. Certain spectacular manifestations—the awarding of medals, the reception of dictators at the White House, and so forth—reinforced this feeling. The growing number of American firms in Latin America created animosity in the business world.

These feelings were dramatically expressed during the visit of Vice President Richard M. Nixon to Latin America in 1958, which was accompanied by violent anti-American demonstrations (many of them staged, to be sure). All this roused Washington from its indifference and forced it to realize that the situation in Latin America could become difficult for the United States. A short time later, the Fidel Castro regime was established in Cuba; it was violently anti-American, aroused great sympathy throughout Latin America, and alarmed the United States. In Latin American eyes, at least, the change in attitude that was becoming evident in Washington in the late 1950's was attributable primarily to a reaction against Nixon's reception and the fear of Castro. To rise above these suspicions, something much more positive and far-reaching was needed. That "something" was the Alliance for Progress, together with the personality of John F. Kennedy.

What made President Kennedy different from his predecessors in the White House was his new interpretation of the American national interest in Latin America. Before Kennedy, this interest had been seen as that of maintaining order in Latin America; it therefore coincided with the interests of the oligarchic groups. Kennedy believed that the interests of the United States coincided with the interests of the populist movements and with the social changes that were tending to make Latin America a society similar—in principle—to that of the United States. For in the twentieth century, the only revolutionary society in the world has been the American; this society has exerted an influence for social change independently of the official policy of the government and even, perhaps, of the wishes of the people of the United States. The traditional U.S. diplomacy in Latin America had tended to counterbalance the influence of American society; Kennedy wanted to turn that influence to advantage.

The result of this new way of looking at the national interest—which was less clear and sharp than suggested here, and subject to many contradictory influences—was the Alliance for Progress. The Alliance gathered up the aspirations of Latin American populism and tried to inject them with American techniques. The Alliance—as it was conceived—had for its object the financing of social change; that is, it sought to fill the gaps that are produced in every economy as a consequence of structural changes: a transitory drop in agricultural production resulting from agrarian reform, withdrawal of investments and flight of capital because of fiscal reforms, and so forth. In short, the Alliance was entrusted with the task of financing a peaceful revolution in Latin America.

The concept of the Alliance for Progress was based on the assumption that the oligarchic forces would accept change, for three reasons: fear of Castroism, pressure from the United States, and pressure from the populist movements. Events proved this to be a bad calculation. Castroism, to the extent that American diplomacy contained and isolated it, especially after October, 1962, ceased to be a threat; American pressure was of no avail in an epoch in which any small country could defy the United States (or the Soviet Union) with impunity; and the populist movements were unable to arouse the middle sectors from their passivity. The only thing left to sustain the Alliance was the possibility of exerting pressure from below, of awaking and organizing the submerged masses. But American diplomacy either did not dare desire this or, having desired it, could do nothing without the collaboration of elements in Latin America that were capable of working among the submerged masses. And at the time, these elements did not exist.

President Kennedy realized that the problems of the Latin American nations should be dealt with on a continental level (something his immediate predecessor had also been aware of, although in a vague way). But the forces favorable to continentalization in Latin America had lost the initiative because of their integration into the oligarchic system and because of the narrow nationalism that had begun to dominate over the continental ideas of populism. Moreover, from the beginning, the large countries sought to limit continentalization, since bilateral dealings were more favorable for them. The support of continentalization came only from the medium-sized and small countries, and even here the support came more from certain populist forces than from the governments.

The Alliance, as an official plan, inevitably had to be carried out through government channels. But except in a few countries, the governments of Latin America were in the hands of groups favorable to the continuation of the system whose replacement the Alliance intended to finance and accelerate. In short, the Alliance had a flaw in principle: it expected to bring about the suicide of a social system, something that has never happened. Thus, within a few years after the Alliance had begun its operations, the Latin American governments had divested it of content and had converted it into merely another plan for aid.

The result of all this has been that the Alliance, although its machinery and phraseology have survived, has been changed into a plan for economic and technical aid but not for social change. The oligarchic system, after incorporating into itself the middle sectors of society, also incorporated the Alliance. This was not done through any government conspiracy or conscious plan. It was the result of the spontaneous action of the oligarchic governments, the inability of the experts to understand the social possibilities of the Alliance, the passivity of the forces that favored social change, and the tendency of every bureaucracy to perpetuate itself and to bureaucratize whatever is put in its charge.

This does not mean that the concept of the Alliance was wrong; what defeated it were its procedures and its Latin American allies (the governments). It is possible to predict that when the forces of change—middle sectors collaborating with the submerged masses—once again feel frustrated and want to alter the social structure, the concepts of the Alliance will prove useful, and it is possible to hope that, when this happens, there will be synchronization between these forces and American policy. But until this does happen, Latin America will continue to be an oligarchic society, at once chaotic and immobile, with an ever more modern façade and an ever more anachronistic structure.

The Alliance for Progress

The ideas that the Kennedy administration and the Latin American populist movements held in common attained official form at the Punta del Este conference of August, 1961. But even before that time, some preparatory steps had been taken which show that the Alliance was not an artificial or utopian creation but one that responded to pressing needs. That Vice President Nixon's visit and Castroism helped to make the United States aware of these needs cannot be doubted, but this does not alter the fact that the Alliance was an attempt to satisfy these needs. Had Castro not existed, it is possible that the Alliance would have taken longer, but it is virtually certain that a similar plan would eventually have been prepared.

The preparatory steps included Brazilian President Juscelino Kubitschek's proposal for an Operation Pan America, in 1958. As a result of this proposal, there was established a Committee of Twenty-One in the Organization of American States to propose new methods of development. Then, in 1959, there was the creation of the Inter-American Development Bank (IDB), which the United States had formerly opposed but now supported. There were also the Act of Bogotá of 1960, the result of a conference in the Colombian capital that set objectives for social development and was signed by all the countries of the inter-American system except Cuba; President Kennedy's proposal of a ten-year development plan in March, 1961; and the establishment of a Fund for Social Progress in the IDB, with contributions by the United States, in June, 1961.

In August, 1961, a conference in Punta del Este, Uruguay, approved the charter of a new agency for development; its name, the Alliance for Progress, had been suggested by Kennedy in a campaign speech. The charter was signed by all the governments of the inter-American system except Cuba, although that country did take part in the discussions.

The fundamental debate at the Punta del Este conference (although this usually took place in the corridors) was over two questions: whether development should be based primarily on a change in the terms of trade (that is, higher prices for Latin American exports), or in measures of a social character, whose object would be the participation in the benefits of progress by the bulk of the Latin American population; and whether the measures for development should be planned, and, if so, whether this planning should be on a national or a continental level. The large Latin American countries succeeded in imposing a decision in favor of national planning. The United States agreed to contribute $1 billion a year for ten years to the Alliance, and the Latin American countries agreed to effect reforms, particularly agrarian and fiscal ones. A committee of nine specialists within the inter-American system was established; this committee was to review the development plans presented by the various countries. No country would receive aid from the Alliance without the committee's approval of its plan. A year later, the U.S. congress passed a new clause of the Foreign Assistance Act dealing with the Alliance, and a new post was created, that of Coordinator for the Alliance. Teodoro Moscoso (b. 1910) of Puerto Rico was appointed coordinator.

It soon became evident that the Alliance was not reaching the people. The populist movements, which should have supported it, were afraid that if they did so too openly they would be accused of being agents of "American imperialism."

The governments effected colonializing measures they called agrarian reforms (Chile, Peru), and adopted systems of tax collection they called fiscal reforms, and considered these moves as giving them the right to receive aid from the Alliance. In June, 1963, two former presidents, Juscelino Kubitschek of Brazil and Alberto Lleras Camargo (b. 1906) of Colombia, drafted a report on the Alliance in which they affirmed that the governments were not carrying out the reforms they had promised. In November, 1963, it was decided to create a new organization, the Inter-American Committee for the Alliance for Progress (CIAP), composed of persons nominated by the governments but not as national representatives, which would be entrusted with coordinating all the activities of the Alliance. In 1966, the Committee of Nine resigned, considering that it no longer had any function.

When it became apparent that the Alliance was being sabotaged by the Latin American governments, which (with some exceptions) did not want social change, the Americans began to exert pressure and, in this way, the Alliance was altered, little by little, from a plan for collaboration into a plan for bilateral agreements. Moreover, the diversity of responsibilities kept the pressure from being effective. In addition to the Committee of Nine and the CIAP, there were the Inter-American Economic and Social Council of the OAS, the Agency for International Development, the Inter-American Development Bank, and the International Monetary Fund; there were also the Export-Import Bank of the United States, and the Department of Economic and Social Affairs of the Pan American Union. A luxuriant bureaucracy of administrators and experts was created which, once it became evident that the real objects of the Alliance could not be attained, went about converting the plans into simple measures for aid, to justify its existence and to find something to do.

Of the $2 billion to be contributed annually to the Alliance, it was thought that 55 per cent would be contributed directly by the United States, 15 per cent by international organizations, 15 per cent by private American investors, and the remaining 15 per cent by public and private sources in Western Europe and Japan. These extrahemisphere contributions did not materialize; moreover, the United States concentrated on the Alliance all the funds that previously had been employed in aid to Latin America, so that in reality the funds for financing social change were much more limited than they appeared.

The objective set by the Alliance was the achievement of a 2.5 per cent per capita growth rate, which would mean, at the end of ten years, an increase of $80 per year in the average per capita income. For this, it was estimated that a total investment of $100 billion was required, of which, it was (optimistically) anticipated, $80 billion would be generated in Latin America. Of the remaining $20 billion, $3 billion ($300 million per year) was to come from private American investment. But these figures have never been reached, and in the past ten years, the per capita growth rate has been only 1.5 per cent.

The Alliance has helped to achieve agrarian reforms in Chile, Peru, and Colombia, all very moderate and so slowly enforced that they have scarcely had any effect (the only effective agrarian reform, that in Venezuela, had begun earlier). It has brought about tax reforms in most of the countries; in general, these reforms have raised income taxes and improved the methods of tax collection, but without reducing the indirect taxes or really taxing the latifundios. Numerous schools, highways, hospitals, and water systems have been built. There has been a relative increase (or a lower decrease than anticipated, depending on the country) of private American investment, through a system by which the American government insures investors against expropriation. Emergency aid has been given to maintain the solvency of Latin American governments in cases of budget deficits and to contain inflation, or lower the rate of its increase, in Chile, Brazil, and Argentina.

With the exception of agrarian and tax reforms, however, these results have nothing to do with the objectives of the Alliance. The social structure has not been changed, and the Alliance has had no political effects in the sense of consolidating democratic forms of government. The United States has made an effort to counter this tendency by means of programs that directly affect the people—credits to cooperatives and unions, encouragement of community development—but these programs are too limited to revitalize the Alliance as such. Whatever pressure could have been caused by the ten-year limit for the Alliance disappeared in 1964, when President Lyndon B. Johnson promised that the Alliance would continue after 1971—and thus permitted the Latin American governments to show themselves still more indifferent to social questions.

The Alliance had at least one virtue: it gave respectability to certain previously taboo ideas—planning, tax reform, land reform, community development, popular participation, and, eventually, Latin American integration and a common market. Yet, at the very time that these ideas were being accepted, the governments and the technicians were denaturalizing them and converting them into mere phrases to cover up the old tradition of aid through official organizations, aid that rarely reached the people.

It may be said that the only important change that occurred in Latin America between 1960 and the present was the short-lived Latin American policy of the United States under President Kennedy. The case of Cuba is not extraneous to this change.

The Case of Cuba

American intervention in Cuba's war of independence deprived the Cubans of the feeling that they had freed themselves by their own efforts—although in fact they were winning the war by themselves—and the Platt Amendment, which gave the United States the right to intervene in Cuba, accustomed them to considering the American reaction before they took a decision or passed a law.

In 1933, after a series of interventions, dictatorships, and ineffectual governments, the Cubans rose up, overthrew the dictator Gerardo Machado (1871–1939), and established a democratic and reformist government. The then Sergeant Fulgencio Batista effected a coup against it and became the island's dominant political figure. Batista always had the support of the Communists, who allied themselves with him in several elections, provided him with a minister, and received frequent aid and a free field for propagandizing and organizing—even when they were nominally outlawed—while democratic forces were being persecuted.

In the brief period 1944–52, in which the Auténtico party

won power through elections, there was considerable improvement in living conditions and absolute liberty, but also a great deal of corruption. This disgusted the Cubans, who meekly accepted a new coup by Batista in 1952. But they soon reacted against the new dictatorship. The students organized terrorist groups in the cities, and on July 26, 1953, a group led by Fidel Castro (b. 1927)—a lawyer and the son of a landowning family—tried to seize an army barracks in Santiago. Defeated, Castro was sentenced to fifteen years in jail; he was released in Batista's general amnesty of May, 1955, and went to Mexico. There he organized an expedition to Cuba (in a boat named the *Granma*), landed near Santiago in December, 1956, and in a battle with the Batista forces lost all but twelve of his eighty-two men. With the survivors, he began a guerrilla campaign in the Sierra Maestra. For two years his activity was limited, but as urban resistance to Batista increased—without any help from the unions or the Communists—the guerrilla bands grew. The corrupt army crumbled, and, with very little real fighting, the regime collapsed. On December 31, 1958, Batista fled the country, and on January 8, 1959, Castro entered Havana.

Castro established a revolutionary regime that gave the peasants land and promised a series of social reforms. The regime was dominated by the personality of Castro, who was passionate, egocentric, and without any political experience. It was disorganized, did not call elections, and was unable to form a true party out of the July 26th Movement, which had been created almost spontaneously out of those who did not want a return to the old discredited parties. Castro did not accept the aid offered by the United States (for the purpose of wiping out the memory of aid earlier given Batista), and he took repressive measures not only against Batista's henchmen but also against union leaders and democratic politicians. These actions led many of his supporters to abandon him; some left the island, others were jailed. Castro imposed Communist leadership on the Cuban Workers' Confederation (CTC) and gradually, as he saw his isolation increasing, began to accept aid from the Communists. He steadfastly refused to hold elections, saying that the tremendous demonstrations of support by his partisans constituted a "direct democracy." And his regime became increasingly anti-American.

As a reaction against the anti-Americanism of Castro, there was an anti-Castro campaign in the United States, where he was soon accused of being a Communist. When Castro ordered the American- and British-owned oil companies in Cuba to refine Russian oil, the companies refused; he expropriated them. The United States then reduced the quota on Cuban sugar, which was permitted to enter the country at a price above that of the world market. The Soviet Union offered to buy this sugar. Castro then nationalized various American and foreign firms, as well as major Cuban firms. In September, 1960, Cuba complained to the United Nations of American "acts of economic aggression." On January 3, 1961, the United States broke off diplomatic relations with the Castro government.

To get the workers to accept voluntarily the privations necessary for the financing of the Cuban economy (relinquishment of vacations, overtime pay, and other gains won by the unions after years of hard struggle), Castro stepped up his anti-American propaganda, in order to make the "Yankee menace" justify the sacrifices he was asking. This, in turn, played into the hands of those elements in the United States that demanded a solution by force. The Eisenhower administration authorized the training of groups of Cuban exiles, who were arriving in ever greater numbers in Miami. The result, as we have seen, was the abortive Bay of Pigs invasion of April 17, 1961.

Meanwhile, Castro revised his agrarian reforms, taking away land from the peasants and organizing state farms. Police activity increased in equal measure with the activities of various anti-Castro movements. Castro reorganized the political system. His 26th of July Movement was absorbed into a single government party, the Integrated Revolutionary Organizations (ORI), which in 1965 became the Communist Party of Cuba. In its political and economic system, Cuba seemed more and more like a country of the Soviet bloc. Castro's political concepts had more in common with those of the Chinese Communists than with those of the Russian; but in the conflict between Moscow and Peking, Castro sided with Moscow because the Soviet Union and the countries of Eastern Europe were supplying him with economic and military aid, as well as furnishing machinery, credit, technicians, and markets in the attempt to industrialize the island. (In a speech on December 1, 1961, Castro announced that he was a Marxist-Leninist and would be one until the last day of his life, although many people considered this a statement made solely for the purpose of maintaining his prestige with the Communists.)

The emotions aroused by the Cuban experience make any attempt to evaluate it difficult. There is no doubt that the bulk of the Cuban population supports Castro, although this support is becoming a matter of routine as time goes on. There is also no doubt that some of Castro's measures have promoted greater equality and a general feeling of dignity among Cubans. The spirit of dependency on the United States has disappeared—although one might ask whether extreme anti-Americanism does not constitute a perpetuation of this dependency in different form. There has been considerable development of education (although without freedom of instruction and without university autonomy), and of public housing.

On the other hand, the standard of living of the peasants and workers has worsened in comparison with that before 1959, as capital formation has been achieved via underconsumption. The economy has not been diversified, and continues to depend fundamentally on sugar exports. The degree of political liberties and guarantees is greatly inferior to that which prevailed before and even during the Batista dictatorship; there is in Cuba today no independent judiciary, no freedom of speech, no right of assembly. There is artistic liberty (within fixed limits) for the intellectuals, to a greater extent than in other Communist-governed countries.

What seems undeniable is that the people have no voice in the government, or any likelihood of having one in the future. Despite what it says in its propaganda, the regime is basically an oligarchic one, in which a political bureaucracy of the middle class and intellectuals has replaced the landowners and military men who previously monopolized power. Cuba is an example of a paternalistic, middle-class dictatorship, and it constitutes proof that a revolution made by the middle class, without the participation of the masses in its leadership, does not necessarily mean the end of the oligarchic system but may merely substitute one oligarchic personnel for another. What gives power now is not ownership of land or military rank but standing within the single party. Power still does not belong to the people. The regime, precisely because it has never been willing to recognize popular participation, and because it has had to impose sacrifices when the emotional climate for making voluntary ones disappeared, has been gradually converted into a typical totalitarian regime based on a systematic police-state organization, propaganda, and control.

Nevertheless, the regime may be considered established, and it is even possible to predict that the generation educated under Castro will be less open to the idea of reconciliation with the United States than the generation that seized power in 1959. Cuban exiles have become a part of the life of countries that have received them (chiefly the United States, but also Latin America and Spain). They no longer have any influence in Cuba, and are losing what they had in the United States, where their wish to solve their problems by invasion has ceased to find encouragement at the official level. The only thing that will make possible the disappearance of the Castro regime in the not too remote future is internal decomposition, or an agreement between the United States and the Soviet Union that will induce Moscow to abandon Castro completely. Or it could be that Castro will undertake a new adventure in Latin America that will induce Washington and the Latin American governments to use force against his regime.

The United States has tried to isolate Cuba through recourse to the Organization of American States. A conference of ministers of foreign relations in August, 1960, at San José, condemned extracontinental attempts at intervention in the Americas, and another, in 1962, expelled the Castro regime from the inter-American system. Efforts to establish a blockade of Cuba have found no support in Europe or in Canada, which continue to trade with Cuba, although under U.S. pressure all the countries of the hemisphere except Mexico broke off relations with Castro in 1964.

In October, 1962, President Kennedy announced that the Soviet Union had installed rockets in Cuba and that the hemisphere was in consequence exposed to Soviet nuclear weapons. The OAS immediately supported the measures adopted by Kennedy—a blockade of all Soviet arms shipments to Cuba—and the Russians, in the face of the strong American reaction, acknowledged that they had placed rockets in Cuba (which they had earlier denied). Castro at first declared that he had not known of the presence of the Soviet rockets on the island, and later stated that they had been installed at his suggestion. In any event, the Soviet withdrawal of the missiles, and the negative role played by Castro in the crisis, caused the loss of a great deal of prestige Castroism had won in Latin America.

The Normalization of Disorder

When Castro came into power in 1959, the Latin American political situation was at the height of its period of transformation. The fall of Batista was not the beginning of a wave of democratization but its culmination. Other dictatorships had fallen previously, as we have seen, and this had created an especially favorable situation for the exertion of influence in favor of social change.

In Argentina, where Perón fell in 1955, two military governments returned to the traditional policy of the oligarchy, that of discouraging industrialization. The inflation that had begun under Perón became worse. In 1958, Arturo Frondizi (b. 1908), of the Intransigent Radical Party, proposed to integrate the Peronists (who had received 2 million votes) into a democratic system and to promote development while controlling inflation. But in 1963, following some electoral successes of the Peronists, to whom Frondizi had restored legal status, the army staged a coup and replaced Frondizi with his vice president. In 1963, the popular Radical Arturo Illia (b. 1901) was elected president. In 1965, a Peronist success at the polls again induced the army to stage a coup; this time it remained in power, outlawed political parties, and established a regime of totalitarian, anti-Semitic tendencies, which handed over the economy to a group of bankers, closed the credit unions, ended university autonomy, reached an agreement with the majority of the Peronist union leaders, and, among other things, forbade kissing in public parks. The people were disillusioned and indifferent. Many "new leftists," however, cooperated with the military, for they were convinced that the regime would become increasing anti-American.

In Peru, the elections of 1962 were won by the APRA candidate, Víctor Raúl Haya de la Torre, but the military staged a coup to prevent Haya's inauguration. For the first time in the history of its relations with Latin America, Washington refused to recognize the government created by the coup and cut off aid; this prevented reprisals which the military was preparing and forced it to hold new elections in 1963. In these, the candidate favored by the military, the architect Fernando Belaúnde (b. 1912), leader of a makeshift party of technocratic tendencies, was elected. Belaúnde, together with the Communists, was one of the few who had supported the coup of 1962. The opposition parties won the majority in congress, however, and in 1965 they passed a moderate agrarian reform law, which the government unwillingly and cautiously enforced. But in 1968, the army staged a new coup to prevent the congressional investigation of a smuggling scandal, in which many members of the military were involved; to disguise the real reason for the coup, the junta expropriated the International Petroleum Company, a subsidiary of Standard Oil Company (New Jersey). In early 1969, the military government seized an American fishing boat off the Peruvian coast. These extreme nationalistic actions gained the military government the support of many new left elements.

In Venezuela, in December, 1959, a part of the navy rebelled against the dictatorship of Pérez Jiménez. There was a general strike, groups of armed civilians fought the police in the streets, and the dictator fled. After a year of provisional government, Rómulo Betancourt, founder of Democratic Action, was elected president. Betancourt succeeded in passing and enforcing an agrarian-reform law that not only gave land to the peasants but took political power away from the latifundists. He won better terms from the oil companies and accelerated the process of industrialization.

During his five-year term, Betancourt struggled with guerrilla action and terrorism incited by Castro, conspiracies set afoot by the Dominican dictator Trujillo, attempted coups by Castroite elements and military allies, and Castroite groups within his own party. Nevertheless, Betancourt, supported by the Christian Democratic party (COPEI), became the first elected president in the history of Venezuela to finish his term of office. In 1964, Betancourt was succeeded by Raúl Leoni, also a member of Democratic Action. In the elections of 1968, a Christian Democrat, Rafael Caldera (b. 1917), was elected president. It marked the first time in the history of the country that the government had handed over power to the opposition candidate.

Venezuela has undergone a period of change, growth, and political apprenticeship that has been marked by disturbances and a certain amount of corruption. Many problems remain, for example, those caused by rapid urbanization, such as slums and unemployment. But Venezuela furnishes an example of a victorious populist movement that, thanks to a few days of struggle against the dictatorship, has succeeded in effecting reforms and in giving the people participation in government. It was the unions, many of whose militant elements were armed, that prevented the success of the military coups, since the officers realized that this time they could not succeed without a fight. And it was the peasants—more than the army—who frustrated the activity of the guerrillas, who were seen as men who wanted to take away the lands the peasants had received, or hoped to receive, as a result of the agrarian reform. The Venezuelan regime is far from being ideal, but in the context of the country's history it constitutes a considerable first step toward the establishment of a democracy that will be social as well as political.

The last of the old-style dictators to fall was Rafael Leónidas Trujillo of the Dominican Republic. In 1960, Trujillo organized an attempt on the life of Venezuelan President Betancourt, whom he considered a dangerous opponent. Betancourt was seriously wounded. Venezuela denounced this intervention before the OAS, which voted in 1960 to break off diplomatic relations with Trujillo and establish economic sanctions against him. The United States broke off diplomatic relations with the Dominican Republic, but never invoked economic sanctions against the dictatorship it had supported for three decades. Trujillo did not frighten, however. He invited a group of Communists to form a party, the Dominican Popular Movement, and even flirted with Castro. But a group of former underlings assassinated him in May, 1961.

The country now entered a strange situation. The rural

population, which had looked up to Trujillo as a kind of severe father, mourned the dictator. The middle class and the oligarchy—which had served Trujillo but were irritated with him because he gave them no power—thought the time had come to take control themselves. After the Trujillo family had made an unsuccessful attempt to remain in power by a coup, and after the resignation of Vice President Joaquín Balaguer (b. 1906), a Council of State, formed of members of the oligarchy, was set up. It was sure it would win the elections scheduled for the end of 1962. But the winner was an exiled writer, Juan Bosch (b. 1909), leader of the Dominican Revolutionary Party (PRD), which had populist tendencies. Bosch was in office only seven months. During that time, the congress approved a constitution but not an agrarian-reform law. When it was about to do so, the army, in September, 1963, staged a coup, on the pretext that Bosch had refused to outlaw the Communist Party; in fact, he had not done so because the Communists were not strong and because he did not want to encourage a guerrilla movement. The United States refused to recognize the new dictatorial government, called the Triumvirate; it did so only after the death of President Kennedy.

In 1965, the dictatorial government came into conflict with the military over a question of privilege. One sector of the army staged a coup, but the other fought in the streets to proclaim the re-establishment of the constitution. The civil war lasted for some weeks, during which the United States, under the false impression that the Communists were dominating the constitutional forces, sent in a force of marines (see Chapter VII). Elections were held in 1966, and Balaguer was victorious over Bosch. Bosch, who had remained in Puerto Rico throughout the civil war, did not leave his house during the campaign for fear of assassination. (He subsequently went to Spain, and has advocated "dictatorships with popular support" as the government best-suited to Latin America.) Conditions are ripe for the renewal of civil war in the Dominican Republic, for the military is still strong, the oligarchy is still lusting for power, and the people are in very bad economic straits.

The situation in Colombia holds an equal potential for violence. After the fall of General Rojas Pinilla, in 1957, the

Conservatives and Liberals agreed to alternate in power for a period of sixteen years; it was thought that this would bring peace. But the roots of unrest were not political but social. Since there have been no structural reforms—an agrarian reform approved in 1964 was not likely to be enforced—the uneasy situation has continued, the surviving Liberal guerrillas have been made use of by various Communist groups, and the country is in a state of uncertainty by no means favorable to progress.

We have seen that in Bolivia, in 1964, there was a military coup against the elected government of Paz Estenssoro, although the country did not revert to the social situation that preceded the 1952 revolution. Militarism is so deeply rooted in Latin American political tradition that it arises even in the very heart of a popular revolution.

In Ecuador, following the forced resignation of the demagogic Velasco Ibarra, in 1961, Vice President Julio Arosemena (b. 1919) succeeded to power. He was deposed in 1963 by a military coup. The military tried to effect a moderate agrarian reform and was in turn forced to resign in 1966 by a union of the oligarchic parties, which has not introduced any reform of the country's social structure.

The situation is no better in Brazil. In August, 1961, President Jânio Quadros (b. 1917), whose election had raised high hopes, unexpectedly resigned after only seven months in office, for reasons still unexplained. He was succeeded by Vice President João Goulart (b. 1918). Goulart, leader of the Brazilian Labor Party (PTB), was viewed with considerable distrust, for he was considered a demagogue with Peronist leanings. Congress opposed his succession to the presidency, but the army forced it to comply with the constitution. Congress then modified the constitution, changing the presidential system into a parliamentary one. Once in office, Goulart gathered around him the most demagogic elements of his party and allowed Communists to head many of the most important unions. Goulart, himself a large landowner, promulgated an agrarian-reform law; the reform consisted in giving the peasants the lands along the railroads, but even this farce frightened the landholders, who saw to it that there was no further talk of this law, or of any other.

Then in 1965, Goulart supported a group of minor naval officers and enlisted men who had mutinied against their superiors. The military accused the president of being under Communist control, and staged a coup. Neither the unions, the political parties, nor the Communists came to the defense of the regime, and Goulart went into exile. General Humberto Castelo Branco (1900–67) was elected president by the chamber of deputies. He reformed the constitution, dissolved the old political parties and organized two new ones—one for the government, one in opposition—and began a fight against inflation by anti-union measures. In 1967, he called elections that were won by the military candidate, General Artur Costa e Silva. In December, 1968, Costa e Silva assumed dictatorial powers, suspended parliament, and took away the political rights of many of his opponents.

Even in Chile, with its solid democratic tradition, disorder has become the normal situation. In 1964, the Christian Democratic Party (founded shortly before World War II) won the elections, thanks to the support of the conservatives, who feared a victory by the Popular Action Front (FRAP), made up of Socialists and Communists. Eduardo Frei (b. 1909) was elected president. But the Christian Democrats were in the minority in the senate, which for nearly three years defeated passage of the agrarian reform law; it was finally put into effect in 1967. In late 1964, Frei had reached an agreement with all the American-owned copper companies except Anaconda* to give the state the majority of their stock, thereby "Chileanizing" the chief source of export income. Led by the Socialists, the miners' union immediately called a long strike, which brought the country a loss of $30 million, despite the fact that the funds from the copper exports were to be used to finance agrarian reform. Allied against the Christian Democrats were the right—Conservatives and Liberals now united in a National Union; the middle-class Radical Party; and the Socialist-Communist alliance. This opposition radicalized a great part of the Christian Democrats. But although the Christian Democrats put their men into many

* In June, 1969, the Chilean government and Anaconda agreed on the terms for the gradual nationalization of the Anaconda mines.

government posts and, for the first time in the history of the country, organized a large number of peasants, they have been unable to supplant the Communists and Socialists in the leadership of the chief unions. Chilean Communists have opposed Castro, because they favor the electoral road to power, while the Socialists are pro-Castro because in reality they are more nationalist than Marxist. The politically oriented strikes against Frei, and the abandonment of cultivation by many landholders who want to sabotage agrarian reform, have put the country in a difficult economic situation.

In Honduras, the liberal government of Dr. Ramón Villeda Morales (b. 1909) was overthrown by a coup staged by Colonel Oswaldo López Arellano in 1963, on the eve of the elections. There was no possibility of effecting any agrarian reform, although some good social legislation had been enacted. In Nicaragua, Anastasio Somoza, Jr. (b. 1925), the son of the general, had himself elected president in 1967, replacing a friend of the Somoza family as head of state. In Guatemala, the head of the Revolutionary Party, Mario Méndez Montenegro, was assassinated in 1965; the following year his brother, Julio César, was elected president, despite the opposition of the incumbent dictator, Colonel Enrique Peralta, who supported a military candidate. But the military, claiming the threat of Communist and Maoist guerrillas and extreme rightist terrorists, has prevented César from offering a plan for agrarian reform—although this would be the best way to isolate the guerrillas. In Panama, in 1968, the military took over after the election to the presidency of a candidate they opposed; they established a civilian government of technicians that was in fact under the control of the army (which in Panama is called the national guard). Finally, in Haiti, François Duvalier (b. 1907), elected president for life in 1964, heads a reign of terror, governs with the aid of voodoo, and has virtually isolated the country, while he mocks American pressure to relinquish power.

Political disorder, then, is a normal feature of Latin American life. It is not considered anomalous or exceptional. The situation would seem to have been ripe for Castro to exert considerable and decisive influence. Why did Castro waste the opportunity, and who can take advantage of it?

Nationalism and Stability

The romantic aspects of Castro's adventure gave him enormous influence throughout Latin America. In 1959 and 1960, guerrilla wars erupted—some aided by Cuba, but many spontaneous—in Panama, Guatemala, and Nicaragua, and groups of exiles organized invasions of Paraguay and the Dominican Republic. The Latin American governments soon put a stop to all this. At the time, however, it would have been possible to coordinate efforts and pressures and to form a continental social revolutionary movement. The populist movements and the numerous reformist groups were ready to accept the leadership of Castro, and the United States, for the first time in its history, was disposed to support such a movement—or at least not to oppose it.

But Castro, as we have seen, made mistakes in Cuba, and he then did what the Russians did in Stalin's time: while he was changing his regime into a totalitarian one—inevitable when one wants to leap from "feudalism" to "socialism"—he used his international influence for the service of his own regime. He annoyed the United States, which had begun to isolate Cuba, and assailed the only democratic government then trying to effect social reforms—that of Venezuela—whose success would have meant the end of Castro's pretension that social change in Latin America could be effected only by the methods used in Cuba. When he failed in Venezuela, Castro helped other guerrilla movements in Peru, Guatemala, and Bolivia. In 1967, he tried to reactivate the Venezuela guerrillas, in order to prevent negotiations between the government and the Communists, who wanted to return to legal status.

The basic ideas of "Castroism" were formulated by the Argentine Ernesto Che Guevara (1928–67). An ex-Trotskyite and profoundly anti-American, Guevara was Castro's principal counsellor from 1959 until he disappeared from Havana in 1965. In 1967, he led a guerrilla band in Bolivia, and in October of that year he was taken prisoner and killed by Bolivian military forces. According to his diary, which was released by Castro in 1968, he had not found any support among the Bolivian peasants.

In the thinking of Guevara, it is not necessary to have revolutionary conditions for a successful guerrilla war, nor is it necessary that the people have a desire to fight, or aspirations to social change; all that is needed is for the guerrillas to be technically prepared, for by their mere presence and activity they can create the conditions favorable for revolution. This concept is fundamentally paternalistic, for it attributes a tutelary function to the guerrilla fighters: they know better than the people what is good for them.

Two works which, although written by Frenchmen, have had considerable repercussions in Latin America, indicate the heart of the thinking of these revolutionary paternalists. In one, Henri Edmé, a French Marxist and friend of Jean-Paul Sartre, says that American "neoimperialism" is a powerful social force that is industrializing Latin America, extending agrarian reforms, and offering the impoverished people a better future. This has prevented the revolution from being an "imminent, inevitable, and triumphant reality." In order to win the masses to socialism, it is necessary for the revolutionaries to take this reality into account. It is easy to see that—although Edmé's description is far from corresponding to Latin American reality—the important thing for him is not improving the living conditions of the masses but "winning the masses for socialism." That is, the doctrinaire objective—revolution—is more important than the well-being of the Latin Americans. Revolution for revolution's sake, so to speak.

The same idea of revolution per se, without objective, is found in a book by the Frenchman Régis Debray, *Revolution in the Revolution?* Debray maintains that guerrilla fighting should be the starting point of revolution; one should not worry about a program, a party (the guerrillas will generate the party), or the existence of revolutionary situations (these will arise as a consequence of guerrilla activity).

It would not be an exaggeration to describe these views as "revolutionary militarism." In both cases, the people play no role at all. This concept naturally attracts those elements of society that feel frustrated in their own tutelary aspirations: intellectuals, pseudo-intellectuals, professionals, students, sectors of the middle class, that is, all those who feel that they constitute an elite but who have not succeeded in winning the privileges and power of an elite. The intellectual's feeling of superiority, together with guilt complexes and aspiration to power, is the motive of this kind of paternalism by violence.*

For years, the groups described above followed the Communist slogans, although they did not join the Communist parties, which they considered too elementary and to whose discipline they did not care to submit. They were inspired more by anti-Americanism than by sympathy for the Communist program; this made them view favorably whatever disturbed Washington. Moreover, they were attracted by the privileges granted intellectuals and technicians in Communist regimes. The same motives later attracted them to Castroism, when the Soviet appeal began to wane. In 1966, Castro tried to organize these groups into a Latin American Solidarity Organization, created by a tricontinental conference that met in Havana for the purpose of forming an international force that would support him in his relations with the Soviet Union and in his opposition to the United States. Clearly, as happened earlier in Russia and China, a frustrated revolution is having recourse, for national ends, to the revolutionary movements of other countries.

Today, these elements form a series of rival groups that accuse one another of being traitors and cowards: pro-Chinese Communists, extreme nationalists, Castroites, and neo-Marxists. Disillusioned with the Soviet Union, they find their theoretical inspiration in the French and Italian new left and, lately, in the American.

The actual strength of these groups is minimal, but because they are made up primarily of intellectuals and students they are articulate, noisy, and find ways of making themselves heard. Their capacity for propaganda is greatly superior to their capacity for action. They possess a considerable advantage in the fact that they offer a sense of mission to those elements that feel insecure and isolated. Many students who join the guerrillas in good faith, and even at the risk of their lives, believe they will be able to win power, although in reality they are creating conditions favorable to

* Henri Edmé, "Damping the Fires of Revolution," in *Atlas*, November, 1966; Régis Debray, *Revolution in the Revolution?* (New York, 1967).

military coups. Other components of these groups, and many who support them without taking an active part in them, are able to satisfy their consciences without having to risk anything to better the living conditions of their own people.

The truth is that no one really asks himself whether Latin America is going through a revolutionary phase, or of what this Latin American "revolution" everyone is talking about consists. This vagueness allows each one to find, in the idea of revolution, the satisfaction of his own aspirations.

But except for the groups mentioned above, these aspirations are really very moderate. What most Latin Americans of today mean when they speak of revolution is the destruction of obstacles that have impeded their country's progress toward a way of life similar to that in the United States. What the Latin American who speaks of revolution would like to do is to establish a regime that is fundamentally capitalistic (that is, opposed to the feudal regime of the landholding oligarchy), politically democratic, economically mixed (with both public and private investment, and state planning), and socially capable of integrating the inhabitants of each country into a national entity.

Precisely for this reason, Latin America is living through a period of intense nationalism. During the eighteenth century, there was what could be called a diversified nationalism: reaction against Spain by the liberals, against the Protestant Anglo-Saxon countries by the conservatives, and against neighboring countries over boundaries. At the beginning of the present century, it took a new form: anti-imperialism. In the countries of the Plata basin, where British investment and trade were decisive economic factors, an anti-British campaign was set afoot. This was later joined by an anti-American campaign all over the continent, as a reaction against the various interventions of the United States.

There had always been distrust of the United States, beginning with Bolívar. But there had also been a current of sympathy for the United States: nineteenth-century thinkers said that Latin America ought to imitate the United States; others proposed that Protestant ministers be brought in to counteract the influence of the Catholic Church; and there were many attempts to transplant the American educational system.

But by the beginning of the twentieth century, a new image of the United States had become dominant. It was expressed by the Uruguayan José Enrique Rodó (1872–1917), in his book *Ariel*. The United States, Rodó said, was materialistic; it was not interested in culture but only in money and technological progress, and it would go to any lengths to extend its influence and to exploit other countries. This image of a "crude people" is still predominant in the oligarchy and the middle class. Among the submerged masses, on the other hand, the image of the United States—where there is any—is one that excites vague sympathy, because it is associated with the smiling tourist who gives tips, or with machinery and "gadgets," or with what is shown in films and on television. But the oligarchy sees in the United States a factor in the disorganization of its society and the promoter—especially under Kennedy—of revolution; the merchants see it as a competitor, as does the industrialist, who fears that if his industry prospers he will be under pressure to accept American capital. The intellectual, though he is interested in American culture, rejects the political and economic influence of the United States and transmits his feelings to students and to his readers. Yet everywhere there is imitation of American ways of life and techniques. This in itself explains much of the resentment against the United States, for it is well known that one tends to destroy or deprecate the very thing one is imitating.

There are, of course, historical and economic bases for many of the anti-American arguments, but these cannot explain the extent of anti-Americanism. Nor can the campaigns of the Communists and Castroites, who maintain that social change is impossible in Latin America without the prior success of the struggle against imperialism. We must search deeper for an explanation. Perhaps it is to be found in the fact that the Latin American countries, owing to the oligarchic nature of their society—which prevents the integration of the entire population into modern political, economic, and social life—have not reached the stage of being nations. In a time in which the most industrialized countries are nations, and even take the next step by forming supranational associations, the Latin Americans compensate for their feeling that their countries are not really nations by displaying a verbal, emotional, and flamboyant nationalism.

At the same time, a scapegoat is found for the failure to speed up the integration of nationality, for not having destroyed the obstacles to the formation of nationality (the oligarchic system being foremost). In the last century, this scapegoat role was filled by Spain, the Protestant countries, or the next-door country; today, it is filled by the United States.

The United States is blamed for everything. If there is a crisis, it is the fault of the United States, and if prosperity makes it impossible to find a parking space for one's car, that is the fault of the United States too. If the United States gives economic aid, it is doing so to serve its own interests; but if it does not, then the poverty of the people is thrown in its face. If birth-control methods are not popularized, it is because the United States wants the population explosion to keep Latin America poor; but if the United States supports birth-control programs, then it is accused of "bedroom imperialism" and of wanting to destroy the revolutionary effects of population pressure. If the United States does not break off relations with the dictatorships, it is supporting them; but if it does break off relations, it is intervening in the country's internal affairs.

Of course, the oligarchic governments, when they are not interested in a problem, or when they want to conceal a scandal, impute it to the United States. Thus many Latin Americans find it easy to ignore these problems, since until American influence disappears nothing can be solved. Such nationalism has led to open sympathy and even support for the adversaries of the United States, even when they are also adversaries of Latin America. The Nazis, and later the Soviet Union, were able to capitalize on this deep prejudice against the United States. In 1960, for example, the Soviet Union began to dump wolframite on the world market, which threatened the interests of several Latin American countries that sold this mineral; but almost no one said that this was so, and many believed that the United States was responsible.

Anti-Americanism is, to some degree, a logical and a transitory situation: the image of the United States will change with the conversion of the Latin American countries into nations; that is, in the same measure as social change allows the integration of the whole population into a national unity. And although this situation may seem unjust, it should not cause too much concern except that it so often misleads American diplomacy. For years, American diplomats believed that they had an ally in the oligarchic groups, who despised the United States; they then thought they had allies in the middle class, who envied the United States; perhaps in the future they will come to see their allies in the submerged masses, the only ones who so far have not shown hostility to the United States.

There is a great deal of talk about the desire for stability in Latin America, and this is said as if stability and order were synonymous. Latin American society is very stable, as is proved by its being essentially the same now as it was a century and a half ago. But precisely because it is stable and is not adapted to new demands and to change, it is a disorderly society. The less stability there is, that is to say, the more adaptation to the realities of the world, the more order there will be. The more stability, the more disorder. Or, in other words, where there is social stability there is also political instability, and where we find social instability, as in the United States, we also find political stability. If the United States—for whatever reasons—is interested in an orderly Latin America, it should accept and encourage everything that contributes to making Latin American society less stable but more flexible.

But who wants Latin American society to be really flexible?

For or Against Social Change?

It is useful here to recall the words of the historian E. H. Carr: "Every society is an arena of social conflicts, and those individuals who range themselves against existing authority are not less products and reflections of the society than those who uphold it."*

The enemies of the Latin American oligarchical society, who believe that within this society there can be no progress for the benefit of everyone, and who think that the social structure must be changed if development is to be achieved, were born and educated in the same oligarchic society. Their culture, their concepts, their psychology, their aspirations are

* E. H. Carr, *What Is History?* (New York, 1962), p. 65.

products of the society they want to change. Not only is their opposition to the oligarchic society a product of that society, but it is expressed in forms that are also products of that society. In this sense, it could be said that the struggle against the oligarchic society assumes a form imposed by the oligarchic society itself.

Since indifference toward the masses has been one of the traits of the oligarchic society—an indifference that has been only a mask for the use of the submerged masses as a source of capital—it is easy to understand that many opponents of the oligarchic society continue to show indifference to the masses and still think of them as the logical source of investment. And since the oligarchic society has always relied on the state to solve the problems of its individual members, and to resolve the differences among rival political groups (often by making use of the armed forces), it is not surprising that many opponents of that society believe that the state is able to bring about social change by itself, and even that, in this task, the state may be represented by the armed forces. If in that society the cult of personality has predominated in politics, as a result of generations of seeing politics as the rivalry between oligarchic families who have dragged their dependents into the fight, it is to be expected that there will be a personality cult in the struggle *against* the oligarchic society. If nationalism as a substitute for nationality has been an unfailing characteristic of the oligarchic society, it is likely that nationalism will play an important role in the struggle against it. Nor should it surprise us that there are Latin Americans who invoke violence as the best way of changing the oligarchic society, since this society has frequently had recourse to violence to maintain and defend itself.

The oligarchic groups, of course, do not desire profound change. They would prefer to limit change to technical progress, by this means keeping the middle sectors satisfied, but without modifying in any way whatever the condition of the submerged masses, who are indispensable to the functioning of their system. Certain segments of the oligarchic groups, however—especially those in banking and industry—are disposed to make concessions, for example, colonization plans that might be called agrarian reforms and that would lighten the population pressure in the rural areas. But these groups are a minority. The obstinate opposition to any change in land ownership continues. Although from time to time there are waves of alarms among the oligarchic groups, in general they are confident that as long as the middle sectors remain satisfied economically, they are in no real danger.

At the present time, the middle sectors are not pressing for change. But it is possible to anticipate a point at which it will no longer be possible to squeeze the submerged masses; the economic rise of the middle sectors will be checked, and they will be forced to exert pressure on the only social group capable of providing income—the oligarchy. Because the oligarchy will refuse to give up its privileges, the middle sectors will bring pressure to bear for structural change. There then will appear a division between those who seek to bring about change in order to establish a democratic system, with the collaboration of the submerged masses, whom they will arouse and organize; and those who seek to establish a tutelary or paternalistic system, using the submerged masses as a lever but without giving them a share of power.

The populist movements have not resolved the contradiction between their program of social change and the lack of genuine interest in it among the middle sectors that form their base of support. Even organized labor shows no desire to develop activities that would put it in a position to exert pressure for social change, for except in a few cases (Venezuela, Peru, Colombia), it has done nothing to organize the peasants, the Indian communities, or the slum dwellers.

Nothing very different has happened in a new movement, Christian Democracy, which has arisen in recent years. Although Catholic groups with interest in social problems have been active for several decades, only with the development of the Venezuelan COPEI after 1959 and with the electoral success of the Chilean Christian Democrats in 1964 has this movement acquired any importance. The Christian Democrats want a society that is neither capitalist nor Communist but communalist. The community should be the basis of society, and the channel to popular participation in government. (It is interesting that there is a greater tendency to elitism, to paternalism, in the Christian Democratic labor movement than there is among the populist elements.) The

Christian Democrats have the support of youthful segments of the Church, although the hierarchies in general continue to be very traditionalist. In a few countries (Chile, Colombia, parts of Ecuador and Peru), the Church has begun to divide its lands, but in others it clings to its wealth and its traditional collaboration with the oligarchy. An example of this division in the Church is found in the life of Camilo Torres (1929–66), a Colombian priest who went over to the guerrillas and died with them. Other priests in Colombia and Guatemala have been expelled from their parishes for organizing cooperatives. The Jesuits, however, have worked openly with the Chilean Christian Democrats, and others have helped to organize the peasants in the Brazilan Northeast. In some countries, notably in Brazil and Argentina, the military governments have put a Communist label on all churchmen, from priests to bishops, who have been active in social matters.

The populists and the Christian Democrats want social change based on popular participation. A second group—young businessmen, technicians, and intellectuals—consists of those who will ally themselves with military men of technocratic outlook and try to produce a revolution from above. This, by its very nature, will result in totalitarian government and collaboration with the various Communist groups. These are the groups who want speedy modernization and believe it cannot be attained by democratic methods. They will accept capital formation effected by underconsumption and overexploitation, because they will not be the ones who will consume less and work more, but will, on the contrary, be the direct beneficiaries of the sacrifices made by the bulk of the population. They are also aggressively nationalistic, for they find in nationalism the justification of such sacrifices, the psychological mechanism for their enforcement, and the lever for mobilizing support. Of course, this is a rationalization of a mental and political process that is much less clear-cut, particularly in the minds of its champions.

The Latin American Communists are badly divided. On one side are those faithful to the Moscow line, who retain control of all the official parties; these are generally weak, except in Chile. For the Moscow-line Communists, the situation is a difficult one. They cannot openly condemn or sabotage the guerrilla operations backed by Castro—whose regime they support at the same time that they disagree with the guerrilla tactics—because they consider conditions ripe for democratic conquest of power in certain countries of Latin America. Actually, the Communists are not interested at the moment in taking power, because this does not suit Moscow's current diplomatic attitude. It must not be forgotten that in Latin America the Communist movement is thoroughly bureaucratized and that there are no cases of independence with respect to Moscow; hence the affirmation that the Latin American Communists are the instruments of Soviet diplomacy is still valid.

The pro-Chinese Communists, who broke off from the official Communist parties, have made little progress. Apparently, Peking does not consider conditions ripe for revolution in Latin America, and therefore does not give much help to its partisans on the continent. Some of those who feel inclined toward Peking's theories, and disillusioned by Soviet policy, have been attracted by minuscule Trotskyite groups or by no less minuscule nuclei of neo-Marxists. These groups have no real influence, but they are noisy, aggressive, and make some impression; their support comes from intellectuals and students.

The students (whom we shall examine in greater detail in Chapter IX) constitute a pressure group of some importance, although they are losing influence in the same measure as they are becoming radical, because their radicalism isolates them from the people. Most students belong to groups of the new left, although Christian Democracy is also influential among them, especially in Chile and Venezuela. Although they want social change, they are more attracted by anti-imperialistic propaganda and extremist positions than by work among the masses. Elitist and paternalistic tendencies are very strong among them, although they are not conscious of this.

These tendencies are much more conscious among the military, which is also divided. On one side are the old-style officers who favor military coups without any attendant risk. On the other are the younger officers who want to effect reforms but whose technocratic ideas put them in the ranks of the paternalists; they too could become allies of the Communists or Castroites, all the more because anti-Americanism is so strong among them (especially among those who have studied in the United States).

There are also certain social groups—or subgroups, rather—that are arising: the industrial technicians, the specialists in planning, the managers of nationalized firms, the government economists, and other elements who tend to see all problems as functions of their specialty, without relating them to the social situation as a whole. For this reason, these groups, politically, may end up as allies, or even inspirers, of such technocratic-paternalistic tendencies as attract the middle sectors.

There remain the submerged masses. It cannot be said that they live altogether with their backs turned on politics. There are small numbers of them—organized by the populist, Communist, and Christian Democratic movements—who are aware that the masses are the ones chiefly in need of social change. But, in general, the peasants and the uprooted city-dwellers have not been educated politically or made aware of their own interests. They are an available mass, who will follow the first one who calls to them: demagogue, military man, Castroite, or populist. It is the oligarchy's good fortune that (with the exception of the populists) these elements do not know how to talk to the masses and have no interest in mobilizing them. But the situation might change with the appearance of a few leaders capable of appealing to the masses.

As we see, the forces at work are the same as they were two generations ago, but their positions have changed and so has their ideological justification. The military still wants power, but neo-militarism justifies this ambition with the desire to bring about revolution from above. The intellectuals and professionals, frustrated in a society in which they have a certain well-being but no power, continue to demand changes that will permit them to guide, order, and regulate, but now they justify these aspirations with neo-Marxism or Castroism. The middle sectors continue to want a greater share in profits and power, but now they justify this with a nationalism that is no longer the vainglorious kind of former days but is aggressive and rationalized as anti-imperialism. The oligarchic forces continue to desire social immobility, but instead of calling themselves conservatives they too call themselves nationalists; their nationalism is exclusivist and chauvinistic. The populists and the Christian Democrats continue to want peaceful social change, democratic regimes, and continental unity. But because these old formulas have lost prestige, they have adopted the slogans "Revolution in Liberty" or "Libertarian Revolution."

Latin American politics resembles a polka danced to the rhythm of the twist. The truth is that there are very few people in Latin America who consider that development—economic and political, as well as social—can be achieved only through the participation of the masses. And this raises the question of how to speed up development—a question to which, so far, no one has given an answer that has won general support.

How Can Development Be Accelerated?

Between 1960 and 1965, the average income of the peoples of the industrialized countries increased by $175 a year. In Latin America, the increase was $40. During the same period, investment in Latin America grew at an annual rate of 3.3 per cent while the population was growing at the rate of 2.7 per cent; thus every year the capital available for each Latin American has increased by little more than half of one per cent. Every year, a minimum of 1 million Latin Americans must be absorbed into the labor market. But to provide a new job means an investment of $5,000, so that a minimum of $5 billion is needed annually merely to put young Latin Americans to work. But Latin America has available only $3.3 billion a year. To increase the annual rate of growth to 2.5 per cent (which would require forty years to double the very low living standard of today, which even then would still be low), it would be necessary to double the 3.3 per cent annual rate of increase in investments.*

Presented in this form, the problem of Latin American development is reduced to deciding who is to furnish the supplementary investment that is indispensable for bettering the living conditions of the Latin Americans. In other words, how is capital to be formed? The answer to this question is

* Figures supplied by the Inter-American Development Bank in 1967.

not economic, but social and political. For the question of who must pay, the rich or the poor—or, if you prefer, which should be invested, money or work—is not an economic problem but a political and social one.

The vast majority of Latin Americans recognize the need for economic development. Most Latin Americans also recognize the need for social change. But they differ on whether social change should be a result, or a condition, of development.

There are many people who believe that the development of Latin America, which until now has happened almost spontaneously, one might say through inertia, will continue in the same way. Moreover, this group says, economic development itself will lead imperceptibly to social change: the oligarchic system will gradually be eaten away by industrialization, urbanization, and the proletarianization of the peasantry and will eventually disappear. If the middle sectors have been growing steadily until the present, they say, there is no reason why they should not continue to do so and to absorb ever larger segments of the submerged masses. This absorption, in turn, will weaken the oligarchic system, will dilute and deform it until it eventually disappears. It is not possible to predict how long this evolution will take, although it will doubtless require several generations. But since there has been no desire for change among the submerged masses, nor any revolutionary forces able to effect change swiftly, this evolution may be permitted to occur, regardless of how long it takes. The only important thing is to continue to industrialize, to strengthen the economic infrastructure, and to pass legislation encouraging this evolution. For the rest, the evolution itself will create conditions that will, little by little, make a democratic political system possible. The people will be getting an education and preparing to share power. Meanwhile, we must resign ourselves to the continuation of the present conditions, to the submerged masses' being the source of capital, and console ourselves with the idea that the volume of these masses will diminish in proportion as they are incorporated into the middle sectors. This position, which concerns itself entirely with economic problems, could be summed up in these words written by an American in Panama, but which might have been those of a Latin American businessman:

The biggest problem down here in Latin America is economic. The social improvements sought by the Alliance for Progress and others are those found generally in the more developed countries of the world. A much sounder fiscal base is required to support social changes and it would seem difficult to expect much progress in this field when Latin economies are hard put to maintain a few public services now offered.

South American countries need help to expand and integrate their economies. Our policy should aim at building up their gross national product so that they can better afford (and continue maintaining, which is important) the social and infrastructural improvements which are so necessary for their proper development.

This is where the United States—through its business and farming communities—can and, I think, would, help if given government encouragement and guarantees. Reduced aid programs can then follow, or even go hand in hand with this economic build-up, but they cannot lead it.*

The supporters of this position are called *desarrollistas* ("developists"). In reality, their position could be described as one of *laissez faire*, although they do not generally advocate a *laissez faire* policy in strictly economic matters.

A second group consists of those who consider that development should proceed as quickly as possible and that it is necessary to bring about a revolution from above, since to hope that the "natural" economic process will produce change is equivalent to refusing to see this change, and particularly, to direct it. These elements feel as frustrated in the society today (despite the fact that they occupy a relatively privileged place within it) as the *desarrollistas* feel satisfied. They consider themselves the moving force in cultural and economic life, feel that they are better trained than the members of the government and the oligarchs, and that it would be fitting for them to exercise power for the benefit of the people. They do not believe that democratic methods will serve in Latin America. Until now, this "revolutionary" paternalistic attitude, which holds no place for the masses and which, therefore, has no desire to permit the free play of social forces, but wants to dominate and channel them, has been shared by very different groups. They have included, on the one hand, intellectuals, the new left, neo-Marxists, Castro-

* Letter of John H. M. Scribner to *The New York Times,* April 30, 1967.

ites, all advocates of violence and guerrilla warfare, and the Moscow-line Communists, advocates of political and conspiratory action; and, on the other, technocrats in business and the military who favor "progressive" military coups. As has been said earlier, all these groups could unite at a future time.

A third group consists of the democratic political movements, supported by a part of the middle class and by the labor movement. These groups want development speeded up by peaceful means. They believe that political action—supported, at times, by violence or by popular pressure—will be able to make the oligarchy give ground. And they hope that, with the support of the United States, they will be able to establish an effective government and prevent the military from overthrowing it. They want to effect gradual and legal social reforms, and are confident that with these they will arouse the submerged masses.

In the past, these movements knew how to appeal to the masses; but they have lost their dynamism and aggressiveness, and many of their members have come to the conclusion that a form of paternalism is needed to enable the masses to benefit from development. The difference between their paternalism and that of the group cited above is that they propose to take the masses out of their inertia, whereas the former group has for its object "saving" the masses while leaving them inert. Another, and very important, difference is that the "revolutionary" and technocratic paternalists want the masses to pay for the cost of development, whereas the populists prefer the oligarchy to do so, through normal capital investment. The political consequences of the two positions are also quite different: paternalism, "revolutionary" or technocratic, will lead to totalitarianism and eventually to alliance or collaboration with the Communists, whereas populism, even in its paternalistic forms, seeks to create a democratic system and therefore will reject collaboration with the Communists.

We have seen that the majority of the active elements of Latin American society are advocates of a tutored development, in one form or another. It might be said that the enormous submerged mass frightens or discourages them, that they have no confidence in the people's capacity to discover their own interests and defend them—or, on the other hand, that they have too much confidence in this capacity and do not want to run the risk of having the people actually hold power.

But there are other elements—unorganized, scattered—who have kept the faith in the people that characterized the early populist movement and who find in the people the only means of accelerating economic growth without running the risk of this acceleration's leading to totalitarianism. These elements believe that social change and economic development must go hand in hand. In the future, they may create their own movement or may succeed in attracting the populist movements to their point of view. But, as of the present, they are a minority.

The reasoning of these elements, whom we may call revolutionary populists, is as follows: the forces that formerly favored revolution have become part of the oligarchy; when they again find themselves frustrated they will try to use the submerged masses to destroy the oligarchic system and to establish a system that will lead to totalitarianism or, at best, to paternalism that is outwardly democratic but excludes the masses from any participation in government. Without that participation, there can be no genuine development—which, by definition, should have as a consequence not only political but also social democratization. There may be technological progress and industrialization; but if there is no political participation, there will not be any real social change but only a change of ruling personnel. The system will continue to be an oligarchic one, with the intellectuals, the technicians, and possibly the military replacing the landholders as the monopolizers of political power. Only with the participation of the submerged masses can there be hope of creating conditions in which it will be possible to find solutions to the problems of development; and, at the same time, only in the participation of the masses are there guarantees against the danger that the masses will pay for development through underconsumption and overexploitation.

Moreover, the revolutionary populists say, the principal obstacles to development—lack of education, inertia, low productivity, low consumption, high birth rate—are derived from the very condition of the submerged masses. It is logical, then, that only by bringing the submerged masses to the surface of society—or, better said, by helping them to bring themselves to the surface—will it be possible to create conditions favorable to development. Otherwise, in order to produce these conditions, it will be necessary to submit the masses to forms of pressure and control that will differ from serfdom only in the technical and legal means that are employed. And these means will prove more costly (and, in the long run, self-defeating) than the minimal risk of arousing the masses and giving them a just share of power. It must not be forgotten that development, by whatever means it is accomplished, will inevitably destroy what remains of the popular social structure: Indian communes, villages, the cacique system, the *patrón* system. These traditional institutions will have to be replaced by new ones. But those that are imposed by force will necessarily be less efficient than those that arise spontaneously from the people. Here, too, participation by the masses is a guarantee of order and efficiency.

The interests of the United States coincide with the interests of the submerged masses, who, as we have said, want a society fundamentally similar to the American. The United States, then, should aid a development program for Latin America that is based on popular participation. But this participation will not be possible without first awakening in the masses an awareness of their interests. Poverty does not produce revolutionaries, but frustration does. It is necessary, therefore, to make the masses aware of their capacities, to make them feel frustrated, so that they will want to change the social system in which they live. There are in the middle class, in the old populist movement, in the labor movement, and even among businessmen, intellectuals, and students, elements who feel this way, and who can go to the people and arouse and organize them—without any paternalism, hoping that leaders will then arise from among the masses. This would be neither disinterestedness nor missionary spirit (although it would satisfy the missionary spirit these groups have) but simple self-interest, because among the masses is to be found the only guarantee that development in Latin America can be realized without a decrease in individual liberties and political freedom.

How shall the masses exert pressure for change? This will

depend, as it always has in history, on the methods the enemies of change employ to oppose it. If they use legal means, the pressure will be produced by legal means; if they use violence, it will be met with violence. Those who favor this point of view consider that, with all the risks it may entail, it is the least dangerous way so far proposed for speeding development, and the only method that will have positive political consequences (more democracy and less vulnerability to demagogic or Communist propaganda). For the United States, they add, it would have the advantage of being the only method that would lessen anti-Americanism instead of increasing it.

On broad lines, these are the different ideas regarding development that are being discussed in Latin America. All of them (for want of anything better) accept the usual technical methods: foreign aid, strengthening of the infrastructure, agrarian reform, industrialization, combined public and private investment, control of both public and private international investment, more or less strict state control of the economy, and economic planning. What distinguishes the various groups is not their preference for one or the other of these methods, but the ends for which these methods are to be used, and for whose benefit.

What are the factors of change? They are to be sought not so much in deliberate political action, or in aid programs, as in the pressures spontaneously generated in a static society such as that of Latin America when it comes into contact with dynamic influences. One factor of change, for instance, is technological progress, which upsets the old local structures. Another factor is the population explosion, which produces unemployed masses and the tensions peculiar to slums. Another factor is the existence of considerable groups that we might call "available," that is, that have no social function and are not integrated into the ruling group; they include the middle class, especially the intellectuals and professionals, as well as the mass of the people. It may be said that the influence of the United States—economic, technical, and cultural—is always a factor in change, independently of the policy of the United States and of those who transmit this influence. An American firm may not desire change, but to the extent to which it introduces modern techniques of production, marketing, and advertising, it exerts an influence favorable to change.

These factors of change generate problems, because Latin American society is not flexible enough to absorb these pressures and convert them into positive factors. The most positive thing about them is that they make passivity more dangerous than action. But these factors of change in turn produce obstacles.

The principal one is the population explosion. The population growth (discussed in Chapter II) neutralizes the results of the increase in production; it necessitates an ever greater production increase to raise—or even to maintain—the living standard of Latin Americans. Because this population growth takes place primarily in rural areas and among the uprooted, the result is regression in the living conditions of the submerged masses and a sharpening of the economic differences between the various social groups. It also makes more difficult and expensive the spreading of education, general as well as technical, which is necessary for industrialization.

The population growth adds an extraordinary complication to the solution of problems that a few decades ago could have been solved with relative ease. This is especially true of agrarian reform. If the population is increasing and the amount of arable land is not, any agrarian-reform plan will accelerate the emigration to the city of the peasants to whom no land can be distributed; if the plan is successful, the mechanization of agriculture will create a surplus of farm labor, which will also emigrate to the urban centers. This means, today, that there can be no possibility of success for an agrarian-reform plan that is not accompanied by plans for rapid industrialization to give employment to the surplus rural population. Since the cities are already overpopulated, industry must be decentralized; this in turn will have to be accompanied by a rapid development of the provincial infrastructure: roads, electricity, schools, housing, hospitals. (If Latin American integration becomes a reality, and if it is not limited solely to problems of trade, it could help to solve, or at least to palliate, the effects of the population explosion, through transfers of population to sparsely settled fertile regions and the opening to cooperative exploitation of regions until now wild or abandoned).

The most important studies of population growth have been made in Puerto Rico. It has been found there that a high birth rate is not caused by religious beliefs but by deeply rooted social concepts that bestow prestige on men and women who have many children. In agricultural societies, children have always been an investment, since they help in cultivating the land. But even when they cease to be profitable, parents will continue to be influenced by the old concepts of prestige. It appears that only social mobility, together with an improvement of living conditions, has any effect on fertility.

The problem, then, consists in a race between the increase of population and the increase of available goods. But if the population increase is to lose the race, social change will be necessary; for even supposing that the amount of available goods increases rapidly, if these goods are not distributed among the masses, the high birth rate will continue. And even so, it will take several generations before the change of living standards and of cultural mores will produce the desired effect upon the birth rate. Thus, it is essential to achieve an economic growth rate that is both rapid and sustained.

At one time, Washington believed that Puerto Rico could serve as a model for development in Latin America. But Puerto Rico's development has been realized under special conditions not found elsewhere on the continent: an exceptional amount of American aid, tax exemptions, the ability of its population to emigrate freely to the United States, and so forth. But there is a lesson applicable to Latin America in Puerto Rico: the island's development could not begin until the mass of the peasants were aroused and allowed to share in power. It was this, accomplished by the Popular Democratic Party of Luis Muñoz Marín (b. 1918), that created favorable conditions for the initiation of development plans and an agrarian reform that destroyed the island's oligarchic system and led to the relative prosperity of today. Puerto Rico also enjoyed another exceptional condition: it had no army that could neutralize the popular will for change once it was aroused and organized.

The existence of a military, which absorbs a high percentage of the national budget that might otherwise be used to promote the infrastructure, is one cause of Latin America's slowness in development.

But a long list of other causes could be drawn up:

The passivity of the majority of the population, which does not believe promises (and often never hears them) and which does not benefit by the greater part of the measures that are adopted.

The caste system, which stifles initiative.

The extreme poverty of the greater part of the population, which lives in a subsistence economy that does not even permit it to think of running the risk of innovation.

The tendency of social measures to favor the poorer (but relatively privileged) part of the middle and working classes, rather than the submerged masses; this is especially true in the matter of housing.

The belief that the Cuban or the American model is suited to Latin America, when in reality the Latin Americans, although they want a society like the American one, want it according to their own specifications, and whereas even those who support Castro do not want the Cuban system applied to their country.

Nationalism, which prevents the search for continental solutions to the basic problems of development. . . .

But it is clear that problems that at first glance seem purely technical take on a social and political character. Hence another obstacle to development is the tenacity with which economists, experts, technicians, and even politicians —in both Latin America and the United States—insist on treating with economic remedies what are really diseases of the social structure. As long as this way of looking at the problem persists, there is little possibility that what are considered solutions will be anything but patchwork.

CHAPTER IX

What Do Latin Americans Think?

On Labor Day in 1933, Fulgencio Batista, a sergeant in the Cuban army, took advantage of the revolutionary climate that had developed in the country after the fall of the Machado dictatorship, staged a coup, and seized power. Batista sent for the United States ambassador to inform him of the fact but had great difficulty finding him, for the diplomat could not conceive of there being a coup on Labor Day. It had not occurred to him that this holiday was not observed in Cuba; he thought it was universal. When he was finally found, on the golf course, he hastened in bad humor to the presidential palace and came face to face with Batista, in his sergeant's uniform, with an unbuttoned jacket and a broad smile on his face. The ambassador—who had never seen the man everyone on the island had pointed out as the inevitable next head of state—sincerely wanted a democratic regime in Cuba. Thinking he could unseat Batista swiftly, he told him that the American government was not accustomed to dealing with sergeants. Batista burst out laughing and called to one of the colonels around him.

"Give me your jacket, buddy," he shouted. And while the colonel was taking off his jacket, Batista did the same. He put on the colonel's jacket with its gold braid, turned to the ambassador, smiled, and said:

"Now I am a colonel and we can talk about serious matters."

This story sums up, better than many learned studies, the difficulty a North American has in understanding Latin Americans. It is no easier for the people of the south to understand those from the northern part of the hemisphere. A long catalog could be made of the clichés in circulation about one or the other. For example, it is common to hear the following observations about Latin Americans from the executive of an American firm in Latin America: "They are just no good. To improve, they would have to change completely, and that seems impossible. If they would only stop breeding like rabbits. Things always go badly here—nothing works well, telephones or plumbing. They don't do anything the way we do. How can they talk about democracy? They aren't ready for it. What they need is a dictatorship that will teach them to conduct themselves with some discipline. . . ." And if you listen to a Latin American who has returned from the United States, you hear another list of clichés: "They are nice people, but so rude and stolid. They don't know what good food is. The women are very pretty, but they are always smiling until it becomes a bore. You never can find what you want in the shops. Nobody knows how to sell things. The machines in the United States are efficient, but the people don't work very hard. . . ."

There is, in the relations between the two peoples, a mixture of contempt and admiration, of envy and sympathy. The Latin American imitates the American's way of life (at least in the cities), and at the same time that he criticizes the United States for its materialism, he is very much concerned with his own material comfort. He gets along with the Americans personally because he tells them what he thinks they would like to hear. The American, for his part, cannot understand how such affable friends, who make him so welcome in their homes, can at the same time be so violently anti-American. The American envies—without saying so—the unpreoccupied, happy life and ease of communication of many Latin Americans, and even their (imaginary) Don Juanism. The Latin American envies—without ever saying so—the comforts and wealth of the American, the security of his existence, the guarantees afforded by his political system. But when they speak of one another's countries, they mention American racial segregation instead of the struggle to end it, and Latin American inefficiency rather than the fact that things work despite it.

There is too great a difference in living standards for any real interchange.* For the American, a new car every two or three years is following the current of the economy; for the Latin American, it would mean impoverishing the country's reserves. The American works hours in his office in order to be able to buy a new car when the engine in the old one begins to fail. The Latin American works hours repairing his car so that the engine will not wear out.

The people who have made and been shaped by Latin American society, so stable in its disorder, which Americans do not understand because it is so alien to them, and which Latin Americans do not need to understand because it is their own, are not a simple folk who may be shown in a schematized outline, but very complicated. This is as true of the daily life of the masses as of the pirouettings of the intellectuals.

Way of Life

In the United States the rich, the middle class, and the poor have a way of life, a manner of behavior and conventions common to all (except, perhaps, in the slums and in certain backward regions). All of them, at any rate, live in the twentieth century. In Latin America we find, side by side, customs and ways of life belonging to different historical periods and diverse cultural traditions. The people in the cities do not live materially very differently from Americans in urban areas. The air is less polluted (although not a great deal less), there are fewer gadgets, but there are no fundamental differences. But between an uprooted city dweller in

* For this reason, it should be pointed out that invitations to study in or visit the United States do not promote friendship but deepen enmity, for it is virtually impossible for Latin Americans to identify themselves with American realities—they are too different.

Rio de Janeiro and an inhabitant of the slums of New York, between an Andean peasant and a Nebraska farmer, between the inhabitant of a small town in Guatemala and a small town in the American Mid-West, the differences are measured in centuries. Hence there cannot be a single Latin American way of life.

There are, however, certain social customs that are common to great areas of the population and that help us to understand the history and the problems that have been described in the preceding chapters.

In general, it may be said that in his social life the Latin American is extremely egocentric. In the Indian communes, of course, cooperation is the very basis of existence, although there too it is slowly disintegrating under the pressure of the population explosion and industrialization. But most Latin Americans do not bother themselves about the problems of their neighborhood or their town. The middle-class Latin American, especially, prefers to debate the great national or international issues rather than to cope with the details of collective daily life. *Madrugarle*—the Mexican phrase for getting ahead—is a proof of cleverness, and to be cleverer than one's neighbor is indispensable for self-respect, prosperity, and even for survival.

The only community with which the Latin American feels identified is the family. The Latin American family is a very large, tightly closed circle, composed not only of relatives but of friends who have witnessed the family ceremonies of baptism, marriage, and so forth—and who are called *compadres* and *comadres*. Often, especially in rural areas, the family is almost endogamous. (Sicilian customs in matters of sex, love, and marriage, when they are shown on the screen in Latin America, do not evoke the same astonished reaction that they do in the United States.) Families are usually large, averaging from five to eight members; from 65 to 80 per cent of the Latin American population belongs to families of five or more members.

Family life centers around the wife. Submissive to her husband in important matters, it is she who makes the daily decisions and who often holds the family together and even supports it when the father abandons it temporarily—or permanently. The man, except in the upper-income and oligarchic families, resents family ties, and if he does not break them he weakens them by multiplication, that is, by having along with his legitimate family, his *casa chica,* or love nest; and this is true of all social levels and even when the "legitimate" family is so by custom and not by law. In many countries, however, the *amasiato,* or de facto union, is recognized by law.

The traditional double standard for men and women, which has predominated in both Iberia and Latin America, continues, although the two standards are slowly approaching each other. In the cities, at least, the woman tends to behave more and more as she does in industrial societies. She has the right to vote in all Latin American countries (although the franchise is exercised only, as a rule, among the middle class), and she works in industry, in business, and in government. The number of business and professional women is steadily growing, and it is not unusual to find women deputies, governors, and ministers. In Argentina, 25 per cent of all jobs are held by women; in Mexico, 20 per cent. But it is less than 10 per cent in the remaining countries.

The transformation of the urban woman has been very rapid. Ecuador was the first Latin American country to give women the vote, in 1929; in 1950, women had the vote in ten of the twenty countries; by 1960, they were denied it only in Paraguay, which granted it shortly thereafter. Along with this has gone a profound change in women's attitudes toward sex, the home, and cultural life. In the cities, it is no longer necessary to have a chaperon along in order to go out with a sweetheart; in the provinces, the traditional customs survive, although there, too, they are slowly disappearing. It may be said that the Latin American woman has shown greater capacity than the man for changing and adapting herself to new ways. Perhaps this is because the man—who enjoys a liberty in his family life infinitely greater than that of the North American—did not have much to gain by change, whereas the woman did. But it should be emphasized that these changes affect only a minority; the women of the rural areas and the slums continue to shoulder the burden of the home, the family, and often of gainful work.

One manifestation of the importance of the wife in the home—and also of the abundance of servants—is Latin American cuisine. Derived from the Spanish, but with local additions, particularly the use of piquant condiments, it is an important part of family life. Drinking is important in the wine-making countries (Chile and Argentina), and, to a lesser extent, in brandy-producing countries (Mexico with its tequila, the Andes countries with their pisco) and those making rum (on the tropical coasts), although inadequate diet often makes the Latin American a poor drinker. Such a diet is based on rice and beans in the Caribbean, on corn in Mexico and Central America, on potatoes in the Andes. Only in the Plata region is the diet composed of wheat and meat.

Except in the extreme south of the continent, most major Latin American cities are located in the interior; the Latin American has always turned his back on the sea. The cities he built had streets in the form of a checkerboard, with a central plaza on which the church and the city hall (or the viceroy's palace, later the presidential palace) faced each other. On the opposite sides were the houses of the town's most distinguished families. It is to this central plaza that people hasten at nightfall and on fiesta days, to stroll, listen to music, or sit in the sidewalk cafés. The American city, on the other hand, is strung out on both sides of a highway, and its equivalent of the Latin American *plaza mayor* is Main Street. The former is planned, the latter makeshift. The plaza is for meeting, strolling, talking; the Main Street is for the purpose of getting somewhere. Perhaps this symbolizes the fundamental difference between the two cultures.

The speech of the people in the plaza is a very important element in their lives, much more so than in the United States. The good talker is appreciated and respected in Latin America; to be a fluent conversationalist and orator is essential for a career in politics or even in business.

The Portuguese spoken in Brazil is softer than that spoken in Portugal, and the same is true of the Castilian of Latin America and that of Spain. Latin American Spanish and Portuguese are not only slower and more melodious, but also richer. They have acquired words and expressions from the Indian languages, from English, from the languages of the immigrants. Some of these words have a history: *gringo*—that is, a citizen of the United States—derives from a ballad sung by the soldiers who invaded Mexico in 1847, "Green Grows the Grass." Latin American Spanish has been enriched by many words of Quechua origin in the south and of Nahuatl, the Aztec language, in the north: for example, it is from the Quechua word *anta,* or copper-colored, that we get the name of the Andes. The influence of the Indian languages is not only in the vocabulary but also in grammar; for instance, Andeans who have had Aymará or Quechua nurses speak a Spanish almost without prepositions, since those languages have very few of them. In Cuba, many words of African origin are current in popular speech.

But the true richness of the language lies in its metaphors and expressions. Very classic, even anachronistic, Castilian and Portuguese are spoken by the Creole families, but the language of the middle class has become popularized, has gathered all the accumulated experiences of the people. That is why there are so many untranslatable Latin American novels; often the translator does not understand the language, for it is composed not of words but of expressions and metaphors. A Mexican will say *"está bruja"* to indicate that he has no money, and outside of Mexico no one will know what he means. To deceive in Mexico is "to give someone soup with your finger." A man in love is "flying low." The Brazilian worker calls the official of his union a "horse blanket."

The Latin American has a ceremonial feeling about life, the legacy of both Indian and Iberian societies. He likes gift-giving, which may explain the spread of the North American institutions of Santa Claus and Christmas celebrations. He delights in filling his life with flowers, colored paper, scraps of cloth, lights, and images.

Good manners are more widespread than in the United States, and one must not fail to observe certain rituals: not to accept an invitation the first time it is extended; not to speak to anyone without giving him his title—a beggar, for example, is *el señor mendigo,* "Mister Beggar." You must offer your house to a visitor, telling him that he is in his own home. One must not refuse an invitation to drink or eat in a public place, must never forget to express thanks on every occasion, and must ask permission to take one's leave.

This ceremonial sense is also found in folklore and customs. Latin America is the only part of the West in which folklore has retained a certain popularity, in which it is not a mere museum piece. The traditional dances of Spanish origin are true ceremonial dances, and in many folk songs we find formulas that are in current use in social intercourse.

It should be said that the Latin American has no respect for ritual in activities that are not traditional. Thus ceremonious behavior persists at bullfights (in countries where they are permitted: Mexico, Venezuela, and Colombia), but it is not to be found in sports—soccer, which is the most popular, and baseball, which is gaining on it—whose public is frequently explosive in its passion. Nor does it exist in the way Latin Americans drive automobiles. But in traditional activities—at work or at play—ceremoniousness reappears on all social levels, although the tendency among the middle class is to imitate Americans and in the oligarchic and very rich groups to imitate the English.

Little of the above applies to the great population groups that are Indian, or culturally Indian. The existence of this mass of people who speak their own language, who do not take much part in the market economy, and who live on the fringes of the nations' life, constitutes a problem as much cultural as economic and social.

About half a century ago, certain Latin Americans began to concern themselves with the Indian population, and from this concern arose what has been called *indigenismo,* the movement aimed at incorporating the Indians into modern life.

Indigenismo was a reaction to the consequences that the concept of equality before the law had for the Indians. There have been various schools of *indigenismo:* one has favored a cultural approach to the problem, that of westernizing the Indian, beginning with his language. Some have thought that a beginning should be made on the economic plane, giving the Indian land and freeing him from servitude. Others have wanted to preserve the Indian and his customs, isolating and protecting him in order that he might follow his own evolution. Between the two world wars, it was fashionable in certain intellectual circles for women to dress "Indian style," which was really a way of dressing adapted from that of Spain in the sixteenth century, and there was a tendency to glorify everything Indian. Still others have seen in the Indian communes (especially in Peru) the model of a new agrarian structure; at one time, the Communists advocated the formation of Aymaran and Mayan republics.

Indigenismo has concentrated on obtaining protective legislation, which has gradually been passed in nearly all countries with a significant Indian population; but this legislation has been only slowly and feebly enforced, since the existence of Indian masses in virtual servitude is to the advantage of many interests. The Inter-American Indian Institute, a specialized branch of the OAS, with headquarters in Mexico, has tried to foster this activity and to help organize Indian Institutes in countries where they are needed.

The Indians are, unquestionably, the most underprivileged part of the submerged masses. Their existence has often served as a pretext for opposition to change, because it is said that they are incapable of making progress. The truth is otherwise: there is "encouraging evidence that, where Indians live under conditions of greater independence and freedom as they do in indigenous nonhacienda communities, changes in attitudes, values and behavior are occurring at a faster rate."*

But despite the studies of anthropologists and the activity of educators, physicians, and sociologists, a coherent approach to the Indian problem has not yet been achieved. Nor, for that matter, has much progress been made toward eliminating another major obstacle to progress in Latin America: illiteracy.

Poverty as Educator

A large part of the Latin American population is illiterate. Much more so in reality than on paper. According to the most recent statistics, about 40 per cent of the Latin American population over fifteen years of age cannot read or write. Of course, the percentage of illiteracy varies from country to country: it is low (under 20 per cent) in Argentina, Costa

* Allan Holmberg: "Changing Community Attitudes and Values in Peru: A Case Study in Guided Change," in *Social Change in Latin America Today* (New York, 1960).

Rica, Chile, and Uruguay; medium (from 20 to 30 per cent) in Mexico and Venezuela; and high (more than 40 per cent) in the remaining countries.

Nearly all the Latin American countries provide for free and compulsory education, but they are seldom able to fulfill the second part of the provision. Only 16 per cent of the Latin American population attends school; since about half the population is under twenty years of age, we can see how low this figure is. The number of children who are not in school is sometimes greater than the number who are (Ecuador, El Salvador, Honduras, Haiti, the Dominican Republic). The percentage of dropouts is very high: only about 15 per cent of those who enter elementary school go on to high school; only about 5 per cent receive higher education. To take care of all children of school age, it would be necessary to more than triple the number of teachers and schools. There are at present double and triple sessions, since the majority of pupils can attend school only at certain times in the day. Nevertheless, some progress has been made. In the last ten years, in which the population has risen 2.8 per cent a year, school registration has increased by 7.2 per cent.

The education budget is often a matter of chance. In Colombia, for example, teachers' salaries are paid with the income from the provincial monopolies on liquors. Elsewhere, the educational budget is extremely low; in the Dominican Republic, under its first democratic government, in 1963, it was $16 million, about as much as an American university with 10,000 students spends in a year. There are countries in which the share of the budget earmarked for the armed forces is greater than that allotted to education (Argentina, Brazil, Chile, Colombia, Ecuador, Haiti, Peru); in some of these countries, there are more soldiers than teachers (Argentina, Chile, Ecuador, Nicaragua, Peru). Everywhere, teachers receive very low salaries, and teacher-training is mediocre.

Not only is there a shortage of teachers and of schools, but in many places the buildings are old and lack modern equipment. In a few countries (Mexico, Uruguay), the children receive free books; in the majority, they do not get anything. Nor do their parents have any voice in the way the schools are run; the educational systems are in the hands of the authorities.

The educational systems are generally based on the European model. They are composed of primary education (from six to eight years); secondary education (two to four years, generally designed to prepare for entry into the university); and higher education (universites and technical schools, from four to eight years). In some countries, there are special schools for Indians, in which their own language is taught in addition to the national one. In recent years, there has also been a growth in the number of vocational schools. For the children of the rich there are private schools, most of them run by the Church; it also is not unusual for foreign colonies—especially the American, French, and German—to have their own schools.

A few countries have good educational systems: Chile (at least in the cities), Uruguay, and especially Argentina, where Domingo Faustino Sarmiento (1811–88) asked his friend the American educator Horace Mann to send teachers to establish a modern school system. Thanks to Sarmiento's efforts, Argentina was able to absorb without difficulty the great mass of immigrants it received. But on the whole, it may be said that education continues to be a privilege of the middle and upper classes. Cuba is an exception, for under the Castro regime there has been considerable encouragement of education. Nevertheless, in early 1969, Castro complained of advances in illiteracy.

For years, it was fashionable to undertake anti-illiteracy campaigns in an attempt to teach adults to read and write. Although spectacular results were claimed, experience has shown that they are short-lived. It is not enough to teach reading and writing to adults living in an isolated village if they do not feel the need to use this knowledge, if they do not have access to newspapers and books or find in their local society any stimulus to reading.

A glance at newspaper circulation figures is enough to make one realize that this stimulus is concentrated in the cities. In all of Latin America, 1,122 dailies are published (their information coming almost exclusively from the American news services). But in only five countries (Argentina, Chile, Panama, Uruguay, and Venezuela) are more than 100 copies sold per 1,000 inhabitants; in five (Bolivia, Guatemala, Haiti, Honduras, and the Dominican Republic), the proportion is less than 30 per 1,000 inhabitants. With the exception of a few great traditional papers, the press is in general provincial and sensational. No paper has a printing of more than 250,000 copies. There is no censorship of the press, but the dictators close down newspapers when the latter oppose them. Government announcements constitute an important source of income, and this, combined with the interests of the newspaper owners, exerts an indirect censorship. The majority of the press is rightist, but it numbers among its contributors many members of the new left, to whom it gives full freedom of expression. There are few party newspapers, although every political party, union, or group has its weekly or its little magazine. There are several independent weeklies of the *Life* or *Time* variety, which denounce as "imperialistic penetration" the Spanish- or Portuguese-language editions of American magazines.

It is natural that, with a high percentage of illiterates, radio, television, and the motion pictures should find a favorable climate, despite the high cost of radio and television sets. In the villages, the people meet at a home or in a café to follow the television or radio programs on the only set in the community. Transistors have made it possible to have radios in many places where there is no electricity.

Most radio and television stations are privately owned, although a few are university-owned, particularly in Chile. The level of the programs is very low, and except for the news programs (which are rarely objective) there are no public service or cultural programs. Moreover, there is censorship of films, radio, and television, especially in sexual matters. But if educational radio and TV are in their early stages, the number of commercial stations has grown rapidly: there are 740 in Brazil, 380 in Mexico, 125 in Colombia, 125 in Ecuador, 100 in Chile, 60 in Argentina. The growth of television has been fantastic: in 1955 there were, in all Latin America, 619,000 receivers and 32 broadcasting stations. Ten years later, these figures had risen to 6.6 million and 217, respectively. But in 1955 the number of TV sets was 10 per cent of those in the world; in 1965, it was only 7 per cent. Argentina has 3 TV stations but Brazil has 20, Colombia 14, Cuba (before 1959), 19, and Mexico, 23. It may be estimated that, on an average, one-third of the Latin American population is "exposed" to radio or television and in Argentina, Chile, Uruguay, and Venezuela, one-half or more.

The abundance of illiterates and semi-illiterates has also helped the formation of the film industry in Argentina, Mexico, and Brazil. Mexico is ninth in the world in the volume of films produced. The quality of Latin American productions has depreciated; although some directors have produced first-rate works and achieved international fame, the bulk of cinema production is limited to the Spanish-speaking market.

The educational system is lamentable, then, in a continent that is being industrialized and therefore needs a trained labor force, and one in which the masses, in order to exercise their political rights, need civic and elementary education.

The Formalization of Life

A great deal has been written about the individualism of Latin Americans, and it is believed that this is one cause of the disorder that has characterized the history of their countries. Yet, it is possible that the Latin American is an individualist precisely because that is the only—or the least difficult—way of escaping an extremely formalized existence.

Before the coming of the Spaniards, the Indians lived in a society under the control of priest-kings. The Spaniards came from an authoritarian society that was a genuine bureaucratic despotism (although it had democratic institutions for a base). The colonies were extremely bureaucratic, from the organization of the first expeditions of the conquistadors to the establishment of the juntas that fought for independence. And the life of the independent Latin American countries has been characterized by a rigid regimentation.

The Aztec and Inca societies were also very legalistic. The Spaniards and Portuguese had an obsession for the juridical, and the oligarchic societies that succeeded them cloaked themselves in legalisms, even in their most shameless moments of dictatorship or demagogy.

The Spanish juridical tradition is rooted in Roman law, and Latin American juridical life has been inspired by Roman law, interpreted by colonial jurists, and modernized by the Napoleonic Code. The written law is more important than jurisprudence, the letter more important than the spirit, the text more than the interpretation. This accounts for the abundance of constitutions and laws in Latin America. It is not unusual for a country—whether it has a legislature or a dictator is of little importance—to turn out a thousand laws in a year. So it is not strange that the legal profession has so many members or that it is the way to success in politics, commerce, and even literature.

The judicial systems, however, resemble not those of Europe but of the United States, even in their names: many countries, for instance, have district and circuit courts. Thus we have the paradox of a machinery that is intended to afford a flexible interpretation of the law but that assumes the duty of applying it rigidly. Moreover, changes of political regimes often mean changes in judicial posts. One of the first things many dictators do is to appoint new justices of the supreme court. This court is not, as a rule, responsible for enforcing respect of constitutional guarantees, but a court of final appeal.

The Latin American codices are excellent juridical exercises: clear, logical, minutely detailed. But they have little to do with real life. A manifestation of this pettifogging spirit is found in the constitutional provision—common to all Latin American countries—that permits the executive to set aside constitutional guarantees in times of national disorder—that is, precisely when there is most need of these guarantees. Another manifestation is the penal system, which is everywhere very modern on paper (some countries even permit family visits to prisoners), but which in reality is a mixture of tolerance and brutality, offering no hope of rehabilitation. The death penalty exists in most countries, but it is enforced only for political motives (under dictatorships) or in cases of crimes that have inflamed public opinion.

But what makes the law slow, costly, and discriminatory is its class character. Justice—even in the few countries where the judiciary is really independent of the executive power—is a gentleman's justice, which considers that its primary mission is to protect the *señores* and which pays little attention to the problems of the common people. The military and the clergy enjoy special privileges under the law; the poor are at the mercy of the judicial bureaucracy. Although the law recognizes individual rights, it has little concern with guaranteeing them. What it does guarantee is the authority of the paterfamilias, of the state, of ownership. All this reinforces the habit of mind of the ruling classes which considers that problems can be solved by laws—and which in itself contributes to perpetuating the problems—and at the same time increases popular skepticism concerning the law. The public has little respect for the law and prefers to settle its own quarrels, sometimes by appealing to the arbitration of a respected person, sometimes by taking the law into its own hands.*

This mixture of respect and contempt for the law is found everywhere. But everywhere the letter of the law is respected, and appearances are kept up. Keeping up appearances is as important in politics as it is in private life. "There must be no scandal" seems to be the motto of the politician—and it has been, and in many places still is, the motto of the Church.

During the nineteenth century, the Latin American Church fought for its privileges, but it did not increase its prestige or contribute anything to Latin American culture. It was a Church closed to innovation, in which there was not a single theologian of distinction. The Church supported the established order, the dictatorships, and latifundism. The state granted it privileges when the conservatives were in power and withdrew them under the liberals. In countries where the liberals held power for long periods, the Church is not rich; in other countries, it still figures among the great landowners. The priests, particularly in rural areas, led a not very prosperous existence, surrounded by their children; their duties were more administrative than spiritual.

The Catholicism of the common people was one of ritual and superstition. The religion of the ruling classes was extremely rigid in sexual matters, extremely lax in matters of money and relations with "inferiors." The ruling groups have not been very generous to the Church, however—unless it has been with public funds—for there are few charitable foundations or donations to the Church (although they are

---

* Justice in Latin America has always been a class matter. In Chile, in the first years after independence, a person who circulated "gloomy rumors" was punished with 200 lashes if he was of "low class" and with banishment from the city—but no lashes—if he belonged to a higher class. Carrying arms without permission was punishable by a fine of twenty-five pesos, but a person of "low class"—possibly on the assumption that he would be unable to pay—was punished instead with twenty-five lashes.

more plentiful than bequests for cultural purposes). One might sum up by saying that nineteenth-century Latin American religious life was sterile.

Things have changed in the present one. There has been a growing number of priests and laymen interested in social problems, who formed the nuclei of today's Christian Democratic movement. But except for these groups, intellectual and religious life have had no interrelation, despite the existence of Catholic universities and the Church's control of most private schools.

But the Church is present everywhere in Latin America: in schools, courtrooms, barracks. Eleven countries have separation of Church and state—Brazil, Chile, Cuba, Ecuador, El Salvador, Guatemala, Honduras, Mexico, Nicaragua, and Uruguay—but in only a few of these is the constitutional provision complied with. In a number of Latin American countries, the Church has managed to prevent divorce and the recognition of illegitimate children. Despite the power of the Church, however, there are few calls to the priesthood. Half a century ago, there were 16,000 priests, or one for every 5,000 inhabitants; today, there are 37,000 or one for every 5,500 inhabitants. One-third of the priests are not Latin Americans; half of that third are Spaniards.

The oligarchic groups are composed of practicing Catholics. In the middle class there are grades ranging from traditionalist Catholics to "progressive" Catholics (atheists), indifferent Catholics, and a small number of Protestants. Among the common people we find the same kind of syncretism that characterized the religious life of the people in colonial times. Support of the Church on the part of the oligarchy (even when it is combined with a certain skepticism about religion, at least among the men) and anticlericalism on the part of the middle class (although it is not incompatible with adherence to Catholicism) are paralleled in the submerged masses by mistrust of the parish priest together with submission to him as one of the "authorities." These "authorities" include the mayor, judge, police officer, and teacher, and are the only contact the submerged masses have with the state and the rest of society.

Latin American life is thus regimented by a law that does not reflect it and by a purely external religion. Political life is also conditioned by the habits engendered by the oligarchic system. In that system, for more than a century, politics consisted in the rivalries of different families for power, each with its clientele, its serfs, its friends in the army and in the bureaucracy. Latin Americans are accustomed to thinking not in terms of ideas and programs but of personalities and labels: So-and-So, of such-and-such a coastal family, was a liberal; So-and-So, of such-and-such a family of the sierra, was a conservative. From this tradition arose personalism, the cult of personality, which is so often considered the basis of Latin American politics.

The political, labor, or any other kind of *líder*—and it is significant that this Anglo-Saxon word has replaced the Spanish *dirigente*—is an outgrowth of the *patrón*, the owner or administrator of the hacienda. The *líder*, like the *patrón*, must be a just man (or at least appear to be so). He must be severe and inflexible, but amiable and paternal. And he must be a *macho*, a he-man, if he wants to enter politics, where many dangers lie in wait for him, the greatest of which is that he may be thought timid or cowardly.* In municipal life, there is the cacique, the local strong man who attracts the people of a village to one or another band and whose masculinity impresses those of the opposite band.

A consequence of the personality cult is continuism, or self-perpetuation in office, the tendency of chiefs of state to stay in power. Perhaps half the coups and rebellions in Latin America have taken place not to win power but to hold on to it, or, on the other hand, to prevent someone from remaining in power when constitutionally he ought to relinquish it. The Mexican Revolution began with the slogan "No re-election," and the constitutions of many Latin American countries forbid re-election, at least for one term after the president leaves office. To prevent self-perpetuation in office has been one of the obsessions of democratic movements.

The mushrooming political parties are another unconscious imitation of the political habits of the oligarchy. In 1965, there were 193 political parties in the twenty countries

---

* The *líder* sometimes goes to incredible extremes to maintain his prestige or prove his good faith. An ex-president of Uruguay, Baltasar Brum (1883–1933), committed suicide in the street to protest the inauguration of the dictator Gabriel Terra. The *líder* of the Cuban Ortodoxo party, Eduardo Chibás (1907–51), launched a radio campaign against political corruption and, to protest the public's indifference, shot himself to death before the microphone.

of Latin America. Argentina had the most, with twenty-nine (subsequently, these were all dissolved by the military dictatorship); Peru had nineteen; Panama, fourteen; Brazil, thirteen (these were later reduced to two by the military government of Castelo Branco); and Nicaragua, twelve (although the Somoza family has ruled for the last forty years). Cuba and Haiti, on the other hand, had one each. Although some of these parties are mass organizations, many are mere splinter groups that are active only at election time or when a coup is to be approved or disapproved. The Communist Party has been outlawed in most countries, but this has never kept the Communists from operating freely, since their "illegality" has existed mainly on paper.

We must bear in mind that in normal times only a small part of the population is interested in politics or takes any part in political life, even by voting. In Chile, a very politically conscious country with a high level of literacy, only 15 per cent of the population took part in the most recent elections. In Argentina, 45 per cent participated in the most recent elections. In countries where an attempt was made to oust the dominant group, the percentage was greater: 33 per cent in the Dominican Republic, 30 per cent in Nicaragua. In Uruguay and Venezuela, where political passions run high, the percentage reached 36 and 34, respectively. But in the other countries it was less than 30 per cent. Even in countries that consider themselves politically minded—Peru, Costa Rica, Colombia—it did not reach 20 per cent. Guatemala, El Salvador, and Honduras, with 14 per cent, were at the bottom of the list. Statistics show that these percentages have no relation to literacy, but on the other hand do have a definite relation to the degree of oligarchic domination: the more oligarchic a country, the lower its rate of participation in elections.

It is easy to criticize these political ways and to say that as long as they persist there can be no progress. But the Latin American—a product of many things, among them the oligarchic system—is what he is. And with this Latin American, Latin America has to change and progress. Only when Latin America changes will its political habits change. What makes law, religion, and political habits combine to regiment the

Latin American's life and to limit his initiative and freedom is the fact that the laws, religious customs, and political habits have not issued from him but are the product of alien influences imposed on majorities by minorities.

It is possible that these minorities constitute the chief limitation encountered by the Latin American. They are not wholly peculiar to Latin America, although there they are more visibly manifest and operate with extraordinary virulence. There are elites in every society, and in all nonindustrialized societies the elites aspire to the monopoly of power. But in Asia and Africa, the elites are very European, quite different from the rest of the people. In Latin America—perhaps because it is halfway to industrialization—the elites are very Latin American.

Again, this can be explained by the character of the society. If that society depends entirely on an elite—the oligarchy—it is natural that those who are below the oligarchy but above the submerged mass should imitate this elite and should also form, or think that they form, an elite: and this consciousness of being one is what really constitutes an elite. Every elite believes that it has the best solution to the problems of the country, which it believes itself qualified to impose "for the good of the country." Common to all elites is contempt of the people and a feeling of paternalism toward them. At present, there are no ideological differences among the various Latin American elites—with the exception, obviously, of the elite that is in power and which, consequently, opposes all the others, although this opposition consists in trying to win them over by giving them a small share of power.

There are elites of businessmen, of the military, of the clergy, of the bureaucracy, of the technicians, of the intellectuals and professional men. Another elite is emerging, made up of experts in development, economics, and administration; we might call this the elite of the public managerial class, in contradistinction to the managers and economists of private enterprise. Finally, there are elites of political leaders, heads of unions and employers' organizations, and so forth—in short, all those who, over and above the interests and ideologies they represent, have aspirations in common. Because of the great fluidity of the middle sectors, of which these elites are a part, and because of the low incomes that often compel members of the group to exercise two or three functions, these elites, in many individual cases, are superimposed: there are some who are at once bureaucrats, political leaders, and poets; or business and military men; or professional men and managers.

In the previous chapters, we have seen these various elites in action, and have seen how they have changed their positions and tactics. But there is one elite of which little has been said: the students and intellectuals.

Students and Intellectuals

The North American is aware of the existence of Latin American students through reports of their violent strikes; the intellectuals are known by a few books translated into English and through the manifestoes they sign to protest some act by Washington. But these are only a few of the activities of this elite, which exhibits very contradictory characteristics.

The intellectual in Latin America enjoys a high degree of social prestige, if not always a decent standard of living. He is respected, he is listened to, and he exerts influence on other social groups, although rarely on the government. The term intellectual is not limited to writers and professors, but extends also to artists and professional men: teachers, engineers, physicians, lawyers, technicians, architects, and economists all regard themselves, and are regarded, as intellectuals. And students know that when they are graduated they, too, will be included among the intellectuals and will form part of this elite.

The first step toward understanding this elite is to know that 1 out of every 750 Latin American young men enters a university, and that 1 in 50 who enter comes from a worker or peasant family. And only 15 out of every 100 professors and professional men have fathers who are workers or peasants. The difference in proportion is explained by the fact that for many intellectual activities it is not necessary to have a degree, and also by the fact that the percentage of dropouts is much higher among students from well-to-do families than among those from poor ones.

In general, tuition costs are relatively low—much lower than in the United States—and many students work; but even so, the university is a closed field for the middle class (the sons of the rich usually study abroad). The state devotes very little money to higher education; the majority of professors are miserably paid and teach only part time, making their living from their professional activities. In recent years, many governments have begun to build university cities, not only to modernize the universities, which were housed in inadequate and ancient buildings, but also in the belief that by removing the universities from the centers of the cities they could prevent student riots. (They have been wrong about that.) The small-town university campus did not exist in Latin America until a few years ago.

The training the student receives in the university is mediocre, although there are some signs of improvement, thanks in part to the aid given by international organizations and American foundations, and the collaboration of universities in the United States. But above all, it is out of date, with very little relation to Latin American needs and social realities.

The Latin American student—whether he seeks a *licentiate* (similar to the American B.A.) or a Ph.D. degree—does not study courses but careers, and he cannot elect his courses but must adjust himself to a curriculum fixed for his given field of study. He leaves the university a lawyer, a physician, a historian.

Forty-two per cent of Latin American students study law or engineering (against 16 per cent in the United States); 1.5 per cent study the natural sciences (11.6 in the United States); 54 per cent the humanities, education, and so forth (68 per cent in the United States). In all Latin American universities, the school with the greatest number of students is the law school.

Technical courses are generally not given in the universities, but in separate schools of engineering, architecture, and so on. The schools of agriculture—in countries that are still primarily agricultural—are small and antiquated. The study of agriculture attracts only 2 per cent of the students, and that of engineering only 10 per cent. In the field of technical education, where there are twice as many students as in universities, four-fifths of the students pursue courses related to commerce and business administration and only one-fifth pursue industrial courses.*

Plainly, students are not being prepared to be useful in development, or, better said, the majority of students do not show any interest in taking part, as professionals, in development.

In general, Latin American university education does not in the least concern itself with Latin America. The social sciences are taught on the basis of imported concepts completely alien to the social realities of Latin America. And although in the leading American universities (and, to a lesser extent, in those of Europe) there are courses dealing with Latin American issues, there are none in Latin American countries. Latin American students are more familiar with the works of Sartre and with modern American literature than with the works of authors from a neighboring country. The libraries are inadequate to remedy this lack.

For some years, it has been customary to send the best students (or the sons of the most influential fathers) to the United States or to Europe, to prepare them for teaching careers. These students usually hold American or European scholarships, for the Latin American governments give few. The practice accentuates the difference between education and reality, for what is learned in the United States or Europe can be adapted to use in Latin America only by a great act of the imagination.

Many university students drop out along the way to devote themselves to business or the bureaucracy (the latter in accordance with the proverb that sets as the highest goal, "to

---

* Statistics are always inexact, but even so they make clear the lack of balance between the humanities and technical fields. Venezuela, a country whose development is fairly advanced and which has a democratic regime, has 60,000 professionals: 10,000 engineers; 2,300 chemists; 20,000 teachers; 3,000 lawyers; 13,000 physicians; and 4,000 artists and writers. In Mexico, out of 206,000 professional men, only 18,000 are engineers, but there are 11,000 lawyers, and no fewer than 34,000 artists and writers. In Brazil, out of 410,000 professional men, we find only 37,000 engineers, but there are 96,000 lawyers and 23,000 artists and writers.

Many development specialists seem to believe that there is little progress because there are so few engineers, and many laws because there are so many lawyers. But the truth is that there are few engineers because there is little progress, and that lawyers proliferate because there are so many laws. The lack of balance among the specialists indicates what a lack of balance there is in reality.

be born with a scholarship, live as a bureaucrat, and die on a pension"). The large number of dropouts creates a situation prejudicial to students who take degrees: there is a shortage of middle-level professional men, and this obliges the most brilliant and well-trained, those who should play creative roles in their professions, to fill posts and assume activities that would normally be suited to professional men of medium grade.

It is not unusual for such men to migrate to the United States or to Europe, where they receive higher pay and better working conditions. Between 1962 and 1967, 3,000 high-level Latin American professional men emigrated to the United States; they were educated at a cost of about $60 million. When there is a dictatorship, the emigration is aggravated by the exile of many intellectuals who oppose the regime. The only people who do not emigrate are the military men, among whom is developing a type of well-trained technical officer who finds the army equipment superior to that furnished by the university.

Thus it is not strange that scientific research, although there are some brilliant figures in it, plays a secondary part in university life and in the cultural life of Latin America. There are about 250,000 Latin American scientists, many of whom can devote themselves only to part-time research, some because research does not yield enough for a living and others because, as has been mentioned, they must fulfill the functions of the middle-grade professionals.

The very fact that there are only two foundations to promote scientific research (one in Argentina and the other in Venezuela) indicates the degree of indifference to scientific activity. If, however, a Latin American scientist, despite everything, succeeds in gaining an international reputation—like the Argentine biologist Bernardo A. Houssay (b. 1887), who won the Nobel Prize for medicine in 1947—everyone boasts about him as if they had all been his sponsors. Nor is it insignificant that most of the great archaeological discoveries have been made by foreigners: Machu Picchu (Peru) was discovered by Hiram Bingham in 1911; San Agustín (Colombia) by Agostino Codazzi in 1857; Tiahuanaco by Wendell C. Bennett in 1932; and the *cenotes* of Yucatán by Edward H. Thompson in the last century. However, in recent years

Latin American archaeologists have received some aid and encouragement and have made such important discoveries as that of Monte Albán (Mexico), found by Alfonso Caso in 1931.

It has been said that the quality of university teaching in Latin America suffers because of its politicization. No doubt the excess of this in recent years—notably since the establishment of the Castro regime—is prejudicial to education. But we must remember that Latin American universities have traditionally been centers of political activity. This was precisely because, in an oligarchic society, the university was one of the few places in which ideological politics could be carried on. Even in colonial times, it was in the universities that works forbidden by the Church were read, and it was there that the works of Tom Paine and the French encyclopedists were circulated. Later, the universities were the field of dispute between liberals and conservatives; the majority of the students were conservatives, and from their ranks were recruited the groups that attacked the strikers in Buenos Aires and demonstrated in favor of the dictator Huerta in Mexico.

But in the present century, the signs changed. Toward the end of World War I, there arose the so-called university reform movement. Begun at the University of Córdoba (Argentina) in 1918, by Gabriel del Mazo (1894–1969), it soon spread to other universities. This movement, which found strong public support, asked for the autonomy of the universities from the governments; the latter should be limited to supplying funds but should not have any control over the naming of professors, the curriculum, etc. All this was intended to guarantee academic freedom. The movement also asked inviolability of the university grounds, the modernization of programs of study, and so forth. These objectives were gradually attained, and the students began to organize their associations, to hold elections, and to share in the government of the various schools.

Little by little, however, the student elections took on a political color as the political parties struggled to dominate the student associations. Communists, nationalists, populists, Christian Democrats, and later Castroites, pro-Chinese Communists, Trotskyites, neo-Marxists, the new left, presented their candidates. Strictly academic problems lost their importance as the active minority of the students began to organize public demonstrations, sign manifestoes, battle with the police, and call strikes over national and international problems. Some universities—the Central University of Venezuela, for instance—have been changed into virtual reserve barracks for guerrillas in recent years, taking advantage of the university privileges forbidding the police to enter university grounds (one of the demands of the university reform movement). It is revealing that the populist movements, which ask the students to work among the people, have less influence than the extreme rightist movements or than those inspired by the Communists, Castroites, and neo-Marxists. It is also significant that there is nothing like a Latin American Peace Corps.

This is easy to understand. The student wants a sense of mission, which the Communists and the Castroites give him. But, at the same time, as a member of the elite, he wants power and does not want to yield it to the masses, to whom he feels superior. He wants to help the people but in an unconsciously paternalistic fashion. The theoretical justification of this aspiration is not found in populism but in the type of Marxism offered him by the Castroites, the Communists, and even the extreme nationalists.

It should not be imagined, however, that the political activity of the students is frivolous. Their activity is often a forerunner of more widespread action and has an influence on public opinion. To some extent, the students have been the barometer of public opinion (although it appears that they are steadily becoming less so). In Cuba, students were effective in the fight for independence, and in the struggle against the dictatorships of Machado and Batista. In Peru, they were very active in opposing the dictatorship of Leguía. In Chile, they supported the Socialist Republic of 1932. In Venezuela, they formed the vanguard against the dictator Juan Vicente Gómez, and after his death founded the democratic parties. They formed the same vanguard in Guatemala against the Ubico dictatorship. Perón was never able to silence them, nor were the dictators who came after World War II.

But today, students show the same enthusiasm in combating regimes that are more or less democratic—with the purpose not of improving them but of destroying them. It is students who form the guerrilla bands (where there are any), and who were dedicated to terrorism in Venezuela. In fact, the students have followed the same evolution as the middle class: from revolutionaries with the people they have become revolutionaries without the people. They formerly had the sympathy of the people; now they are isolated from them.

But they still find support in those who were students before them: the intellectuals. For the latter live under the same contradictions as the students: they too want a sense of mission, of social usefulness, but they are more or less integrated into the oligarchic system. Often they are part of the bureaucracy—particularly the diplomatic service—or enjoy the privileges, posts, and aid of the government. They do not feel any real solidarity with the people. As an elite, they want to direct, guide, and control, and they are convinced that they have the remedies for the evils besetting their country. Not to be able to apply these frustrates them, and if they are not as available as the students, it is for practical reasons (the risk of losing salaries, family, social position) rather than for political or moral ones.

This frustration is understandable, since students and intellectuals, despite the dynamism of their protests, have exerted little influence on the politics of their countries. They do, however, exert a by no means contemptible influence on the manner of thinking of the middle class, especially of the youngest and most technocratic—businessmen, military men, government executives—since they contribute to the latter the ideological rationalization and justification of their aspirations. Naturally, neither the one nor the other realizes this, and they sincerely believe in the purity and disinterestedness of their motives and theories. But these are derived from their political impotence, their contempt for the people, and their belief that they are superior.

All this is expressed in a form of nationalism with a Marxist vocabulary which at once satisfies their consciences, their elitism, and their intelligence. It also keeps alive the conviction of their superiority, since this nationalism finds an echo in broad sections of public opinion and is tolerated—even regarded favorably—by the oligarchic groups, which find it an inoffensive outlet for the energies and dissatisfactions of the public-opinion stratum.

The Latin American intellectual has, in general, adopted "extremist" positions. He was liberal and anticlerical in the nineteenth century and populist in the first half of the twentieth. Today, he is anti-American, sympathetic to Castro (although to a lesser degree than the students), and considers himself a socialist. But only a minority of intellectuals are militantly active in neo-Marxist or Castroist groups; the majority have sided with the Christian Democrats, the populists, and other democratic groups, although they have no influence on these movements and do not reflect the parties' doctrines in their writings. Latin American intellectuals have always been involved with politics and were *engagés* long before Jean-Paul Sartre made this word fashionable. They have acted with courage against dictatorships in every period, and have frequently suffered persecution, prison, and exile. But, like the students, they have been losing contact with the people.

To judge by appearances, the Communist influence among intellectuals and students is considerable. But the truth is that the Communist movement has never been decisive in Latin America. The changes that have occurred, the movements that have appeared, the revolutions—including the Cuban—have all taken place without the participation of the Communists. Possibly it is this marginal character that explains Communism's influence among intellectuals, who also feel that they are marginal, who know they have had no influence on the recent history of their countries, and who have aspirations that coincide with what Communism offers them. But, in this sense, it might be said that, instead of there being a Communist influence among intellectuals, what we really have is the influence of the aspirations, resentments, elitism, and paternalism of the intellectuals upon the Latin American Communist movement, which helps to explain its ineffectiveness at moments when everything looked favorable for it.

It is difficult to give a picture of the beliefs of the Latin American intellectual, but a few principal traits may be emphasized. He believes in the superiority of the spiritual over the material (and reproaches the United States for its materialism). He tends to seek interpretations of the national character, preferring psychological explanations to historical ones. He is attracted by style—which explains the disproportionate influence of the Spanish philosopher José Ortega y Gasset—and seeks a doctrine that will resolve his basic contradiction (which explains his ready acceptance of Marxism). He is convinced that a synthesis of Eastern and Western cultures is being achieved in Latin America, that Latin America will emerge as the "savior race" of the world, and that social change is fundamentally cultural and psychological. Like intellectuals everywhere, he is prone to follow ideological and stylistic fashions.

The intellectual always lives in a vacuum chamber. In Latin America, the chamber is very small. There are few readers of books, few who attend lectures, and few who buy paintings. The intellectual tries to be in the vanguard; he imports the latest styles, and "naturalizes" them—but he elicits a response from very limited groups, although they are growing in proportion as the more well-to-do middle class expands.

The theater is limited almost entirely to the experimental, and does not reach the urban masses. Most publishers are poor, and books are circulated only in the country in which they are published. The average book is printed in an edition of one or two thousand copies; if it reaches 10,000, it is a best seller. If it is circulated outside the country, or is translated into English or French, its author is virtually deified.*

A few figures will give an idea of the atmosphere in which the Latin American intellectual lives and creates. It has been said that in Colombia even taxi drivers write poetry, and Bogotá was called the Athens of Spanish America. Well: in October, 1966, there were published in Colombia ten books by that country's authors: four novels, two books of poetry, two of essays, one on law, and one of drama. In the same month, in the entire country, there were 112 cultural events, two-thirds of them in the capital. Among these were eighteen poetry readings, fourteen lectures on politics, ten on religion, and eight on science. There were also sixty-three concerts, ten orchestral (and one of these by a foreign orchestra). Sim-

---

* The number of titles that appear in the only countries with a publishing industry worthy of the name is growing, however. In Brazil, the average over five years was 5,500 a year; in Argentina, 4,500; in Mexico, 1,800; in Chile, 1,500. Half of these were translations, one-third were novels, another third were technical works, and the rest were works in the fields of the humanities, economics, and politics.

ilarly, there were sixty-five theatrical performances (one-third of them for children) and forty-two art exhibits. Argentina and Mexico—whose capitals are, in a way, the "Paris" of the Latin American intellectual or artist, who does not feel consecrated until he has been accepted by them—would show higher figures. But Colombia may serve as an average example.

Despite this situation (which is less discouraging now than it was a quarter of a century ago), there are many literary reviews, the universities publish specialized journals, and authors write more and more. The cultural atmosphere, although its extent is limited, is much more favorable than it was in the past. But the intensity of intellectual creation has always been considerable.

Cultural Expression

The literature and art of Latin America, which have been the subject of more studies than have its history and social problems, may be viewed from several perspectives.* It would be possible to trace the changes of literary style from the mystical and mythological style of the Aztecs, through conceptualism and neo-classicism, to the baroque style of the colonial period, the romantic and Gallicized neo-neo-classicism of the nineteenth century, until we reach modernism, social realism, and the retarded "Joyceanism" of the present. But this would be of small help in understanding the measure in which cultural expression reflects anything really Latin American.

Nor would it help us much to point out the successive influences: Spanish and Portuguese in colonial times, and through it the Renaissance and the dogmatism of the Counter-Reformation at one and the same time; the French encyclopedists and Tom Paine in the period before and immediately after independence. Then came the French lib-

---

* Here only the major cultural tendencies of Latin America will be discussed. For further information, the reader may consult Pedro Henríquez Ureña, *A Concise History of Latin American Culture* (New York, 1966); Jean Franco, *The Modern Culture of Latin America: Society and the Artist* (New York, 1967); and Germán Arciniegas, *Latin America, a Cultural History* (New York, 1967). These three works contain bibliographies of Latin American literature translated into English and of English-language studies of Latin American arts and letters.

eral philosophers, the English economists, and the French romantics, in the mid-nineteenth century; English and French positivism and, in reaction against them, the philosophy of Bergson in the second half of the nineteenth century and the beginning of the present one. After these came the influence of the American novel, surrealism, Ortega y Gasset, Marxism, the theories of Keynes, Edmund Wilson, Camus, existentialism. We could also point out the influence of German expressionism on the painters of the years between the two wars; or that of the California style, derived from the style of colonial Mexico (itself derived from the Andalusian), on the houses of the *nouveaux-riches* of today. In the matter of styles and influences, Latin America's cultural expression is no different from that of any other Western culture. But there are certain aspects of it that are its very own and that give it personality.

The Discovery and the Conquest occupied an exceptional period in history. It is probable that never have so many magnificent deeds been heaped up, did so many outstanding figures emerge, and were so many new things found in such a short space of time. This period is also one of the best documented in history. Not only did the friars write accounts of what they saw, studies of the cultures they encountered, and grammars of the languages they learned, but the chief actors themselves—from Columbus and Cortés down to the captains of the expeditions—wrote chronicles of their deeds. And these were no mere accounts for home consumption but genuine histories, with analyses of peoples, personalities, and events, with denunciation of crime and plunder, as well as compassion for the sufferings and appreciation of the heroism of both sides. These chronicles are perhaps the first examples of modern realistic literature. Although written by Spaniards and Portuguese, they are a product of the American reality and they form the very beginning of the literature of Latin America. But after them, and until the eighteenth century, everything that was produced was merely Iberian.

In the eighteenth century, in accordance with the encyclopedist spirit, a new curiosity about things American was awakened. The Jesuits spoke of *la patria*, scientists studied the New World's geography, botany, and zoology. Americans were discovering their America, but they were still not expressing it. The colonial intellectual did not imitate his Spanish or Portuguese counterpart; he *was* a Spanish or Portuguese intellectual who lived in, or was born in, the New World. The great figures of colonial literature in the drama, in poetry, in mysticism, have their place in Spanish and Portuguese literary history; in some cases, in fact, they furnished that literature with its first modern epics.

What is truly Latin American must be sought in the plastic arts and in architecture, where we do not find great names but great works. It was Spanish and Portuguese artisans, working with the Indians, teaching them their techniques and absorbing their tastes, who produced the churrigueresque churches and the sober, solid palaces of the viceroys, and who decorated them with statues, carvings, and portraits that, without ceasing to be Iberian, are yet American. The baroque art of Quito and Mexico City is different from that of Spain, just as the palaces and houses of Lima are different from those of Seville, even though they are built on the Andalusian model, with their glazed tile central patios. Curiously, there was no monumental sculpture in this period, except for the astonishing figures of the prophets by the Brazilian leper Antônio Francisco Lisboa (1730–1814), called "Aleijadinho." And it is still more curious that no novel of any real value was written during the entire colonial period.

Nor was any written in most of the nineteenth century, to the point at which it was said that Latin America was "a novel without novelists." The post-independence novelist either confined himself to romantic narratives of things that could have happened to Europeans, or lost himself in folkloric descriptions that smothered the plot under an excess of local color. Until the end of the nineteenth century, the only original products of Latin America were those of the essayists, who wrote long histories or tried to find solutions to the cultural and political problems of the continent—although seldom to its social problems. Neither in the plastic arts, nor in music, nor in architecture did the nineteenth century bring forth anything that was interesting for its Latin American character. Whatever was written, painted, built, or composed was intended for a tiny Europeanizing minority, which regarded things Latin American with contempt, which had no interest in archaeology and still less in the survival of the popular arts, the refuge of all that was indigenous to the culture of the period. What has survived from the nineteenth century are not novels, paintings, buildings, or symphonies, but the histories of Lucas Alamán and Lorenzo de Zavala (1788–1836) of Mexico, the works of Faustino Sarmiento of Argentina, the legends of Ricardo Palma (1833–1919) of Peru. Many others played respectable roles, but they might be included in the cultural history of any European country.

Not until the end of the nineteenth century do writers appear whose work could not be confused with that of men from other countries. The emergence of intellectuals who could only be Latin American coincides with the awakening of interest in social problems. This allows of the suggestion that the intellectual sterility of the nineteenth century, and of the greater part of the colonial period—sterility in the sense only of a lack of the representative, of an absence of Latin American personality—was a result of the fact that the intellectuals accepted the social system and hence could not reflect reality but had to create fictions for consumption by their privileged little world. They were very Latin American in their customs, their politics, their personal reactions, and their interests, but not in their creative activity. This is true even of the language; in the nineteenth century, the spoken language of Latin America had become very much differentiated from that of the motherland, but the written language was the same.

It was precisely by means of its language that Latin America found its way to cultural expression. The Nicaraguan Rubén Darío (1867–1916) began a renovation in poetry that had a decisive influence not only in Latin America but also in Spain; this was the so-called Modernist movement, which reformed techniques and images. The reform was soon extended to prose writing. Novels completely new to Latin America were published; often baroque and of a tropical luxuriance, they described with brutal realism the life of peoples who had never before interested the men of letters: the Negroes, the Indians, the rubber-harvesters. Among those who won entry for Latin America in literature and the arts were the novelists Ciro Alegría (1909–67) of Peru, with *El mundo es ancho y ajeno* (*Broad and Alien is the World*);

Eustasio Rivera (1889–1928) of Colombia, with *La Voragine* (*The Vortex*); Miguel Angel Asturias (b. 1899) of Guatemala, with *El Señor Presidente;** Jorge Amado (b. 1912) of Brazil, with *Jubiaba;* Mariano Azuela (1873–1952) of Mexico, with *Los de Abajo* (*The Underdogs*); Rómulo Gallegos (1884–1969) of Venezuela, with *Reinaldo Solar;* José Lins do Rego (1901–57) of Brazil, with *Bangue;* Jorge Icaza (b. 1906) of Ecuador, with *Huasipungo;* Alejo Carpentier (b. 1904) of Cuba, with *Ecue-Yamba O;* Ricardo Guiraldes (1886–1927) of Argentina, with *Don Segundo Sombra;* the Colombian Gabriel García Márquez (b. 1917), with *Cien años de Soledad.* There were also the poet Luis Palés Matos (1898–1959) of Puerto Rico; the muralists José Clemente Orozco (1883–1949), Diego Rivera (1886–1957), and David A. Siqueiros (b. 1896), all of Mexico.

There were also the poets César Vallejo (1893–1938) of Peru, Vicente Huidobro (1894–1948) of Chile, Jorge Luis Borges (b. 1899) of Argentina, Pablo Neruda (Neftalí Reyes) (b. 1904) of Chile, and Octavio Paz (b. 1914) of Mexico; the composers Heitor Villa-Lobos (1887–1959) of Brazil, Carlos Chávez (b. 1899) of Mexico, and Alberto Ginastera (b. 1916) of Argentina; the painters Candido Portinari (1903–62) of Brazil, Rufino Tamayo (b. 1899) of Mexico, and Wilfredo Lam (b. 1902) of Cuba; and the architects of Brasília and of Mexico's University City. All these artists have universalized with imagination and experimentation what the preceding generation nationalized by means of realism: the existence of Latin America.

The essayists of the turn of the century, following José Enrique Rodó of Uruguay and his *Ariel,* felt superior to American "materialism" (only to fall into the racist thinking that Latin America had not made progress because of the "burden of the Indian"). But those of the period after World War I, led by José Carlos Mariátegui (1895–1930) of Peru and Gilberto Freyre (b. 1900) of Brazil, "discovered" the Indian, the Negro, and social problems. In the same way, those of today are obsessed with the search for the feeling of being Latin American (or Argentine, Mexican, Paraguayan, Nic-

---

* Asturias received the Nobel Prize for Literature in 1967. The only other Latin American writer to receive this award was the Chilean poet Gabriela Mistral (1889–1957), in 1945.

araguan), of defining their national and continental character.

But no one has been satisfied with what he has found. The social reality of the novelists, the psychological reality of the poets and essayists, and even the plastic reality of the painters are not what the intellectuals would like to have found. They aspire to change these realities. In fact, the desire for change arose earlier among intellectuals than among politicians. While liberals and conservatives still dispute, there have already been writers who have foreseen more fundamental disputes.

A very meaningful word in Latin America is the *pensador*. The *pensador* is one who deals with general concepts; he is the interpreter, the man who generates ideas. He is usually not a politician, although his thoughts have political consequences. He is not interested in the individual, in classes, or in groups but only in the great entities: the nation, the continent, the hemisphere. The *pensadores* affirm that social change should derive from the "national character," the "national culture," the "national spirit." An Argentine *pensador*, for instance, will say that a gaucho breathes under the starched shirt of the *porteño* (a resident of Buenos Aires). Any change, at any rate, must be fundamentally spiritual; only a change in attitudes can produce political change, and a revolution is not genuine unless it brings with it a change in moral values. Curiously, this is affirmed even by Marxist thinkers like Mariátegui.

But does Latin America have the potential for changing its moral values? Here the *pensadores* differ among themselves. They are critical of the past: history is lamentable, a burden, in which false appearances cover up the "true national reality," the "authentic national spirit." But there are also those who are pessimistic about the future, who feel that the Latin Americans are incapable of self-government, that Latin America will oscillate between despotism and freedom. The more optimistic believe in progress, believe that change is inevitable. All would agree with what was written by the Mexican poet Octavio Paz:

> Some people claim that the only differences between the North American and ourselves are economic. That is, they are rich and we are poor, and while their legacy is Democracy, Capi-

talism and the Industrial Revolution, ours is the Counter-reformation, Monopoly and Feudalism. But however influential the systems of production may be in the shaping of a culture, I refuse to believe that as soon as we have heavy industry and are free of all economic imperialism, the differences will vanish. In fact, I look for the opposite to happen. . . .*

And this hope synthesizes the history, problems, and contradictions of Latin America that have made this introduction to its people such a long one.

* Octavio Paz, *The Labyrinth of Solitude* (New York, 1961), p. 21.

Reading List

General

ROBERT J. ALEXANDER, *Today's Latin America* (2d rev. ed.; New York, 1968). JAMES BRYCE, *South America: Observations and Impressions* (New York, 1913). LEWIS HANKE, *Modern Latin America: Continent in Ferment*, 2 vols. (Princeton, N.J., 1959). FRANK MACSHANE (ed.), *Impressions of Latin America: Five Centuries of Travel and Adventure by English and North American Writers* (New York, 1963). HARRY ROBINSON, *Latin America: A Geographical Survey* (rev. ed.; New York, 1967). WILLIAM LYTLE SCHURZ, *Latin America: A Descriptive Survey* (rev. ed.; New York, 1967); and *This New World: The Civilization of Latin America* (New York, 1954). FRANK TANNENBAUM, *Ten Keys to Latin America* (New York, 1962). CLAUDIO VÉLIZ (ed.), *Latin America and the Caribbean: A Handbook* (New York, 1968).

General History

HELEN M. BAILEY and ABRAHAM P. NASATIR, *Latin America: The Development of Its Civilization* (Englewood Cliffs, N.J., 1960). JOHN F. BANNON, *History of the Americas*, 2 vols. (2d ed.; New York, 1963). JOHN F. BANNON and PETER M. DUNNE, *Latin America: An Historical Survey* (Milwaukee, 1963). HERBERT E. BOLTON, *Wider Horizons of American History* (New York, 1939). JOHN ARMSTRONG CROW, *The Epic of Latin America* (Garden City, N.Y., 1948). DONALD M. DOZER, *Latin America: An Interpretative History* (New York, 1962). JOHN E.

FAGG, *Latin America: A General History* (New York, 1963). LEWIS HANKE, *Do the Americas Have a Common History?* (New York, 1964). HUBERT HERRING, *A History of Latin America from the Beginnings to the Present* (3d ed.; New York, 1968). BENJAMIN KEEN (ed.), *Americans All: The Story of Our Latin American Neighbors* (New York, 1966); and (ed.), *Readings in Latin American Civilization: 1492 to the Present* (2d ed.; Boston, 1967). DANA GARDNER MUNRO, *The Latin American Republics: A History* (New York, 1950). GEORGE PENDLE, *A History of Latin America* (Baltimore, 1963). J. FRED RIPPY, *Latin America: A Modern History* (Ann Arbor, Mich., 1958). CURTIS A. WILGUS and RAUL D'ECA, *An Outline-History of Latin America* (New York, 1963). DONALD E. WORCESTER and WENDELL G. SHAEFFER, *The Growth and Culture of Latin America* (New York, 1956).

Precolonial Period

IGNACIO BERNAL, *Mexico Before Cortez: Art, History, and Legend,* trans. by WILLIS BARNSTONE (Garden City, N.Y., 1963). HIRAM BINGHAM, *Lost City of the Incas: The Story of Machu Picchu and Its Builders* (New York, 1948). G. H. S. BUSHNELL, *The First Americans: The Pre-Columbian Civilizations* (New York, 1968). ALFONSO CASO, *The Aztecs: People of the Sun,* trans. by LOWELL DUNHAM (Norman, Okla., 1958). MIGUEL COVARRUBIAS, *Indian Art of Mexico and Central America* (New York, 1957). GARCILASO DE LA VEGA, *The Incas: Royal Commentaries of the Inca Garcilaso de la Vega, 1539-1616,* tr. by MARIA JOLAS from the French ed. (New York, 1961). CLEMENTS ROBERT MARKHAM, *Cuzco: A Journey to the Ancient Capital of Peru* (London, 1856). J. ALDEN MASON, *The Ancient Civilizations of Peru* (Baltimore, 1957). PHILIP AINSWORTH MEANS, *Ancient Civilizations of the Andes* (New York, 1936). SILVANNUS G. MORLEY, *The Ancient Maya,* rev. by G. W. BRAINERD (Stanford, Calif., 1956). FREDERICK PETERSON, *Ancient Mexico: An Introduction to the Pre-Hispanic Cultures* (New York, 1959). LAURETTE SEJOURNÉ, *Burning Water: Thought and Religion in Ancient Mexico,* trans. by IRENE NICHOLSON (New York, 1956). JOHN ERIC THOMPSON, *The Rise and Fall of Maya Civilization* (Norman, Okla., 1956). GEORGE CLAPP VAILLANT, *The Aztecs of Mexico,* rev. by S. B. VAILLANT (New York, 1962). VICTOR VON HAGEN, *The Ancient Sun Kingdoms of the Americas: Aztec, Maya, Inca* (Cleveland, 1961). E. R. WOLF, *Sons of the Shaking Earth* (Chicago, 1959).

Colonial Period

GERMÁN ARCINIEGAS, *Amerigo and the New World: The Life and Times of Amerigo Vespucci,* tr. by HARRIET DE ONÍS (New York, 1955). HUBERT HOWE BANCROFT, *The Conquest of Mexico* (San Francisco, 1883–88). HERNANDO CORTÉS, *Conquest: Dispatches of Cortés from the New World,* ed. by IRWIN R. BLACKER and HARRY M. ROSEN (New York, 1962). BERNAL DÍAZ DEL CASTILLO, *The Discovery and Conquest of Mexico, 1517–1521,* tr. and with an introduction and notes by A. P. MAUDSLAY (New York, 1956). PATRICIA DE FUENTES (ed. and tr.), *The Conquistadors: First-Person Accounts of the Conquest of Mexico* (New York, 1963). LILLIAN E. FISHER, *The Last Inca Revolt, 1780-83* (Norman, Okla., 1965). GARCILASO DE LA VEGA, *The Florida of the Inca,* tr. and ed. by JOHN GRIER VARNER and JEANNETTE JOHNSON VARNER (Austin, Texas, 1951). CHARLES GIBSON, *The Aztecs Under Spanish Rule* (Stanford, Calif., 1964); and (ed.), *The Spanish Tradition in America* (Columbia, S.C., 1968). LEWIS HANKE, *The Spanish Struggle for Justice in the Conquest of America* (Philadelphia, 1949). C. H. HARING, *The Spanish Empire in America* (New York, 1947). ROBERT A. HUMPHREYS and JOHN LYNCH (eds.), *The Origins of the Latin American Revolutions, 1808–1826: European Influences or American Nationalism* (New York, 1965). BENJAMIN KEEN (trans. and ed.), *Life of the Admiral Christopher Columbus by His Son Ferdinand* (New Brunswick, N.J., 1959). SALVADOR DE MADARIAGA, *The Fall of the Spanish American Empire* (New York, 1948); and *The Rise of the Spanish American Empire* (New York, 1947). MAGNUS MÖRNER, *The Expulsion of the Jesuits from Latin America* (New York, 1965). RICHARD M. MORSE (ed.), *The Bandeirantes: The Historical Role of the Brazilian Pathfinders* (New York, 1965). J. H. PARRY, *The Spanish Seaborne Empire* (New York, 1966). WILLIAM H. PRESCOTT, *The Conquest of Mexico* (various eds.; first published, New York, 1843; a paperback ed. has been published as *History of the Conquest of Mexico*); and *The Conquest of Peru* (various eds.; first published, 1847; a paperback ed. has been published under the same title, partly abridged and rev. by VICTOR W. VON HAGEN). CECIL ROTH, *The Spanish Inquisition* (New York, 1964). BERNARDINO DE SAHAGÚN, *A General History of the Things of New Spain,* trans. from the Aztec with notes and illustrations by ARTHUR J. O. ANDERSON and CHARLES E. DIBBLE, 10 vols. (Santa Fe, N.M., 1950-61). WILLIAM LYTLE SCHURZ, *The Manila Galleon* (New York, 1939). ROBERT SOUTHEY, *History of Brazil,* 3 vols. (London, 1810–19). JORGE JUAN and ANTONIO DE ULLOA, *A Voyage to South America,* tr. by JOHN ADAMS, 2 vols. (London, 1806; an abridged paperback ed. has been published).

Government and Politics

MILDRED ADAMS (ed.), *Latin America: Evolution or Explosion?* (New York, 1963). VÍCTOR ALBA, *Nationalists Without Nations: The Oligarchy Versus the People in Latin America* (New York, 1968). ROBERT J. ALEXANDER, *Communism in Latin America* (New Brunswick, N.J., 1957); and *Latin American Politics and Government* (New York, 1965); and Charles O. Porter, *The Struggle for Democracy in Latin America* (New York, 1961). GABRIEL ALMOND and JAMES S. COLEMAN (eds.), *The Politics of the Developing Areas* (Princeton, N.J., 1960). CHARLES W. ANDERSON, *Politics and Economic Change in Latin America* (Princeton, N.J., 1967). GERMÁN ARCINIEGAS, *The State of Latin America* (New York, 1952). WILLARD F. BARBER and C. NEALE RONNING, *Internal Security and Military Power: Counterinsurgency and Civic Action in Latin America* (Athens, Ohio, 1966). JAMES L. BUSEY, *Latin America, Political Institutions and Processes* (New York, 1963). HAROLD E. DAVIS, *Makers of Democracy in Latin America* (New York, 1945). RUSSELL H. FITZGIBBON (ed.), *The Constitutions of the Americas* (Chicago, 1948). JOHN GERASSI, *The Great Fear in Latin America* (rev. ed.; New York, 1965). R. A. GÓMEZ, *Government and Politics in Latin America* (New York, 1960). HUGH M. HAMILL, JR. (ed.), *Dictatorship in Spanish*

America (New York, 1965). JOHN J. JOHNSTON, *The Military and Society in Latin America* (Stanford, Calif., 1964); and *Political Change in Latin America: The Emergence of the Middle Sectors* (Stanford, Calif., 1958); and (ed.), *Continuity and Change in Latin America* (Stanford, Calif., 1964). JOHN H. KAUTSKY (ed.), *Political Change in Underdeveloped Countries: Nationalism and Communism* (New York, 1962); ROBERT C. KINGSBURY and RONALD M. SCHNEIDER, *An Atlas of Latin American Affairs* (New York, 1965). EDWIN LIEUWEN, *Arms and Politics in Latin America* (New York, 1961); and *Generals vs. Presidents: Neomilitarism in Latin America* (New York, 1964). JOSEPH MAIER and RICHARD W. WEATHERHEAD (eds.), *Politics of Change in Latin America* (New York, 1964). JOHN D. MARTZ (ed.), *The Dynamics of Change in Latin American Politics* (Englewood Cliffs, N.J., 1965). GERARD MASUR, *Nationalism in Latin America: Diversity and Unity* (New York, 1966). LUIS MERCIER VEGA, *Roads to Power in Latin America*, trans. ROBERT ROWLAND (New York, 1969). MARTIN C. NEEDLER, *Latin American Politics in Perspective* (Princeton, N.J., 1963); and *Political Systems of Latin America* (Princeton, N.J., 1964). WILLIAM W. PIERSON and FEDERICO G. GIL, *Governments of Latin America* (New York, 1957). KARL M. SCHMITT and DAVID D. BURKS, *Evolution or Chaos: Dynamics of Latin American Government and Politics* (New York, 1963). TAD SZULC, *Twilight of the Tyrants* (New York, 1959); and *The Winds of Revolution: Latin America Today—And Tomorrow* (rev. ed.; New York, 1965). ROBERT D. TOMASEK (ed.), *Latin American Politics: Studies of the Contemporary Scene* (New York, 1966). CLAUDIO VÉLIZ (ed.), *Politics of Conformity in Latin America* (New York, 1967). ARTHUR P. WHITAKER and DAVID C. JORDAN, *Nationalism in Contemporary Latin America* (New York, 1966). EDWARD J. WILLIAMS, *Latin American Christian Democratic Parties* (Knoxville, Tenn., 1967).

Economic Questions

MARVIN D. BERNSTEIN (ed.), *Foreign Investments in Latin America: Cases and Attitudes* (New York, 1966). WENDELL GORDON, *The Political Economy of Latin America* (New York, 1965). ALBERT O. HIRSCHMAN, *Journeys Toward Progress: Studies of Economic Policy-Making in Latin America* (New York, 1963). PRESTON E. JAMES, *Latin America: An Economic Geography* (3d ed.; New York, 1959). ALBERT T. LAUTERBACH, *Enterprise in Latin America: Business Attitudes in a Developing Economy* (Ithaca, N.Y., 1966). STACY MAY and GALO PLAZA LASSO, *The United Fruit Company in Latin America* (Washington, D.C., 1958). VÍCTOR L. URQUIDI, *The Challenge of Development in Latin America*, trans. by MARJORY M. URQUIDI (New York, 1964). RAYMOND VERNON (ed.), *How Latin America Views the U.S. Investor* (New York, 1966). MIGUEL S. WIONCZEK (ed.), *Latin American Economic Integration* (New York, 1966). JOHN R. WISH, *Economic Development in Latin America: An Annotated Bibliography* (New York, 1965).

Social Questions

RICHARD N. ADAMS et al., *Social Change in Latin America Today: Its Implications for United States Policy* (New York, 1960). LUIS E.

AGUILAR, *Marxism in Latin America* (New York, 1968). VÍCTOR ALBA, *Politics and the Labor Movement in Latin America* (Stanford, Calif., 1968). ROBERT J. ALEXANDER, *Labor Relations in Argentina, Brazil, and Chile* (New York, 1962); and *Organized Labor in Latin America* (New York, 1965). MARGARET BATES (ed.), *The Migration of Peoples to Latin America* (Washington, D.C., 1957). BEN G. BURNETT and MOISES POBLETE TRONCOSO, *The Rise of the Latin American Labor Movement*. M. M. and JOHN J. CONSIDINE (eds.), *The Church in the New Latin America* (Notre Dame, Ind., 1965). WILLIAM V. D'ANTONIO and FREDERICK B. PIKE, *Religion, Revolution, and Reform: New Forces for Change in Latin America* (New York, 1964). REGIS DEBRAY, *Revolution in the Revolution: Armed and Political Struggle in Latin America* (New York, 1967). LESLIE DEWART, *Christianity and Revolution: The Lesson of Cuba* (New York, 1962). DONALD K. EMMERSON (ed.), *Students and Politics in Developing Nations* (New York, 1968). WILLIAM H. FORM and A. A. BLUM, *Industrial Relations and Social Change in Latin America* (Gainesville, Fla., 1965). ERNESTO CHE GUEVARA, *Guerrilla Warfare* (New York, 1961); and *Reminiscences of the Cuban Revolutionary War* (New York, 1968). GERMÁN GUZMAN, *Camilo Torres* (New York, 1969). PHILIP M. HAUSER (ed.), *Urbanization in Latin America* (New York, 1961). DANIEL JAMES (ed.), *The Complete Bolivian Diaries of Che Guevara and Other Captured Documents* (New York, 1968). JOHN J. JOHNSON, *Social Change in Latin America* (New York, 1960). SEYMOUR MARTIN LIPSET and ALDO SOLARI (eds.), *Elites in Latin America* (New York, 1967). J. LLOYD MECHAM, *Church and State in Latin America* (rev. ed.; Chapel Hill, N.C., 1966). FREDERICK B. PIKE, *The Conflict Between Church and State in Latin America* (New York, 1964); and (ed.), *Freedom and Reform in Latin America* (Notre Dame, Ind., 1959). KALMAN H. SILVERT, *The Conflict Society: Reaction and Revolution in Latin America* (New York, 1961). T. LYNN SMITH (ed.), *Agrarian Reform in Latin America* (New York, 1965). J. MAYONE STYCOS and JORGE ARIAS (eds.), *Population Dilemma in Latin America* (Washington, D.C., 1966). FRANK TANNENBAUM, *Slave and Citizen: The Negro in the Americas* (New York, 1947). CLAUDIO VÉLIZ (ed.), *Obstacles to Change in Latin America* (New York, 1965). CHARLES WAGLEY and MARVIN HARRIS, *Minorities in the New World: Six Case Studies* (New York, 1958).

International Relations

VÍCTOR ALBA, *Alliance Without Allies: The Mythology of Progress in Latin America* (New York, 1965). JUAN JOSÉ AREVALO, *The Shark and the Sardines*, tr. by JUNE COBB and RAUL OSEGUEDA (New York, 1961). NORMAN A. BAILEY, *Latin America in World Politics* (New York, 1967); and (ed.), *Latin America: Politics, Economics, and Hemispheric Security* (New York, 1965). SAMUEL F. BEMIS, *The Latin American Policy of the United States: An Historical Interpretation* (New York, 1943). ADOLF A. BERLE, *Latin America: Diplomacy and Reality* (New York, 1962). DONALD DOZER (ed.), *The Monroe Doctrine: Its Modern Significance* (New York, 1965). JOHN C. DREIER, *The Organization of American States and the Hemisphere Crisis* (New York, 1962); and (ed.), *The Alliance for Progress: Problems and Perspectives* (Baltimore, 1962). MILTON S. EISENHOWER, *The Wine Is Bitter: The United*

States and Latin America (Garden City, N.Y., 1963). ALTON FRYE, Nazi Germany and the American Hemisphere, 1933-41 (New Haven, Conn., 1967). ALFONSO GARCÍA ROBLES, The Denuclearization of Latin America (New York, 1967). LINCOLN GORDON, A New Deal for Latin America: The Alliance for Progress (Cambridge, Mass., 1963). JOHN A. HOUSTON, Latin America in the United Nations (New York, 1956). EDWIN LIEUWEN, U.S. Policy in Latin America: A Short History (New York, 1965). HERBERT L. MATTHEWS, The United States and Latin America (2d ed.; New York, 1963). J. LLOYD MECHAM, A Survey of United States–Latin American Relations (Boston, 1965); and The United States and Inter-American Security (Austin, Texas, 1961). J. WARREN NYSTROM and NATHAN A. HAVERSTICK, The Alliance for Progress (Princeton, N.J., 1966). DEXTER PERKINS, History of the Monroe Doctrine (rev. ed.; Boston, 1955); and The United States and Latin America (Baton Rouge, La., 1961). O. CARLOS STOETZER, The Organization of American States: An Introduction (New York, 1965). ANN VAN WYNEN THOMAS and A. J. THOMAS, JR., Non-Intervention: The Law and Its Import in the Americas (Dallas, 1956). ARTHUR P. WHITAKER, The United States and the Independence of Latin America, 1800–1830 (New York, 1964); and The Western Hemisphere Idea: Its Rise and Decline (Ithaca, N.Y., 1954).

Cultural Life

GERMÁN ARCINIEGAS (ed.), The Green Continent: A Comprehensive View of Latin America by Its Leading Writers, trans. by HARRIET DE ONÍS et al. (New York, 1944); and Latin America: A Cultural History (New York, 1967). LEOPOLDO CASTEDO, A History of Latin American Art and Architecture: From Pre-Columbian Times to the Present, trans. and ed. by PHYLLIS FREEMAN (New York, 1969). WILLIAM REX CRAWFORD, A Century of Latin American Thought (rev. ed.; Cambridge, Mass., 1961). JEAN FRANCO, The Modern Culture of Latin America: Society and the Artist (New York, 1967). PEDRO HENRÍQUEZ UREÑA, A Concise History of Latin American Culture, trans. and with a supplementary chapter by GILBERT CHASE (New York, 1966); and Literary Currents in Hispanic America (Cambridge, Mass., 1945). WILLIS KNAPP JONES, Behind Spanish American Footlights (Austin, Texas, 1965). MARIANO PICÓN-SALAS, A Cultural History of Spanish America: From Conquest to Independence, trans. by IRVING A. LEONARD (Berkeley, Calif., 1962). HARRIET DE ONÍS (ed. and trans.), The Golden Land: An Anthology of Latin American Folklore in Literature (rev. ed.; New York, 1961). ARTHUR P. WHITAKER (ed.), Latin America and the Enlightenment (New York, 1942).

Argentina

ROBERT J. ALEXANDER, An Introduction to Argentina (New York, 1969); and The Perón Era (New York, 1951). GEORGE I. BLANKSTEN, Perón's Argentina (Chicago, 1953). JOHN J. KENNEDY, Catholicism, Nationalism, and Democracy in Argentina (Notre Dame, Ind., 1958). F. A. KIRKPATRICK, A History of the Argentine Republic (Cambridge, Mass., 1931). RICARDO LEVENE, A History of Argentina, trans. and ed. by W. S.

ROBERTSON (Chapel Hill, N.C., 1937). MADALINE W. NICHOLS, *The Gaucho* (Durham, N.C., 1942). GEORGE PENDLE, *Argentina* (3d ed.; New York, 1963). TOMÁS FILLOL, *Social Factors in Economic Development: The Argentine Case* (Cambridge, Mass., 1961). JOSÉ LUIS ROMERO, *A History of Argentine Political Thought* (Stanford, Calif., 1963). DOMINGO FAUSTINO SARMIENTO, *Life in the Argentine Republic in the Days of the Tyrants: Or, Civilization and Barbarism,* trans. by MRS. HORACE MANN (New York, 1868). JAMES R. SCOBIE, *Argentina: A City and a Nation* (New York, 1964). ARTHUR P. WHITAKER, *Argentina* (Englewood Cliffs, N.J., 1964).

Bolivia

ROBERT J. ALEXANDER, *The Bolivian National Revolution* (New Brunswick, N.J., 1958). CHARLES W. ARNADE, *The Emergence of the Republic of Bolivia* (Gainesville, Fla., 1957). O. E. LEONARD, *Bolivia: Land, People, Institutions* (Washington, D.C., 1952). HAROLD OSBORNE, *Bolivia: A Land Divided* (3d ed., New York, 1964). C. H. ZONDAG, *The Bolivian Economy, 1952–65* (New York, 1966).

Brazil

FERNANDO DE AZEVEDO, *Brazilian Culture: An Introduction to the Study of Culture in Brazil,* trans. by W. REX CRAWFORD (New York, 1950). JOSÉ MARÍA BELLO, *A History of Modern Brazil, 1889–1964,* trans. by J. L. TAYLOR and with a new concluding chapter by ROLLIE E. POPPINO (Stanford, Calif., 1966). E. BRADFORD BURNS, *Nationalism in Brazil* (New York, 1968); and (ed.), *A Documentary History of Brazil* (New York, 1966). JOÃO PANDIA CALOGERAS, *A History of Brazil,* trans. and ed. by P. A. MARTIN (Chapel Hill, N.C., 1939). EUCLIDES DA CUNHA, *Rebellion in the Backlands (Os Sertoes),* trans. by SAMUEL PUTNAM (Chicago, 1957). GILBERTO FREYRE, *Brazil: An Interpretation* (New York, 1945); and *The Masters and the Slaves: A Study in the Development of the Brazilian Civilization,* trans. by SAMUEL PUTNAM (2d ed.; New York, 1956); and *New World in the Tropics: The Culture of Modern Brazil* (New York, 1959). CELSO FURTADO, *The Economic Growth of Brazil: A Survey from Colonial to Modern Times,* trans. by RICARDO W. DE AGUIAR and ERIC CHARLES DRYSDALE (Berkeley, Calif., 1963). CLARENCE H. HARING, *Empire in Brazil: A New World Experiment with Monarchy* (Cambridge, Mass., 1958). KARL LOWENSTEIN, *Brazil Under Vargas* (New York, 1942). CAROLINE MARÍA DE JESÚS, *Child of the Dark,* trans. by DAVID ST. CLAIR (New York, 1962). CLODOMIR VIANNA MOOG, *Bandeirantes and Pioneers,* trans. by HARRIET DE ONÍS (New York, 1964). ROLLIE E. POPPINO, *Brazil: The Land and the People* (New York, 1968). SAMUEL PUTNAM, *Marvelous Journey: Four Centuries of Brazilian Literature* (New York, 1948). WILLIAM LYTLE SCHURZ, *Brazil, the Infinite Country* (New York, 1961). THOMAS E. SKIDMORE, *Politics in Brazil, 1930–1964: An Experiment in Democracy* (New York, 1967). T. LYNN SMITH, *Brazil: People and Institutions* (3d ed.; Baton Rouge, La., 1963); and ALEXANDER MARCHANT (eds.), *Brazil: Portrait of Half a Continent* (New York, 1951). CHARLES WAGLEY, *Amazon Town: A Study of Man in the Tropics* (New York, 1953); and *An Introduction to Brazil* (New York, 1963).

The Caribbean and Central America

RICHARD N. ADAMS, *Cultural Survey of Panama-Nicaragua-Guatemala-El Salvador-Honduras* (Washington, D.C., 1957). GERMÁN ARCINIEGAS, *Caribbean: Sea of the New World,* tr. by HARRIET DE ONÍS (New York, 1946). JOHN EDWIN FAGG, *Cuba, Haiti, and the Dominican Republic* (Englewood Cliffs, N.J., 1965). JOHN D. MARTZ, *Central America, the Crisis and the Challenge* (Chapel Hill, N.C., 1959). F. D. PARKER, *The Central American Republics* (New York, 1964). DEXTER PERKINS, *The United States and the Caribbean* (Cambridge, Mass., 1947).

Chile

GILBERT J. BUTLAND, *Chile: An Outline of Its Geography, Economics, and Politics* (3d ed.; New York, 1953). ERNA FERGUSSON, *Chile* (New York, 1943). LUIS GALDAMES, *A History of Chile,* trans. and ed. by I. J. COX (Chapel Hill, N.C., 1941). FEDERICO G. GIL, *The Political System of Chile* (Boston, 1966). ERNST HALPERIN, *Nationalism and Communism in Chile* (Cambridge, Mass., 1965). GEORGE M. MCBRIDE, *Chile: Land and Society* (New York, 1936). GEORGE PENDLE, *The Land and People of Chile* (New York, 1960). FREDERICK PIKE, *Chile and the United States, 1880–1962: The Emergence of Chile's Social Crisis and the Challenge to U.S. Diplomacy* (Notre Dame, Ind., 1963). JOHN REESE STEVENSON, *The Chilean Popular Front* (Philadelphia, 1942).

Colombia

HARRY BERNSTEIN, *Venezuela and Colombia* (Englewood Cliffs, N.J., 1964). ORLANDO FALS-BORDA, *Peasant Society in the Colombian Andes* (Gainesville, Fla., 1955). VERNON LEE FLUHARTY, *Dance of the Millions: Military Rule and the Social Revolution in Colombia, 1930–1956* (Pittsburgh, 1957). JESÚS MARÍA HENAO and GERARDO ARRUBLA, *A History of Colombia,* trans. and ed. by J. FRED RIPPY (Chapel Hill, N.C., 1938). PAT M. HOLT, *Colombia Today—And Tomorrow* (New York, 1964). JOHN D. MARTZ, *Colombia: A Contemporary Political Survey* (Chapel Hill, N.C., 1962).

Costa Rica

JOHN and MAVIS BIESANZ, *Costa Rican Life* (New York, 1944). CHESTER LLOYD JONES, *Costa Rica and the Civilization in the Caribbean* (Madison, Wisc., 1935).

Cuba

FIDEL CASTRO, *History Will Absolve Me,* trans. from the Spanish (New York, 1961). THEODORE DRAPER, *Castro's Revolution: Myths and Realities* (New York, 1962); and *Castroism: Theory and Practice* (New York, 1965). BORIS GOLDENBERG, *The Cuban Revolution and Latin*

America (New York, 1965). RUFO LOPEZ-FRESQUET, *My Fourteen Months with Castro* (Cleveland, 1966). KARL E. MEYER and TAD SZULC, *The Cuban Invasion: The Chronicle of a Disaster* (New York, 1962). ESTEBAN MONTEJO, *The Autobiography of a Runaway Slave*, ed. by MIGUEL BARNET and trans. by JOCASTA INNES (New York, 1968). FERNANDO ORTIZ, *Cuban Counterpoint: Tobacco and Sugar*, trans. by HARRIET DE ONÍS (New York, 1947). DUDLEY SEERS *et al.*, *Cuba: The Economic and Social Revolution* (Chapel Hill, N.C., 1964). ROBERT FREEMAN SMITH, *Background to Revolution: The Development of Modern Cuba* (New York, 1966).

The Dominican Republic

JUAN BOSCH, *The Unfinished Experiment: Democracy in the Dominican Republic* (New York, 1965). JAMES A. CLARK, *The Church and the Crisis in the Dominican Republic* (Westminster, Md., 1967). ROBERT D. CRASSWELLER, *Trujillo: The Life and Times of a Caribbean Dictator* (New York, 1966). ALBERT C. HICKS, *Blood in the Streets: The Life and Rule of Trujillo* (New York, 1946). DAN KURZMAN, *Santo Domingo: Revolt of the Damned* (New York, 1965). JOHN BARTLOW MARTIN, *Overtaken by Events: The Dominican Crisis from the Fall of Trujillo to the Civil War* (Garden City, N.Y., 1966). SELDEN RODMAN, *Quisqueya: A History of the Dominican Republic* (Seattle, Wash., 1964). TAD SZULC, *Dominican Diary* (New York, 1965). SUMNER WELLES, *Naboth's Vineyard: The Dominican Republic, 1884–1924,* 2 vols. (New York, 1928). HOWARD J. WIARDA, *The Dominican Republic: Nation in Transition* (New York, 1969).

Ecuador

GEORGE I. BLANKSTEN, *Ecuador: Constitutions and Caudillos* (Berkeley, Calif., 1951). ALBERT B. FRANKLIN, *Ecuador: Portrait of a People* (New York, 1943). LILO LINKE, *Ecuador: Country of Contrasts* (3d ed.; New York, 1960). M. C. Needler, *Anatomy of a Coup d'Etat: Ecuador 1963* (Washington, D.C., 1964). NORMAN E. WHITTEN, JR., *Class, Kinship, and Power in an Ecuadorian Town* (Stanford, Calif., 1959).

El Salvador

LILLY DE JONGH OSBOURNE, *Four Keys to El Salvador* (New York, 1956).

Guatemala

ERNA FERGUSSON, *Guatemala* (New York, 1937). C. L. JONES, *Guatemala, Past and Present* (Minneapolis, 1940). RONALD M. SCHNEIDER, *Communism in Guatemala, 1944-54* (New York, 1958). KALMAN H. SILVERT, *A Study in Government: Guatemala* (New Orleans, 1954). NATHAN L. WHETTEN, *Guatemala: The Land and the People* (New Haven, Conn., 1961).

Haiti

H. P. DAVIS, *Black Democracy* (rev. ed.; New York, 1936). M. J. HERSKOVITS, *Life in a Haitian Valley* (New York, 1937). C. L. R. JAMES, *The Black Jacobins: Toussaint L'Ouverture and the Santo Domingo Revolution* (2d ed.; New York, 1963). ALFRED MÉTRAUX, *Haiti: Black Peasants and Voodoo*, tr. by PETER LENGYEL (New York, 1960). SELDEN RODMAN, *Haiti: The Black Republic* (New York, 1954).

Mexico

VÍCTOR ALBA, *The Mexicans: The Making of a Nation* (New York, 1967). HUBERT HOWE BANCROFT, *History of Mexico* (New York, 1914). FRANK R. BRANDENBERG, *The Making of Modern Mexico* (Englewood Cliffs, N.J., 1964). ANITA BRENNER and GEORGE R. LEIGHTON, *The Wind that Swept Mexico: The History of the Mexican Revolution, 1910–1942* (New York, 1943). FRANK CANCIAN, *Economics and Prestige in a Maya Community* (Stanford, Calif., 1965). STUART CHASE, *Mexico: A Study of Two Americas* (New York, 1937). HOWARD F. CLINE, *Mexico: Revolution to Evolution, 1940–1960* (New York, 1962). MARTIN LUIS GUZMAN, *Memoirs of Pancho Villa*, trans. by V. TAYLOR (Austin, Texas, 1965). OSCAR LEWIS, *Children of Sanchez: Autobiography of a Mexican Family* (New York, 1961). GEORGE MCCUTCHEN MCBRIDE, *The Land Systems of Mexico* (New York, 1923). L. VINCENT PADGETT, *The Mexican Political System* (Boston, 1966). HENRY B. PARKES, *A History of Mexico* (rev. ed., Boston, 1960). OCTAVIO PAZ, *The Labyrinth of Solitude: Life and Thought in Mexico*, trans. by LYSANDER KEMP (New York, 1962). J. R. POWELL, *The Mexican Petroleum Industry, 1938–50* (Berkeley, Calif., 1956). ROBERT E. QUIRK, *The Mexican Revolution* (New York, 1963); and *Mexico* (Englewood Cliffs, N.J., 1960). SAMUEL RAMOS, *Profile of Man and Culture in Mexico*, trans. by PETER G. EARLE (New York, 1963). GUSTAV REGLER, *A Land Bewitched: Mexico in the Shadow of the Centuries*, trans. by CONSTANTINE FITZGIBBON (London, 1955). ROBERT RICARD, *The Spiritual Conquest of Mexico* (Berkeley, Calif., 1966). CLARENCE O. SENIOR, *Land Reform and Democracy* (Gainesville, Fla., 1958). FRANK TANNENBAUM, *The Mexican Agrarian Revolution* (New York, 1929); and *Mexico: The Struggle for Peace and Bread* (New York, 1950). NATHANIEL WEYL and SYLVIA WEYL, *The Reconquest of Mexico: The Years of Lázaro Cárdenas* (New York, 1939). NATHAN L. WHETTEN, *Rural Mexico* (Chicago, 1948). JOHN WOMACK, JR., *Zapata and the Mexican Revolution* (New York, 1969).

Nicaragua

A. H. Z. CARR, *The World and William Walker* (New York, 1963). ISAAC J. COX, *Nicaragua and the United States, 1909–1927* (Boston, 1927). NEILL MACAULAY, *The Sandino Affair* (Chicago, 1967).

Panama

JOHN BIESANZ and MAVIS BIESANZ, *The People of Panama* (New York, 1955). DAVID HOWARTH, *Panama* (New York, 1966). GERSTLE MACK, *The Land Divided: A History of the Panama Canal and Other Isthmian Canal Projects* (New York, 1944). JOSEPH L. SCHOTT, *Rails Across Panama: The Story of the Building of the Panama Railroad, 1849–1855* (New York, 1967).

Paraguay

ARTHUR E. ELLIOT, *Paraguay: Its Cultural Heritage, Social Conditions, and Education* (New York, 1931). GEORGE PENDLE, *Paraguay* (3d ed.; New York, 1967). J. RENGGER and I. LONGCHAMP, *The Reign of Doctor Joseph Gaspard Roderick de Francia in Paraguay* (London, 1827). C. A. WASHBURN, *History of Paraguay*, 2 vols. (Boston, 1871).

Peru

HARRY KANTOR, *The Ideology and Program of the Peruvian Aprista Movement* (Berkeley, Calif., 1953). HAROLD OSBORNE, *Indians of the Andes: Aymaras and Quechuas* (Cambridge, Mass., 1952). JAMES L. PAYNE, *Labor and Politics in Peru: The System of Political Bargaining* (New Haven, Conn., 1965). FREDERICK B. PIKE, *The Modern History of Peru* (New York, 1967). GEORGE WOODCOCK, *Incas and Other People* (London, 1967).

Uruguay

MARVIN ALISKY, *Uruguay: A Contemporary Survey* (New York, 1969). R. H. FITZGIBBON, *Uruguay: Portrait of a Democracy* (New Brunswick, N.J., 1954). GEORGE PENDLE, *Uruguay, South America's First Welfare State* (3d ed.; New York, 1963). JOHN STREET, *Artigas and the Emancipation of Uruguay* (Cambridge, Mass., 1959). PHILIP B. TAYLOR, *Government and Politics of Uruguay* (New Orleans, 1962).

Venezuela

ROBERT J. ALEXANDER, *The Venezuelan Democratic Revolution: A Profile of the Regime of Rómulo Betancourt* (New Brunswick, N.J., 1964). HARRY BERNSTEIN, *Venezuela and Colombia* (Englewood Cliffs, N.J., 1964). ROBERT L. GILMORE, *Caudillism and Militarism in Venezuela—1810–1910* (Athens, Ohio, 1964). EDWIN LIEUWEN, *Petroleum in Venezuela: A History* (Berkeley, Calif., 1954); and *Venezuela* (London, 1962). W. D. MARSLAND and A. L. MARSLAND, *Venezuela Through Its History* (New York, 1954). JOHN D. MARTZ, *Acción Democrática: Evolution of a Modern Political Party in Venezuela* (Princeton, N.J., 1966).

Index

ABC countries, 264
AD, *see* Democratic Action party
AFL-CIO, 248; *see also* American Federation of Labor, Congress of Industrial Organizations
Agency for International Development, 226, 297
Agrarian reform, 131, 150, 153, 185, 186, 199, 206, 217, 229, 232, 307, 308, 329, 330; in Bolivia, 283, 284; in Brazil, 308; in Chile, 309, 310; in Colombia, 308; in Cuba, 300, 301; in Guatemala, 250, 285, 310; in Honduras, 310; in Mexico, 165, 166, 167, 168, 170, 186; in Puerto Rico, 331; in Peru, 305; in Venezuela, 280, 298, 305, 306; and Alliance for Progress, 293, 296, 297, 298, 299
Agriculture, 6–7, 9, 13–14, 123, 212–15; investment in 214–15, 218|n; in precolonial era, 49, 53–54, 57; *see also* Agrarian reform
Aguinaldo, Emilio, 246
Aguirre, Lope de, 83
Air transport, 8, 198
Alamán, Lucas, 90n, 121, 134, 364
Alberdi, Juan Bautista, 28

Alegría, Ciro, 364
Alemán, Miguel, 280
Alembert, d', Jean Le Rond, 80
Alessandri, Arturo, 150, 156
Alexander VI, Pope, 75–76
Alfaro, Eloy, 134
Alliance for Progress, 153, 184, 245, 273, 278, 293–99
Almagro, Diego de, 63, 81
Altar Desert, 10
Alvarado, Pedro de, 64
Alves, Antônio de Castro, 119
Amado, Jorge, 365
Amat, viceroy of Peru, 28
Amazon, River, 7–8, 9; Amazon Valley, 58
Ameghino, Florentino, 18
American Federation of Labor (AFL), 148, 149; *see also* AFL-CIO
American Revolutionary Popular Alliance (APRA) (Peru), 152, 280, 305
American Treaty of Pacific Settlement (Bogotá Pact), 274, 275–76
Anaconda Company, 217, 309
Anarchists, 145–46, 164
Andrada e Silva, José Bonifácio de, 97
Antequera, José, 91

Anti-Americanism, 45, 126, 152-53, 238, 251, 252, 253, 277, 287, 288, 290, 292-93, 314-17, 329, 359
Antigua, 12
Antilles, 27, 119
APRA, *see* American Revolutionary Popular Alliance
Arabs, in Spain, 13, 22, 24, 67, 69-70, 81
Arana, Francisco, 285
Aranda, Count of, 95
Araucanians, 21, 59, 64, 82
Arawaks, 58
Arbenz, Jacobo, 250, 251, 285, 286
Archaeology, 18, 46, 51, 355-56, 363
Arcos Ariegui, Santiago, 145
Arévalo, Juan José, 250, 280, 285
Argentina, 6, 7, 11, 14, 15, 16, 129, 240; population of, 26, 29, 30, 31, 37, 39; precolonial, 51, 55, 59; in colonial era, 79; independence of, 100; government and politics in, 46, 108, 109, 111, 113, 129-30, 136, 145, 146, 147, 148, 150, 154, 155, 159, 161, 162, 256, 257, 279, 280, 283, 286-88, 291; socio-economic conditions in, 8, 14, 33, 37, 39, 41, 42, 49, 113, 114, 115, 117, 118, 122, 123, 124, 125, 126, 141, 142*n*, 145, 148, 173, 174, 175, 176*n*, 178, 179, 180, 186, 187-88, 189, 190, 194, 198, 200, 201, 202, 203, 204, 205, 206, 207, 209, 213, 214, 215, 216, 218*n*, 224, 229, 230, 231, 298, 338, 341, 342, 343, 344, 345, 355, 360; foreign relations of, 235, 236, 239, 260, 261, 262, 264, 265, 266, 275
Arguedas, Alcides, 183
Arosemena, Julio, 308
Art and architecture, 78, 361, 363, 365; pre-Columbian, 51, 52, 54, 55, 57, 78
Artigas, José Gervasio, 101
Assis, Machado de, 36,
Association of Latin American Union Workers (ATLAS), 149
Asturias, Miguel Angel, 365
Asunción, 62, 78, 82, 90-91
Atacama Desert, 10
Atahualpa, 63, 77
Atlantis, 18
Atzcapotzalco, 53
Auténtico party (Cuba), 152, 299-300
Automobiles; 340; production of, 216; import of, 158, 192, 201
Avila Camacho, Manuel, 168
Ayacucho, battle of, 101
Aymarás, 13, 55
Aztecs, 18, 20, 21, 51, 53-54, 56, 57, 59, 62, 63, 75, 215, 345
Azuela, Mariano, 365

Bahia, 93, 95
Bajío, 14
Bakunin, Mikhail, 145
Balaguer, Joaquín, 307
Balaio, Manuel, 89
Balboa, Vasco Núñez de, 60, 63
Balmaceda, Jose María, 109, 130
"Banana republics," 257
Bananas, 13, 14*n*, 26, 224
Bandeirantes, 68*n*, 85, 89
Banks, banking, 124, 200, 202-3
Barrientos, René, 284
Barrios, Justo Rufino, 132
Bastida, Micaela, 87
Batista, Fulgencio, 155, 251, 279, 282, 299, 300, 304, 333-34, 357
Batlle y Ordóñez, José, 150
Bay of Pigs invasion, 251, 268, 301
Bayano, 88
Belaúnde Terry, Fernando, 305
Belgium, investments in Latin America, 124, 125
Belize, *see* British Honduras
Beltrán, Manuela, 91
Benalcázar, Sebastián de, 64, 82-83
Benavente, Toribio de (Motolinía), 78
Bennett, Wendell C., 355
Bergson, Henri, 362
Bernay, 95
Betancourt, Rómulo, 274, 280, 305-6
Bidlack Treaty, 244, 247
Bilbao, Francisco, 145
Bingham, Hiram, 355
Blaine, James G., 270
Board of Trade (*Casa de Contratación*), 72
Bogotá, 7, 9, 10, 62, 64, 91, 94, 96, 360
Bogotá Pact, *see* American Treaty of Pacific Settlement
Bohórquez, Pedro, 86
Bolívar, Simón, 99, 100-101, 102, 103, 105, 107, 128, 131, 146, 242, 261, 314; distrust of United States, 235, 262
Bolivia, 7, 9, 10, 13, 15, 16; population of, 22, 32; precolonial, 48, 55, 59; in colonial era, 65, 87; independence of, 101; government and politics in, 112, 135, 152, 153, 156, 258, 277, 278, 280, 283-85, 308, 311; socio-economic conditions in, 49, 105, 113, 114, 115, 116, 118, 123, 142*n*, 146, 174, 198, 201, 202, 203, 205*n*, 206, 207, 211*n*, 213, 215, 217, 218*n*, 224, 228; 230, 231, 269, 343; foreign relations of, 107, 160, 260, 261, 262, 264, 266, 268
Books, 78, 342, 343, 352, 360
Borges, Jorge Luis, 365
Bosch, Juan, 251, 307
Boundary disputes, 107, 260-61
Boyacá, battle of, 100

Index

Brasília, 365
Brazil, 5, 6, 7, 13, 14, 16, 47, 129, 238, 240; population of, 22, 24, 26–27, 28, 29, 31, 32, 39, 105; discovery of, 61; in colonial era, 25, 26, 63, 68–69, 73, 79, 85, 88–89, 92–93, 94, 95; independence of, 97, 108; government and politics in, 108, 109, 112, 113, 133, 136n, 145, 146, 154, 156, 159, 161–62, 257, 258, 265, 279, 280, 282, 308–9, 320, 348, 350; socio-economic conditions in, 8, 34, 35, 36–37, 39, 42, 113, 114, 115, 118, 119–20, 121–22, 123, 126, 141, 142n, 146, 147–48, 174, 175, 176, 179, 180, 186, 189, 190, 194, 198, 201, 202, 203, 204, 205, 207, 209, 213, 214, 215, 216, 218n, 220, 223, 225, 227n, 228, 230, 231, 298, 342, 344, 345, 354n; foreign policy of, 160, 235, 236, 237, 260, 261, 264, 266, 267, 268, 275
British Guiana, 93; *see also* Guyana
British Honduras (Belize), 27, 93, 180, 260
Brum, Baltasar, 349n
Bryan-Chamorro Treaty, 249
Budgets, government, 122, 178, 190, 204–6
Buenaventura Baez, 132
Buenos Aires, 6, 7, 9, 10, 14, 17, 27, 31, 40, 41n, 62, 90, 94, 101, 114, 118, 120, 123, 129, 136, 145, 177, 209, 229, 356, 366
Bunge, Octavio, 183
Bustamente Rivero, Luis, 280, 282

Caballero y Góngora, Antonio, 91
Cabeza de Vaca, Alvar Núñez, 61–62
Cabildos, 66–67, 98, 99
Cabildos abiertos, 23–24, 66
Caboto, Giovanni (John Cabot), 60
Caboto, Sebastian, 27
Cabral, Pedro Alvares, 61
Cádiz, 72, 96, 98
Calchaquíes, 86
Caldera, Rafael, 306
California, 28, 80, 125
Callao, 9, 88
Calles, Plutarco Elías, 29, 167
Calvo, Carlos, 263
"Camelot" plan, 255
Campos, Roberto de Oliveira, 185, 207
Camus, Albert, 362
Canada, 303; investments in Latin America, 124, 125; trade with Latin America, 22; aid to Latin America, 228
Candau, Marcolino G., 269
Canek, Jacinto, 86
Canudos wars, 113

Capital, lack of, 209–12, 229, 323–24; *see also* Foreign capital, Investments
Caracas, 6, 36, 41n, 100, 158, 177
Cárdenas, Lázaro, 167–68
Carías, Tiburcio, 156, 283
Caribbean nations, 12, 15, 93, 235, 264; population of, 27, 39; precolonial, 58; in colonial era, 92; socio-economic conditions in, 141, 338; British interventions in, 237–38, 239; U.S. interventions in, 238, 239, 243, 244, 248
Caribs, 58–59
Carpentier, Alejo, 365
Carr, E. H., 317
Carranza, Venustiano, 165, 166, 167
Carrera, Rafael, 132
Cartagena, 92
Carvajal, Luis de, 28
Caso, Alfonso, 356
Castelo Branco, Humberto, 309, 350
Castilla, Ramón, 130
Castillo Armas, Carlos, 250–51, 286
Castro, Fidel, 44, 136, 169, 237, 246, 251, 252, 263, 265, 268, 282, 292, 295, 300–304 *passim,* 305, 306, 310, 311, 313, 332, 343, 356, 359
Castro, Lope García de, 85
Castroism, Castroites, 293, 295, 304, 305, 311–14 *passim,* 315, 322, 325–26, 356, 357
Catalans, in America, 28, 94
Catavi, 87
Catherine II, Empress of Russia, 96
Catholic Church, 46, 71, 72, 140, 141, 314; in colonial America, 74–81, 94, 95, 356; as property-owner, 79, 109–13 *passim,* 188, 320, 347; Church-state relations, 109–13 *passim,* 124, 130–35 *passim,* 138, 163, 188, 229, 287–88, 347, 348; support of dictatorships, 157, 287, 290, 291, 320, 347; and social change, 320, 348; and education, 131, 133, 287, 343, 348
Cattle-raising, 14, 212
Caudillos, caudillism, 103, 106, 127–37, 154–55, 158; *see also* Militarism
Central America, 5, 235; population of, 39; precolonial, 19, 51, 53; in colonial era, 26, 60, 88; independence of, 102, 105; union of, 102, 131–32; government and politics in, 106, 111, 131–32, 161; socio-economic conditions in, 121, 141, 176, 198, 199, 217, 230–31, 257, 261, 338; U.S. interventions in, 243, 244; *see also individual countries*
Central American Bank for Economic Integration (BCIE), 228, 231

Central American Common Market (CACM), 176, 184, 230–31
Central Intelligence Agency (CIA), 251, 256
Central Treaty Organization (CENTO), 267
Cerro de Pasco, 8
Chaco War, 156, 160, 260, 266, 271
Chamizal, 260
Chapultepec, Act of, 272
Charles III, King of Spain, 72, 73, 83, 94, 95
Charles V, Emperor (Charles I, King of Spain), 25, 69, 76
Chávez, Carlos, 365
Chavín, 55
Chechenetes, 59
Chibás, Eduardo, 349n
Chibchas, 58
Chichén Itzá, 51
Chicle, 9, 134, 180, 219
Chile, 6, 7, 10, 12, 14, 15, 16, 27, 240; population of, 28, 29, 31, 39; precolonial, 59; in colonial era, 21, 70, 82, 84, 86, 92, 95; independence of, 101; government and politics in, 106, 109, 130, 140, 146, 147, 150, 154, 156, 158, 161, 162, 278, 280, 283, 297, 309–10, 319, 320, 321, 342, 348, 350, 357; socio-economic conditions in, 33, 39, 41, 42, 114, 118, 122, 123, 140, 145, 174, 175, 177, 178, 180, 186, 198, 201, 202, 206, 207, 209, 213, 215, 217, 218n, 225, 229, 230, 231, 298, 338, 343, 344, 345, 347n, 360n; foreign relations of, 107, 236, 260, 261, 262, 264, 265, 268
Chimús, 55
China, 4, 19; immigration from, 7, 29, 31, 34n, 119
China, Communist, 228, 301; and Latin American Communists, 313, 321, 356
Chirianás, 59
Christian Democratic movement, 149, 319–20, 321, 322, 323, 348, 356, 359
Christian Democratic Party (Chile), 309–10, 319
Christian Democratic party (COPEI) (Venezuela), 305, 319
Christophe, Henri, 132
Cities, 6, 29, 110, 119, 177, 178, 195, 196, 213, 335, 353; in colonial era, 9, 23, 60, 61, 64, 65–66, 69, 92, 237; growth of, 40–42, 123, 306, 330; plan of, 66, 338
Claver, Pedro (Saint Peter Claver), 87
Clavijero, Francisco Xavier, 81
Clay, Lucius, 258
Clayton-Bulwer Treaty, 244

Coal, 15, 16, 49
Codazzi, Agostino, 355
Coffee, 13, 121, 122, 125, 133, 222, 224, 225, 227
Colombia, 8, 13, 16, 107, 340; population of, 27; precolonial, 48, 57–58; in colonial era, 70, 86, 90, 91, 96; independence of, 100; government and politics in, 108, 111, 130–31, 140, 160, 162, 278, 279, 282, 319, 320, 350; socio-economic conditions in, 14, 42, 45n, 116, 117, 118, 121, 122, 140, 142n, 174, 176, 177, 179, 197, 198, 201, 205n, 207, 208, 217, 230, 231, 298, 307–8, 342, 344, 360; foreign relations of, 160, 235, 244, 247, 260, 262, 265, 266, 268
Colón, 247
Columbus, Christopher, 13, 27, 60, 65, 67, 76, 81, 362
Columbus, Ferdinand, 65
Communist parties, movement, 35, 50, 144, 145, 146–47, 151, 153, 154, 283, 285–86, 305, 307, 308, 309, 310, 313, 315, 320–22, 326, 329, 341, 356, 357; formation of, 146; and labor movement, 148, 149, 150, 278–79; support of dictatorships, 159, 282, 290–91, 299, 306; outlawing of, 290, 350; and Castro regime, 299, 300, 301, 302, 320–21; pro-Chinese, 313, 321, 356; and intellectuals, 312–13, 359–60; lack of influence of, 359–60
Concepción, 12, 209
Condorcanqui, José Gabriel, 86–87
Confederation of Latin American Unions (CSLA), 148
Confederation of Latin American Workers (CTAL), 148–49, 278, 279
Congress of Industrial Organizations (CIO), 149; *see also* AFL–CIO
Conquistadors, 14, 18, 20, 22–25, 59, 60–68 *passim*, 74, 80, 81, 82, 362
Copán, 51
Copper, 15, 16, 215, 217, 222, 224; nationalization of, in Chile, 164, 309
Corn, 13, 14, 189, 213, 222, 338
Coro, 88
Coronado, Francisco Vásquez de, 62
Cortés, Hernán, 62–63, 64, 67, 81, 362
Cortés, Martín, 82
Costa e Silva, Artur, 309
Costa Rica, 12, 19, 274; population of, 38–39; government and politics in, 132, 152, 162, 278, 279, 280, 283, 285, 350; socio-economic conditions in, 33, 34n, 38–39, 142n, 174, 199, 201, 205n, 341–42; foreign relations of, 235, 260, 262, 266

INDEX 383

Cotton, 10, 13, 117, 222, 224, 225, 227n
Council of the Indies, 26, 65, 68, 70, 72
Cuauhtémoc, 46
Cuba, 13, 19, 275; population of, 24, 26, 27, 30, 31, 39; discovery of, 60; in colonial era, 61, 62, 70; independence of, 102, 234, 243, 245–46; government and politics in, 136n, 152, 155, 160, 162, 277, 279, 280, 282, 290, 292, 299–304, 311, 333–34, 348, 349n, 350, 357; socio-economic conditions in, 34n, 35, 37, 39, 41, 44, 119, 121, 142n, 145, 146, 199, 201, 213, 217, 223, 228, 231, 343, 344; foreign relations of, 235, 237, 263, 267, 268, 269; U.S. interventions in, 245–47, 249, 251, 268
Cuban missile crisis, 255, 265, 268, 303–4
Cuenca, 79
Cuernavaca, 63
Cunha, Euclides da, 183
Curaçao, 93
Currencies, 200–201, 207
Cuzco, 40, 55, 57, 86, 87
Czechoslovakia, 250, 285

Darío, Rubén, 364
Darien, see Panama, in colonial era
De Soto, Hernando, 62
Debray, Régis, 312
Delgado, José Matías, 132
Democratic Action party (AD) (Venezuela), 152, 280, 305, 306
Dessalines, Jean Jacques, 97, 108, 132
Díaz, Porfirio, 38, 113, 135, 163, 164, 165, 204
Díaz del Castillo, Bernal, 62, 65
Díaz de Solís, Juan, 61
Diderot, Denis, 80
Diet, 13, 338; inadequacy of, 115, 143, 176–77
Diseases, 9, 11–12, 76, 178
Disraeli, Benjamin, 238
Dominican Republic, 25; population of, 27, 39; in colonial era, 92; independence of, 102, 243; government and politics in, 132–33, 152, 156, 158, 160, 162, 244, 254, 257, 274, 279, 280, 283, 306–7, 311, 350; socio-economic conditions in, 35, 39, 118n, 146, 174, 176, 178, 195, 200, 201, 217, 230, 342, 343; foreign relations of, 270; U.S. interventions in, 245, 249, 251–52, 268
Dominican Revolutionary Party (PRD) (Dominican Republic), 152, 251, 252, 307

Drago, Luis María, 263
Drago Doctrine, 263, 265
Drake, Francis, 88
Dutch, in America, 13, 26, 73, 89, 92, 93
Dutch West India Company, 92, 93
Dutra, Eurico Gaspar, 280
Duvalier, François, 156, 310

Earthquakes, 12
Echeverría, Esteban, 145
Economic Commission for Latin America (ECLA), 175–76, 184–85, 208, 211, 269
Economic development, 172–73, 276, 323–32; Latin American views on, 182–86, 324–29; and social change, 324–29, 332; and Alliance for Progress, 277–78, 297–98
Ecuador, 12, 13, 14, 16, 19; population of, 22, 27, 32; precolonial, 48, 51, 55, 58; in colonial era, 79; independence of, 100; government and politics in, 11–12, 133–34, 138, 140, 156, 162, 280, 282, 308, 320, 337, 348; socio-economic conditions in, 33, 115, 116, 117, 118, 140, 142n, 146, 174, 175, 180, 198, 201, 205n, 211n, 213, 217, 223, 230, 231, 269, 342, 344; foreign relations of, 260, 262, 267, 268
Edmé, Henri, 312
Education, 327, 330, 342–43, 345; state aid to, 190, 204, 205, 302, 342, 353
Egypt, 4, 18, 159, 239
Eisenhower, Dwight D., 290, 292, 301
El Dorado, search for, 58, 62, 64, 83
El Salvador, 19; population of 38; government and politics in, 107, 132, 138, 155, 160, 280, 283, 348, 350; socio-economic conditions in, 38, 142n, 174, 175, 178, 201, 205n, 211n, 213, 342; foreign relations of, 262
Elcano, Juan Sebastian, 61
Elections, 103, 108–9, 150, 157, 279; popular participation in, 153, 350; in colonial America, 66–67
Encina, Francisco, 183
Encomienda system, 68, 76, 81–82, 83, 84, 85, 94, 115, 116
España, José María, 96
Estrada, Genaro, 263
Estrada Cabrera, Manuel, 132, 135
Estrada Doctrine, 263
Export-Import Bank, 226, 297

Family life, 43, 336–37
Febrerismo (Paraguay), 152
Federmann, Nicolaus, 64

Ferdinand VII, King of Spain, 98, 99, 101
Figueres, José, 280
Fishing, 215
Flores, Juan José, 133
Flores Magón, Ricardo, 164, 165
Florida, 6, 58, 61, 70, 92, 93, 241
Foodstuffs, 115, 192, 213, 223, 224
Foreign aid, 184, 221, 225–29, 329
Foreign capital, 124–26, 163, 169, 189, 190, 217–20, 238, 239, 256–60; impact of, 214, 217, 218, 221; criticisms of, 218–19, 257–60; regulations on, 219–21
Fourier, Charles, 145
France, 49, 130, 161, 225; in colonial Latin America, 13, 26, 92, 93; and Latin American independence movements, 96, 97; interventions in Latin America, 108, 134, 163, 234, 238, 239; investments in Latin America, 125, 202, 217; influence of, on Latin America, 108, 110, 111, 239, 240, 361–62; immigration from, 28, 144, 243
Francia, José Gaspar Rodríguez de, 101, 129
Franco, Francisco, 169, 237, 246
Franco-Prussian War, 135
Frei Montalva, Eduardo, 231, 309, 310
French Guiana, 93
French language, 4
French Revolution, 96, 97, 240
Freyre, Gilberto, 36, 365
Frondizi, Arturo, 304
Fruit industry, 198, 199, 217, 257
Furtado, Celso, 186

Gadsden Purchase, 243
Galán, Antonio, 118
Gálan, José Antonio, 91, 118
Gallegos, Rómulo, 280, 281, 365
Gama, Luiz da, 119
Gandhi, Mohandas K., 45
Ganza, Zumba, 89
García, Alejo, 63
García Moreno, Gabriel, 112, 133
General Labor Federation (CGT) (Argentina), 149, 286
George, Henry, 151
Germany, 46, 135, 225, 287; investments in Latin America, 125, 202, 217, 239; aid to Latin America, 228; in World War II, 235–36, 239–40, 279; immigration from, 27, 30, 31, 144, 236, 240
Ginastera, Alberto, 365
Gold, 15, 58, 63, 68n, 75, 83, 88, 121, 133, 145, 200, 201, 203, 210

Gómara, López de, 82
Gómez, Juan Vicente, 113, 155, 158, 200, 357
Gómez, Laureano, 282
Gómez Farías, Valentín, 134
Gompers, Samuel, 148
Gondra Treaty (Treaty to Avoid or Prevent Conflicts Between the American States), 271
González Prada, Manuel, 35
González Videla, Gabriel, 280
Good Neighbor Policy, 241, 245, 251, 278
GOU, see Group of United Officers
Goulart, João, 308-9
Grace, W. R., and Company, 217
Grammusset, 95
Gran Chaco, 10
Gran Colombia, 100, 103, 105, 107, 241
Grant, Ulysses S., 245
Grau Sanmartín, Ramón, 280
Great Britain, 45, 111, 126, 130, 161, 188, 225, 244, 262; in colonial Latin America, 13, 26, 92, 93; and Latin American independence movements, 95, 96, 99, 233; interventions in Latin America, 237–39; investments in Latin America, 124–25, 129, 168, 202, 217, 238, 287; immigration from, 29
Grijalva, Juan de, 62
Group of United Officers (GOU) (Argentina), 159, 286
Guadalupe Hidalgo, Treaty of, 243
Gual, Manuel, 96
Guanajuato, 16
Guaranís, 59, 79, 86, 129
Guatemala, 12, 13; population of, 22, 32, 39; precolonial, 48, 51; in colonial period, 70; independence of, 102; government and politics in, 132, 135, 155, 280, 283, 285–86, 310, 311, 348, 350, 357; socio-economic conditions in, 34, 39, 116, 117, 118, 142n, 174, 176, 180, 199, 201, 205n, 213, 336, 343; foreign relations of, 235, 260, 267, 268; U.S. intervention in, 245, 250–51, 262
Guayaquil, 82, 101
Guerrero, Vicente, 102
Guevara, Ernesto Che, 311–12
Guiraldes, Ricardo, 365
Guipuzcoana company, 73, 90, 100
Guyana, 27, 35; see also British Guiana
Guzmán, Antonio Leocadio, 108n, 131
Guzmán Blanco, Antonio, 131, 135

Hague Conferences, see International Peace Conferences

INDEX

Haiti, 25, 47; population of, 26, 27, 38; in colonial era, 60, 92; independence of, 97, 241; government and politics in, 108, 132, 156, 160, 162, 254, 279, 283, 310, 350; socio-economic conditions in, 34, 38, 119, 142n, 146, 174, 176, 178, 201, 213, 219-20, 342, 343; foreign relations of, 235; U.S. intervention in, 249
Havana, 41n, 92, 121, 246
Hay-Herrán Treaty, 247
Hay-Pauncefote Treaty, 244
Haya de la Torre, Víctor Raúl, 151, 154, 183, 264n, 305
Hayes, Rutherford B., 244
Hernández, José, 37
Hernández de Córdoba, Francisco, 62
Hernández Girón, Francisco, 82, 83
Hernández Martínez, Maximiliano, 155
Herrera, Felipe, 228
Heureaux, Ulises, 35, 133
Hickenlooper Amendment, 227
Hidalgo, Miguel, 102
Hispaniola, 25, 60, 61, 76, 92, 93, 102; see also Dominican Republic, Haiti
Hitler, Adolf, 240
Hoil, Juan José, 52
Holy Alliance, 236, 239, 242
Honduras, 19; precolonial, 51; government and politics in, 107, 132, 156, 162, 244n, 280, 283, 310, 348, 350; socio-economic conditions in, 142n, 174, 176, 177, 178, 199, 201, 203, 205n, 342, 343; foreign relations of, 235, 260, 274
Housing, 177, 178, 181
Houssay, Bernardo A., 355
Huastecs, 52
Huayna Capac, 63
Huerta, Victoriano, 165, 166, 248, 356
Huidobro, Vicente, 365
Huitzilopochtli, 53
Humboldt, Alexander von, 16, 74
Humboldt Current, 10-11
Hurricanes, 12, 66
Hydroelectric power, 10, 49

Ibáñez del Campo, Carlos, 156, 283
Icaza, Jorge, 365
Iguala Plan, 102
Iguazu, Mt., 12
Illia, Arturo, 304
Illiteracy, 34n, 142, 153, 341-45 passim
Immigration: in colonial era, 27-28; after independence, 28-31, 39, 122, 124, 144, 187
Incas, 20, 21, 49, 51, 55-57, 58, 63, 75, 86, 215, 345
Income, per capita, 174-76, 323

Indigenismo, 340-41
India, 4, 25, 60, 61
Indians: before the Conquest, 35, 48, 50-60, 345; in colonial era, 26, 32, 36, 38, 65, 66, 68, 75-80, 81-82, 84-87; in independent Latin America, 21-22, 32, 33, 105, 111, 112, 114, 117, 141, 142, 164, 188, 319, 340-41, 365; see also individual tribes
Industrialization: in the nineteenth century, 12-13, 120-24, 137, 187-89; in the twentieth century, 172, 184, 215-17, 277, 324, 329, 330
Inflation, 179, 185, 186, 202, 206-9
Ingenieros, José, 37
Inquisition, in America, 28, 71, 102
Institutional Revolutionary Party (PRI) (Mexico), 152, 167
Inter-American Committee for the Alliance for Progress (CIAP), 297
Inter-American Development Bank (IDB), 177, 225, 228, 295-96, 297
Inter-American Peace Committee, 275-76
Inter-American Regional Workers' Organization (ORIT), 149
Inter-American system, 269-76; and Cuba, 303-4
Inter-American Treaty of Reciprocal Assistance (Rio Treaty), 274-75
Inter-American Workers' Organization (CIT), 149
International Bank for Reconstruction and Development (World Bank), 228
International Coffee Agreement, 227
International Confederation of Free Trade Unions (ICFTU), 149
International Labor Organization (ILO), 269
International Monetary Fund (IMF), 201, 202, 207-8, 258, 297
International Peace Conferences (the Hague Conferences): *(1899)*, 265; *(1907)*, 263, 265
International Petroleum Company, 305
International Workers of the World (IWW), 165
Investments: domestic, 120-21, 168, 189, 209-12; foreign, 124-26, 163, 169, 189, 190, 209, 211, 214-15, 217-21, 238, 239; public, 197-200, 209, 210-11, 329; and Alliance for Progress, 297-98; see also Foreign capital
Irigoyen, Hipólito, 150, 155
Iron ore, 15, 16, 215, 218, 222, 224
Irrigation, 10, 214; in precolonial era, 57

Isabella I, Queen of Spain, 76
Italy, 25, 49, 80, 81, 161, 225, 279, 287; investments in Latin America, 202, 217; immigration from, 27-28, 30, 31, 144
Itúrbide, Agustín de, 102, 107–08, 264
Itzcoatl, 53
Ixtaccihuatl, 54

Jagan, Cheddi, 35
Jamaica, 60, 81, 93, 100
Japan, 19, 49, 214, 236, 297; investments in Latin America, 125, 217; trade with Latin America, 223, 224, 225; immigration from, 7, 29, 34n, 236
Jefferson, Thomas, 243
Jesuits: in colonial era, 78–79, 80, 86, 96, 362; expulsion from America, 80–81, 94, 95, 129; in twentieth century, 320
Jews: in Spain, 22, 24; in Latin America, 28, 30
Jiménez de Quesada, Gonzalo, 62, 64
Jívaros, 58
João VI, King of Portugal, 97
Johnson, Lyndon B., 231, 255, 299
Juan, Jorge, 74, 80
Juárez, Benito, 38, 134–35, 242–43
Judicial system, 345–47
Junín, battle of, 101
Justo, Juan B., 151

Kennecott Copper Corporation, 217
Kennedy, John F., 251, 252, 254, 291–99 *passim*, 303, 304, 307, 315
Keynes, John Maynard, 186, 362
Kind, Eusebius, 80
Kingsborough, Lord, 18
Korea, immigration from, 29
Korean War, 160, 236, 268, 289
Kubitschek, Juscelino, 264, 295, 297

La Malinche, 62
La Paz, 9, 35, 65
Labor movement, 143–50, 153, 196, 200, 257, 259, 277, 278, 279, 281, 290–91, 306, 319, 328; in Mexican Revolution, 166, 169; and Perón, 148, 149, 286-87; *see also* Social legislation
Lam, Wilfredo, 365
Land ownership, 103, 105, 109–10, 112–15, 163, 164, 213, 214, 319, 347; in colonial era, 67; and political power, 103, 105, 168n; *see also* Agrarian reform
Lardizábal, Miguel, 98

Las Casas, Bartolomé de, 36, 76
Latin American Confederation of Christian Trade Unionists (CLASC), 149
Latin American Free Trade Association (LAFTA), 230, 231
Latin American Solidarity Organization (OLAS), 313
Lawrence, D. H., 11
League of Nations, 265–66
Lebanon, immigration from, 29
Lechín, Juan, 29, 283, 284
Leguía, Augusto, 155, 357
Lenin, Nikolai, 146, 152
Leoni, Raúl, 306
Lesseps, Ferdinand de, 247
Leticia, 266
Lima, 6, 35, 36, 40, 41n, 65, 79, 86, 101, 177, 181, 209, 363
Lincoln, Abraham, 243
Liniers, Santiago, 28
Lisboa, Antônio Francisco ("Aleijadinho"), 363
Lisbon, 24, 67
Literature, 64–65, 361–65; pre-Columbian, 19, 51, 54, 57, 78
Liverpool, Lord, 96
Lleras Camargo, Alberto, 297
Lodge, Henry Cabot, 250
Lombardo Toledano, Vicente, 149
Lombart, Guillen, 95
López, Carlos Antonio, 129
López, Francisco Solano, 129
López Arellano, Oswaldo, 310
López Contreras, Eleazar, 155
Lotteries, 44, 205
Louisiana, 70, 93
Lumber industry, 15, 214
Luque, Fernando de, 63

Machado, Gerardo, 155, 246, 299, 357
Machinery: production of, 216; import of, 201, 223
Machu Picchu, 57, 355
McKinley, William, 245–46
Madero, Francisco I., 164, 165
Magallanicos, 59
Magdalena River, 10
Magellan, Ferdinand, 60
Mahan, Alfred T., 244
Maine (battleship), 246
Maipú, battle of, 101
Males, 26-27
Manabís, 58
Managua, 181
Manaus, 121
Manco Capac, 55
Manco Capac II, 63
Mann, Horace, 343

Maracaibo, Lake, 10
Marañons, 83
Maria I, Queen of Portugal, 94
Mariátegui, José Carlos, 151, 365, 366
Márquez, Gabriel García, 365
Martín de Anglería, Pedro, 65
Marx, Karl, 145, 146
Marxism, Marxists, 151, 153, 184n, 186, 321, 322, 325, 356, 357, 358, 359, 362, 366
Matarazzo United Industries, 194
Matto Grosso, 16
Maximilian, Emperor of Mexico, 108, 111, 113, 134, 166, 238, 239, 242
Mayas, 13, 18, 29, 49, 51-52, 54, 57, 58, 85-86, 164
Mazo, Gabriel del, 356
Medical services, 174, 178
Medina Angarita, Isaías, 155, 280
Melgarejo, Mariano, 112, 135
Méndez Montenegro, Julio César, 310
Méndez Montenegro, Mario, 310
Mendoza, 8
Mendoza, Andrés Hurtado de, 85
Mendoza, Antonio de, 85
Mendoza, Pedro de, 62
Mennonites, 30
Mérida, 92
Mexican Regional Federation of Labor (CROM), 148
Mexican Revolution, 38, 114, 135, 163-71, 258, 261, 262n, 264, 349
Mexico, 7, 10, 11, 12, 14, 15, 16, 340; population of, 22, 28, 29, 30, 31, 32, 39, 105; precolonial, 19, 20, 48, 51-54, 57, 59; conquest of, 62-63, 65, 81; in colonial era, 26, 28, 61, 62, 70, 72, 77, 78, 79, 81, 82, 84, 85, 86, 87, 90, 95, 120; independence of, 21, 100, 101-2; government and politics in, 106, 107-8, 109, 111, 112, 113, 133, 134-35, 146, 147, 151, 152, 163-71, 238, 239, 242-43, 244, 254, 280, 283, 348, 349; socio-economic conditions in, 8, 21, 33, 37-38, 39, 42, 113, 114, 118, 120-21, 122, 123, 124, 141, 142n, 143, 145, 146, 147, 169, 173, 174, 175, 180, 181, 186, 189, 194, 198, 199, 200, 201, 202, 203, 204, 206, 209, 213, 214, 215, 216, 217, 218n, 219, 220, 224, 230, 337, 338, 341, 342, 345, 354n, 360n; foreign relations of, 160, 169, 234, 235, 237, 243, 254n, 260, 261, 262, 263, 264, 265, 266, 267, 268, 275; U.S. interventions in, 248-49, 252; see also Mexican Revolution
Mexico City, 6, 7, 9, 40, 41n, 52, 53, 54, 79, 85, 145, 177, 179, 209, 363

Miguel, 88
Military, militarism, 106, 291, 154-63, 281, 321-22, 326, 331-32, 351, 352; technocratic, 159, 162, 320, 321-22, 326; and the United States, 161, 255-56; in Argentina, 155, 159, 161-62, 275, 280, 286, 287-88, 304; in Bolivia, 156, 280, 283, 284, 308; in Brazil, 156, 159, 162, 275, 279, 282, 308-9; in Chile, 156, 158, 162, 279; in Colombia, 160, 282; in Costa Rica, 162; in Cuba, 155, 280, 282, 300; in Dominican Republic, 156, 158, 160, 162, 251-52, 280, 283, 306, 307; in Ecuador, 280, 282; in El Salvador, 155, 160, 280, 283; in Guatemala, 155, 280, 285, 286, 310; in Haiti, 156, 162; in Honduras, 156, 162, 280, 283, 310; in Mexico, 162; in Nicaragua, 155-56, 162, 280, 283, 310; in Paraguay, 156, 162, 275, 280, 282; in Peru, 155, 158, 162, 280, 282, 305; in Uruguay, 156, 162; in Venezuela, 155, 158, 162, 280, 281-82, 305
Minas Gerais, 16, 89
Mining, 9, 15-16, 123, 197-98, 212, 215, 219, 220, 224; investment in, 122, 124, 217; in colonial era, 15, 73, 84, 122, 187
Miranda, Francisco de, 96
Mistral, Gabriela (pseudonymn of Lucila Godoy Alcayaga), 365n
Mitla, 52
Mixtecs, 52
MNR, see Nationalist Revolutionary Movement
Moctezuma I, 54
Moctezuma II, 63
Molina, Alonso de, 25
Mompó, Fernando, 91
Monagas, José Tadeo, 131
Monroe, James, 242
Monroe Doctrine, 235, 238, 239, 242-43, 250, 266
Montalvo, Juan, 133-34
Monte Albán, 52, 356
Monterrey, 28, 209
Montes, Ismael, 112
Montevideo, 10, 41n, 230, 231
Montevideo, Treaty of, 230, 231
Morazán, Francisco, 132
Morelos, José María, 102, 118
Moreno, Gabriel René, 37
Mormons, 30
Moscoso, Teodoro, 296
Mosquera, Tomás Cipriano de, 131
Mozambique, 26
Muñoz Marín, Luis, 331

Nabuco, Joaquím, 119
Nahuatl language, 18, 53, 339
Nancera, Marquis of, 84
Napoleon I, 69, 93, 97, 98, 135
Napoleon III, 134, 135
Nariño, Antonio, 96
Nasser, Gamal Abdel, 159
National Liberation Party (PLN) (Costa Rica), 152, 280
Nationalist Revolutionary Movement (MNR) (Bolivia), 152, 283–84
Nazcas, 55
Negroes, 7, 18, 32, 365; in colonial era, 24, 25–27, 36, 76, 87–89; discrimination against, 34, 35, 36–37
Neruda, Pablo, 365
Netherlands, 228; *see also* Dutch, in America
Netzahualcoyotl, 54
New Freiburg, 121
New Granada, *see* Colombia, in colonial era
New Laws (1542), 76, 81–83 *passim*, 84
New Spain, *see* Mexico, in colonial era
Newspapers, 141, 343–44
Nicaragua, 3, 19; government and politics in, 107, 124, 155–6, 160, 244, 279, 280, 283, 310, 311, 348, 350; socio-economic conditions in, 118n, 174n, 176, 201, 205n, 342; foreign relations of, 235, 260, 274; U.S. interventions in, 248, 249
Nixon, Richard M., 292, 295
North Atlantic Treaty Organization (NATO), 267
Núñez, Rafael, 131

O'Higgins, Bernardo, 27, 101
O'Neill, Eugene, 132
Obregón, Alvaro, 166, 167
Odría, Manuel, 35, 158, 282
Oil, 16, 49, 124, 167–68, 197, 200, 215, 217, 220, 222, 223, 224, 256, 257, 301; nationalization of, in Mexico, 167–68, 198, 199; nationalization of, in Brazil, 258
Olid, Cristóbal de, 81
Olmecs, 51
Onas, 59
Olney, Richard, 238
Organization of American States (OAS), 252, 267–68, 272–76, 295, 297, 303, 306, 341
Oribe, Manuel, 130
Orinoco river, 8, 10, 58, 59, 83
Orozco, José Clemente, 365
Ortega y Gasset, José, 359, 362

Ortiz, Fernando, 37
Ortodoxo party (Cuba), 152, 349n
Otomís, 52
Ovando, Nicolás de, 76
Oviedo, Gonzalo Fernández de, 65

Pachuca, 16
Pacific War, 260
Páez, José Antonio, 131
Paine, Thomas, 356, 361
Palés Matos, Luis, 365
Palma, Ricardo, 364
Palmares, 88
Palos de Moguer, 60
Pan-American Federation of Labor (COPA), 148, 149
Pan-American Highway, 8
Panama, 8, 19; population of, 32; in colonial era, 61, 92; independence of, 107, 234, 239, 247; government and politics in, 140, 162, 310, 311, 350; socio-economic conditions in, 118n, 140, 142n, 174, 177, 178, 199, 201, 203, 219, 230, 343; relations with United States, 247–48, 260; *see also* Panama Canal
Panama, Congress of (1826), 107, 235, 242, 262, 269
Panama Canal, 107, 237, 247–48
Panama City, 41n
Paraguay, 10; population of, 30; pre-colonial, 59; in colonial era, 78–79, 84; independence of, 101; government and politics in, 128–29, 138, 152, 153, 156, 278, 280, 282–83, 311, 337; socio-economic conditions in, 114, 117, 118, 142n, 174, 176, 177, 178, 180, 201, 230, 231; foreign relations of, 129, 160, 260, 261, 266, 275
Paraná river, 8, 9–10, 62
Pardo, Manuel, 130
Patagonia, 10, 95
Patiño, Simón, 35
Paterson, William, 92
Paz, Octavio, 365, 366
Paz Estenssoro, Víctor, 283, 284, 308
Peace Corps, 226, 357
Peçanha, Nilo, 36
Pedro I, Emperor of Brazil, 97, 133
Pedro II, Emperor of Brazil, 133
Peralta, Enrique, 310
Pérez Jiménez, Marcos, 218, 254, 264, 282, 305
Pernambuco, 89, 93
Perón, Eva Duarte de, 287, 288
Perón, Juan Domingo, 30, 136n, 148, 149, 159, 190, 264, 286–89, 304, 357
Peronism, Peronists, 46, 148, 149, 264, 287, 288, 304, 308

Pershing, John J., 249
Peru, 5, 9, 10, 12, 13, 15, 16; population of, 22, 27, 28, 32, 105; precolonial, 20, 48, 55, 59; conquest of, 63–64, 81, 83; in colonial era, 28, 70, 79, 80, 82, 84, 85, 86–87, 91; independence of, 100–101; government and politics in, 103, 107, 109, 130, 140, 151, 152, 153, 154, 155, 158, 161, 162, 254, 256, 279, 280, 281, 282, 290, 297, 298, 305, 311, 319, 320, 350, 357; socio-economic conditions in, 21, 42, 114, 116, 117, 118, 122, 123, 126, 140, 146, 174, 175, 176, 179, 197, 201, 205n, 206, 207, 209, 213, 215, 217, 223, 224, 230, 231, 269, 341, 342; foreign relations of, 235, 236, 260, 261, 262, 264, 265, 266
Petén, 51
Petropolis, 121
Philip II, King of Spain, 28, 83
Philippine Islands, 61, 102
Piérola, Nicolás de, 130
Pisco, Antonio, 91
Pizarro, Francisco, 63, 64, 67, 81
Pizarro, Gonzalo, 63, 82
Platt Amendment, 246, 247, 299
Plaza Lasso, Galo, 268, 280
PLN, *see* National Liberation Party
Political parties, 103, 106, 145–46, 150–51, 349–50; *see also under individual parties*
Polk, James K., 243
Pombal, Prime Minister, 95
Ponce de León, Juan, 61
Popocatepetl, 54
Population, growth of, 38–40, 329, 330-31
Populism, populists, 144, 151–54, 278, 279, 281, 283, 311, 319, 320, 322, 323, 327–28, 356
Porras, Francisco de, 81
Portales, Diego, 130
Portinari, Candido, 365
Portugal: discovery and colonization of Brazil, 5, 20, 22-25, 26, 36, 60, 61, 68–69, 73, 74, 76, 92, 94, 95, 345, 361, 362–63; loss of Brazil, 97; relations with independent Brazil, 237, 267; immigration from, 27, 31, 32
Portuguese language, 4, 22, 49, 338–39, 344, 345, 364
Potatoes, 13, 338
Prado, Manuel, 279
PRD, *see* Dominican Revolutionary Party
Prebisch, Raúl, 184
PRI, *see* Institutional Revolutionary Party

Prieto, Guillermo, 164
Primo de Rivera, Miguel, 240
Prío Socarrás, Carlos, 282
Progreso, 92
Puelches, 59
Puerto Rico, 60, 61, 70, 102, 118, 246, 296, 307, 331
Purúes, 59

Quadros, Jânio, 308
Quechua language, 56, 339
Quechuas, *see* Incas
Querétaro, 134, 166
Quetzalcoatl, 11, 52, 53
Quiroga, Juan Facundo, 129
Quito, 57, 64, 79, 80, 95, 363

Race relations, 32-38
Radical parties, 144, 150–51, 154
Radio and television, 143, 344–45
Railroads, 8, 122, 124, 125, 129, 132, 168, 190n, 198
Rainfall, 11
Ramos, Artur, 36
Recife, 6, 93
Rego, José Lins do, 365
Requerimiento, 75
"Rex Americana" plan, 255
Rhodakanaty, Polonio C., 145
Rice, 13, 117, 338
Rio Branco, Baron of, 119
Rio Branco Law, 119
Rio Grande, 5
Rio de Janeiro, 7, 9, 69, 73, 93, 95, 177, 336
Río de la Plata, 7, 10, 61, 62, 67, 70, 88, 92
Rio Treaty, *see* Inter-American Treaty of Reciprocal Assistance
Rivadavia, Bernardino, 129
Rivera, Diego, 365
Rivera, Fructuoso, 130
Rivera, José Eustasio, 365
Rivera, Payo Enríquez de, 84
Rivet, Paul, 19n
Roads and highways, 8, 122, 190n; precolonial, 57
Rodó, José Enrique, 315, 365
Rojas Pinilla, Gustavo, 282, 307
Roosevelt, Franklin D., 168, 244, 245, 246, 249, 250, 251, 252, 278
Roosevelt, Theodore, 239, 245, 247
Rosario Sánchez, Francisco del, 35
Rosas, Juan Manuel de, 46, 111, 129–30, 136, 239
Rubber, 9, 13, 121, 122, 180, 219

Sáenz Peña, Roque, 150
Sahagún, Bernardino de, 78
Salinas Grandes, Lake, 10

San Agustín, 355
San José, 12, 41n
San Juan, 6
San Lorenzo de los Negros, 88
San Martí, José de, 88, 100–101, 102, 103
Sandino, Augusto César, 249
Santa Anna, Antonio López de, 134, 135
Santa Cruz Espejo, Francisco Eugenio de, 95–96
Santana, Pedro, 132
Santiago de Chile, 8, 64, 90, 177, 209, 269
Santiago del Principe, 88
Santo Domingo, 35, 251, 252
Santos, Juan, 86
São Paulo, 89, 121, 123, 209, 229
Sarmiento, Domingo Faustino, 343, 364
Sartre, Jean-Paul, 312, 359
Scientific research, 355
Sepúlveda, Juan Gínes de, 75
Serra, Junípero, 28, 80
Servitude, systems of, 115–18
Seville, 65, 67, 70, 72, 76, 363
SIAM di Tella, 194
Siles Salinas, Luis Adolfo, 284
Siles Zuazo, Hernán, 284
Silver, 15, 16, 73, 200, 210
"Simpático" plan, 255
Siqueiros, David A., 365
Sirionós, 58
Slavery, 25–27, 76, 87–88, 112; abolition of, 27, 118–20, 122
Slums, 118, 174, 175, 177, 196, 306, 329
Social legislation, 147–48, 179–81
Socialist parties, 118, 145–46, 233
Socorro, 91
Somoza, Anastasio, 155–56, 249, 279, 283, 350
Somoza, Anastasio, Jr., 156, 310, 350
Somoza, Luis, 156, 350
Soulouque, Faustin, 108
Southeast Asia Treaty Organization (SEATO), 267
Souza, Irineu Evangelista de (Viscount Mauá), 121
Souza, Martim Afonso de, 68
Soviet Union, 7, 41, 46, 148–49, 279, 281, 283, 316; and inter-American relations, 266-68; economic relations with Latin America, 223, 224, 228; and Cuba, 251, 301, 303, 304; and Latin American Communist parties, 250, 251, 313, 320–21
Spain, 48, 80, 81, 110, 111, 139, 154, 162, 234, 235, 242, 243, 245, 246, 316, 364; discovery and conquest of America, 5, 9, 19, 20, 21, 22–25, 40, 46, 59–65, 75–76, 87; colonization of America, 12–13, 14, 15, 21, 23, 25–26, 46, 47, 50, 65–73, 74, 76, 92, 93, 94–95, 345, 361, 362–63; loss of colonies, 48, 98–103, 121; relations with independent American states, 234, 236–37, 240; immigration from, 27, 30, 31, 32, 71n, 112, 144; investments in Latin America, 125; aid to Latin America, 228; *see also* Spanish America
Spanish America: administration of, 69-73, 74, 89-90, 94, 345; economy of, 12, 14, 15, 72–73, 94, 187, 210; land ownership in, 67, 68, 113; the Church in, 77–81; society in, 5, 23–25, 38, 40, 44, 66–67, 68, 74, 338, 345, 356; the arts in, 361, 362–63; rebellions in, 81–91, 233; foreign interventions in, 92–93, 237; independence of, 93–99
Spanish Civil War, 30, 169, 237
Spanish language, 4, 22, 49, 143, 338–39, 344, 364
Spanish-American War, 125, 245–46
Standard Fruit Company, 217
Steel industry, 215–16, 229
Stroessner, Alfredo, 282
Students, 141, 315, 352-58 *passim;* political activism of, 277, 280, 321, 356–58
Sudan, 27
Sugar, 13, 14, 26, 69, 94, 117, 121, 176n, 217, 222, 224, 229, 301, 302
Surinam, 13, 93
Switzerland, 3, 161, 225, 228
Syria, immigration from, 29

Tacuba, 53
Tamayo, Rufino, 365
Tarascans, 52
Taudonnet, Eugène, 145
Taxes, 122, 187, 191, 200, 205–6; in colonial era, 72-73, 79, 87, 89-90, 91, 94; tax reform, 206, 295, 296, 297, 298, 299
Tehuelches, 59
Tenochtitlán, 40, 53, 62, 81
Teotihuacán, 52
Terra, Gabriel, 156, 349n
Texas, 7, 61, 134, 146, 243
Texcoco, 53, 54, 78
Textiles, 121, 216, 227
Tezcatlipoca, 53
Thompson, Edward H., 355
Tiahuanaco, 54, 57, 355
Tiahuanacos, 54–55

Tierra del Fuego, 10, 59, 114
Tin, 15, 35, 217, 222, 224; nationalization of, in Bolivia, 198, 200, 283, 284
Titicaca, Lake, 10, 54, 55
Tlaxcaltecs, 52, 62
Tobacco, 13, 26, 78, 94, 121, 222, 224
Toltecs, 52, 54
Torres, Camilo, 320
Torres Bodet, Jaime, 269
Toscanás, 58
Tourism, 198, 222n
Toussaint L'Ouverture, Pierre Dominique, 97
Trade: international, 184, 185, 217, 221–25, 234, 296; inter-American, 230; in colonial era, 72, 94, 98
Trinidad, 4, 93, 96
Triple Alliance, War of the, 79, 260
Trujillo Molina, Rafael Leonidas, 35, 156, 158, 200, 249, 251, 268, 279, 305, 306–7
Truman, Harry, 225, 292
Tucumán, 86
Tula, 52
Tumbes, 64
Tupac Amaru, 86–87, 91

Ubico, Jorge, 155, 285, 357
Ulloa, Antonio de, 74, 80
Unemployment, 178–79
UNESCO, 269
United Fruit Company, 217, 250, 285
United Nations, 30, 184, 185, 225, 236, 266–69, 275, 301
United States, 6, 7, 8, 10, 29, 33, 39, 41, 42, 43, 45n, 47, 48, 49, 50, 74, 123, 126, 169, 172, 175, 177, 179, 180, 181, 182, 184, 191, 193, 201, 202, 204, 205, 208, 261, 262, 263, 265, 267, 302, 335, 353, 354; and Latin American independence movements, 99, 233, 240–41; Latin American policy of, 241–60 *passim*, 267–68, 303–4, 305, 307; interventions in Latin America, 134, 163, 234, 240, 243–52, 299, 301, 307; and inter-American diplomacy, 235, 269–76, 303–4; trade with Latin America, 221, 222, 224, 225; aid to Latin America, 225, 226–27, 231, 254, 256, 258, 283–84, 294–98 *passim*; and development and social change in Latin America, 278, 279, 281, 291–99 *passim*, 315, 328, 329, 331; military, and Latin America, 160–61, 255–56; investments in Latin America, 125, 168, 199, 217–21, 256–60, 290, 309; attempts to imitate, by Latin Americans, 108, 109, 110, 111, 139, 183, 187, 189, 314; views of, Latin American, 45, 47, 152–53, 170, 235, 265, 290, 315–17, 322, 324–25; immigration from, 29
Universities, 30, 352-58 *passim;* in colonial era, 48, 78; university reform movement, 356–57
Uros, 58
Urquidi, Víctor, 186
Uruguay, 3, 13, 31, 129; population of, 28, 31, 39; in colonial era, 80, 88; independence of, 101; government and politics in, 106, 109, 130, 145, 146, 147, 156, 162, 174, 203, 278, 283, 348, 349n, 350; socio-economic conditions in, 14, 33, 39, 41, 118, 124, 125, 145, 176, 178, 188, 201, 215n, 218n, 224, 230, 231, 342, 343, 345; foreign relations of, 260
Uruguay River, 10
Uxmal, 51

Valdivia, Pedro de, 64
Vallejo, César, 365
Valparaíso, 9, 236
Vargas, Getúlio, 136n, 147, 156, 159, 190, 279, 280, 282
Vasconcelos, José, 37
Vega Florida, Count of, 95
Velasco Ibarra, José María, 282, 308
Velásquez, Diego de, 62, 81
Venezuela, 10, 15, 16, 340; population of, 27, 39; precolonial, 58; discovery and conquest of, 60, 64; in colonial era, 70, 73, 76, 88, 90, 94, 96; independence of, 100; government and politics in, 106, 108, 111, 112–13, 131, 135, 152, 153, 155, 158, 162, 173, 174, 258, 263, 277, 280, 281–82, 290, 298, 305–6, 311, 319, 321, 350, 357, 358; socio-economic conditions in, 14, 39, 41, 42, 113, 114, 115, 116–17, 118, 123, 141, 142n, 146, 175, 176, 177, 180, 198, 200, 201, 203, 205n, 206, 211n, 213, 215, 217, 218n, 220, 224, 230, 231, 342, 343, 345, 354n, 355; foreign relations of, 238–39, 254n, 260, 262, 265, 268
Ventas, 51
Veracruz, 7, 51, 62, 248
Versailles, Treaty of, 265
Vespucci, Amerigo, 27
Victoria, Queen of England, 135
Vikings, 60
Villa, Francisco (Pancho), 165, 166, 249
Villa-Lobos, Heitor, 365

Villava, Victorián de, 94
Villeda Morales, Ramón, 310
Vitoria, Francisco de, 75
Volcanoes, 12

Walker, William, 244, 262
Waris, 55
Water transport, 8, 10
Watling Island, 60
Wheat, 13, 14, 188, 189, 205, 213, 222, 230, 338
Wickham, Henry, 13
Wilson, Edmund, 362
Wilson, Henry Lane, 165
Women, position of, 43, 124, 180, 336–37; in colonial era, 24
World Bank, *see* International Bank for Reconstruction and Development
World Federation of Trade Unions (WFTU), 149
World Health Organization (WHO), 269
World War I, 30n, 50, 146, 160, 183, 239, 356, 365; Latin America's role in, 160, 235
World War II, 30, 31, 139, 147, 148, 153, 155, 161, 184, 185, 201, 204, 217, 218, 220, 239, 245, 248, 250, 254, 257, 264, 265, 271, 272, 277, 357; Latin America's role in, 160, 235–36

Xavier, Joaquim José da Silva (Tiradentes), 89

Yanga, 88
Yapuras, 59
Yaquis, 21, 59
Yucatán, 29, 51, 63, 86, 92, 244, 355
Ypiranga, Cry of, 97

Zapata, Emiliano, 165, 166
Zapotecs, 52
Zavala, Lorenzo de, 364
Zumárraga, Juan de, 78
Zúñiga y Velasco, López de, 84